Jeff Duntemann Series Editor

VISUAL BASIC 5 Web Development

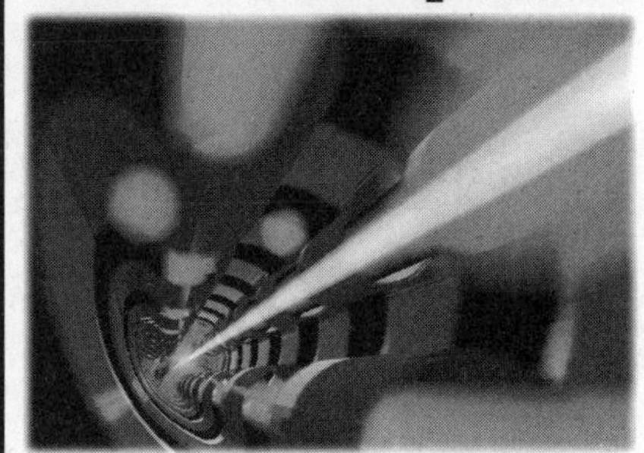

Scott Jarol

an International Thomson Publishing company I(T)P®

Albany, NY • Belmont, CA • Bonn • Boston • Cincinnati • Detroit • Johannesburg • London
Madrid • Melbourne • Mexico City • New York • Paris • Singapore • Tokyo • Toronto • Washington

Publisher	**Keith Weiskamp**
Project Editor	**Toni Zuccarini**
Cover Artist	**Performance Design/Gary Smith**
Cover Design	**Anthony Stock**
Interior Design	**Nicole Colon**
Layout Production	**ProImage**
Copy Editor	**Maggie Miskell**
Proofreader	**Eric Kingsbury**
Indexer	**Diane Cook**

High Performance Visual Basic 5 Web Development

1-57610-063-4

The Coriolis Group, Inc.
An International Thomson Publishing Company
14455 N. Hayden Road, Suite 220
Scottsdale, Arizona 85260

602/483-0192
FAX 602/483-0193
http://www.coriolis.com

Printed in the United States of America
10 9 8 7 6 5 4 3 2 1

This book is dedicated to my mother, Ila Jarol, and to the memory of my father, Leslie George Jarol.

Acknowledgments

This project took place during the most difficult time I've ever experienced in my life, and I could not have completed it without the support of some exceptional people. First I wish to thank Ryan, Kristen, and Claudia once again for their patience.

Thanks also to Keith Weiskamp and Jeff Duntemann for their relentless support of my writing and their unflagging confidence.

Several people contributed their technical expertise. Markus Roberts deserves co-author credit for his remarkable contributions. I also stole many substantial ideas from David Friedel, a Webmaster's Webmaster. I am indebted to Robert Denny, the inventor of Windows CGI, whose work serves as the foundation of most Visual Basic CGI programming, including my own, and to his publisher, O'Reilly & Associates, Inc., for permission to use and include his CGI32.BAS code module. I'm afraid I pestered a few other people as I pondered the intricacies of Internet programming, including Chris Coppola, Dan Haygood, and Larion Vasilkovsky, who shared their knowledge freely and enthusiastically.

I wish to thank my editors, Scott Palmer and Toni Zuccarini, for taking the heat for me, and for coping with my perpetually revised schedule.

Thanks Mom, for all that you have taught me, and for insisting that I never lose confidence and that I should pursue the highest standards permitted by my abilities.

Finally, I wish to thank Marisa Lynn Peña, without whose strength I might never have completed this project. I love you, Misa.

A Note From Jeff Duntemann

Programmers (especially those just coming up to speed) often challenge one another with questions like, "How good are your tools?" There was a time when this was a valid question. Compilers, debuggers, servers, database engines, and all the rest were just coming out of the Stone Age. There were tremendous variations in quality and power from one tool to another. If you bet on the wrong toolset, you could be working harder than you needed to—or worse.

Today, the more pertinent question might be "How good are *you*?" Relentless competition has given today's developer tools tremendous depth and amazing quality, such that a journeyman programmer is highly unlikely to push such tools to the limit. Long before your tools hit the wall, *you* will—unless you go the distance to learn everything you can about the tools that you use, and refine the skill with which you use them.

The Coriolis Group's High Performance series was designed to help you take your tools *deep*. These books explain the advanced tool features that the intro books just can't cover, and provide heavy-duty projects that force you to think through the development process at an expert's level—using those head muscles that lie behind everything we could call skill.

You could discover this knowledge by beating your head against the technology, and trying things randomly until they work. Or you can benefit from the experience of our authors, who've been up this learning curve before and took notes along the way. We've chosen the topics, the authors, and the approaches carefully to ensure that you don't get mired in introductory material you don't need and irrelevant technology that you can't use.

The goal is to take you and your chosen toolset as far as you choose to go. You've already got high-performance tools. Here's to your success at becoming and remaining a high-performance developer.

—Jeff Duntemann

Contents

Introduction

With all the programming languages, scripting languages, HTML tags, APIs, object specifications, media viewers, plug-ins, and applets that are out there, a Web developer could find himself on an ActiveX buzz after Shocking himself with too much Java. The popularization of the World Wide Web has sparked a firestorm of technological innovation, inundating Web developers with an embarrassment of riches. With so many options, overlap was inevitable, and therein lies confusion. The number of technologies that address any particular problem can be overwhelming—just take an inventory of the available online database publishing tools. Microsoft alone has offered several overlapping technologies, ranging from database engines and interfaces to scripting languages to HTML editing tools.

As if the explosion of competing technologies weren't enough, the hottest debate among Web developers revolves around cross-platform compatibility—the question of whether all Web sites and their features should look and function equally well regardless of the client computer, operating system, or browser used to visit them. Adversaries argue the trade-off between universal solutions and technologies that exploit more advanced, platform-specific features, such as Windows 95's DirectX sound and graphics systems.

For those of us who just need to bring our Web sites online, the options can be intimidating. How many programming languages and media preparation tools can one Webmaster master? Ideally we'd like to find solutions that leverage our knowledge from one task to another. Imagine a programming language that would let us build all kinds of Web applications, including database-driven CGI applications, browser plug-ins, client scripts, and various other Internet utilities and services. That language may just be Visual Basic.

While it's true that programs we write in Visual Basic currently will run only in a Windows 95 or Windows NT environment, don't be put off by that limitation. If your application does not require cross-platform compatibility, then Visual Basic may be the only programming language you'll ever need. Between its powerful built-in features, easy access to the Windows APIs, and extensive third-party support in the form of ActiveX components, Visual Basic delivers the muscle we need to create killer Windows applications—networked or otherwise. And even if your application does need to function on all client platforms, you'll find that Visual Basic still offers the best way to implement the server-based elements of your Web or Internet site. Visual Basic features a rich set of tools for developing server-side applications, such as database-driven CGI scripts and special-purpose Internet servers, replacing reams of obscure Perl script and C code. If you've chosen to implement your site on a Windows-based server, Visual Basic should be a part of your toolkit.

While Visual Basic may not qualify as the Rosetta Stone of Internet technology, the Visual Basic family of languages—which now includes Visual Basic 5, Visual Basic for Applications, and VBScript—does support an extensive and exciting range of Web and Internet programming solutions.

Chapter Overview

We'll begin our exploration of Visual Basic 5 Web programming with a "Jump Start." In Chapter 1 we'll test some of Visual Basic's latest Internet programming features, including ActiveX programming, and the Winsock control.

In Chapter 2 we'll pause while we try to develop some perspective on all of Visual Basic's Internet and Web programming options.

In Chapter 3 we'll use the spanking new Internet Transfer Control to implement a Web Robot, a special Web client that wanders the Web seeking documents that match our specifications. Chapter 4 then describes in detail the nifty parser used by the Web Robot to analyze document contents against a search string.

In Chapters 5 and 6 we'll implement another kind of Internet client, a news reader. Unlike most news clients, however, this one will incorporate the text parser we developed in Chapter 4, making it the Smart News Reader, and a close relative of the Web Robot. We'll also take another look at the Winsock control, using it to implement the Network News Transfer Protocol. By the time you finish this project you'll be ready to write your own suite of Internet utilities.

Chapters 7 and 8 introduce Visual Basic CGI programming. Visual Basic's built-in database capabilities make it a snap to develop database-driven Web sites. By using a handy code library developed by Robert Denny—author of the popular WebSite

Web server product (published by O'Reilly & Associates, Inc.)—we'll write CGI scripts in Visual Basic that demonstrate how we can encapsulate an entire Web site—even a commerce site—in a single executable file. We'll also talk about how to solve one of the stickiest CGI problems, establishing persistent client states. (You may want to pour yourself a glass of milk, we'll be serving *cookies.*)

In Chapter 9 we'll tackle Visual Basic's newest centerpiece: developing ActiveX controls. We'll build an ActiveX control from the ground up and talk about some of the special considerations that affect controls destined for the Web.

Finally, in Chapter 10 we'll write our own custom Internet application, a chat system with separate client and server components. Once we get the basic system working we'll convert the client into an ActiveX control that will download, install, and run itself automatically on the user's computer, all within a Web document.

Let's get started.

Jump Start

CHAPTER 1

Visual Basic 5 makes it easier than ever to write all kinds of Web and Internet applications. Get started right now with a handful of simple programs that demonstrate the power and flexibility of this remarkable programming system.

Jump Start

Visual Basic offers a handful of features that will have a profound impact on Web and Internet software development. As in every previous release, version 5 delivers powerful new tools that simplify once-arcane programming tasks. This time, the wizards from Redmond have wired Visual Basic for cyberspace by fortifying it with three key technologies:

- Support for ActiveX development
- The Winsock Control
- The Internet Transport Control

Let's take a quick tour through some of the ways that Visual Basic brings Web programming down to earth.

A New World Of ActiveX

The first three releases of Visual Basic were based on a new control architecture—the VBX—designed specifically to provide extensive third-party support for the language in the form of custom controls. By version 4, Visual Basic's creators had merged their vision with the more general approach being taken by Microsoft's architects of Object Linking and Embedding (OLE) technology. Visual Basic now supports two kinds of controls: its own intrinsic controls, encapsulating standard Windows controls such as scroll bars and drop-down boxes; and OCX controls that comply with the ActiveX specification, an architecture for universally interchangeable program components.

Microsoft practices what they preach. Most of the new applications emerging from Redmond are aggregates of ActiveX components, many of which we can re-use in our own applications. Internet Explorer 3.0, for example, is based on an ActiveX control that retrieves and displays HTML documents from the Web. If you have installed Internet Explorer 3.0 on your system, you can easily incorporate that control into your own Visual Basic projects.

An Instant Web Browser

Open Visual Basic 5 and start a Standard EXE project. Stretch out the form displayed in the initial form designer window so you have a little room to work with, as shown in Figure 1.1.

Place the cursor over the Toolbox and right click to display its context menu. Then select Components to display the Components dialog box, as shown in Figure 1.2.

Select the Controls tab to display the list of controls installed and registered on your computer. As you scroll through the list of available components, you'll notice a few that begin with the initials IE. Those are controls installed by Internet Explorer that you can re-use in your own projects. The Internet Explorer WebBrowser control, however, is located further down the list in a component called Microsoft Internet Controls. When you select it, the dialog box will display its location, usually something like C:\WINDOWS\SYSTEM\SHDOCVW.DLL. Although the WebBrowser control is located in a DLL rather than an OCX, it is nevertheless an OLE component. After selecting the Microsoft Internet Controls component, click OK to close the dialog box. The control will then appear in the Toolbox, represented by a small file folder under a magnifying glass, as shown in Figure 1.3.

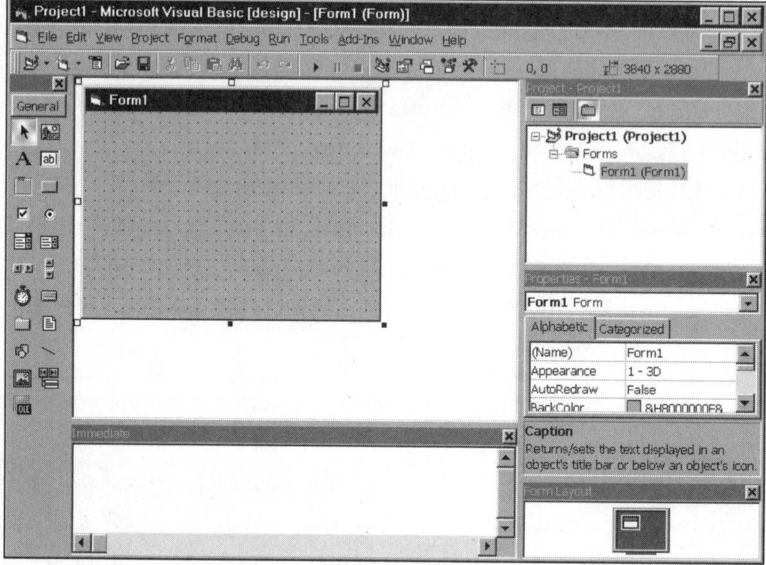

Figure 1.1
The Visual Basic 5 development environment with a new form designer.

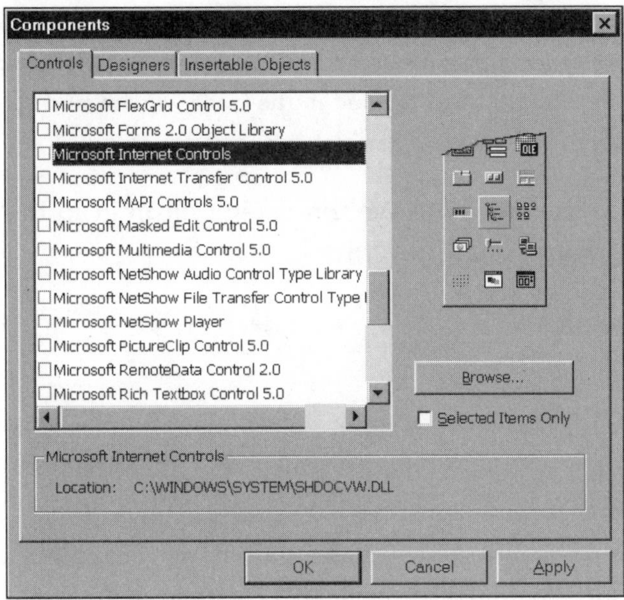

Figure 1.2

The Visual Basic 5 Components dialog box.

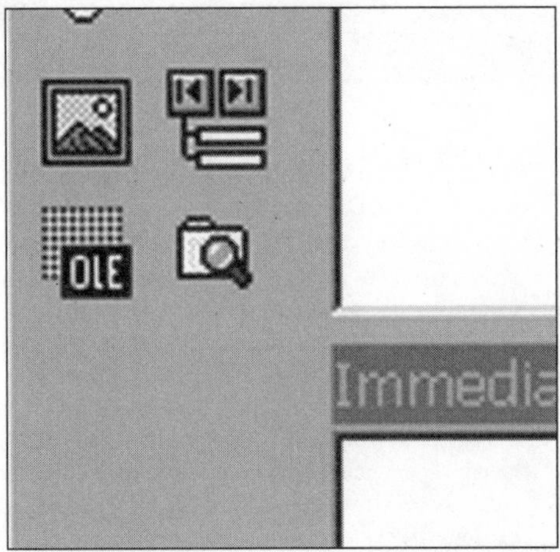

Figure 1.3

The browser control as it appears in the Visual Basic Toolbox.

Select the newly added control from the Toolbox and drop an instance of it onto the form, stretching it to occupy most of the available space. Next, double click the form itself to open the **Form_Load**() method in the Code window and add a call to the WebBrowser control's **Navigate**() method, as shown in Listing 1.1.

Listing 1.1 Activating the WebBrowser control from the **Form_Load()** event.

```
Private Sub Form_Load()
    WebBrowser1.Navigate "http://www.mediaterra.com"
    End Sub
```

Activate your TCP/IP connection to the Internet, then run the program. It should load and display the Web document specified in the **Form_Load**() event procedure, as shown in Figure 1.4.

With the Internet Explorer WebBrowser control, we could build a multimedia application with a user interface based on HTML and ActiveX component technology that restricts users to the content we specify. We could even build hybrid products that seamlessly integrate CD-ROM and Web-based content. ActiveX com-

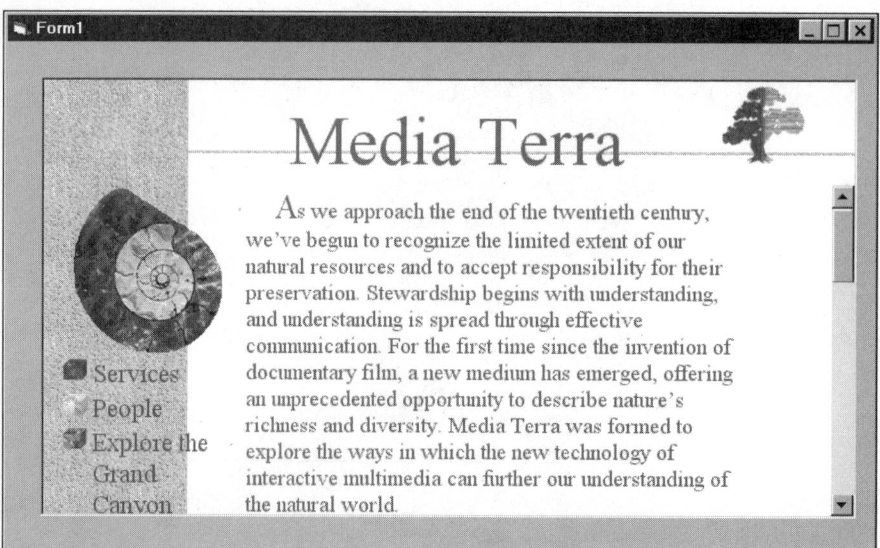

Figure 1.4
The WebBrowser ActiveX control in action.

ponents contribute new resources to the operating system, making them available not only to the application for which they were originally designed, but to all other applications as well.

Visual Basic 4 introduced support for ActiveX controls—at least for their use within Visual Basic applications. To create new controls, however, you still needed expertise in a more complex language such as C++. However, Visual Basic 5 now enables us to build ActiveX controls in Visual Basic itself.

Instant ActiveX Controls

In Chapter 9, we'll take a detailed look at the control creation process. For now, let's see just how easy it can be to build our own ActiveX controls.

Select File|New Project from the Visual Basic menu, and select ActiveX Control as the project type. The first thing you will see is the UserControl designer, as shown in Figure 1.5. Like a Form, a UserControl object is a background on which you can visually design your control—either by populating it with other pre-existing controls or by drawing with graphics methods.

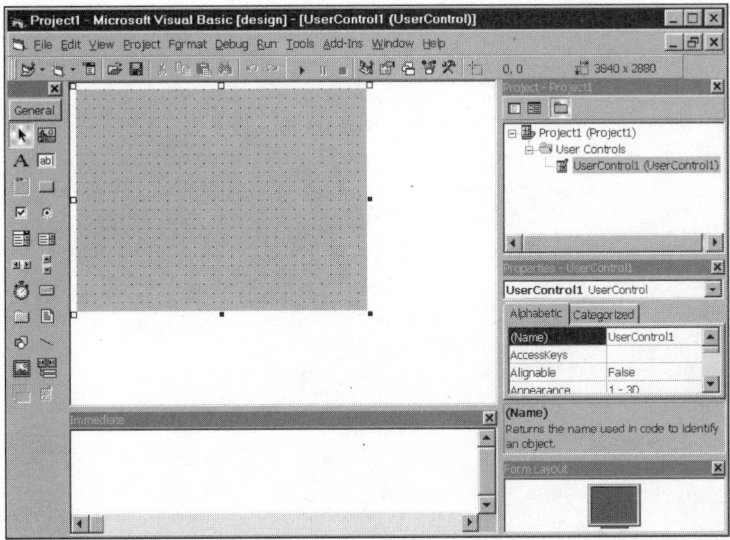

Figure 1.5

Visual Basic displaying a new UserControl designer.

Before we proceed, let's assign some names. In the Properties window, set the **Name** property of the UserControl to **MarqueeControl**. From the Visual Basic menu, select Project|Project1 Properties. In the Project Properties dialog box, set the Project Name to MarqueeControlProject. Finally, save the project with the file names MarqueeControlProject.VBP and MarqueeControl.CTL.

For this simple project, we'll use a PictureBox control and a Timer to create a traveling marquee, as shown in Figure 1.6. Drop a Timer control on the UserControl designer. Leave its **Name** property at its default value, **Timer1**, and set its **Interval** property to **50**. Next, place a single PictureBox on the UserControl designer, stretching it to fill the entire UserControl object. Set its **Name** property to **pbMarquee**, and set its **BorderStyle** property to **1 - Fixed Single**. The code for the project is shown in Listing 1.2.

Listing 1.2 The complete listing of MarqueeControl.CTL.

```
Option Explicit
Private TextXPos As Long
Private TextTop As Long
Private TextSize As Long

Const Caption = "What?! Another marquee?"

Private Sub Timer1_Timer()
    If Ambient.UserMode Then
        pbMarquee.Cls
        If (TextXPos + pbMarquee.TextWidth(Caption)) < 0 Then
            TextXPos = pbMarquee.ScaleWidth
          End If
        TextXPos = TextXPos - 25
        pbMarquee.CurrentX = TextXPos
        pbMarquee.CurrentY = TextTop
        pbMarquee.Print Caption
      End If
    End Sub

Private Sub UserControl_Resize()
    TextXPos = pbMarquee.ScaleWidth
    pbMarquee.Left = 0
    pbMarquee.Width = UserControl.ScaleWidth
    pbMarquee.Top = 0
    pbMarquee.Height = UserControl.ScaleHeight
```

```
    pbMarquee.FontSize = pbMarquee.ScaleY _
        (pbMarquee.ScaleHeight * 0.8, vbTwips, vbPoints)
    TextTop = (pbMarquee.ScaleHeight \ 2) - _
        (pbMarquee.TextHeight("A") \ 2)
    If Ambient.UserMode Then
        Timer1.Enabled = True
      Else
        Timer1.Enabled = False
      End If
    End Sub

Private Sub UserControl_Terminate()
    Timer1.Enabled = False
    End Sub
```

The real activity of this control all takes place in the **Timer1_Timer**() event procedure. This simple procedure first calls the **Cls**() method to erase the current contents of **pbMarquee.** After setting the PictureBox's current coordinates, it uses the **Print**() method to display the string specified in the constant **Caption**, gradually sliding it to the left with each timer tick until it runs completely off the left edge. It then starts the process over again at the right edge.

Type in the code from Listing 1.2. This code defines a completely functional—although not terribly useful—ActiveX control. To test it, select File|Add Project from the Visual Basic menu, and add a Standard EXE project. It is not necessary to name or save the Standard EXE project or its Form.

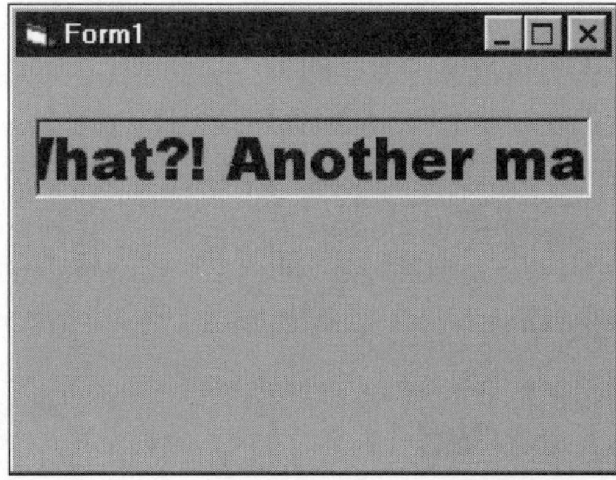

Figure 1.6
A simple ActiveX marquee control in action.

When you close the UserControl designer for the **MarqueeControl**, Visual Basic will compile and register a temporary version of the control. You may then select the control in the Toolbox and draw an instance on the Form. Run the Standard EXE program to activate the new control.

To change the message displayed by the control, first close the runtime version of the Form. Then, in the Project Explorer, right click the **MarqueeControl** object and select View Code. You may then modify the contents of **Caption** before running the Standard EXE project again.

Although Visual Basic makes it easy to create a basic ActiveX control, any truly useful control will likely need to expose various properties, events, and methods. And writing a complete control can become rather complicated. In Chapter 9, we'll explore some of the subtleties of control creation, and we'll see just what it takes to get a custom ActiveX control working in a Web document.

Internet Communications With Winsock

The Internet's mystique of complexity derives mainly from the number and diversity of applications that use the Internet to exchange information. These include the systems that distribute email and news and, most of all, the World Wide Web. The Internet itself, however, remains a simple digital network with a well-defined, reliable communication protocol.

In recognition of that fundamental simplicity, the Windows 95 and Windows NT operating systems offer a standard interface to the Internet known as *Windows Sockets*, or *Winsock*. Visual Basic, in turn, offers a standard interface to Winsock through its Winsock ActiveX control. The purpose of Winsock is almost trivially simple: to enable two or more Internet nodes to establish a connection and exchange data—any data. Let's put together a simple application that demonstrates this process.

The Winsock Server

In this project we'll use the TCP protocol to establish a connection between two nodes, a client and a server. For an actual Internet application, we would likely write two separate applications. But for now, we'll build the client and server into two separate Forms within a single application.

Open a new Standard EXE project. We'll begin by implementing the Winsock server, as shown in Figure 1.7. We'll need five controls, which are listed in Table 1.1.

Listening For A Winsock Connection

Each server application that exists on the Internet is identified uniquely by two numbers: its IP address and the port on which it listens for a connection request. Any Internet node—in other words, a computer at a particular IP address—can run multiple servers, as long as each server listens on a unique port. In the server's **Form_Load**() event procedure, shown in Listing 1.3, we'll set the Winsock control's

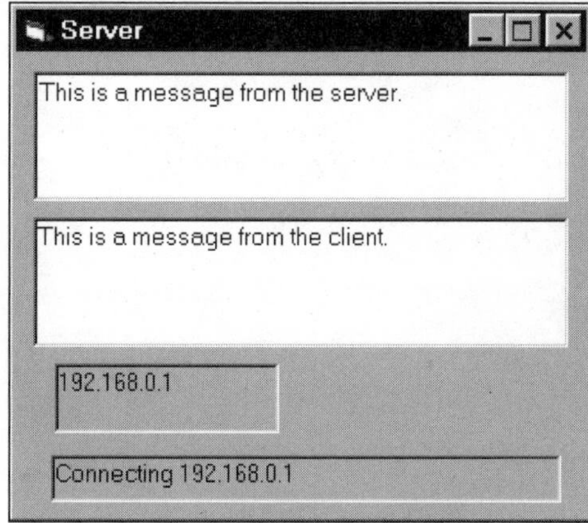

Figure 1.7
frmServer from WinsockExperiment1.VBP.

Table 1.1 The controls in frmServer1.FRM.

Name	Type	Property	Value
lblDataReceived	Label	Caption	""
lblIPAddress	Label	Caption	""
lblStatus	Label	Caption	""
sktTCPChatServer	Winsock	Protocol	0 - sckTCPProtocol
txtDataToSend	TextBox	MultiLine	True

LocalPort number to the arbitrary value 1600. We do not set the IP address, since it is determined by the computer on which the server runs. To activate the server, we call its **Listen()** method, which causes it to begin monitoring the Internet for connection requests.

Listing 1.3 The complete listing of frmServer1.FRM from the project WinsockExperiment1.VBP.

```
Option Explicit

Private Sub Form_Load()
    frmClient.Show
    sktTCPChatServer.LocalPort = 1600 ' Set the local port.
    sktTCPChatServer.Listen           ' Use the Listen method.
    lblIPAddress.Caption = sktTCPChatServer.LocalIP
    lblStatus.Caption = "Host Name: " & _
        sktTCPChatServer.LocalHostName
    End Sub


Private Sub Form_QueryUnload(Cancel As Integer, _
                             UnloadMode As Integer)
    Dim ArrayIndex As Integer

    Unload frmClient
    End Sub

Private Sub sktTCPChatServer_Close()
    lblStatus.Caption = _
        "Disconnecting from " & sktTCPChatServer.RemoteHostIP

    ' Return to listening state.
    sktTCPChatServer.Close
    sktTCPChatServer.LocalPort = 1600
    sktTCPChatServer.Listen

    End Sub

Private Sub sktTCPChatServer_ConnectionRequest _
               (ByVal requestID As Long)
    Dim Dummy As String

    If sktTCPChatServer.State <> sckClosed Then
        sktTCPChatServer.Close
      End If
```

```
    sktTCPChatServer.Accept requestID
    lblStatus.Caption = "Connecting " & _
        sktTCPChatServer.RemoteHostIP
    End Sub

Private Sub sktTCPChatServer_DataArrival(ByVal bytesTotal As Long)
    Dim DataReceived As String
    sktTCPChatServer.GetData DataReceived, vbString
    If CStr(DataReceived) = "QUIT" Then
        sktTCPChatServer_Close
      Else
        lblDataReceived.Caption = DataReceived
      End If

    End Sub

Private Sub txtDataToSend_Change()
    sktTCPChatServer.SendData txtDataToSend.Text
    End Sub
```

Making The Winsock Connection

When a client sends a connection request to the appropriate IP address and port number, the Winsock control will raise its **ConnectionRequest** event. In the **sktTCPChatServer_ConnectionRequest()** event procedure, we establish the connection between the client and the server by calling the Winsock control's **Accept()** method, passing it the **requestID** received as an argument to the event procedure.

Exchanging Data

To send data to the client, we use the Winsock control's **SendData()** method, as shown in the event procedure **txtDataToSend_Change()** in Listing 1.3. When the Winsock control receives data from the client, it fires its **DataArrival()** event procedure, also shown in Listing 1.3, signaling us to use its **GetData()** method to retrieve the data from its communications buffer.

The Winsock Client

For the client, shown in Figure 1.8, we'll create a Form similar to the server, with two text boxes to display incoming and outgoing messages. We'll add a pair of CommandButtons to control the connection to the server. Altogether, **frmClient** will require six controls, as listed in Table 1.2.

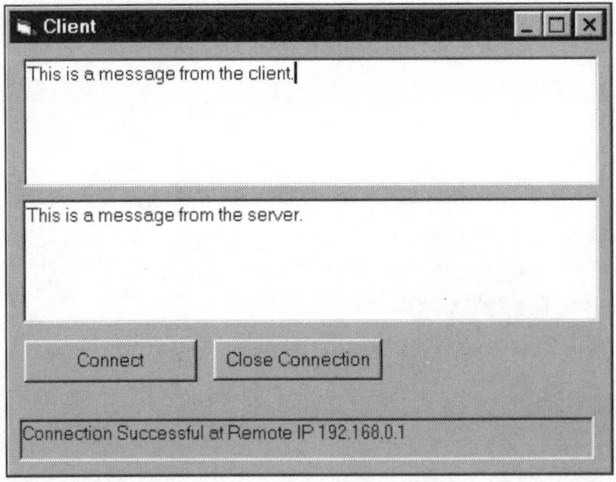

Figure 1.8
frmClient from WinsockExperiment1.VBP.

Table 1.2 The controls in frmClient1.FRM.

Name	Type	Property	Value
cmdCloseConnection	CommandButton	Caption	"Connect"
cmdConnect	CommandButton	Caption	"Close Connection"
lblStatus	Label	Caption	""
sktTCPChatClient	Winsock	Protocol	0 - sckTCPProtocol
txtDataReceived	Label	MultiLine	True
txtDataToSend	TextBox	MultiLine	True

Connecting To The Server

The main difference between the client and the server is determined by how the connection is established. While the server listens for a connection request, the client uses the Winsock control's **Connect()** method—along with its **RemoteHost** and **RemotePort** properties—to transmit a connection request. In this program, the server and client reside on the same computer, so we set **RemoteHost** to the **LocalIP** detected by the Winsock control. In **frmClient**, the connection request is performed by the **cmdConnect_Click()** event procedure, shown in Listing 1.4.

Listing 1.4 The complete listing of frmClient1.FRM from the project WinsockExperiment1.VBP.

```
Option Explicit

Private Sub cmdCloseConnection_Click()
    lblStatus.Caption = "Closing Connection"
    ' Don't terminate the connection like this:
    '     sktTCPChatClient.Close
    sktTCPChatClient.SendData "QUIT"
    End Sub

Private Sub cmdConnect_Click()
    If sktTCPChatClient.State <> sckClosed Then
        sktTCPChatClient.Close
      End If
    With sktTCPChatClient
        .RemoteHost = sktTCPChatClient.LocalIP
        .RemotePort = 1600
        End With
    sktTCPChatClient.Connect
    End Sub

Private Sub Form_Load()
    lblStatus.Caption = "Local IP Address: " & _
        sktTCPChatClient.LocalIP
    End Sub

Private Sub Form_QueryUnload(Cancel As Integer, _
                             UnloadMode As Integer)
    sktTCPChatClient.Close
    End Sub

Private Sub sktTCPChatClient_Close()
    sktTCPChatClient.Close
    Do
        lblStatus.Caption = "Status: " & _
            sktTCPChatClient.State
        DoEvents
        Loop Until sktTCPChatClient.State = sckClosed
    End Sub

Private Sub sktTCPChatClient_Connect()
    If sktTCPChatClient.State = sckConnected Then
```

```
        lblStatus.Caption = "Connection Successful at Remote IP " & _
            sktTCPChatClient.RemoteHostIP
        End If

    End Sub

Private Sub sktTCPChatClient_DataArrival(ByVal bytesTotal As Long)
    Dim vtData As Variant

    sktTCPChatClient.GetData vtData, vbString
    txtReceived.Text = vtData
    End Sub

Private Sub txtDataToSend_Change()
    sktTCPChatClient.SendData txtDataToSend.Text
    End Sub
```

When we close the connection in the **cmdCloseConnection_Click()** event procedure, shown in Listing 1.4, notice that we don't call the Winsock control's **Close()** method. Instead, we send the string "QUIT". We then let the server perform the actual disconnection by calling its **Close()** method. The order of connection and close operations can affect the usability and reliability of a Winsock application. We'll discuss these issues in more detail when we expand the Winsock Chat application in Chapter 10.

To exchange data with the server, the client uses the same Winsock methods used by the server. To transmit data to the server, it calls the Winsock control's **SendData()** method. To retrieve data received from the server, it calls the Winsock control's **GetData()** method within the **DataArrival()** event procedure.

A Handful Of Powerful Tools

In this quick introduction to Visual Basic's Internet programming features, we've explored two of Visual Basic's most valuable tools. We've seen that it's now possible to write our own ActiveX components, which we can use to expand our Web sites with rich interactivity and lively multimedia. We've also seen how we can use the Winsock ActiveX control to write Internet applications and services that are capable of exchanging information across the Internet, anywhere in the world. In the coming chapters, we'll investigate other Visual Basic features that will help us enrich our Internet and Web experiences—both as users and as publishers.

HIGH PERFORMANCE

Visual Basic And The Internet

CHAPTER 2

Visual Basic may become the most popular programming language of all time. It does a little of everything—which is good news for Web and Internet programmers anxious to design exciting, new online sites and services.

Visual Basic And The Internet

Internet programming encompasses so many diverse disciplines that it may seem senseless to gather them together under a single roof. Nevertheless, the roof exists—we know it as the World Wide Web. The Web is rapidly becoming the universal distribution and navigation system for all types of networked applications and information, from the promotional Web sites published by global mega-companies like Coca-Cola, Twentieth Century Fox, and Chevrolet, to internal accounting systems distributed on corporate intranets. To paint the same kind of Web face on such diverse applications, developers have had to master a few fundamental technologies: Hypertext Markup Language (HTML), the Common Gateway Interface (CGI), object embedding, client-side scripting, and TCP communications—not to mention various layout and design skills.

Web and Internet programming tends to fall into two categories: client-side and server-side applications. For example, CGI scripts are programs that run under the control of a Web server, usually providing database services in the form of data collection or publishing. On the other hand, we tend to think of ActiveX controls as visual components we can add to Web pages to help users navigate our sites and to display multimedia elements. But that distinction begins to crumble when we begin writing more complex applications.

For example, we could write groupware utilities, such as video conferencing and shared whiteboard simulators, that users might access through linked documents on the Internet or a corporate intranet. Such applications often require special programs for both the server and the client machine. The server may run as an independent application on a computer somewhere on the Internet, managing connections and dispatching data. The client, activated by navigating to the correct Uniform Resource Locator (URL), may consist of a scripted Web document populated with Java applets or ActiveX controls, or it may be a single monolithic ActiveX control. It could even be an ActiveX document.

Internet programming today runs the gamut from Internet-specific applications such as email and Usenet news, to corporate information systems that offer a Web-compatible user interface.

Web And Internet Programming

In this book, we'll explore four general types of Internet programming:

- Internet utilities such as Web robots and News readers
- Client/server applications that exchange data over the Internet
- CGI and database publishing
- ActiveX control development

Internet Utilities

The Internet community today shares information in countless ways, but its most popular services (including email, Usenet news, Gopher, and the World Wide Web) conform to widely adopted standards, as described in a series of documents called *Requests for Comments* (RFCs). By following the specifications for any particular Internet service, we can write our own custom servers and client utilities for these services. For example, you may wish to write your own email program with features that filter out unwanted junk mail, or that send automated responses to messages that contain specific keywords.

While all Internet services exchange their data with the Internet Protocol (IP), each application defines a secondary, higher-level protocol that consists of various commands and responses. Most of these application protocols are text-based, meaning that the client communicates with the server by sending it ordinary verbal commands such as "POST" and "QUIT". To implement one of these protocols, we can use the Winsock ActiveX control to send and receive the text commands and responses. A typical Internet client utility consists of a user interface wrapped around a protocol handler. For example, an email client displays a list of message subject headers sent or received by the client, allowing the user to display existing messages or compose and transmit new messages. All the commands and messages sent and received by the email client travel across the Internet as plain text, formatted precisely as prescribed by the appropriate RFC. The unique qualities of your custom clients will be defined largely by how well they represent the server's commands and responses to the user, and by the other operations they perform on the data received.

New Internet Applications

Along with the well-known Internet services described above, the Internet serves as the data conduit for untold numbers of custom applications. The applications you write are not limited to those defined by the published standards. The Internet is just a public digital communications medium. As long as you comply with the TCP/IP and UDP/IP standards for transmitting data across the Internet (conveniently handled for us by the Winsock control), you may send any kind of data you wish. Of course, sending data in custom formats is useless unless someone out there can receive and interpret it. Thus, a custom Internet application requires at least two nodes that understand each other.

As we demonstrated in Chapter 1, the Winsock control performs generic Internet communications, so we can use it to implement any type of custom client and server applications. If you wish, you can even build globally distributed database applications. Just remember that the Internet is used by millions of people—and some of them have nefarious tendencies. Always practice safe networking.

CGI And Database Publishing

The Web may have started as a means of publishing and cross-referencing documents, but it's rapidly becoming a major means of distributing and collecting data. The Common Gateway Interface (CGI) was created to enable Webmasters to collect information about visitors to their sites. It was a simple idea: add some tags to HTML that would display a few input fields and use a piggyback protocol to transmit the entered information back to the Web server. The server would, in turn, hand the data off to a simple program—or script—which would add it to a database.

CGI has considerably outgrown its creators' early intent. Thousands of Web sites now use CGI—or variations on CGI—to offer all kinds of services, from tracking overnight deliveries to selling khaki pants and sandals. And now, with the rich resources of Visual Basic and Windows operating systems, CGI programming is easier and more flexible than ever.

With the tools built into Visual Basic, it's possible to write even the most ambitious database-driven Web sites. The Coriolis Group's site (visit **http://www.coriolis.com**), for example (designed and implemented by Coriolis' own Web wizard, David Friedel), is written entirely in Visual Basic (see Figure 2.1). Besides offering content from Coriolis' magazine, *Visual Developer*, the site also provides information on all of The Coriolis Group's books and accepts orders through an online shopping cart system. The CGI code for the Coriolis Group Web site is contained entirely within a single Visual Basic EXE.

With a well-crafted Visual Basic CGI program, you can build a Web site that automatically formats and displays your content without ever writing a static HTML document.

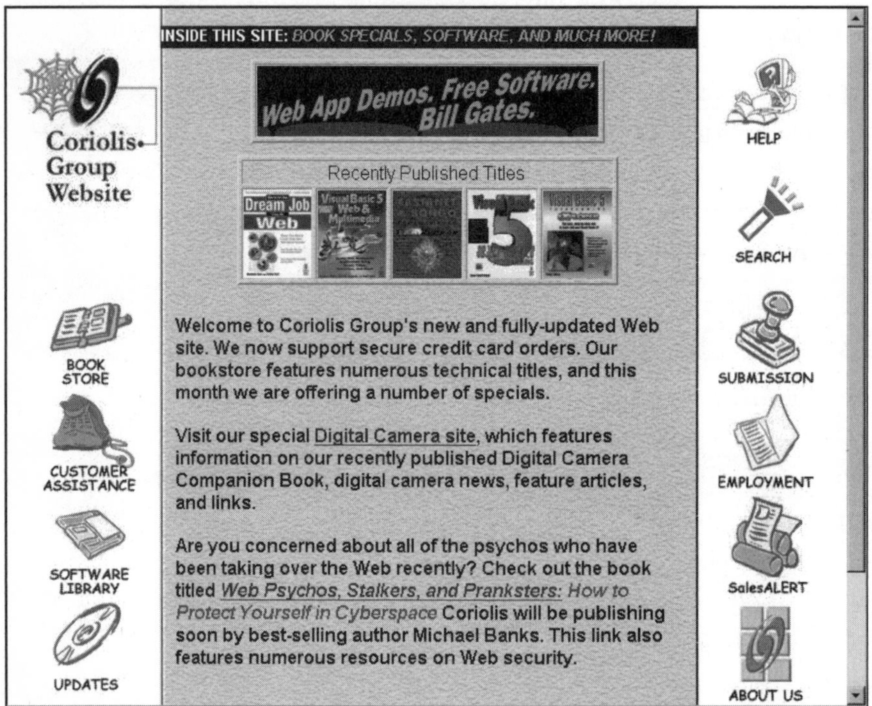

Figure 2.1
The Coriolis Group's Web site.

ActiveX Web Controls

Most of the recent developments in Web technology have focused on the user experience at the browser level. The introduction of the Java programming language promised more lively presentations. Java applets are supposed to bring all kinds of multimedia events to life—from 3D animations to streaming video and CD-quality sound—with complete platform independence. Unfortunately, the real world has so far proven that the performance demands of such ambitious applications often exceed the least-common-denominator capabilities of all the client systems that live on the Web.

For Web applets to assume the role expected of them, they needed a little refinement. First, they needed a uniform interface specification that would enable Web developers to orchestrate their action through client-side scripts. Second, they needed access to the more advanced features of the operating systems on which they were supposed to run. Most members of the Internet community agreed on the need for standards, but the idea of throwing out universal compatibility has raised a considerable ruckus.

Despite this resistance, however, Microsoft introduced their own specification for Web component objects—an outgrowth of Windows OLE technology—which they named ActiveX. While the ActiveX control specification does not exclude Java as a Web programming language, it does eschew the Java ideal of absolute cross-platform compatibility. (The Microsoft Java development system, Visual J++, even includes a complete object model to support the development of Windows-specific applications.) Microsoft has already introduced an ActiveX specification for the Apple Macintosh operating system (and they say they intend to support Unix as well); nonetheless, it remains true that any given ActiveX component is designed at the source code level to run on a specific target platform.

So why should ActiveX excite us? Because the ActiveX specification, combined with a tool like Visual Basic, enables us to create dynamic (or "active" as they say in Redmond) content for the Web that leverages all the resources of the Windows operating systems, including built-in support for high-speed 3D graphics and sound.

Mix And Match Technology

The boundaries between these Internet technologies are not absolute. As we'll see later in this book, it's possible to create all kinds of interdependent applications. Using the Web as a delivery system, we can

- write not only Internet-based applications, but standalone products that simply install and update themselves across the network.
- construct our client application as an ActiveX control rather than as a Standard EXE.
- open secondary channels of communication between the client and server to provide an even greater degree of interactivity between the client and the database server.

The dust has not even begun to settle yet. Opportunity abounds for creative networked applications. We'll soon see how Visual Basic 5 makes it easier than ever to stake a claim in the expanding online market.

A Word About Objects

For all the incompatibilities and competitive approaches among Web developers and their tools of choice, one methodology appears to draw praise from members of most denominations—Object-Oriented Programming, or OOP.

You'll know that you've grokked OOP when you start swearing at Visual Basic's object shortcomings. To be fair, Visual Basic's designers are caught in a conundrum. Basic is supposed to be a friendly language, offering enough power to write useful high-level applications without requiring the meticulous attention to technical details demanded by C++. In fact, Visual Basic has always had objects—forms and controls. The idea was to supply enough prefabricated objects to make it possible to build useful Windows applications, and to provide a standard control architecture with which C programmers could create new custom controls.

That idea worked pretty well. Thousands of controls have become available from hundreds of developers, offering everything from multimedia functions to word processing to animal-shaped push buttons. Suddenly Basic programmers grew fat on an embarrassment of riches, and they were content. And then it happened: Visual Basic's designers gave us our first taste of native Visual Basic object classes in Visual Basic 4.

Visual Basic Object Classes

Object classes enable us to declare a special data type that can support all the traditional elements, or members, familiar to programmers who work in other OOP languages, including properties, methods, and events. In some ways, a Visual Basic object class resembles a code module. We can still declare module-level variables and any number of general procedures or functions. We can even declare a special kind of procedure, called a **Property** procedure, which offers a more powerful way to define the class's properties. The main difference between an object class and a code module lies in the way they are used.

A code module simply enables us to combine useful code, constants, and global variables into re-useable libraries. When we add a code module to a Visual Basic project, we can call any of its procedures or functions from any other module in the project. To use an object class, however, we must declare an instance of that class. We can then set or retrieve the property values belonging to that class instance and apply its method procedures and functions completely independently of all other instances of the same class. In other words, an object class declares a kind of super user-defined data type.

Object classes enable us to model the behavior of either real world or abstract processes and objects by combining their traits and behavior into a self-contained module.

Limitations Of Visual Basic Objects

In visual programming, most of the work revolves around assigning behavior to the controls. In Visual Basic, that can sometimes make it difficult to design clean object classes. For example, what do you do when the class you're creating is intended to extend the behavior of a control? If Visual Basic supported inheritance, you could declare a new control class based on the existing class, then add your own methods and properties. But because Visual Basic doesn't support inheritance, we end up writing code modules with procedures to perform tasks on data extracted from controls. So, we manipulate data by passing it to procedures instead of asking objects to update their data: procedural code as opposed to object-oriented code.

One way to skirt this particular limitation is to define a new ActiveX control based on a single constituent control, adding whatever code you wish in the UserControl module to extend the constituent control's features—a kind of visual inheritance.

This approach will often enable us to derive our own control classes from existing controls, which would be the only way to accomplish the task in any language unless we had the source code to the original control.

Unfortunately, it still isn't possible to define object class hierarchies for non-control objects. Many applications define families of object types to represent their data. One classic textbook example is a graphics class, which defines a generic graphic object with a pair of methods called **Draw()** and **Erase()**. From this parent class, we declare a subclass called **Line**, which implements its own unique **Draw()** and **Erase()** methods. From **Line**, we derive **Square**, which again implements the methods in a way that draws its namesake shape. And so on. For each child class, we need to write code only for those procedures unique to that object; all other methods are called directly from the nearest ancestor that implements them. For example, the **Line** object may implement a method that draws line segments between two points. The **Square** object could use the same method, located in the **Line** class, to draw its own four sides. In Visual Basic projects, however, no such inheritance exists, so we need to duplicate common code from one class to another. When we decide to modify a commonly used procedure, we need to repeat the changes on each class.

Despite these limitations, Visual Basic object classes provide many of the benefits of object-oriented programming.

Sharing Objects

Each object-oriented programming (OOP) language implements object technology in its own way. By the time you compile a program written in Microsoft Visual C++ or Borland Delphi, the objects have lost their identity. They've become just so much machine code. The purpose of ActiveX technology—and other similar technologies—is to enable objects built in any language to retain their identity as objects, even after they're compiled, so they may be used as objects by other programs written in the same or any other language. ActiveX controls and ActiveX servers are two kinds of "shareable" objects. Any Windows programming language that supports the ActiveX specification—from Borland's Delphi to the Visual Basic macro languages built into Microsoft's Office 97 applications—can use these public objects, regardless of the language in which they were originally written.

Who Needs Pointers?

There's another benefit to Visual Basic's object support—one that is often overlooked. The C programmer's short list of Visual Basic's shortcomings often bemoans its lack of *pointers*. Pointers provide a way to explicitly access particular portions of memory. While the contents of a variable are automatically stored at some indeterminate location in memory, selected and managed by the language's own runtime kernel, a pointer provides the actual memory address of a variable. On their own, variable pointers have little value—it's much easier to let the language kernel and operating system worry about the storage details. But when used together, pointer addresses become a potent tool for data modeling.

In languages like C and Pascal, we can use pointers to assemble *data structures* that organize data in ways that make them more useful. The simplest compound data structure is known as a *linked list*. In a linked list, each data element contains at least one pointer, which specifies the location of the next item in the list. The actual position of each item in memory doesn't make any difference, because we read the items in order according to the daisychain defined by their pointers.

Visual Basic offers plenty of ways to store lists of information. Traditionally, Basic programmers have used arrays for this purpose. But arrays don't work well for all purposes. For one thing, arrays don't shrink and expand easily. Sure, you can **ReDim** them—you can even preserve existing values—that is, unless they're full of holes. But to insert an item into the middle of an array, you need to move all the later elements out of the way. On the other hand, to insert an element into a linked list, you just write it to memory and swap pointers with the existing elements at the insertion point. And because each data element can contain multiple pointers, linked structures can become much more elaborate than the simple lists and tables described by arrays.

Although Visual Basic does not directly support pointers, its object features offer most of the same benefits. An object variable in Visual Basic does not actually contain the object itself, but a reference to an object in memory. Object references serve the same purpose as the memory addresses stored in pointer variables: they provide an indirect reference to the data element. To build a linked list with objects, you can declare a class that includes an object property that references objects of its own class.

You then use that property in each instance of the class to store the reference to the next instance in the list:

```
VERSION 1.0 CLASS
BEGIN
  MultiUse = -1  'True
END
Attribute VB_Name = "MyListClass"
Attribute VB_GlobalNameSpace = False
Attribute VB_Creatable = True
Attribute VB_PredeclaredId = False
Attribute VB_Exposed = False
Option Explicit

Public MyData As String
Public NextElement As MyListClass

Public Sub InsertElement(NewElement As MyListClass)
    Set NewElement.NextElement = Me.NextElement
    Set Me.NextElement = NewElement
    End Sub
```

C and Pascal programmers, even those from the BOOP era (Before Object-Oriented Programming), have long enjoyed the benefits of data modeling, or data abstraction. And while the Visual Basic, object-oriented approach to data abstraction may seem like a work-around for its lack of pointers, it actually embraces the ideals of object-oriented programming. Regardless of the language, OOP eschews memory pointers in favor of object references.

In many of the projects in this book, we'll use Visual Basic object classes to construct some sophisticated data structures. If you're new to data modeling, you'll find that it offers elegant solutions to complex problems. And if you have experience with these techniques, you'll see that you needn't sacrifice them to work in Visual Basic.

Ready To Go

In Chapter 1, we tried out a couple of Visual Basic 5's key Internet technologies. In the chapters that follow, we'll explore these features in much greater depth, incorporating along the way some of the most advanced capabilities of this remarkably flexible programming system.

Just The Facts

CHAPTER 3

Tired of surfing? Unleash your own electronic detectives to hunt down the stuff you need—automatically.

Just The Facts

Each day more information slips away into the abyss known as the World Wide Web. The Web's global, paperless, freely-distributed, hyperlinked free-for-all is supposed to make information more accessible. But the hyperlinks that helped make the Web famous often loop back on themselves, or dead-end in "Weblands" that have long since vanished. Many Web pages drift undiscovered in the deepest recesses of the "docuverse"—unreferenced by other, more frequently visited pages. To find sites otherwise lost among lengthy or broken link chains, search services have become indispensible. But even the best of these often spit out long lists of Web documents cluttered with marginal or irrelevant matches. Worse yet, search services often miss many Web pages. Why? Their creators may have failed to notify the services that they exist, or the services' own indexing systems have yet to stumble across them. To be fair, the search services face a monumental task. To remain current, they need to discover and index the thousands of new pages that go online every day. But that's not all. They have to revisit each site as frequently as possible to determine whether the documents have changed—or, for that matter, whether they even still exist.

So when you're after the latest information, especially on more obscure topics (i.e., anything not about computers or the Internet itself), you may need to sniff it out yourself. So why not take advantage of the same technology used by the big boys? Most search services gather their information in one or both of two ways: by submission from the author or publisher, or by traveling the Web with a program that automatically extracts and follows the hyperlinks from each page it visits. These automated systems form a class of applications known collectively as Web *walkers, crawlers, spiders,* or *robots.*

By combining a few of the techniques we've explored in previous chapters with some new tricks, we can build our own Web robots to uncover some of the Web's better-kept secrets. In this chapter, we'll begin by writing a simple program to demonstrate how to retrieve Web documents with the Hypertext Transfer Protocol (HTTP). Then we'll build a Web Explorer that will extract the links from Web documents and display them in a tree view. Finally, we'll expand that program to incorporate automatic Web traversal and search string matching.

Agents And Bots

In addition to walkers, crawlers, spiders, and robots, you may have heard the term *agent* to describe automatic search programs. The definition of these various terms depends on who you ask.

To "technotopians," agents are diligent assistants—programs endowed with enough intelligence to understand our needs and interests. Like experienced secretaries, they anticipate us, locating and retrieving information before we request it, sometimes before we even *realize* we need it. As wonderful as this might sound, agents of this ilk still reside more in the imagination than on anyone's hard disk.

To more pragmatic programmers, an agent is simply a program that travels from server to server, following explicit instructions to gather specific kinds of information and send it home. Some agents can even clone themselves across the network to run independently and simultaneously on numerous servers. The other term, robot—or *webot*, or just *bot*—applies to a program that stays put on the operator's own system, requesting information from remote servers just as a human operator would—only faster, and with considerably less sleep. Right now, agents don't really exist on the Internet, at least not legitimately. They behave a little too much like viruses, making it difficult for system administrators to guard against malicious or poorly behaved programs that drift in from the Internet. Robots, however, are proliferating so rapidly that the Internet community has been forced to develop a code of ethics to keep them from overwhelming their servers with requests.

Whether you aspire to create full-fledged, intelligent agents or just simple-minded but obedient robots, you'll need to understand and implement the basic mechanics of Web traversal.

Grabbing Documents With HTTP

Most activity on the Web depends on the Hypertext Transfer Protocol. Like the other higher-level Internet protocols we've discussed in earlier chapters, HTTP depends on the TCP/IP protocol to transfer requests and responses across the Internet. HTTP data is nothing more than a bunch of bits, just like any other data traveling the Net. The interpretation of those requests and responses is up to the programs running on either end of the connection—specifically, the Web server and Web browser. Without servers and browsers, there is no Web.

Although you won't need an intimate knowledge of HTTP to understand and expand the projects in this chapter, a little background will make it easier. Once you've mastered the basics, you can develop more sophisticated applications that take advantage of the protocol's more advanced features.

Requesting A Document

HTTP is one of the easiest Internet protocols to implement. After you've established a connection to a server, you just send a string containing the **Get** method

```
"Get /anysubdirectory/…/anydocument.htm"
```

followed by a carriage return and line feed. If the server locates the requested document, it begins sending it to the client. The client grabs the chunks that come across the Internet and assembles them back into a complete document, then saves or displays it.

Headers And Their Fields

The Get method string is actually a field, belonging to an HTTP request header. Along with the *method field*, you may send various optional *request fields*, each ending with a carriage return and line feed. For example, most Web browsers now identify themselves with a request field called *User-Agent:*

```
User-Agent: Mozilla/2.0 (compatible; MSIE 3.0B; Windows 95)
```

This User-Agent field identifies the browser as Microsoft Internet Explorer 3.0 for Windows 95, which is compatible with Mozilla 2.0, otherwise known as Netscape Navigator. The User-Agent field for Netscape Navigator 2.0 itself looks like this:

```
User-Agent: Mozilla/2.0 (Win95; I)
```

Some servers use the information in the User-Agent field to respond to each browser with documents designed specifically for that client. Another header field, *Accept,* tells the server what types of data the client will accept.

No matter how many fields it includes, however, the request header is just a block of text transferred from one IP address to another using TCP/IP.

The server's response also begins with a header—appropriately called a *response header*—which includes a status line, followed by various fields such as Content-type, Last-modified, and Content-length. The header is separated from the data, or *object*, with a blank line—a double carriage return and line feed sequence—as shown in Listing 3.1.

Listing 3.1 A typical HTTP response header.

```
HTTP/1.0 200 Document follows
Date: Wed, 11 Sep 1996 22:28:18 GMT
Server: Apache/1.1.1
Content-type: text/html
Content-length: 4294
Last-modified: Thu, 15 Aug 1996 19:10:46 GMT
```

Here Comes The Data

The data object immediately follows the header, as part of the continuing byte stream. Usually, documents of more than just a few bytes arrive in multiple chunks. Each time a new chunk arrives, the Windows Socket notifies the client that it has received a block of data. The client application then accepts that chunk and appends it to its buffer. The client knows when it has received the entire object either by comparing the number of bytes received to the value passed in the Content-length response header field, or by waiting for the server to close the connection. So the whole thing—header and data object combined—comes from the server as a single transmission. If the client application is quick enough, it can split off the header as it arrives. If not, it can wait until it has collected the entire document, then interpret the header to determine what type of data it has received.

Learn More About HTTP

For more information on HTTP, see the Web site of the World Wide Web Consortium at http://www.w3.org. The Consortium not only manages Web standards but publishes numerous technical articles, along with Web news and announcements.

Of course, several things can interrupt this data exchange, or at least slow it down. The server may not respond at all, which cancels the entire operation. Errors can also crop up after the request or reply have begun. Which only proves that the simplest protocol can still become pretty hairy. Fortunately, the Inet ActiveX control organizes the entire process into a set of Visual Basic compatible properties, events, and methods.

HTTP In Action

In this simple project, we'll use the Inet ActiveX control to request and receive HTML documents from Web servers.

To run this program, establish your connection to the Internet, and run the HTTP experiment project, called HTTPExp1, from the book's CD-ROM. The program's only form (shown in Figure 3.1) will display four controls, one of which is just a label.

Enter the URL of any HTML or text document—*not* the URL of a media object, such as a GIF or AIF file—into the URL TextBox and click "Perform Request." The program will first locate the specified Web server and then request the document. As the document arrives, block by block, it will appear in the text box control. You may cancel the transfer by clicking the command button again. The text box will display the actual HTML source of the requested document.

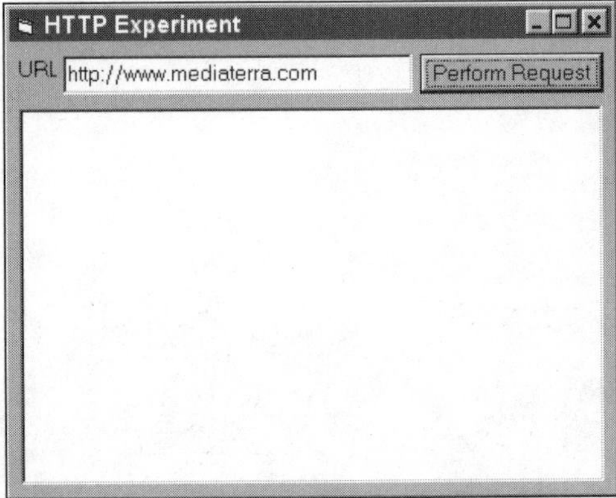

Figure 3.1
The project HTTPExp1 at runtime.

Designing The HTTP Experiment Form

This project is contained entirely within a single form and includes five controls, listed in Table 3.1. The Internet Transfer Control (called the Inet control) will perform all the HTTP operations. The two different types of text controls will display the current URL and the downloaded document text. The command button both activates and cancels the operation of the Inet control.

If you build this project from scratch—or build any other project that uses the Inet control—you'll need to add it to the Visual Basic Toolbox. For this project and the others in this chapter, you'll also need the RichTextBox control. To add these controls, either right click the Toolbox and select Components from the popup menu, or select Project Components from the main menu. Next, select the Microsoft Internet Transfer Control and the Microsoft RichTextBox control (as shown in Figure 3.2) and click OK. If you open the existing project files from the companion CD-ROM, VB will add these controls to its toolbox automatically.

Performing An HTTP Document Transfer

The event procedure **cmdPerformRequest_Click()**, shown in Listing 3.2, toggles the CommandButton's caption, and either activates or deactivates **Inet1**. The

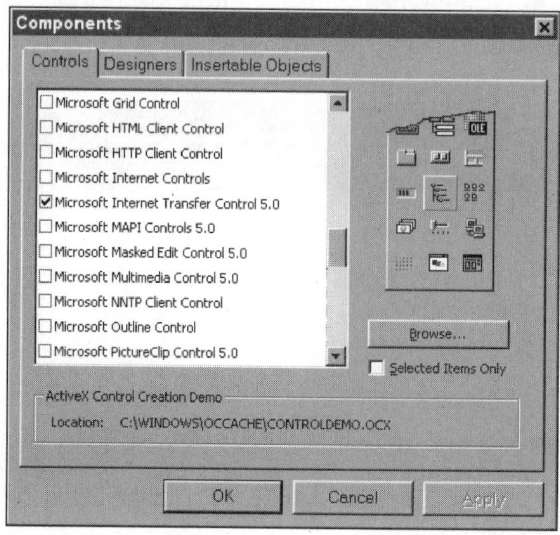

Figure 3.2
Adding controls to the VB Toolbox.

Table 3.1 The controls and properties for the form frmHTTPExp1.

Control Name	Type	Properties	Value
frmHTTPExp1	Form	Caption	"HTTP Experiment"
cmdPerformRequest	CommandButton	Caption	"Perform Request"
Inet1	Inet	Protocol	4 - icHTTP
lblURL	Label	Caption	"URL:"
txtOutput	RichTextBox	Text	""
txtURL	TextBox	Text	"http://www.mediaterra.com"

form-level boolean variable, **bPerformingRequest**, keeps track of the current status of the Inet control.

Listing 3.2 The complete listing of frmHTTPExp1.FRM from the project HTTP1.VBP.

```
Option Explicit

Dim bPerformingRequest As Boolean

Private Sub cmdPerformRequest_Click()
    On Error GoTo Error
    If bPerformingRequest Then
        Inet1.Cancel
        bPerformingRequest = False
        cmdPerformRequest.Caption = "Perform Request"
      Else
        txtOutput.Text = ""
        bPerformingRequest = True
        cmdPerformRequest.Caption = "Cancel Request"
        Inet1.Execute txtURL.Text
      End If
    Exit Sub

Error:
    MsgBox "Unable to Contact Host" & vbCrLf & _
           "Check URL.", vbCritical, "HTTP Error"
    End Sub


Private Sub Form_Resize()
    If Me.WindowState = vbMinimized Then
```

```
        Exit Sub
      End If
    If Me.ScaleWidth < _
        (lblURL.Width + _
         cmdPerformRequest.Width + _
         200 + 3 * 72) Then
        Me.Width = lblURL.Width + _
            cmdPerformRequest.Width + _
            500 + 4 * 72 + 4
    End If
    If Me.ScaleHeight < _
        (txtOutput.Top + 500 + 72) Then
        Me.Height = txtOutput.Top + 500 + 72
    End If
    lblURL.Left = 72
    txtURL.Left = lblURL.Left + lblURL.Width + 72
    txtURL.Width = Me.ScaleWidth - _
        (txtURL.Left + cmdPerformRequest.Width + 144)
    cmdPerformRequest.Left = Me.ScaleWidth - _
        (cmdPerformRequest.Width + 72)
    txtOutput.Left = 72
    txtOutput.Width = Me.ScaleWidth - 144
    txtOutput.Height = Me.ScaleHeight - _
        (txtOutput.Top + 72)
    End Sub

Private Sub Inet1_StateChanged(ByVal State As Integer)
    Dim Loc As Long
    Dim sHeaderValue As String
    Dim vtData As Variant
    Dim vtBinaryData As Variant

    Select Case State
      Case icNone
      Case icResolvingHost
      Case icHostResolved
      Case icConnecting
      Case icConnected
        Loc = InStr(Inet1.URL, ":80")
        If Loc > 0 Then
            txtURL.Text = Left(Inet1.URL, Loc - 1) & _
                Mid(Inet1.URL, Loc + 3)
          Else
            txtURL.Text = Inet1.URL
          End If
      Case icRequesting
```

```
        Case icRequestSent
        Case icReceivingResponse
        Case icResponseReceived
        Case icDisconnecting
        Case icDisconnected
        Case icError
        Case icResponseCompleted
          sHeaderValue = Inet1.GetHeader("Content-type")
          If InStr(1, sHeaderValue, "text/", 1) Then
              vtData = Inet1.GetChunk(1024, icString)
              Do While Len(vtData) > 0
                  txtOutput.Text = txtOutput.Text + vtData
                  vtData = Inet1.GetChunk(1024, icString)
                  Loop
            Else
              vtData = Inet1.GetChunk(1024, icByteArray)
              Do While Len(vtData) > 0
                  vtBinaryData = vtBinaryData + vtData
                  vtData = Inet1.GetChunk(1024, icByteArray)
                  Loop
            End If
          bPerformingRequest = False
          cmdPerformRequest.Caption = "Perform Request"
        Case Else
        End Select
    End Sub

Private Sub txtURL_KeyPress(KeyAscii As Integer)
    If KeyAscii = 13 Then
        cmdPerformRequest_Click
      End If
    End Sub
```

All the meaningful activity in this program takes place within the **Inet1_StateChanged**() event procedure. The **State** argument receives a simple integer value that indicates the current status of the current transfer request. Once the Inet control's **Execute**() method has been called, it automatically performs a series of operations, each of which triggers a state change. First, it must determine the IP address of the Web server specified in the given URL, a procedure known as *resolving the host*. It must then try to establish a connection to the host before sending its request. If the host server accepts the connection and the document request, it begins to send the requested document, which triggers one receiving response state change for each block of data transferred. When the entire document has arrived, the control will raise the response completed state. Finally, it disconnects from the server, raising the disconnecting and disconnected states.

In this project, we'll respond to only two of the state change events: **icConnected** and **icResponseCompleted.** Often, the Web server we contact will translate a simplified or *aliased* URL into a more precise URL. After it connects to the server, the Inet control will set its **URL** property to the URL reported by the server. We'll take advantage of the **icConnected** state change to display the actual URL resolved by the Inet control. I've also taken the liberty of slightly simplifying the URL. A complete HTTP URL includes the IP socket number. Normally this value follows the server domain name, separated by a colon:

```
http://www.microsoft.com:80/
```

Because all Web operations on the public Web take place on socket 80, no one ever bothers to include the socket number when they display their URL. However, the Inet control's **URL** property reports the complete legal URL. Since I find this annoying, I prefer to undo some of its handiwork.

Instead of handling each data block as it arrives, which we could do within the **icResponseReceived** state change event, we'll just wait until the entire document has arrived. First, we call the Inet control's **GetHeader**() method to retrieve the value of the Content-type response header field, which identifies the type of data transferred. All Web text files should be preceded by a Content-type header containing a string that begins with "text/". The header for an HTML document will contain "text/HTML". Once we determine whether the data represents text or binary information, we can then use the Inet control's **GetChunk**() method to retrieve the document from its buffer.

GetChunk() takes two arguments: an integer specifying the number of bytes to pull off the front of the buffer, and a data type for the return value (which may specify either a string or a byte array). To retrieve the entire contents of the buffer, we call **GetChunk**() repeatedly within a loop until it returns an empty result.

The Inet control handles all interaction with the Web server. All we need to retrieve a document is its URL. In the next project, we'll use the same simple features of the Inet control to build an application that will trace and display Web document hyperlinks.

Tree The Web

Okay. Now you know how to retrieve a Web document without the aid of Navigator or Internet Explorer—or any other browser, for that matter. You have absolute power, so let's use it. In this section, we'll develop a project called the Visual Basic Web Explorer. If you want a preview, you can load the finished version of the project from the book's CD-ROM.

A Pruned Tree Is A Happy Tree

Because it's hyperlinked, the Web sometimes deludes us into believing that it's well organized. What a bunch of malarkey—it's a rat's nest. But that's fine. All those cross-wired, hot-listed, cool-sited, hyperlinked pages act like a maniacal superhighway system with interchanges running every which way. The more links it contains, the more routes by which to travel. The only drawback is that it's easy to get lost.

To avoid running in circles, we need some way to keep track of where we've already been. To help us manage our offline resources, the Windows 95 Explorer displays a tree view of all the directories on our disk drives, including all network volumes and virtual drives. Directories—or folders, as they are known by those weaned on GUIs—naturally organize themselves into tree structures, so it's no great trick to display them as a tree. But the Web is not a tree. It's not even much of a web—more like a tangled thicket. Nevertheless, a tree turns out to be one of the best search patterns for the Web. We'll call our Web tree project "the Web Explorer."

Each Web document may contain any number of hyperlinks, either to other locations within itself or to other pages anywhere on the Internet. To ensure that we've thoroughly explored all the paths that lead from any given document, we can keep a list of its links. We can then follow the first link to the next page. That page, in turn, may offer several branches of its own. We could explore each of those branches, or return to the first page and advance to its next link. The depth to which we follow any particular path is arbitrary.

If we keep jumping from document to document until we hit a dead end—a page with no further links—we could find ourselves hundreds or thousands of links away from our point of departure. As we select each link, our travel tree sprouts new limbs. Some links will re-appear from time to time. This happens often when you're browsing through a bunch of Web sites about the same or similar subjects; their pages may contain their own lists of recommended links, all pointing to each other. By pruning duplicate links as they appear, we ensure that every branch leads to a unique destination. The tree-shaped map not only charts our adventure, but clearly marks the paths yet untraveled.

Running The Web Explorer

The Web Explorer gives you a way to graphically search the Web for files. If you want to follow along with the steps explained here, locate the Web Explorer on the CD and load it.

At runtime, the Web Explorer displays four principal controls:

- A TextBox in which you may enter new URLs
- A CommandButton to start retrieval of the document at the specified URL
- A tree-diagram view in which you may select and activate URLs already unearthed by the program
- A TextBox that displays the raw text of the latest Web page retrieved

The StatusBar at the bottom of the window displays information about the current HTTP connection, along with the current time and date.

Enter the URL of your favorite Web site in the URL TextBox and click the "Perform Request" button. The program locates the server and begins retrieving the document, updating the main TextBox as new data blocks arrive. When it has received the entire document, it will add its URL and the URLs of all the image files and hyperlinks it contains to the TreeView on the left. To expand one of the newly added document nodes, click it. Once again, the program will retrieve the document at the specified URL and add its links to the TreeView.

Unlike the directory tree on your local hard drive, the tree that grows from your Web explorations does not comprehensively depict the Web's real structure. Let's say, for example, that you visit two Web sites about dogs, each of which contains a hyperlink to the American Kennel Club Web page. To prevent redundancy, that link can appear only at one node in the tree, meaning that it will be listed under whichever dog site you visit first. The Visual Basic Web Explorer does not map the Web; it maps your path *through* the Web.

Designing The Web Explorer Form

In this project, we'll use the TreeView control to map our Web explorations. We'll begin by writing a procedure that extracts all the hyperlinks from a document, using that information to add a new node to the TreeView for each link we find.

We'll add 8 new controls for this project, bringing our total to 13, as shown in Figure 3.3 and listed in Table 3.2. Most of them play supporting roles—only six actually contain event code.

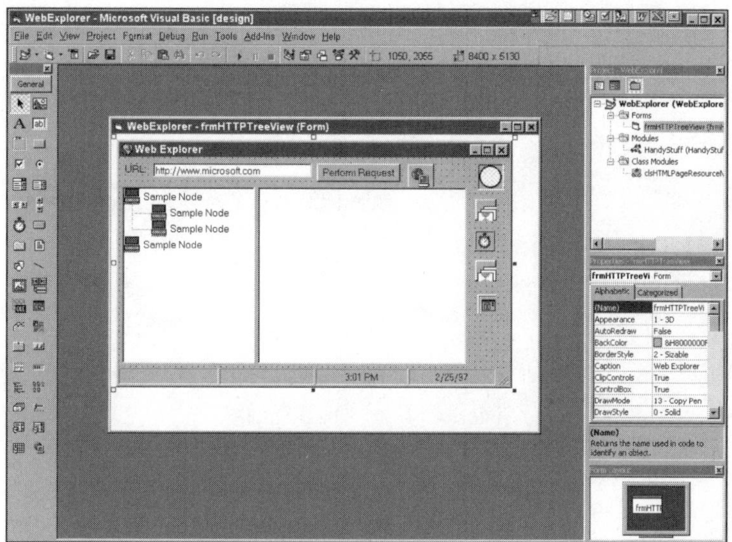

Figure 3.3
The form frmWebExplorer.FRM at design time.

Table 3.2 The controls and properties for the form FRMHTTPTreeView in the Web Explorer.

Control Name	Type	Properties	Value
frmHTTPTreeView	Form	Caption	"Web Explorer"
Inet1	Inet	Protocol	4 - icHTTP
cmdPerformRequest	CommandButton	Caption	"Perform Request"
cmnSaveAs	CommonDialog	CancelError	True
ilBusyIcons	ImageList	(Custom)	

continued

Table 3.2 The controls and properties for the form frmHTTPTreeView in the Web Explorer (continued).

Control Name	Type	Properties	Value
ilTreeIcons	ImageList	(Custom)	
lblURL	Label	Caption	"URL:"
picBusy	PictureBox	Appearance	1 - 3D
	BorderStyle	1 - Fixed Single	
picDivider	PictureBox	Appearance	1 - 3D
	AutoSize	False	
	BackColor	&H00C0C0C0	
	BorderStyle	None	
	MousePointer	9 - Size W E	
sbHTTPStatus	StatusBar	Align	2 - Align Bottom
	Style		0 - Multiple panels
tmrBusy	Timer	Enabled	False
	Interval		500
tvURLTreeView	TreeView	Appearance	1 - 3D
	BorderStyle	1 - Fixed Single	
	Style		7 - Treelines, ...
txtOutput	TextBox	BorderStyle	1 - Fixed Single
	MultiLine	True	
	ScrollBars	3 - Both	
	Text		""
txtURL	TextBox	BorderStyle	1 - Fixed Single
	MultiLine	False	
	ScrollBars	0 - None	
	Text		""

Requesting A Web Document

Beginning with the **cmdPerformRequest_Click()** event procedure (shown in Listing 3.3), you can see that this program handles more detail than the previous example.

Listing 3.3 The **cmdPerformRequest_Click()** event procedure from the Web Explorer project.

```
Private Sub cmdPerformRequest_Click()
    Dim FileExtension As String
    Dim TargetFilename As String
    Dim TempURL As String
    Dim vtBinaryData As Variant
    Dim BinaryData() As Byte
    Const BinaryFileID = 1

    TempURL = txtURL.Text
    If Not URLNormalized(TempURL) Then
        MsgBox "Please enter a valid URL", vbCritical, "Invalid URL"
        Exit Sub
      Else
        txtURL.Text = TempURL
      End If
    If Not bPerformingRequest Then
        FileExtension = Trim(LCase( _
           ExtractFilenameExtensionFromPath(txtURL.Text)))
        Select Case FileExtension
          Case "gif", "jpg"
            BinaryFile = True
            TargetFilename = App.Path & "\" & _
                 ExtractFilenameFromPath(txtURL.Text)
            cmnSaveAs.filename = TargetFilename
            cmnSaveAs.DefaultExt = Right(TargetFilename, 4)
            cmnSaveAs.Filter = "Images(*.bmp;*.gif;*.jpg)"
            cmnSaveAs.CancelError = True
            On Error GoTo Skip
            cmnSaveAs.ShowSave
            bPerformingRequest = True
            cmdPerformRequest.Caption = "Cancel Request"
            txtURL.Enabled = False
            Me.MousePointer = vbHourglass
            tmrBusy.Enabled = True
            FilenameForBinaryData = cmnSaveAs.filename

            BinaryData() = Inet1.OpenURL(txtURL.Text, icByteArray)
            If bPerformingRequest Then
                Open FilenameForBinaryData For Binary As BinaryFileID
                Put BinaryFileID, , BinaryData()
                Close BinaryFileID
```

```
            End If

          ' Alternative way to handle binary files:
          'Inet1.Execute txtURL.Text

          txtURL.Enabled = True
          tmrBusy.Enabled = False
          Me.MousePointer = vbDefault

          ' To use Execute() method on binary files,
          ' remove the following line:
          bPerformingRequest = False

          cmdPerformRequest.Enabled = True
          cmdPerformRequest.Caption = "Perform Request"
Skip:     'User cancelled Save As dialog
        Case Else
          ' This case will handle any HTML document request,
          ' whether or not it includes a filename,
          ' because a URL with no filename will cause the
          ' web server to return its default HTML document
          ' file.

          bPerformingRequest = True
          cmdPerformRequest.Caption = "Cancel Request"
          tmrBusy.Enabled = True
          Me.MousePointer = vbArrowHourglass
          txtURL.Enabled = False
          BinaryFile = False
          txtOutput.Text = ""

          Set PageResources = New clsHTMLPageResourceNode
          txtOutput.Text = ""
          Inet1.Execute txtURL.Text
        End Select
    Else
      Inet1.Cancel
      bPerformingRequest = False
      cmdPerformRequest.Caption = "Perform Request"
      tmrBusy.Enabled = False
      Me.MousePointer = vbDefault
      txtURL.Enabled = True
      Set PageResources = Nothing
    End If
  End Sub
```

Before doing anything else, **cmdPerformRequest_Click**() verifies that the URL entered in the **txtURL** TextBox appears to be valid. It does this by calling the **URLNormalized**() function (shown in Listing 3.4), which is in the code module HandyStuff.BAS. Aside from identifying an actual server, a URL needs to conform to some simple standards. First, it must begin with a numeral or letter. Secondly, it must begin with a protocol identifier (known to the Internet high priesthood as a *scheme*). Lastly, it should end with a slash if it does not end with the name of an *object*—in other words, a filename. Some of these rules can be handled by the Domain Name Server when it tries to resolve the URL to an IP address, and some are handled automatically by the Inet control itself. But it's still possible to trigger a runtime error with a totally bogus URL, so it's best either to reject it or convert it to an acceptable form if possible. If **URLNormalized**() can't recognize or repair the URL, it returns **False**. If the URL passes muster, the string variable passed to the function by reference will contain a valid URL and the function will return **True**.

Listing 3.4 The **URLNormalized()** function from HandyStuff.BAS.

```
Public Function URLNormalized(URL As String) As Boolean
    Dim TempURL As String
    Dim ValidFirstChar As Boolean

    TempURL = URL
    Select Case Asc(Left(TempURL, 1))
      Case 48 To 57
        ValidFirstChar = True
      Case 65 To 90
        ValidFirstChar = True
      Case 97 To 122
        ValidFirstChar = True
      Case Else
        ValidFirstChar = False
      End Select

    If ValidFirstChar Then
        If (InStr(TempURL, "//") = 0) Then
            TempURL = "http://" & TempURL
          End If
        If (Not URLEndsWithFilename(TempURL)) And _
           (Not (Right(TempURL, 1) = "/")) And _
           (InStr(8, TempURL, "/") = 0) Then
            TempURL = TempURL & "/"
```

```
        End If
      URL = TempURL
      URLNormalized = True
    Else
      URLNormalized = False
    End If

  End Function
```

URLNormalized() can't be trusted completely because it cheats. You'll notice that it calls the function **URLEndsWithFilename**(), shown in Listing 3.5 and also located in HandyStuff.BAS. In fact, the analysis performed by this function qualifies as little more than than an educated guess. Let's break it down.

Listing 3.5 The function **URLEndsWithFilename()** from HandyStuff.BAS.

```
Public Function URLEndsWithFilename(URL As String) As Boolean
    Dim Loc As Long

    If Right(URL, 1) = "/" Then
        URLEndsWithFilename = False
      Else
        Loc = InStr(URL, "//")
        If Loc > 0 Then
            If InStr(Loc + 2, URL, "/") > 0 Then
                URLEndsWithFilename = True
              Else
                URLEndsWithFilename = False
              End If
          Else
            URLEndsWithFilename = True
          End If
      End If
    End Function
```

You can begin by eliminating any URL that ends with a forward slash. Next, look for a double forward slash—indicating a complete URL—beginning with a protocol identifier. All *complete* URLs must include a protocol identifier, but many of the URLs that we'll uncover as links within documents won't include the protocol and server identifiers. We'll eventually want to use this function to analyze those *relative* URLs as well, so we'll need to consider both cases. When we do find a double slash, it can't be followed by anything but a server name or IP address. In other words, unless the URL contains another slash somewhere after the double slash, it doesn't end with a filename.

In truth, the only reliable way to tell whether a URL contains a filename—and if so, what type of data it contains—is by asking the Web server for its header. To validate a URL in advance (before contacting the server) or even to determine whether it contains a filename, you have to scrutinize it and hope for the best. It almost always works.

After the URL has been verified or modified, **cmdPerformRequest_Click()** examines **bPerformingRequest** to confirm that a file transfer is not already underway. If not, it calls another function in the HandyStuff.BAS code module, **ExtractFilename ExtensionFromPath()**, shown in Listing 3.6.

Listing 3.6 **ExtractFilenameExtensionFromPath()** from HandyStuff.BAS.

```
Public Function ExtractFilenameExtensionFromPath(ByVal Path As String) As
String
    Dim StringPos As Long

    If Right(Path, 1) = "/" Then
        ExtractFilenameExtensionFromPath = ""
      ElseIf (Left(Right(Path, 4), 1) = ".") Then
        ExtractFilenameExtensionFromPath = Right(Path, 3)
      ElseIf (Left(Right(Path, 5), 1) = ".") Then
        ExtractFilenameExtensionFromPath = Right(Path, 4)
      Else
        ExtractFilenameExtensionFromPath = ""
      End If

    End Function
```

While this function is based on the same foolish assumptions as **URLEndsWith Filename()**, we can easily cope with the consequences, as you'll see shortly.

The bulk of **cmdPerformRequest_Click()** lies within a **Select Case** statement that selects on **FileExtension**. This version of the procedure handles only two general cases, graphics and text. Any file that does not qualify as a GIF or JPG falls through to the **Case Else** clause, where it's treated as text. On the Web, a URL that doesn't contain a filename almost always represents a text file, specifically an HTML file, or even more specifically, a file named Index.Htm or Index.Html. This helpful convention makes it possible to contact almost any Web server with just its server URL.

This lazy method of differentiating between text files and binary files could have some serious consequences, because the Inet control could download an entire binary file—a 10 megabyte video clip, for instance—before we check its Content-type header and reject it. We could test for all known binary filename extensions, but that wouldn't trap file types that have appeared since the program was last updated. The most reliable way to identify the type of data contained within a file is to query the server for header information, which we'll do in the next project.

Except for the code that activates the "Save As" CommonDialog control, most of the code within the two case clauses disables other controls to prevent mishaps during the file transfer. It also activates the animation that acts as a "busy" indicator. Each of the clauses also invokes a different method to initiate its file transfer.

Receiving The File

cmdPerformRequest_Click() calls the function method **Inet1.OpenURL**() to retrieve a binary image file and the procedure method **Inet1.Execute**() to retrieve a text file. **OpenURL**() performs a *synchronous* data transfer, which means that it chugs the entire file in one continuous series of gulps; program execution pauses until **OpenURL**() returns a complete object. When you invoke the **OpenURL**() method of the Inet control, all the state change events will occur on the control except **icResponseCompleted**. That state change is reserved for *asynchronous* transfers performed with the **Execute**() method. When we use the **Execute**() method, the **icResponseCompleted** state change signals us that the Inet control has come to the end of an asynchronous data transfer. **Execute**() does not pause program execution, so we need to monitor the Inet control and collect the contents of its buffer—either as the file downloads (in response to a series of **icResponseReceived** state changes within the Inet control's **StateChanged**() event) or when it has finished (**icResponseCompleted**).

If we use the **OpenURL**() method, we have nothing further to do. We don't even need to implement the **Inet1_StateChanged**() event. If we use the **Execute**() method, however, we need to implement at least one state change handler within the **Inet1_StateChanged**() event procedure, as shown in Listing 3.7.

Listing 3.7 The **Inet1_StateChanged()** event procedure from frmHTTPTreeView.FRM.

```
Private Sub Inet1_StateChanged(ByVal State As Integer)
    Dim Loc As Long
    Dim sHeaderValue As String
    Dim vtDataChunk As Variant
    Dim BinaryData() As Byte
    Dim Offset As Long
    Dim Counter As Long
    Dim BinaryFileID As Integer

    Select Case State
      Case icNone
      Case icResolvingHost
        Debug.Print "Resolving Host"
      Case icHostResolved
        Debug.Print "Host Resolved"
      Case icConnecting
        Debug.Print "Connecting"
      Case icConnected
        Loc = InStr(Inet1.URL, ":80")
        If Loc > 0 Then
            txtURL.Text = Left(Inet1.URL, Loc - 1) & _
                 Mid(Inet1.URL, Loc + 3)
          Else
            txtURL.Text = Inet1.URL
          End If
      Case icRequesting
        Debug.Print "Requesting"
      Case icRequestSent
        Debug.Print "Request Sent"
      Case icReceivingResponse
        Debug.Print "Receiving Response"
      Case icResponseReceived
        Debug.Print "Response Received"
      Case icDisconnecting
        Debug.Print "Disconnecting"
      Case icDisconnected
        Debug.Print "Disconnected"
      Case icError
        Debug.Print "Error"
      Case icResponseCompleted
        Debug.Print "Response Completed"
        sHeaderValue = Inet1.GetHeader("Content-type")
        If (Not BinaryFile) And _
```

```
      InStr(1, sHeaderValue, "text/", 1) Then
      vtDataChunk = Inet1.GetChunk(1024, icString)
      Do While Len(vtDataChunk) > 0
          txtOutput.Text = txtOutput.Text + vtDataChunk
          vtDataChunk = Inet1.GetChunk(1024, icString)
          Loop
    Else
      ' Alternative way to handle binary files.
      ReDim BinaryData(0)
      vtDataChunk = Inet1.GetChunk(1024, icByteArray)
      Do While UBound(vtDataChunk) > 0
          If UBound(BinaryData) = 0 Then
              Offset = 0
            Else
              Offset = UBound(BinaryData) + 1
            End If
          ReDim Preserve BinaryData(LBound(BinaryData) _
              To Offset + UBound(vtDataChunk))
          For Counter = 0 To UBound(vtDataChunk)
              BinaryData(Counter + Offset) = _
                   CByte(vtDataChunk(Counter))
              Next Counter
          vtDataChunk = Inet1.GetChunk(1024, icByteArray)
          Loop
    End If
  If bPerformingRequest Then
      If Not BinaryFile Then
          PageResources.URL = txtURL.Text
          PageResources.AddLinksFromDocument txtOutput.Text, _
              txtURL
          AddLinksToTreeView PageResources
        Else
          ' Alternative way to handle binary files.
          BinaryFileID = FreeFile
          Open FilenameForBinaryData For Binary As BinaryFileID
          Put BinaryFileID, , BinaryData()
          Close BinaryFileID
        End If
      txtURL.Enabled = True
      tmrBusy.Enabled = False
      Me.MousePointer = vbDefault
      bPerformingRequest = False
      cmdPerformRequest.Enabled = True
      cmdPerformRequest.Caption = "Perform Request"
```

```
            End If
        Case Else
        End Select

    End Sub
```

In this program, I have arbitrarily chosen to perform synchronous transfers for binary data, and asynchronous transfers for text data. The **Inet1_StateChanged()** event procedure contains code to handle binary files asynchronously:

```
Else
  ' Alternative way to handle binary files.
  ReDim BinaryData(0)
  vtDataChunk = Inet1.GetChunk(1024, icByteArray)
  Do While UBound(vtDataChunk) > 0
      If UBound(BinaryData) = 0 Then
          Offset = 0
        Else
          Offset = UBound(BinaryData) + 1
        End If
      ReDim Preserve BinaryData(LBound(BinaryData) To Offset + _
          UBound(vtDataChunk))
      For Counter = 0 To UBound(vtDataChunk)
          BinaryData(Counter + Offset) = CByte(vtDataChunk(Counter))
          Next Counter
      vtDataChunk = Inet1.GetChunk(1024, icByteArray)
      Loop
.
.
.
    Else
      ' Alternative way to handle binary files.
      BinaryFileID = FreeFile
      Open FilenameForBinaryData For Binary As BinaryFileID
      Put BinaryFileID, , BinaryData()
      Close BinaryFileID
```

You'll find annotations in **cmdPerformRequest_Click()** that indicate how to use the **Execute()** method for binary files. The reverse is also true: you may use the **OpenURL()** method to retrieve text data. For this program, the simpler **OpenURL()** method might well have worked in all cases. But in other projects, you may need to perform asynchronous transfers. Asynchronous operations are advantageous because they permit the program to continue performing other tasks concurrently with the data transfer, such as playing audio files as they arrive instead of waiting for the entire file to download. The Web Explorer isn't doing anything that requires concurrency, so you could easily (and harmlessly) simplify the program by eliminating all the code that handles asynchronous transfers.

Extracting The Hyperlinks

Next, we'll read through the document we've retrieved and locate all the links it contains. But before we design procedures to perform that task, we'll need a place to store the results. I've chosen to define a class of objects to hold the links. The most significant advantages of this method will become even more apparent when we tackle the next project. But even here, the object-oriented approach again enables us to encapsulate the data and its behavior in a portable, re-usable class module.

An Object With Growth Potential

The class **clsHTMLPageResourceNode** defines an object that represents the links belonging to a Web page, including the page's own location on the Web, as shown in Listing 3.8.

Listing 3.8 The **clsHTMLPageResourceNode** class.

```
Option Explicit

Public Parent As clsHTMLPageResourceNode
Public URL As String
Public Path As String
Public MatchesSearch As Boolean
Public PageLinks As New Collection
Public PageElements As New Collection

Public Function AlreadyContains(TargetNodeKey As String, _
           MatchingNode As clsHTMLPageResourceNode) As Boolean

    Dim WebNode As clsHTMLPageResourceNode
    Dim NodeFound As Boolean

    DoEvents
    NodeFound = (Me.URL = TargetNodeKey)
    If NodeFound Then
        Set MatchingNode = Me
```

```
      Else
        For Each WebNode In Me.PageLinks
            If WebNode.AlreadyContains( _
               TargetNodeKey, MatchingNode) Then
                NodeFound = True
                Exit For
              End If
            Next WebNode
        If Not NodeFound Then
            For Each WebNode In Me.PageElements
                If WebNode.AlreadyContains( _
                    TargetNodeKey, MatchingNode) Then
                    NodeFound = True
                    Exit For
                  End If
                Next WebNode
          End If
      End If
    AlreadyContains = NodeFound
    End Function

Public Sub RemoveLinks()
    ' This recursive procedure removes all
    ' nodes connected to the node on which
    ' the method was first invoked, eliminating
    ' the entire sub-tree.

    Dim WebNode As clsHTMLPageResourceNode

    For Each WebNode In PageLinks
        WebNode.RemoveLinks
        PageLinks.Remove WebNode.URL
        Next WebNode
    For Each WebNode In PageElements
        ' These nodes are always terminal,
        ' i.e., their collections are always
        ' empty, so we can save some time by not
        ' recursing.
        PageElements.Remove WebNode.URL
        Next WebNode

    End Sub

Private Sub Class_Terminate()
    ' As a precaution, remove all items
    ' from the two collections.
```

```
    RemoveLinks
    End Sub

Public Function Root() As clsHTMLPageResourceNode

    If Me.Parent Is Nothing Then
        Set Root = Me
      Else
        Set Root = Me.Parent.Root
      End If

    End Function
```

We'll begin with the **clsHTMLPageResourceNode** properties, but let's skip the **Parent** property for now. We'll come back to it shortly.

The **URL** and **Path** properties hold the full URL and relative path of the page. When you ask the program to retrieve a Web page, you must specify a complete and valid URL. This assures that **URL** and **Path** will contain the same string. Links within a page, however, may contain an abbreviated URL. For example, we might retrieve a document with the following URL:

```
http://www.webserver.com/mainpage.html
```

The document mainpage.html may contain a hyperlink to another page on the same server:

```
<a href="http://www.webserver.com/anotherpage.htm">another page</a>
```

This same link could be expressed in an abbreviated form as:

```
<a href="/anotherpage.htm">another page</a>
```

This shortened version is known as a *relative path*. Only URLs extracted from pages can specify a relative path—a path based on the page's own URL. Complete URLs can become lengthy, which could crowd our TreeView with redundant information. So we'll keep the complete URL as a way to uniquely and fully identify each Web link, and we'll keep the relative path as a way to display concise captions in the TreeView control.

Sure, you could store just the relative path for each link and use the page's own URL to reconstruct a complete link URL on demand. But when we add the links to the

TreeView control, each link will require a unique URL to serve as a *key* value in the TreeView control's **Nodes** collection. We can't depend on a sub-path alone as a unique identifier; it's actually common for pages on many servers to share the same name—especially the default page, Index.html. The names of subdirectories within servers also tend to follow some conventions. So the only way to guarantee a unique file identifier—known in net-speak as a *universal resource identifier (URI)*—is to include its complete URL.

A Web page may contain two types of links: hyperlinks to other pages, and links to other files—such as images, sounds, or other media elements—needed to display the page. We'll store hyperlinks in the **PageLinks** property and links to media files in **PageElements**.

PageLinks and **PageElements** are collections—but collections of what? Once they are populated, they become collections of objects belonging to the class **clsHTMLPageResourceNode.** This means that each object belonging to this class contains two collections of other objects belonging to the same class. So each page resource node contains the seed of a page resource tree. By adding members to either its **PageLinks** or **PageElements** collection, it becomes a tree with two tiers. If we add members to either of the collections belonging to the members added to the first node, the tree grows to three tiers, and so on. Do not confuse this tree with the TreeView control's tree. The TreeView control uses an object class called **Node**, which also forms a tree—but one that is based on a completely different structure. For this project, trees based on **clsHTMLPageResourceNode** will never exceed two tiers—a page node and two collections of link nodes—and will serve only as temporary work spaces. In the next project, we'll extend the function of this tree so that it grows in tandem with the tree displayed in the TreeView control.

The **Parent** property identifies the node to which any given node belongs. The two collections enable us to climb out on the tree's branches; the **Parent** property guides us back toward the root. That doesn't mean much right now, but it's good practice to incorporate two-way links, and the potential value of this property will become clearer when we begin building larger trees for the Web Robot project.

From Document To Tree

Once the Inet control has retrieved a Web document, we create a new instance of **clsHTMLPageResourceNode** and set its **URL** and **Path** properties to the URL of the document. We then pass the document to the object's **AddLinksFromDocument**() method—a brief procedure shown in Listing 3.9.

Listing 3.9 The method **AddLinksFromDocument()** from clsHTMLPageResourceNode.CLS.

```
Public Sub AddLinksFromDocument(Document As String, _
    DocumentURL As String)
    ExtractLinksFromDocument Document, DocumentURL, "href", PageLinks
    ExtractLinksFromDocument Document, DocumentURL, "src", _
        PageElements
    End Sub
```

Although we need to populate two separate collections, the process of identifying links, turning them into new nodes, and adding them to the collections is nearly identical. Instead of writing one long method procedure that performs the same series of steps two times, we'll break the process out into a separate procedure: **ExtractLinks FromDocument**(), shown in Listing 3.10, will remain private to the class.

Listing 3.10 The private procedure **ExtractLinksFromDocument()** from clsHTMLPageResourceNode.CLS.

```
Private Sub ExtractLinksFromDocument(Document As String, _
                                     DocumentURL As String, _
                                     TagParamName As String, _
                                     HostCollection As Collection)

    Dim ParentURL As String
    Dim ServerURL As String
    Dim TargetURL As String
    Dim URLType As String
    Dim StringPos As Long
    Dim CurrentStartPos As Long
    Dim WebNode As clsHTMLPageResourceNode
    Dim ExistingNode As clsHTMLPageResourceNode

    Document = LCase(Document)
    DocumentURL = LCase(DocumentURL)
    ' Extract ParentURL from DocumentURL.
    ParentURL = GetParentURLFrom(DocumentURL)
    ' Extract ServerURL from DocumentURL.
    ServerURL = GetServerURLFrom(DocumentURL)

    CurrentStartPos = 1
    Do
```

```
    TargetURL = GetNextTargetURLFromDocument(Document, _
        CurrentStartPos, TagParamName)
    If TargetURL <> "" Then
        On Error Resume Next
        StringPos = InStr(TargetURL, ":")
        If StringPos > 0 Then
            URLType = Left(TargetURL, StringPos - 1)
            If URLType = "http" Then
                Set WebNode = New clsHTMLPageResourceNode
                Set WebNode.Parent = Me
                WebNode.URL = TargetURL
                WebNode.Path = TargetURL
                If Not WebNode.Root.AlreadyContains( _
                    WebNode.URL, ExistingNode) Then
                    HostCollection.Add WebNode, WebNode.URL
                  End If
              End If
          ElseIf Left(TargetURL, 1) = "/" Then
            Set WebNode = New clsHTMLPageResourceNode
            Set WebNode.Parent = Me
            WebNode.URL = ServerURL & TargetURL
            WebNode.Path = TargetURL
            If Not WebNode.Root.AlreadyContains( _
                WebNode.URL, ExistingNode) Then
                HostCollection.Add WebNode, WebNode.URL
              End If
          Else
            Set WebNode = New clsHTMLPageResourceNode
            Set WebNode.Parent = Me
            WebNode.URL = ParentURL & TargetURL
            WebNode.Path = TargetURL
            If Not WebNode.Root.AlreadyContains( _
                WebNode.URL, ExistingNode) Then
                HostCollection.Add WebNode, WebNode.URL
              End If
          End If
      End If
    Debug.Print "Collection Count: ", HostCollection.Count
    Loop While (CurrentStartPos > 0)
For Each WebNode In HostCollection
    Debug.Print WebNode.URL
    Next WebNode
End Sub
```

AddLinksFromDocument() first calls **ExtractLinksFromDocument()** to fill in the **PageLinks** collection. **ExtractLinksFromDocument()** takes four arguments. The first two specify the HTML document from which to pull the links and the URL—or more precisely, the URI—of that document. The third argument specifies the type of HTML tag parameter from which to take the link URLs. The HTML <A> tag, for example (as shown above), must include an HREF parameter that specifies the target URL of the hyperlink. Whenever we see HREF in the document, we know that the string assigned to it represents a link URL. The procedure's fourth argument specifies the collection to which the function will add the page resource nodes containing the identified URLs.

After converting everything to lower case, the procedure calls a pair of functions in HandyStuff.BAS, shown in Listing 3.11, called **GetParentURLFrom**() and **GetServerURLFrom**().

Listing 3.11 The code for HandyStuff.BAS.

```
Option Explicit

Public Function GetServerURLFrom(URL As String)
    Dim StringPos As Long

    StringPos = InStr(1, URL, "//")
    If StringPos > 0 Then
        StringPos = InStr(StringPos + 2, URL, "/")
        If StringPos > 0 Then
            GetServerURLFrom = Left(URL, StringPos - 1)
          Else
            GetServerURLFrom = URL
          End If
      End If
    End Function

Public Function GetParentURLFrom(URL As String)
    Dim StringPos As Long

    If URLEndsWithFilename(URL) Then
        StringPos = Len(URL)
        Do Until (StringPos = 1) Or (Mid(URL, StringPos, 1) = "/")
            StringPos = StringPos - 1
          Loop
        GetParentURLFrom = Left(URL, StringPos)
      Else
        GetParentURLFrom = URL
      End If
```

```
    End Function
Public Function URLEndsWithFilename(URL As String) As Boolean
    Dim Loc As Long

    If Right(URL, 1) = "/" Then
        URLEndsWithFilename = False
      Else
        Loc = InStr(URL, "//")
        If Loc > 0 Then
            If InStr(Loc + 2, URL, "/") > 0 Then
                URLEndsWithFilename = True
              Else
                URLEndsWithFilename = False
              End If
          Else
            URLEndsWithFilename = True
          End If
      End If
    End Function

Public Function MinLong(A As Long, B As Long) As Long
    If A < B Then
        MinLong = A
    Else
        MinLong = B
    End If
End Function

Public Function MaxLong(A As Long, B As Long) As Long
    If A > B Then
        MaxLong = A
    Else
        MaxLong = B
    End If

End Function

Public Function ExtractFilenameFromPath(ByVal Path As String) _
    As String
    Dim StringPos As Long

    If (Right(Path, 1) <> "/") Then
        StringPos = Len(Path)
        Do While (StringPos > 1) And (Not Mid(Path, StringPos, 1) _
            = "/")
            StringPos = StringPos - 1
            Loop
```

```
        ExtractFilenameFromPath = Right(Path, (Len(Path) - _
            StringPos))
      Else
        ExtractFilenameFromPath = ""
      End If
    End Function

Public Function ExtractFilenameExtensionFromPath( _
    ByVal Path As String) As String
    Dim StringPos As Long

    If Right(Path, 1) = "/" Then
        ExtractFilenameExtensionFromPath = ""
      ElseIf (Left(Right(Path, 4), 1) = ".") Then
        ExtractFilenameExtensionFromPath = Right(Path, 3)
      ElseIf (Left(Right(Path, 5), 1) = ".") Then
        ExtractFilenameExtensionFromPath = Right(Path, 4)
      Else
        ExtractFilenameExtensionFromPath = ""
      End If

    End Function

Public Function URLNormalized(URL As String) As Boolean
    Dim TempURL As String
    Dim ValidFirstChar As Boolean

    TempURL = URL
    Select Case Asc(Left(TempURL, 1))
      Case 48 To 57
        ValidFirstChar = True
      Case 65 To 90
        ValidFirstChar = True
      Case 97 To 122
        ValidFirstChar = True
      Case Else
        ValidFirstChar = False
      End Select

    If ValidFirstChar Then
        If (InStr(TempURL, "//") = 0) Then
            TempURL = "http://" & TempURL
          End If
        If (Not URLEndsWithFilename(TempURL)) And _
           (Not (Right(TempURL, 1) = "/")) And _
           (InStr(8, TempURL, "/") = 0) Then
```

```
        TempURL = TempURL & "/"
      End If
    URL = TempURL
    URLNormalized = True
  Else
    URLNormalized = False
  End If

End Function
```

These functions take the URI of the document as their only argument and return two shortened forms. The first function returns the entire path, excluding the document's own filename. The second function returns just the URL of the server on which the document was found. For example, take the URI:

```
http:/www.microsoft.com/support/news/explorertips.htm
```

The **ParentURL** of this URI would exclude the document filename

```
http:/www.microsoft.com/support/news/
```

and the **ServerURL** would exclude the entire directory path:

```
http:/www.microsoft.com
```

This information will help us reconstruct the full URI for each relative link we find within **Document**.

The remainder of the **ExtractLinksFromDocument**() procedure takes place within a loop that scans forward through **Document**, looking for tag parameters:

```
CurrentStartPos = 1
Do
    TargetURL = GetNextTargetURLFromDocument(Document, _
        CurrentStartPos, TagParamName)
    .
    .
    .
    Loop While (CurrentStartPos > 0)
```

For each **TargetURL** it finds, the procedure considers three possible types of URLs. First, it checks for the presence of a colon, indicating that the URL contains a protocol specifier:

```
If TargetURL <> "" Then
    On Error Resume Next
    StringPos = InStr(TargetURL, ":")
    If StringPos > 0 Then
```

If it finds the protocol specifier "http," it knows that the URL is complete. So it verifies that none of the collections in the tree already contain a node with this URL, and if not, adds it to **HostCollection**—the collection specified in the procedure's fourth argument.

```
URLType = Left(TargetURL, StringPos - 1)
If URLType = "http" Then
    Set WebNode = New clsHTMLPageResourceNode
    Set WebNode.Parent = Me
    WebNode.URL = TargetURL
    WebNode.Path = TargetURL
    If Not WebNode.Root.AlreadyContains( _
        WebNode.URL, ExistingNode) Then
        HostCollection.Add WebNode, WebNode.URL
      End If
  End If
```

Handling Protocol Specifiers Other Than HTTP

This version of the Web Explorer ignores all URLs that contain protocol specifiers other than HTTP. You could, however, modify it to accept others, such as FTP. You would then need to add support for those protocols so the program could download and handle the data it receives when the user selects a node with a non-HTTP URL.

In the second possible case, the **TargetURL** may begin with a forward slash, indicating a URL on the same server as **Document**, but located in a specific directory—which, incidentally, may or may not match the document's own directory. A slash at the beginning of a directory path indicates that the path begins at the root of the server's directory structure. If it finds an opening slash, the procedure constructs a complete URL by appending the **TargetURL** onto the **ServerURL** before adding the node to the **HostCollection**:

```
ElseIf Left(TargetURL, 1) = "/" Then
  Set WebNode = New clsHTMLPageResourceNode
  Set WebNode.Parent = Me
  WebNode.URL = ServerURL & TargetURL
```

```
  WebNode.Path = TargetURL
  If Not WebNode.Root.AlreadyContains(WebNode.URL, ExistingNode) Then
      HostCollection.Add WebNode, WebNode.URL
    End If
```

Finally, in the third case, the URL begins with neither a protocol identifier nor a forward slash, indicating a relative path—one that is relative to the document's own directory. For example, a URL that contains a filename with no directory path and no preceding slash indicates that the document or other file specified in the target URL resides in the same directory as the document containing the hyperlink. If the target URL contains a directory path that does not begin with a forward slash, the specified path lies within the directory of the parent document. So the procedure appends the **TargetURL** to the **ParentURL** before adding the node to the **HostCollection**.

```
Else
  Set WebNode = New clsHTMLPageResourceNode
  Set WebNode.Parent = Me
  WebNode.URL = ParentURL & TargetURL
  WebNode.Path = TargetURL
  If Not WebNode.Root.AlreadyContains(WebNode.URL, ExistingNode) Then
      HostCollection.Add WebNode, WebNode.URL
    End If
```

ExtractLinksFromDocument() loops until the function **GetNextTargetURLFromDocument**(), shown in Listing 3.12, either returns an empty string or reaches the end of the document.

Listing 3.12 The private function **GetNextTargetURLFromDocument()** from clsHTMLPageResourceNode.CLS.

```
Private Function GetNextTargetURLFromDocument(Document As String, _
                                    CurrentStartPos As Long, _
                                    TagParamName As String) As String

    Dim TempURL As String
    Dim EndOfCurrentTagPos As Long
    Dim CurrentEndPos As Long

    TempURL = ""
    CurrentStartPos = InStr(CurrentStartPos, Document, TagParamName)
    If CurrentStartPos > 0 Then
        EndOfCurrentTagPos = InStr(CurrentStartPos, Document, ">")
```

```
      CurrentStartPos = InStr(CurrentStartPos, Document, """")
      If CurrentStartPos > 0 Then
         CurrentStartPos = CurrentStartPos + 1
         CurrentEndPos = InStr(CurrentStartPos, Document, """")
         If (CurrentEndPos > CurrentStartPos) And _
            (CurrentEndPos < EndOfCurrentTagPos) Then
             TempURL = Mid(Document, CurrentStartPos, _
                           CurrentEndPos - CurrentStartPos)
           Else
             CurrentStartPos = EndOfCurrentTagPos
           End If
        End If
    End If
  GetNextTargetURLFromDocument = TempURL

  End Function
```

GetNextTargetURLFromDocument() searches the contents of **Document** for the first occurrence of the specified **TagParamName**—"href", for example—following the given **CurrentStartPos**. If it finds the tag parameter, it locates the end of the current tag by searching for the next greater-than sign. Next, it attempts to identify a pair of quotation marks that lie after the tag parameter and within the boundaries of the tag. The function will return whatever text it finds between the quotation marks.

Although it won't catch every possible error in the tag, limiting the search for quotation marks to the tag's boundaries will catch common tag errors—such as omitting one or both quotation marks—without terminating or bungling the entire search.

The **CurrentStartPos** is passed by reference to **GetNextTargetURLFromDocument**(), so the next time we call it from **ExtractLinksFromDocument**(), the search will begin after the position of the previously located tag parameter.

Methods That Talk To Themselves

ExtractLinksFromDocument() depends on two other methods in the class **clsHTMLPageResourceNode:** the functions named **Root**() and **AlreadyContains**(), shown in Listing 3.13.

Listing 3.13 The public function methods **Root()** and **AlreadyContains()** in clsHTMLPageResourceNode.CLS.

```
Public Function Root() As clsHTMLPageResourceNode

    If Me.Parent Is Nothing Then
        Set Root = Me
      Else
        Set Root = Me.Parent.Root
      End If

    End Function

Public Function AlreadyContains(TargetNodeKey As String, _
           MatchingNode As clsHTMLPageResourceNode) As Boolean

    Dim WebNode As clsHTMLPageResourceNode
    Dim NodeFound As Boolean

    DoEvents
    NodeFound = (Me.URL = TargetNodeKey)
    If NodeFound Then
        Set MatchingNode = Me
      Else
        For Each WebNode In Me.PageLinks
            If WebNode.AlreadyContains( _
                TargetNodeKey, MatchingNode) Then
                NodeFound = True
                Exit For
              End If
            Next WebNode
        If Not NodeFound Then
            For Each WebNode In Me.PageElements
                If WebNode.AlreadyContains( _
                    TargetNodeKey, MatchingNode) Then
                    NodeFound = True
                    Exit For
                  End If
                Next WebNode
          End If
      End If
    AlreadyContains = NodeFound
    End Function
```

You'll recall that objects of the class **clsHTMLPageResourceNode** contain two collections of objects belonging to that same class. As we add new nodes to those collections, the objects organize themselves into a tree. A structure built from elements containing references to other elements of its own type is called a *recursive data structure.* The most efficient way to manipulate such data structures is with recursive procedures or recursive functions such as the method functions **Root()** and **AlreadyContains()**—both of which search the tree, though in two distinctly different ways.

The conventional, or non-recursive, way to search a list is by looping through the elements, checking each member of the list for a match. A recursive procedure, however, steps through a list without looping. The function **Root()** demonstrates the most basic recursive search. Although the page resource nodes form a tree , the links described by their **Parent** properties form a simple daisy-chain, or *linked list,* that ends at the root node. The root node is the only node that has no parent, meaning that its **Parent** property contains no reference to another node object. To locate the root node of a tree built from page resource nodes, we can invoke any node's **Root()** method. If a node's **Parent** property contains a reference to another node, **Root()** tells that node to perform the method **Root()** on itself. If the tree consists of five tiers, for example, and we invoke the **Root()** method on a node in the last tier, then five nodes must perform their **Root()** methods. When the **Root()** method of a node determines that its node contains no **Parent** reference, it returns itself. The next node up the chain, having previously called **Root()** on its own **Parent** property, receives this object reference and passes it along as its own return value. This process cascades up the calling chain until it arrives at the original call, where the calling procedure receives a reference to the root node.

Nodes at the boundaries of a recursive data structure are called *terminal nodes.* A tree of page resource nodes contains two types of terminal nodes, a single root, and all the outermost nodes—those at the ends of the tree's branches.

The function **AlreadyContains()** performs a search in the other direction—out toward the ends of the branches. It also relies on a different terminating condition. To search the branches of the tree, the function needs to loop through each of the node's two collections, invoking each member's own **AlreadyContains()** method. If any page resource node determines that its URL matches the **TargetNodeKey**, it sets its **MatchingNode** argument to reference itself and returns **True**. If that happens, the recursion collapses and returns control to the original calling procedure. If none of the tree nodes match the **TargetNodeKey**, the recursion will have walked through the entire tree before returning **False**.

Remember To Call DoEvents In Recursive Procedures

Although recursive procedures are not loops, they do often perform dozens or hundreds of iterations. If you consider the number of hyperlinks embedded in a typical Web page, you can see how the TreeView can grow rapidly. A tree with just three tiers (a third-order tree) could easily include thousands of nodes. A search of that tree could take considerable time, and without a call to ***DoEvents****, the program will effectively hang until the search ends. In the Web Explorer, this is just an inconvenience. In our next project, you'll see that it would be just as fatal as an infinite loop.*

ExtractLinksFromDocument() prevents duplicate nodes by searching the tree beginning with the root of the current node. In a tree, this happens to be the same for all nodes:

```
If Not WebNode.Root.AlreadyContains(WebNode.URL, ExistingNode) Then
    HostCollection.Add WebNode, WebNode.URL
  End If
```

Displaying Hyperlinks In The TreeView Control

After we've grown a little two-tiered treelet, we need to reveal to the user the precious information stored in the page resource nodes by updating the TreeView control. In Listing 3.14, you'll find the general procedure **AddLinksToTreeView**(), which belongs to the project's only form, **frmHTTPTreeView**. This procedure adds new **Node** objects to the TreeView contol **tvURLTreeView**, based on the **Path** and **URL** properties of the page resource nodes.

Listing 3.14 The general procedure **AddLinksToTreeView()** from frmHTTPTreeView.FRM.

```
Public Sub AddLinksToTreeView(PageResources As clsHTMLPageResourceNode)
    Dim CurrentNode As Node
    Dim Link As clsHTMLPageResourceNode
```

```
On Error Resume Next

Set CurrentNode = tvURLTreeView.Nodes.Add("WWW", tvwChild, _
                                          PageResources.URL, _
                                          PageResources.URL, _
                                          icoSERVER, icoSERVER)
If Not (CurrentNode Is Nothing) Then
    Set ActiveTreeNode = CurrentNode
  End If

For Each Link In PageResources.PageLinks
    If InStr(Link.Path, "http://") > 0 Then
        Set CurrentNode = tvURLTreeView.Nodes.Add _
            (PageResources.URL, tvwChild, _
             Link.URL, Link.Path, _
             icoSERVER, icoSERVER)
      Else
        Set CurrentNode = tvURLTreeView.Nodes.Add _
            (PageResources.URL, tvwChild, _
             Link.URL, Link.Path, _
             icoDOCUMENT, icoDOCUMENT)
      End If
    If Not CurrentNode Is Nothing Then
        CurrentNode.EnsureVisible
      End If
    Next Link

For Each Link In PageResources.PageElements
    Set CurrentNode = tvURLTreeView.Nodes.Add _
        (PageResources.URL, tvwChild, _
         Link.URL, Link.Path, _
         icoIMAGE, icoIMAGE)
    If Not CurrentNode Is Nothing Then
        CurrentNode.EnsureVisible
      End If
    Next Link

End Sub
```

AddLinksToTreeView() adds a new **Node** object to the TreeView control based on the URL property of the root page resource node in the treelet. For each page resource node in the two collections of the root node—**PageLinks** and **PageElements**—it then adds one new child **Node** object to the TreeView control.

The **Add** method of the TreeView control's **Nodes** collection takes as many as six arguments, five of which are optional. We'll use them all, however. The first two arguments, **relative** and **relationship**, determine where the new nodes will be added to the TreeView. The only way to add new nodes to a specific location in the TreeView is by specifying the **key** of an existing node in the first argument, and the relationship between that node and the new node in the second argument. The third argument specifies the **key** value itself. Any node in the TreeView's **Nodes** collection can be identified either by its **Index** value—an automatically assigned integer value—or by a string specified in this argument. The collection requires a unique value for the **key** string of each node, which is why we've retained the complete URL for each page resource node. The fourth argument also takes a string, the string that will appear to the user in the TreeView control. The last two arguments specify which icons to use for the TreeView node in its unselected and selected states, respectively. The integer values passed in these two last arguments actually reference images stored in an associated ImageList control.

To add the root page resource node, we specify "WWW" as the **relative** TreeView node, and the constant **tvwChild** as the **relationship**. To ensure that all our nodes will have a home, we create the node "WWW" at startup, in the **Form_Load**() event (shown in the next section, in Listing 3.15).

To add the **PageLinks** and **PageElements** nodes, we loop through the two collections, passing the **URL** property of the root node as the **relative** and **tvwChild** as the **relationship**.

This procedure takes considerable (yet necessary) liberties with VB's error handling. Since each TreeView node must have a unique **key** value, we can add any given URI only once. But the Web doesn't play by those rules; redundant links are more the norm than the exception. The **On Error Resume Next** statement causes the procedure to simply skip over attempts to add duplicates. For example, if the root page resource node already exists—which will be the case whenever a user selects a node in the TreeView—the first call to **tvURLTreeView.Nodes.Add()** will trigger a runtime error, causing execution to skip to the two **For Each** loops that add the nodes in **PageLinks** and **PageElements**. If any of those nodes exist elsewhere in the tree (also common), it just skips them. The stylistically correct way to handle these exceptions is to catch them before they occur. How? By querying the **Nodes** collection for the new node before attempting to **Add** it. Unfortunately, the **Nodes** collection doesn't support membership queries, so we're stuck with error trapping.

Housekeeping Code

The remainder of the code in this project performs basic housekeeping functions such as sizing and arranging the controls at runtime, and managing the split bar between **tvURLTreeView** and **txtOutput**. (Refer to the event procedures **picDivider_MouseMove()** and **picDivider_MouseUp()** in Listing 3.15.)

In the next project, we'll beef up the Web Explorer, transforming it into a Web Robot by giving it a mind of its own.

Listing 3.15 Support code from frmHTTPTreeView.FRM.

```
Private Sub Form_Load()
    tvURLTreeView.Nodes.Add , , "WWW", "World-Wide Web", _
                            icoROOT, icoROOT
    End Sub

Private Sub Form_Resize()
    If Me.ScaleWidth < _
        (lblURL.Width + _
         cmdPerformRequest.Width + _
         200 + 3 * 60) Then
        Me.Width = lblURL.Width + _
            cmdPerformRequest.Width + _
            500 + 4 * 60 + 4
    End If
    If Me.ScaleHeight < _
        (txtOutput.Top + 500 + 60) Then
        Me.Height = txtOutput.Top + 500 + 60
    End If
    lblURL.Left = 60
    txtURL.Left = lblURL.Left + lblURL.Width + 60
    txtURL.Width = Me.ScaleWidth - _
        (txtURL.Left + cmdPerformRequest.Width + _
            picBusy.Width + 3 * 60)
    cmdPerformRequest.Left = Me.ScaleWidth - _
        (cmdPerformRequest.Width + picBusy.Width + 2 * 60)
    cmdPerformRequest.Height = txtURL.Height
    picBusy.Left = cmdPerformRequest.Left + _
        cmdPerformRequest.Width + 60
    tvURLTreeView.Left = 60
```

```
    tvURLTreeView.Height = Me.ScaleHeight - _
        (sbHTTPStatus.Height + tvURLTreeView.Top + 60)
    txtOutput.Top = tvURLTreeView.Top
    txtOutput.Left = tvURLTreeView.Left + tvURLTreeView.Width + 60
    txtOutput.Width = Me.ScaleWidth - (txtOutput.Left + 60)
    txtOutput.Height = Me.ScaleHeight - _
        (sbHTTPStatus.Height + txtOutput.Top + 60)
    picDivider.Top = tvURLTreeView.Top
    picDivider.Height = tvURLTreeView.Height
    picDivider.Left = tvURLTreeView.Left + tvURLTreeView.Width
    picDivider.Width = 60
    End Sub

Private Sub picDivider_MouseMove(Button As Integer, _
    Shift As Integer, x As Single, y As Single)
    If Button = vbLeftButton Then
        picDivider.Left = _
            MaxLong(200, _
                    MinLong((picDivider.Left + x), _
                            (Me.ScaleWidth - 260)))
      End If

    End Sub

Private Sub picDivider_MouseUp(Button As Integer, _
    Shift As Integer, x As Single, y As Single)
    tvURLTreeView.Width = picDivider.Left - tvURLTreeView.Left
    txtOutput.Left = picDivider.Left + picDivider.Width
    txtOutput.Width = Me.ScaleWidth - (txtOutput.Left + 60)
    End Sub

Private Sub tmrBusy_Timer()
    Static Counter As Integer
    Counter = (Counter + 1) Mod (ilBusyIcons.ListImages.Count)
    picBusy.Picture = ilBusyIcons.ListImages(Counter + 1).Picture
    End Sub

Private Sub tvURLTreeView_NodeClick(ByVal Node As Node)
    If (Node.Key <> Node.Root.Key) And _
       (Not (Node Is ActiveTreeNode)) And _
       (Not bPerformingRequest) Then
        Set ActiveTreeNode = Node
        txtURL.Text = Node.Key
        cmdPerformRequest_Click
      End If
    End Sub
```

```
Private Sub txtURL_KeyPress(KeyAscii As Integer)
    If KeyAscii = 13 Then
        cmdPerformRequest_Click
      End If
    End Sub
```

Building A Web Robot

This program will use the page resource tree to chart its own course through the Web. To ensure that it does our bidding, we'll implant a search filter that we'll discuss in great detail in Chapter 4. We'll also add another recursive procedure, this time not to search the page resource tree, but to build it.

Running The Web Robot

You'll notice some significant differences between the Web Robot and the Web Explorer. Give it a try. Leave the search string empty but set the search depth to 1, enter a URL and select File|Perform Search from the program Menu, or click the Search button on the Toolbar.

Just like the Web Explorer, this program will retrieve the specified Web document and add it to the TreeView. But unlike the Web Explorer, it will not display the document's links.

Next, enter a word in the search string that you know the program will find in the document you just retrieved, then click the document in the TreeView. The program will re-load the document and will display a different icon in the TreeView to indicate a document match.

While the Web Explorer simply extracts and displays hyperlinks, the Web Robot must check each document against the current search string. This means it must retrieve and analyze each document before it can add it to the TreeView.

To see the search in action, increase the search depth to 2 and click the node again. After it re-analyzes the document in the selected node, it will first retrieve and display all its image links. It will then begin retrieving and analyzing each hyperlinked document, adding one at a time to the TreeView. To interrupt the search, select File|Stop Search from the program Menu, or click the Stop button on the Toolbar.

To extend the search, choose one of the outer nodes or increase the search depth and re-select the original URL. To check a branch of existing nodes against a new search string, you'll need to restart the search at their parent node. The Web Robot does not travel back up through the tree to re-evaluate existing nodes; it always works from the selected node toward its child nodes. You'll notice that a well-traveled tree might include nodes that indicate matches to a variety of search strings. To re-analyze an entire tree against a single search string, you'll need to set the search depth to at least the tree's current depth and begin the search at its root.

Designing The Web Robot Form

The form for this project (shown in Figure 3.4) will be based on the form in the Web Explorer, but we'll need to make a few changes. The code for the Web Robot form is shown in Listing 3.16.

Listing 3.16 The complete listing of frmWebRobot.FRM.

```
Option Explicit

Private Dummy As Variant
Private bPerformingRequest As Boolean
Private bPerformingSearch As Boolean
Private bRequestingHeaders As Boolean
Private BinaryFile As Boolean
Private RootWebNode As clsHTMLPageResourceNode
Private ActiveTreeNode As Node
Private bSearchCancelled
Private Analyst As clsDocumentAnalyst
Private TimeOfLastTransfer As Date

' Tree Icon Selectors for ImageList ilTreeIcons
Private Const icoHIT = 1
Private Const icoERROR = 2
Private Const icoSERVER = 3
Private Const icoDOCUMENT = 4
Private Const icoIMAGE = 5
Private Const icoROOT = 6

'Create HTTP Semaphore Flags
Private Type ProtocolTransferSemaphores
    Error As Boolean
    Timeout As Boolean
```

```
    Complete As Boolean
    Connected As Boolean
    ConnectionFailed As Boolean
    Cancelled As Boolean
    Disconnected As Boolean
    End Type

Private HTTPSemaphore As ProtocolTransferSemaphores

Private Sub Form_Load()
    Set RootWebNode = New clsHTMLPageResourceNode
    RootWebNode.URL = "WWW"
    RootWebNode.Path = "World-Wide Web"
    AddNodeToTreeView RootWebNode, icoROOT
    End Sub

Private Sub Form_QueryUnload(Cancel As Integer, _
    UnloadMode As Integer)
    RootWebNode.RemoveLinks
    End Sub

Private Sub Form_Resize()
    If Me.WindowState = vbMinimized Then
        Exit Sub
      End If
    If Me.ScaleWidth < _
        (lblURL.Width + _
         picBusy.Width + _
         200 + 4 * 60) Then
        Me.Width = lblURL.Width + _
            picBusy.Width + _
            500 + 4 * 60 + 4
    End If
    If Me.ScaleHeight < _
        (txtOutput.Top + 500 + 60) Then
        Me.Height = txtOutput.Top + 500 + 60
    End If
    'lblURL.Left = 60
    txtURL.Left = lblURL.Left + lblURL.Width + 60
    txtURL.Width = Me.ScaleWidth - _
        (txtURL.Left + picBusy.Width + 2 * 60)
    picBusy.Left = Me.ScaleWidth - _
        (picBusy.Width + 60)
    lblSearch.Left = lblURL.Left + lblURL.Width - lblSearch.Width
    udSearchDepth.Left = txtURL.Left + txtURL.Width - _
        udSearchDepth.Width
```

```
    txtSearchDepth.Left = udSearchDepth.Left - txtSearchDepth.Width
    lblSearchDepth.Left = txtSearchDepth.Left - _
        lblSearchDepth.Width - 60
    txtSearchString.Left = txtURL.Left
    txtSearchString.Width = lblSearchDepth.Left - _
        (txtSearchString.Left + 2 * 60)
    tvURLTreeView.Left = 60
    tvURLTreeView.Height = Me.ScaleHeight - _
        (sbHTTPStatus.Height + tvURLTreeView.Top + 60)
    txtOutput.Top = tvURLTreeView.Top
    txtOutput.Left = tvURLTreeView.Left + tvURLTreeView.Width + 60
    txtOutput.Width = Me.ScaleWidth - (txtOutput.Left + 60)
    txtOutput.Height = Me.ScaleHeight - _
        (sbHTTPStatus.Height + txtOutput.Top + 60)
    pbDivider.Top = tvURLTreeView.Top
    pbDivider.Height = tvURLTreeView.Height
    pbDivider.Left = tvURLTreeView.Left + tvURLTreeView.Width
    pbDivider.Width = 60
    End Sub

Private Sub Inet1_StateChanged(ByVal State As Integer)
    Dim Loc As Long
    Dim sHeaderValue As String
    Dim vtData As Variant
    Dim vtBinaryData As Variant
    Const BinaryFileNumber = 1

    Select Case State
      Case icNone
        sbHTTPStatus.Panels(1).Text = ""
      Case icResolvingHost
        sbHTTPStatus.Panels(1).Text = "Resolving Host"
      Case icHostResolved
        sbHTTPStatus.Panels(1).Text = "Host Resolved"
      Case icConnecting
        sbHTTPStatus.Panels(2).Text = ""
        sbHTTPStatus.Panels(1).Text = "Connecting"
      Case icConnected
        sbHTTPStatus.Panels(1).Text = "Connected"
        Loc = InStr(Inet1.URL, ":80")
        If Loc > 0 Then
            txtURL.Text = Left(Inet1.URL, Loc - 1) & _
                Mid(Inet1.URL, Loc + 3)
          Else
            txtURL.Text = Inet1.URL
          End If
```

```
Case icRequesting
  sbHTTPStatus.Panels(1).Text = "Requesting"
Case icRequestSent
  sbHTTPStatus.Panels(1).Text = "Request Sent"
Case icReceivingResponse
  sbHTTPStatus.Panels(1).Text = "Receiving Response"
Case icResponseReceived
  sbHTTPStatus.Panels(1).Text = "Response Received"
Case icDisconnecting
  sbHTTPStatus.Panels(1).Text = "Disconnecting"
Case icDisconnected
  sbHTTPStatus.Panels(1).Text = "Disconnected"
  If bPerformingRequest And (Not HTTPSemaphore.Complete) Then
      HTTPSemaphore.ConnectionFailed = True
    End If
Case icError
  sbHTTPStatus.Panels(1).Text = "Error"
  HTTPSemaphore.Error = True
  sbHTTPStatus.Panels(2).Text = "ErrorCode: " & _
      Inet1.ResponseCode & _
      " : " & Inet1.ResponseInfo
Case icResponseCompleted
  sbHTTPStatus.Panels(1).Text = "Response Completed"
  sHeaderValue = Inet1.GetHeader("Content-type")
  If bRequestingHeaders Then
      vtData = Inet1.GetChunk(1024, icString)
      txtOutput.Text = sHeaderValue & vbCrLf & vbCrLf & vtData
    Else
      If (Not BinaryFile) And InStr( _
          1, sHeaderValue, "text/", 1) Then
          'txtOutput.Text = sHeaderValue
          vtData = Inet1.GetChunk(1024, icString)
          Do While Len(vtData) > 0
              txtOutput.Text = txtOutput.Text + vtData
              vtData = Inet1.GetChunk(1024, icString)
              Loop
          bPerformingRequest = False
          HTTPSemaphore.Complete = True
        Else
          ' Could add code here to handle binary files.
        End If
    End If
  HTTPSemaphore.Complete = True
Case Else
End Select
```

```
    End Sub

Private Sub mnuExit_Click()
    Unload Me
    End
    End Sub

Private Sub mnuPerformSearch_Click()
    PerformRequest
    End Sub

Private Sub mnuStopSearch_Click()
    bSearchCancelled = True
    mnuStopSearch.Enabled = False
    tbToolbar.Buttons("btnStop").Enabled = False
    End Sub

Private Sub pbDivider_MouseMove(Button As Integer, _
    Shift As Integer, X As Single, y As Single)
    If Button = vbLeftButton Then
        pbDivider.Left = _
            MaxLong(200, _
                    MinLong((pbDivider.Left + X), _
                            (Me.ScaleWidth - 260)))
    End If

    End Sub

Private Sub pbDivider_MouseUp(Button As Integer, _
    Shift As Integer, X As Single, y As Single)
    tvURLTreeView.Width = pbDivider.Left - tvURLTreeView.Left
    txtOutput.Left = pbDivider.Left + pbDivider.Width
    txtOutput.Width = Me.ScaleWidth - (txtOutput.Left + 60)
    End Sub

Private Sub tbToolbar_ButtonClick(ByVal Button As Button)
    Select Case Button.Key
      Case "btnSearch"
        PerformRequest
      Case "btnStop"
        Inet1.Cancel
        HTTPSemaphore.Cancelled = True
        bSearchCancelled = True
        mnuStopSearch.Enabled = False
        tbToolbar.Buttons("btnStop").Enabled = False
      End Select
```

```
    End Sub

Private Sub tmrBusy_Timer()
    Static Counter As Integer
    Counter = (Counter + 1) Mod (ilBusyIcons.ListImages.Count)
    picBusy.Picture = ilBusyIcons.ListImages(Counter + 1).Picture
    End Sub

Private Sub tvURLTreeView_NodeClick(ByVal Node As Node)
    If (Node.Key <> RootWebNode.URL) And _
       (Not bPerformingSearch) Then
        Set ActiveTreeNode = Node
        txtURL.Text = Node.Key
        PerformRequest
      End If
    End Sub


Private Sub txtURL_KeyPress(KeyAscii As Integer)
    If KeyAscii = 13 Then
        PerformRequest
      End If
    End Sub

Private Sub PerformRequest()
    Dim TempURL As String
    Dim FileExtension As String
    Dim TargetFilename As String
    Dim SearchDepth As Integer
    Dim NewWebNode As clsHTMLPageResourceNode
    Dim ExistingNode As clsHTMLPageResourceNode
    Dim Diplomat As clsDiplomat
    Dim vtBinaryData As Variant
    Dim BinaryData() As Byte
    Dim FilenameForBinaryData As String
    Const BinaryFileID = 1

    If Not ValidSearchDepth(SearchDepth) Then Exit Sub
    TempURL = txtURL.Text
    If Not URLNormalized(TempURL) Then
        MsgBox "Please enter a valid URL", vbCritical, "Invalid URL"
        Exit Sub
      Else
        txtURL.Text = TempURL
      End If
```

```
    If Not bPerformingRequest Then
        FileExtension = Trim(LCase( _
            ExtractFilenameExtensionFromPath(txtURL.Text)))
        Select Case FileExtension
          Case "gif", "jpg"
            BinaryFile = True
            TargetFilename = App.Path & "\" & _
                ExtractFilenameFromPath(txtURL.Text)
            cmnSaveAs.filename = TargetFilename
            cmnSaveAs.DefaultExt = Right(TargetFilename, 4)
            cmnSaveAs.Filter = "Images(*.bmp;*.gif;*.jpg)"
            cmnSaveAs.CancelError = True
            On Error GoTo Skip
            cmnSaveAs.ShowSave
            bPerformingRequest = True
            txtURL.Enabled = False
            mnuPerformSearch.Enabled = False
            mnuStopSearch.Enabled = False
            tbToolbar.Buttons("btnSearch").Enabled = False
            tbToolbar.Buttons("btnStop").Enabled = False
            Me.MousePointer = vbHourglass
            tmrBusy.Enabled = True
            bPerformingSearch = True
            bSearchCancelled = False

            FilenameForBinaryData = cmnSaveAs.filename

            BinaryData() = Inet1.OpenURL(txtURL.Text, icByteArray)
            Open FilenameForBinaryData For Binary As BinaryFileID
            Put BinaryFileID, , BinaryData()
            Close BinaryFileID

            txtURL.Enabled = True
            mnuPerformSearch.Enabled = True
            mnuStopSearch.Enabled = False
            tbToolbar.Buttons("btnSearch").Enabled = True
            tbToolbar.Buttons("btnStop").Enabled = False
            tmrBusy.Enabled = False
            Me.MousePointer = vbDefault
            bPerformingSearch = False
            bPerformingRequest = False

Skip:
          Case Else
            ' This case will handle any HTML document request,
            ' whether or not it includes a filename,
```

```
' because a URL with no filename will cause the
' web server to return its default HTML document
' file.

bPerformingRequest = True
tmrBusy.Enabled = True
Me.MousePointer = vbArrowHourglass
txtURL.Enabled = False
mnuPerformSearch.Enabled = False
mnuStopSearch.Enabled = True
tbToolbar.Buttons("btnSearch").Enabled = False
tbToolbar.Buttons("btnStop").Enabled = True
bPerformingSearch = True
bSearchCancelled = False
BinaryFile = False
txtOutput.Text = ""

Set Analyst = New clsDocumentAnalyst
Analyst.Init txtSearchString.Text
If RootWebNode.AlreadyContains( _
    txtURL.Text, ExistingNode) Then
    Set Diplomat = DispatchNewDiplomat(ExistingNode.URL)
    If Not (Diplomat Is Nothing) Then
        SearchWeb ExistingNode, SearchDepth, Diplomat
      End If
  Else
    Set NewWebNode = New clsHTMLPageResourceNode
    NewWebNode.URL = txtURL.Text
    NewWebNode.Path = txtURL.Text
    Set NewWebNode.Parent = RootWebNode
    Set Diplomat = DispatchNewDiplomat(NewWebNode.URL)
    If Not (Diplomat Is Nothing) Then
        RootWebNode.PageLinks.Add NewWebNode, _
            NewWebNode.URL
        SearchWeb NewWebNode, SearchDepth, Diplomat
      End If
  End If

txtURL.Enabled = True
mnuPerformSearch.Enabled = True
mnuStopSearch.Enabled = False
tbToolbar.Buttons("btnSearch").Enabled = True
tbToolbar.Buttons("btnStop").Enabled = False
tmrBusy.Enabled = False
Me.MousePointer = vbDefault
```

```
            bPerformingSearch = False
            bPerformingRequest = False
          End Select
      End If

    End Sub

Private Function ValidSearchDepth(SearchDepth As Integer)

    ValidSearchDepth = True
    If IsNumeric(txtSearchDepth) Then
        SearchDepth = Val(txtSearchDepth.Text)
        If Not (SearchDepth = Abs(Int(SearchDepth)) And _
            (SearchDepth > 0)) Then
            MsgBox "Please enter an integer value for Search Depth.", _
                   vbOKOnly + vbCritical, _
                   "Invalid Search Depth"
            ValidSearchDepth = False
          End If
      Else
        MsgBox "Please enter an integer value for Search Depth.", _
               vbOKOnly + vbCritical, _
               "Invalid Search Depth"
        ValidSearchDepth = False
      End If

    End Function

Private Sub udSearchDepth_DownClick()
    Dim SearchDepth As Integer

    If ValidSearchDepth(SearchDepth) Then
        SearchDepth = MaxLong(1, SearchDepth - 1)
        txtSearchDepth.Text = Str(SearchDepth)
      End If
    End Sub

Private Sub udSearchDepth_UpClick()
    Dim SearchDepth As Integer

    If ValidSearchDepth(SearchDepth) Then
        SearchDepth = MinLong(SearchDepth + 1, 999)
        txtSearchDepth.Text = Str(SearchDepth)
      End If

    End Sub
```

```
Private Sub SearchWeb(CurrentWebNode As clsHTMLPageResourceNode, _
                      ByVal LevelsToSearch As Integer, _
                      ByVal Diplomat As clsDiplomat)

    Dim WebNode As clsHTMLPageResourceNode
    Dim NodeIcon As Integer
    Dim TempText As String

    ' Evaluate Access Restrictions
    If Diplomat.NewServerURL(CurrentWebNode.URL) Then
        Set Diplomat = DispatchNewDiplomat(CurrentWebNode.URL)
      End If
    If Diplomat.Rejects(CurrentWebNode.URL) Then
        AddNodeToTreeView CurrentWebNode, icoERROR
        Exit Sub
      End If

    If AbleToGetWebDocument(CurrentWebNode.URL) Then
        TimeOfLastTransfer = Now
        CurrentWebNode.MatchesSearch = Analyst.DocumentMatches( _
            txtOutput.Text)
        If CurrentWebNode.MatchesSearch Then
            NodeIcon = icoHIT
          ElseIf InStr(CurrentWebNode.Path, "://") Then
            NodeIcon = icoSERVER
          Else
            NodeIcon = icoDOCUMENT
          End If
        AddNodeToTreeView CurrentWebNode, NodeIcon
        If (LevelsToSearch > 1) Then
            TempText = txtOutput.Text
            ExtractLinksFromDocument TempText, "href", CurrentWebNode
            ExtractLinksFromDocument TempText, "src", CurrentWebNode
            For Each WebNode In CurrentWebNode.PageElements
                DoEvents
                If bSearchCancelled Then Exit For
                AddNodeToTreeView WebNode, icoIMAGE
                Next WebNode
            For Each WebNode In CurrentWebNode.PageLinks
                DoEvents
                If bSearchCancelled Then Exit For
                Do Until DateDiff("s", TimeOfLastTransfer, Now) > 5
                    DoEvents
                    Loop
                SearchWeb WebNode, LevelsToSearch - 1, Diplomat
                Debug.Print "Call SearchWeb "; WebNode.URL
                Next WebNode
```

```
        If bSearchCancelled Then MsgBox "Search Cancelled"
      End If
    Else
      AddNodeToTreeView CurrentWebNode, icoERROR
    End If
  End Sub

Public Sub AddNodeToTreeView(CurrentWebNode As _
    clsHTMLPageResourceNode, TreeNodeIcon As Integer)

    Dim CurrentTreeViewNode As Node
    Dim WebNode As clsHTMLPageResourceNode

    On Error Resume Next
    Set CurrentTreeViewNode = tvURLTreeView.Nodes(CurrentWebNode.URL)
    If CurrentTreeViewNode Is Nothing Then
        If (CurrentWebNode.Parent Is Nothing) Then
            Set CurrentTreeViewNode = tvURLTreeView.Nodes.Add _
                (, , _
                 CurrentWebNode.URL, CurrentWebNode.Path, _
                 TreeNodeIcon, TreeNodeIcon)
          Else
            Set CurrentTreeViewNode = tvURLTreeView.Nodes.Add _
                (CurrentWebNode.Parent.URL, tvwChild, _
                 CurrentWebNode.URL, CurrentWebNode.Path, _
                 TreeNodeIcon, TreeNodeIcon)
          End If
      Else
        tvURLTreeView.Nodes(CurrentWebNode.URL).Image = TreeNodeIcon
        tvURLTreeView.Nodes(CurrentWebNode.URL).SelectedImage = _
            TreeNodeIcon
      End If
    If Not (CurrentTreeViewNode Is Nothing) Then
        Set ActiveTreeNode = CurrentTreeViewNode
        CurrentTreeViewNode.EnsureVisible
      End If

    End Sub

Public Function DispatchNewDiplomat(ByVal URL As String) As _
    clsDiplomat
    Dim AgentFileReceived As Boolean
    Dim Diplomat As clsDiplomat

    URL = GetServerURLFrom(URL)
    AgentFileReceived = AbleToGetWebDocument(URL & "/robots.txt")
```

```
    If HTTPSemaphore.Cancelled Then
        Set DispatchNewDiplomat = Nothing
      Else
        Set Diplomat = New clsDiplomat
        Diplomat.Init URL, txtOutput.Text
        Set DispatchNewDiplomat = Diplomat
      End If
    End Function

Public Function AbleToGetWebDocument(URL As String) As Boolean

    ' Initialize Semaphore Flags.
    HTTPSemaphore.Error = False
    HTTPSemaphore.Timeout = False
    HTTPSemaphore.Connected = False
    HTTPSemaphore.ConnectionFailed = False
    HTTPSemaphore.Complete = False
    HTTPSemaphore.Cancelled = False

    ' Request HTML document retrieval.
    txtOutput.Text = ""
    bPerformingRequest = True

    Inet1.Execute URL

    ' Wait until asynchronous transfer terminates:
    Do
        DoEvents
        Loop Until (HTTPSemaphore.Complete Or _
                    HTTPSemaphore.Cancelled Or _
                    bSearchCancelled)

    ' I also monitored for a ConnectionFailed event:

    '                HTTPSemaphore.ConnectionFailed Or _
    '
    ' but this seemed to fire even when the document transfer
    ' was able to continue and complete successfully,
    ' which caused the program to make the next request
    ' before the previous request had finished, resulting
    ' in an error.

    ' The correct way to detect activity on the Inet control
    ' would be to watch the StillExecuting property. But, at
    ' this writing, this property never indicates True, which
    ' prevents me from using it:
```

```
    'Do While Inet1.StillExecuting
    '    DoEvents
    '    Loop

    AbleToGetWebDocument = HTTPSemaphore.Complete
    End Function

Public Function AbleToGetWebDocumentHeaders(URL As String) As Boolean
    ' Initialize Semaphore Flags.
    HTTPSemaphore.Error = False
    HTTPSemaphore.Timeout = False
    HTTPSemaphore.Connected = False
    HTTPSemaphore.ConnectionFailed = False
    HTTPSemaphore.Complete = False
    HTTPSemaphore.Cancelled = False

    ' Request HTML document header retrieval.
    txtOutput.Text = ""
    bPerformingRequest = True
    bRequestingHeaders = True

    Inet1.Execute URL, "HEAD"

    ' Wait until asynchronous transfer terminates:
    Do
        DoEvents
        Loop Until (HTTPSemaphore.Complete Or _
                    HTTPSemaphore.Cancelled Or _
                    bSearchCancelled)

    bRequestingHeaders = False
    AbleToGetWebDocumentHeaders = HTTPSemaphore.Complete

    End Function

Private Sub ExtractLinksFromDocument(Document As String, _
                           TagParamName As String, _
                           CurrentWebNode As clsHTMLPageResourceNode)
    Dim HostCollection As Collection
    Dim ParentURL As String
    Dim ServerURL As String
    Dim TargetURL As String
    Dim URLType As String
    Dim StringPos As Long
    Dim CurrentStartPos As Long
    Dim WebNode As clsHTMLPageResourceNode
    Dim ExistingNode As clsHTMLPageResourceNode
```

```
Document = LCase(Document)
CurrentWebNode.URL = LCase(CurrentWebNode.URL)
' Extract ParentURL from Document URL.
ParentURL = GetParentURLFrom(CurrentWebNode.URL)
' Extract ServerURL from Document URL.
ServerURL = GetServerURLFrom(CurrentWebNode.URL)

CurrentStartPos = 1
Do
    TargetURL = GetNextTargetURLFromDocument(Document, _
        CurrentStartPos, TagParamName)
    If TargetURL <> "" Then
        On Error Resume Next
        StringPos = InStr(TargetURL, ":")
        If StringPos > 0 Then
            URLType = Left(TargetURL, StringPos - 1)
            If URLType = "http" Then
                Set WebNode = New clsHTMLPageResourceNode
                Set WebNode.Parent = CurrentWebNode
                WebNode.URL = TargetURL
                WebNode.Path = TargetURL
                Set HostCollection = SelectHostCollection( _
                    WebNode.URL, CurrentWebNode)
                If Not (HostCollection Is Nothing) Then
                    If Not WebNode.Root.AlreadyContains( _
                        WebNode.URL, ExistingNode) Then
                        HostCollection.Add WebNode, WebNode.URL
                      End If
                  End If
              End If
          ElseIf Left(TargetURL, 1) = "/" Then
            Set WebNode = New clsHTMLPageResourceNode
            Set WebNode.Parent = CurrentWebNode
            WebNode.URL = ServerURL & TargetURL
            WebNode.Path = TargetURL
            Set HostCollection = SelectHostCollection( _
                WebNode.URL, CurrentWebNode)
            If Not (HostCollection Is Nothing) Then
                If Not WebNode.Root.AlreadyContains( _
                    WebNode.URL, ExistingNode) Then
                    HostCollection.Add WebNode, WebNode.URL
                  End If
              End If
          Else
            Set WebNode = New clsHTMLPageResourceNode
            Set WebNode.Parent = CurrentWebNode
```

```
            WebNode.URL = ParentURL & TargetURL
            WebNode.Path = TargetURL
            Set HostCollection = SelectHostCollection( _
                WebNode.URL, CurrentWebNode)
            If Not (HostCollection Is Nothing) Then
                If Not WebNode.Root.AlreadyContains( _
                    WebNode.URL, ExistingNode) Then
                    HostCollection.Add WebNode, WebNode.URL
                  End If
              End If
          End If
        Debug.Print "Collection Count: ", HostCollection.Count
      Else
        ' No URL found.
      End If 'TargetURL <> ""
    Loop While (CurrentStartPos > 0)
End Sub

Private Function GetNextTargetURLFromDocument(Document As String, _
                                  CurrentStartPos As Long, _
                                  TagParamName As String) As String
    Dim TempURL As String
    Dim EndOfCurrentTagPos As Long
    Dim CurrentEndPos As Long

    TempURL = ""
    CurrentStartPos = InStr(CurrentStartPos, Document, TagParamName)
    If CurrentStartPos > 0 Then
        EndOfCurrentTagPos = InStr(CurrentStartPos, Document, ">")
        CurrentStartPos = InStr(CurrentStartPos, Document, """")
        If CurrentStartPos > 0 Then
            CurrentStartPos = CurrentStartPos + 1
            CurrentEndPos = InStr(CurrentStartPos, Document, """")
            If (CurrentEndPos > CurrentStartPos) And _
               (CurrentEndPos < EndOfCurrentTagPos) Then
                TempURL = Mid(Document, CurrentStartPos, _
                              CurrentEndPos - CurrentStartPos)
              Else
                CurrentStartPos = EndOfCurrentTagPos
              End If
          End If
      End If
    GetNextTargetURLFromDocument = TempURL

    End Function
```

```
Public Function SelectHostCollection(URL As String, _
    WebNode As clsHTMLPageResourceNode) As Collection
    Dim sHeaderValue As String

    If AbleToGetWebDocumentHeaders(URL) Then
        sHeaderValue = Inet1.GetHeader("Content-type")
        If (InStr(1, sHeaderValue, "text/", 1) > 0) Then
            Set SelectHostCollection = WebNode.PageLinks
          Else
            Set SelectHostCollection = WebNode.PageElements
          End If
      Else
        Set SelectHostCollection = Nothing
      End If
    Debug.Print URL
    Debug.Print sHeaderValue
    End Function
```

First, we'll drop the CommandButton in favor of a neater ToolBar, which will also require an ImageList to supply its button icons. Two more TextBox controls will accept and display the search string and search depth. We'll round out those additions with appropriate Labels and an UpDown arrow for a total of seven new controls. Finally, just for the sake of completeness, we'll toss in a totally redundant Menu Bar. The controls and properties are summarized in Table 3.3.

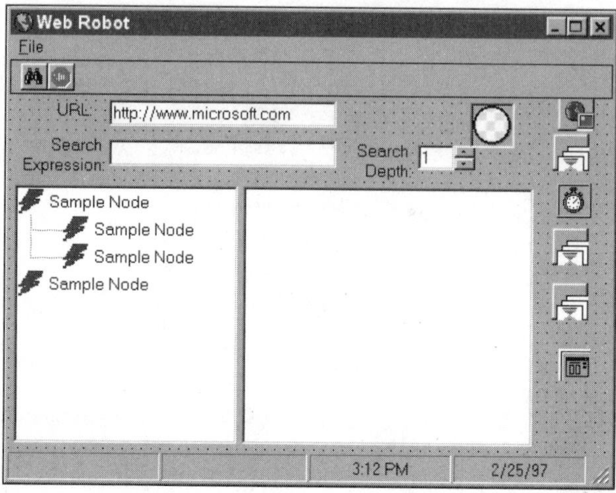

Figure 3.4
The Web Robot form at design time.

Table 3.3 The controls and properties for the form frmWebRobot.

Control Name	Type	Properties	Value
frmWebRobot	Form	Caption	"Web Robot"
Inet1	Inet	Protocol	4 - icHTTP
cmnSaveAs	CommonDialog	CancelError	True
ilBusyIcons	ImageList	(Custom)	
ilTreeIcons	ImageList	(Custom)	
ilToolbarIcons	ImageList	(Custom)	
lblSearch	Label	Alignment	1 - Right Justify
	Caption	"Search Expression:"	
lblSearchDepth	Label	Alignment	1 - Right Justify
	Caption	"Search Depth:"	
lblURL	Label	Caption	"URL:"
mnuExit	Menu	Caption	"&Exit"
	Enabled	True	
mnuFile	Menu	Caption	"&File"
	Enabled	True	
mnuPerformSearch	Menu	Caption	"&Perform Search"
	Enabled	True	
mnuStopSearch	Menu	Caption	"&Stop Search"
	Enabled	False	
picBusy	PictureBox	Appearance	1 - 3D
	BorderStyle	1 - Fixed Single	
picDivider	PictureBox	Appearance	1 - 3D
	AutoSize	False	
	BackColor	&H00C0C0C0	
	BorderStyle	None	
	MousePointer	9 - Size W E	
sbHTTPStatus	StatusBar	Align	2 - Align Bottom
	Style		0 - Multiple panels

continued

Table 3.3 The controls and properties for the form frmWebRobot (continued).

Control Name	Type	Properties	Value
tbToolbar	Toolbar	(Custom)	btnSeparator1
	btnSearch		
	btnStop		
	ImageList	ilToolbarIcons	
	Align		1 - Align Top
	Appearance	1 - 3D	
	BorderStyle	1 - Fixed Single	
tmrBusy	Timer	Enabled	False
	Interval	500	
tvURLTreeView	TreeView	Appearance	1 - 3D
	BorderStyle	1 - Fixed Single	
	Style		7 - Treelines, ...
txtOutput	TextBox	BorderStyle	1 - Fixed Single
	MultiLine	True	
	ScrollBars	3 - Both	
	Text		""
txtSearchDepth	TextBox	BorderStyle	1 - Fixed Single
	MultiLine	False	
	ScrollBars	0 - None	
	Text		""
txtSearchString	TextBox	BorderStyle	1 - Fixed Single
	MultiLine	False	
	ScrollBars	0 - None	
	Text		""
txtURL	TextBox	BorderStyle	1 - Fixed Single
	MultiLine	False	
	ScrollBars	0 - None	
	Text		""
udSearchDepth	UpDown	Orientation	0 - Vertical

Changes To The Form Code

In the Web Explorer, most of the action occurred in the **cmdPerformRequest_Click()** event. For this project, we'll move that code into a general procedure called **PerformRequest()**, shown in Listing 3.17. We can call this from any of three event procedures: **tbToolbar_ButtonClick()**, **mnuPerformSearch_Click()**, and **tvURLTreeView_NodeClick()**.

Listing 3.17 The general procedure **PerformRequest()** from form frmWebRobot.FRM.

```
Private Sub PerformRequest()
    Dim TempURL As String
    Dim FileExtension As String
    Dim TargetFilename As String
    Dim SearchDepth As Integer
    Dim NewWebNode As clsHTMLPageResourceNode
    Dim ExistingNode As clsHTMLPageResourceNode
    Dim Diplomat As clsDiplomat
    Dim vtBinaryData As Variant
    Dim BinaryData() As Byte
    Dim FilenameForBinaryData As String
    Const BinaryFileID = 1

    If Not ValidSearchDepth(SearchDepth) Then Exit Sub
    TempURL = txtURL.Text
    If Not URLNormalized(TempURL) Then
        MsgBox "Please enter a valid URL", vbCritical, "Invalid URL"
        Exit Sub
      Else
        txtURL.Text = TempURL
      End If

    If Not bPerformingRequest Then
        FileExtension = Trim(LCase( _
            ExtractFilenameExtensionFromPath(txtURL.Text)))
        Select Case FileExtension
          Case "gif", "jpg"
            BinaryFile = True
            TargetFilename = App.Path & "\" & _
                ExtractFilenameFromPath(txtURL.Text)
            cmnSaveAs.filename = TargetFilename
            cmnSaveAs.DefaultExt = Right(TargetFilename, 4)
            cmnSaveAs.Filter = "Images(*.bmp;*.gif;*.jpg)"
```

```
        cmnSaveAs.CancelError = True
        On Error GoTo Skip
        cmnSaveAs.ShowSave
        bPerformingRequest = True
        txtURL.Enabled = False
        mnuPerformSearch.Enabled = False
        mnuStopSearch.Enabled = False
        tbToolbar.Buttons("btnSearch").Enabled = False
        tbToolbar.Buttons("btnStop").Enabled = False
        Me.MousePointer = vbHourglass
        tmrBusy.Enabled = True
        bPerformingSearch = True
        bSearchCancelled = False

        FilenameForBinaryData = cmnSaveAs.filename

        BinaryData() = Inet1.OpenURL(txtURL.Text, icByteArray)
        Open FilenameForBinaryData For Binary As BinaryFileID
        Put BinaryFileID, , BinaryData()
        Close BinaryFileID

        txtURL.Enabled = True
        mnuPerformSearch.Enabled = True
        mnuStopSearch.Enabled = False
        tbToolbar.Buttons("btnSearch").Enabled = True
        tbToolbar.Buttons("btnStop").Enabled = False
        tmrBusy.Enabled = False
        Me.MousePointer = vbDefault
        bPerformingSearch = False
        bPerformingRequest = False

Skip:
      Case Else
        ' This case will handle any HTML document request,
        ' whether or not it includes a filename,
        ' because a URL with no filename will cause the
        ' web server to return its default HTML document
        ' file.

        bPerformingRequest = True
        tmrBusy.Enabled = True
        Me.MousePointer = vbArrowHourglass
        txtURL.Enabled = False
        mnuPerformSearch.Enabled = False
        mnuStopSearch.Enabled = True
```

```
        tbToolbar.Buttons("btnSearch").Enabled = False
        tbToolbar.Buttons("btnStop").Enabled = True
        bPerformingSearch = True
        bSearchCancelled = False
        BinaryFile = False
        txtOutput.Text = ""

        Set Analyst = New clsDocumentAnalyst
        Analyst.Init txtSearchString.Text
        If RootWebNode.AlreadyContains(txtURL.Text, _
            ExistingNode) Then
            Set Diplomat = DispatchNewDiplomat(ExistingNode.URL)
            If Not (Diplomat Is Nothing) Then
                SearchWeb ExistingNode, SearchDepth, Diplomat
              End If
          Else
            Set NewWebNode = New clsHTMLPageResourceNode
            NewWebNode.URL = txtURL.Text
            NewWebNode.Path = txtURL.Text
            Set NewWebNode.Parent = RootWebNode
            Set Diplomat = DispatchNewDiplomat(NewWebNode.URL)
            If Not (Diplomat Is Nothing) Then
                RootWebNode.PageLinks.Add NewWebNode, _
                    NewWebNode.URL
                SearchWeb NewWebNode, SearchDepth, Diplomat
              End If
          End If

        txtURL.Enabled = True
        mnuPerformSearch.Enabled = True
        mnuStopSearch.Enabled = False
        tbToolbar.Buttons("btnSearch").Enabled = True
        tbToolbar.Buttons("btnStop").Enabled = False
        tmrBusy.Enabled = False
        Me.MousePointer = vbDefault
        bPerformingSearch = False
        bPerformingRequest = False
      End Select
  End If

End Sub
```

In this version of **PerformRequest()**, the code under **Case "gif", "jpg"** nearly matches the event procedure version in the Web Explorer. The only difference is the addition of the numerous statements that enable and disable the various controls and menu options before the file transfer begins. The **Case Else** clause, however, differs siginificantly.

Here, too, the code has swollen with statements that modifty the **Enabled** properties of several controls. But more importantly, it now calls a new general procedure named **SearchWeb()** and works with three new objects: **RootWebNode, Diplomat,** and **Analyst**.

The **Diplomat** object, described later in the section "Don't Let Your Robots Grow Up To Be Monsters," will act as the Robot's conscience, preventing it from degenerating into a marauder. The **Analyst** object—an instance of the class **clsDocumentAnalyst**, which we'll explore in detail later in Chapter 6—will perform search string matching. The **RootWebNode** makes it practical to keep a complete tree of page resource nodes throughout the current session.

As I mentioned earlier, the Web Robot—unlike the Web Explorer—will retain all of its page resource nodes, constructing an internal tree that grows in parallel with the TreeView **Nodes** collection. The TreeView is just a convenient way to monitor and manage the paths taken by the Web Robot. But you may not always need a TreeView. The tree built from objects of the class **clsHTMLPageResourceNode**—the *page resource tree*—maintains all the information the robot needs to keep itself from running in circles or repeating itself. Because it could accomplish this without all the overhead of a TreeView control, the functional core of the program remains independent of the visual interface. At least that's the philosophical rationalization. But the page resource tree also serves a practical purpose. The TreeView provides little space for data other than what it needs to display itself. By adding properties to **clsHTMLPageResourceNode**, however, it's possible to store all kinds of information in each node—anything from search statistics to time and date stamps to complete page texts. The **RootWebNode** provides an anchor, a home for all other page resource nodes. When you begin a search by clicking an existing node, that node by definition becomes the parent of all the new nodes created during the search. But when you begin a search by typing in an entirely new URL—one that hasn't already appeared in the tree—where do you put it? The **RootWebNode** becomes a foster parent to all these orphan nodes, binding them together into a single tree.

Before beginning the search, **PerformRequest()** creates a new instance of **Analyst**, initializing it with the current Search String as contained in **txtSearchString.Text**.

Incorporating the document search string parser is that simple. Next, it searches the page resource tree, beginning with **RootWebNode**, to determine whether it already contains a page resource node representing the starting URL. If so, it instantiates a new **Diplomat** for that URL with **DispatchNewDiplomat()** and calls **SearchWeb()**:

```
Analyst.Init txtSearchString.Text
Set Analyst = New clsDocumentAnalyst
If RootWebNode.AlreadyContains(txtURL.Text, ExistingNode) Then
   Set Diplomat = DispatchNewDiplomat(ExistingNode.URL)
   SearchWeb ExistingNode, SearchDepth, Diplomat
```

If not, it first sets **NewWebNode** to a new instance of **clsHTMLPageResourceNode**. Then, after setting **Diplomat,** it adds the new page resource node to the tree by adding it to the **PageLinks** collection of **RootWebNode**. Finally, it begins the search, passing the newly created node to **SearchWeb()**:

```
Else
   Set NewWebNode = New clsHTMLPageResourceNode
   NewWebNode.URL = txtURL.Text
   NewWebNode.Path = txtURL.Text
   Set NewWebNode.Parent = RootWebNode
   Set Diplomat = DispatchNewDiplomat(NewWebNode.URL)
   RootWebNode.PageLinks.Add NewWebNode, NewWebNode.URL
   SearchWeb NewWebNode, SearchDepth, Diplomat
End If
```

Roaming The Web

The general procedure **SearchWeb()**, shown in Listing 3.18, performs the actual task of retrieving documents and adding them to both the page resource tree and the TreeView control.

SearchWeb() takes three arguments. The first, **CurrentWebNode**, specifies an object reference to the page resource node at which to begin the search. This can either be an existing node in the page resource tree or a new node created within the calling procedure, **PerformRequest()**. **LevelsToSearch**, an integer, determines how many levels deep to search the current node for linked pages. A value of 1 means to retrieve and analyze only the page referenced by **CurrentWebNode**. A value of 2 means to retrieve and analyze all documents pointed to by hyperlinks in that first page, and so on. In the third argument, **Diplomat**, the procedure receives a reference to an object belonging to the class **clsDiplomat**, which carries a list of access restrictions for the most recently contacted Web server.

Listing 3.18 The general procedure **SearchWeb()** from frmWebRobot.FRM.

```
Private Sub SearchWeb(CurrentWebNode As clsHTMLPageResourceNode, _
                      ByVal LevelsToSearch As Integer, _
                      ByVal Diplomat As clsDiplomat)

    Dim WebNode As clsHTMLPageResourceNode
    Dim NodeIcon As Integer
    Dim TempText As String

    ' Evaluate Access Restrictions
    If Diplomat.NewServerURL(CurrentWebNode.URL) Then
        Set Diplomat = DispatchNewDiplomat(CurrentWebNode.URL)
      End If
    If Diplomat.Rejects(CurrentWebNode.URL) Then
        AddNodeToTreeView CurrentWebNode, icoERROR
        Exit Sub
      End If


    If AbleToGetWebDocument(CurrentWebNode.URL) Then
        TimeOfLastTransfer = Now
        CurrentWebNode.MatchesSearch = _
            Analyst.DocumentMatches(txtOutput.Text)
        If CurrentWebNode.MatchesSearch Then
            NodeIcon = icoHIT
          ElseIf InStr(CurrentWebNode.Path, "://") Then
            NodeIcon = icoSERVER
          Else
            NodeIcon = icoDOCUMENT
          End If
        AddNodeToTreeView CurrentWebNode, NodeIcon
        If (LevelsToSearch > 1) Then
            TempText = txtOutput.Text
            ExtractLinksFromDocument TempText, "href", CurrentWebNode
            ExtractLinksFromDocument TempText, "src", CurrentWebNode
            For Each WebNode In CurrentWebNode.PageElements
                DoEvents
                If bSearchCancelled Then Exit For
```

```
            AddNodeToTreeView WebNode, icoIMAGE
            Next WebNode
        For Each WebNode In CurrentWebNode.PageLinks
            DoEvents
            If bSearchCancelled Then Exit For
            Do Until DateDiff("s", TimeOfLastTransfer, Now) > 5
                DoEvents
                Loop
            SearchWeb WebNode, LevelsToSearch - 1, Diplomat
            Debug.Print "Call SearchWeb "; WebNode.URL
            Next WebNode
        If bSearchCancelled Then MsgBox "Search Cancelled"
      End If
  Else
    AddNodeToTreeView CurrentWebNode, icoERROR
  End If
End Sub
```

Before it can proceed, the search procedure needs to determine whether or not the server permits robot access to the page. If the **CurrentWebNode** belongs to a new server, we must first query the server for its access restrictions by calling **Dispatch NewDiplomat()**:

```
' Evaluate Access Restrictions
If Diplomat.NewServerURL(CurrentWebNode.URL) Then
    Set Diplomat = DispatchNewDiplomat(CurrentWebNode.URL)
  End If
```

Once we have the **Diplomat** properly initialized, we test the current URL with the **Rejects** method of the **Diplomat**. If the server prohibits access to the page, we add it to the TreeView with an icon that indicates an error and exit the procedure:

```
If Diplomat.Rejects(CurrentWebNode.URL) Then
    AddNodeToTreeView CurrentWebNode, icoERROR
    Exit Sub
  End If
```

If the **Diplomat** gives us the green light, we retrieve the document by calling **AbleToGetWebDocument()**, shown in Listing 3.19.

Listing 3.19 The general function **AbleToGetWebDocument()** from frmWebRobot.FRM.

```
Public Function AbleToGetWebDocument(URL As String) As Boolean

    ' Initialize Semaphore Flags.
    HTTPSemaphore.Error = False
    HTTPSemaphore.Timeout = False
    HTTPSemaphore.Connected = False
    HTTPSemaphore.ConnectionFailed = False
    HTTPSemaphore.Complete = False
    HTTPSemaphore.Cancelled = False

    ' Request HTML document retrieval.
    txtOutput.Text = ""
    bPerformingRequest = True

    Inet1.Execute URL

    ' Wait until asynchronous transfer terminates:
    Do
        DoEvents
        Loop Until (HTTPSemaphore.Complete Or _
                    HTTPSemaphore.Cancelled Or _
                    bSearchCancelled)

    ' I also monitored for a ConnectionFailed event:
    '
    '                HTTPSemaphore.ConnectionFailed Or _
    '
    ' but this seemed to fire even when the document transfer
    ' was able to continue and complete successfully,
    ' which caused the program to make the next request
    ' before the previous request had finished, resulting
    ' in an error.

    ' The correct way to detect activity on the Inet control
    ' would be to watch the StillExecuting property. But, at
    ' this writing, this property never indicates True, which
    ' prevents me from using it:
    'Do While Inet1.StillExecuting
    '    DoEvents
    '    Loop

    AbleToGetWebDocument = HTTPSemaphore.Complete
    End Function
```

In the previous project, the Web Explorer, we called the Inet control's **Execute()** method and relinquished control of the program to the Inet control's **StateChanged()** event procedure. Although the transfer was performed asynchronously, the program had nothing else to do—it just waited for a state change of **icResponseCompleted.** The Web Robot, however, depending on how many levels we instruct it to search, may need to carry on an automated traversal of the Web. As soon as it retrieves a document, it may need to extract that document's hyperlinks and perform the entire process all over again for each linked document. To keep the program from proceeding on to the next step before the document transfer has finished, we use a set of *semaphores,* which are just flags that keep track of the current state of the Inet control. **AbleToGetWebDocument()** calls the Inet control's **Execute()** method, then enters a **Do** loop until it detects any of three conditions as indicated by **HTTPSemaphore.Complete**, **HTTPSemaphore.Cancelled**, or **bSearchCancelled.** This little trick effectively converts the Inet control's clever asynchronous file transfer process into a synchronous process, pretty much obliterating any advantage of the asynchronous method.

Watch Those Transfer Errors

*Before moving on, let me confess to one other shortcoming: The procedure **AbleToGetWebDocument()** entirely ignores transfer errors, which would normally be signaled by the **icError** state change event. The Inet control detects and reports a rather large number of error conditions—you'll find them listed as **ErrorConstants** under the **InetCtlsObjects** within the VB Object Browser—not all of which will abort the file transfer. As far as I can tell, the best way to handle transfer errors is to execute the Inet control's **Cancel()** method. You can drop it right into the **Case icError** in the **StateChanged()** event procedure. Otherwise, you'll need to accumulate a list of errors while the control completes the transfer, then sort through them to determine whether you received useable data. It's probably better to just quit and start over.*

After it has retrieved the document, **SearchWeb()** hands it over to the document **Analyst** to see if it matches the Search String. The result—**True** or **False**—is assigned to the **Matches** property of **CurrentWebNode** and indicated by an appropriate icon in the TreeView control:

```
If AbleToGetWebDocument(CurrentWebNode.URL) Then
    TimeOfLastTransfer = Now
```

```
CurrentWebNode.MatchesSearch = Analyst.DocumentMatches( _
    txtOutput.Text)
If CurrentWebNode.MatchesSearch Then
    NodeIcon = icoHIT
  ElseIf InStr(CurrentWebNode.Path, "://") Then
    NodeIcon = icoSERVER
  Else
    NodeIcon = icoDOCUMENT
  End If
AddNodeToTreeView CurrentWebNode, NodeIcon
```

If **LevelsToSearch** is greater than 1, the procedure needs to identify the hyperlinks in the current document. In our Web Explorer project, this task was handled by the method **AddLinksFromDocument**() in the class **clsHTMLPageResourceNode**, and its subordinate procedures, **ExtractLinksFromDocument**() and **GetNextTargetURL FromDocument**(). But there were two major holes in the way the Web Explorer differentiated between document files and binary files, and between the various types of binary files. First, we assumed that **HREF** tag attributes always referenced documents and that **SRC** attributes always referenced binary objects. Both of these assumptions fail frequently. In fact, any **<A>** tag, which uses the **HREF** attibute to identify its link target, may point either to a text file or to a binary object such as a GIF image, or a sound or video clip. On the other hand, the **<FRAME>** tag, which uses the **SRC** attribute to identify the contents of each frame, often identifies a document as its target. The other faulty assumption in the Web Explorer was that we could identify the contents of a file by its filename extension. That will work most of the time. But the Web and HTTP provide a more reliable way to identify files, even those whose names lack extensions. We can actually query the Web server for the response header alone—without the data. We can then check the Content-type header, which identifies what type of data the file contains to determine how, where, and when we want to retrieve the file.

The procedures **ExtractLinksFromDocument**() and **GetNextTargetURLFrom Document**() in the Web Explorer's class **clsHTMLPageResourceNode** never required direct access to the Web. They could perform their functions without ever looking beyond the contents of the text file retrieved by the Inet control. But our Web Robot has to walk through the Web automatically and efficiently, so we'll want these procedures to differentiate more carefully between documents (which are usually small and frequently contain hyperlinks) and binary objects (which are often huge and rarely contain hyperlinks).

We'll still sort the document's links into two collections, **PageElements** and **PageLinks**—both of which are stored in a page resource node. But this program will no longer collate the identified links into the two collections according to the SRC and HREF attributes. Instead, **ExtractLinksFromDocument()** will call a new function, **SelectHostCollection()**. This, in turn, will call the procedure **AbleToGet WebDocumentHeaders()** to retrieve and interpret the Content-type header for each link it extracts from the source document.

AbleToGetWebDocumentHeaders() closely resembles **AbleToGetWebDocument()**, except that we pass the **Inet1.Execute()** method a string, "HEAD," indicating that we want it to retrieve only the response headers from the server; we also set and clear the flag **bRequestingHeaders**. This flag keeps us from performing unnecessary steps in the **icResponseCompleted** case clause in the **Inet1_StateChanged()** event procedure. It's true that we could have dispensed with the procedure **AbleToGet WebDocument()** by simply using the Inet control's **OpenURL()** method instead of **Execute()**. However, to retrieve headers alone, we must use the **Execute()** method. **Execute()** always performs an asynchronous transfer. So regardless of which method we choose to retrieve the files, we need the procedure **AbleToGetWebDocument Headers()**—or something similar—to suspend program execution while we await the response to a request for headers.

Because these functions now depend on an asynchronous operation performed by the Inet control, we need to move **ExtractLinksFromDocument()** and **GetNextTargetURLFromDocument()**—shown back in Listing 3.16—from the class module **clsHTMLPageResourceNode** to the form module **frmWebRobot**.

SearchWeb() calls **ExtractLinksFromDocument()** two times in succession: once to analyze the HREF tag attributes and once to analyze the SRC attributes, building (or rebuilding) the node's **PageElements** and **PageLinks** collections. It then loops through the **PageElements** collection, adding its members to the TreeView:

```
If (LevelsToSearch > 1) Then
    TempText = txtOutput.Text
    ExtractLinksFromDocument TempText, "href", CurrentWebNode
    ExtractLinksFromDocument TempText, "src", CurrentWebNode
    For Each WebNode In CurrentWebNode.PageElements
        DoEvents
        If bSearchCancelled Then Exit For
        AddNodeToTreeView WebNode, icoIMAGE
        Next WebNode
```

SearchWeb() is supposed to perform a search to any specified depth. To advance to the next level of the search tree, it calls itself recursively for each page resource node in the **PageLinks** collection:

```
For Each WebNode In CurrentWebNode.PageLinks
    DoEvents
    If bSearchCancelled Then Exit For
    Do Until DateDiff("s", TimeOfLastTransfer, Now) > 5
        DoEvents
        Loop
    SearchWeb WebNode, LevelsToSearch - 1, Diplomat
    Debug.Print "Call SearchWeb "; WebNode.URL
    Next WebNode
```

The second argument to **SearchWeb()**, **LevelsToSearch,** is passed **ByVal.** Which means that each time the procedure passes **LevelsToSearch - 1** to itself, the next instance of the procedure receives a decremented value. A value of zero in **LevelsToSearch** terminates the recursion, causing control to jump back to the previous level. The second terminating condition occurs when the second **For Each** loop exhausts its **PageLinks** collection. The third terminating condition occurs when the user sets **bSearchCancelled** to **True** by selecting File|Stop Search or by clicking the Stop button on the Toolbar.

The **Diplomat** argument is also passed **ByVal**, but the passing of an object variable by value can have subtler effects than it does for other data types. As with any variable of a primitive type—such as an **Integer** or **String**—or with any variable of a user-defined type, passing an object variable by value means that changing the value of that argument from within the procedure will have no effect outside the procedure. The argument behaves like a local variable. But unlike the fields of a user-defined type, this behavior does not extend to the properties of an object *referenced by* an object variable.

For example, let's define a simple type:

```
Type MyType
    FieldA As Integer
    End Type
```

Now, let's declare a variable of the type **MyType** and pass it to a sub procedure:

```
Dim MyVariable As MyType
MyVariable.FieldA = 0
Debug.Print "The Value of FieldA is ";MyVariable.FieldA
Call AnyProcedure(MyVariable)
Debug.Print "The Value of FieldA is ";MyVariable.FieldA
```

The procedure might look something like this:

```
Sub AnyProcedure(ByVal TheArgument As MyType)
    TheArgument.FieldA = 99
    Debug.Print "The Value of FieldA is ";TheArgument.FieldA
    End Sub
```

The three lines printed in the debug window would look like this:

```
The Value of FieldA is 0
The Value of FieldA is 99
The Value of FieldA is 0
```

Now, instead of a user-defined type, let's declare an object class called **clsMyClass.** This class module will have one property in its declarations section:

```
Option Explicit
Public FieldA As Integer
```

This time, we begin by declaring an instance of **clsMyClass** represented by an object variable called **MyObject**:

```
Dim MyObject As New clsMyClass
MyObject.FieldA = 0
Debug.Print "The Value of FieldA is ";MyObject.FieldA
Call AnyProcedure(MyObject)
Debug.Print "The Value of FieldA is ";MyObject.FieldA
```

The procedure now takes an object reference as its argument:

```
Sub AnyProcedure(ByVal TheArgument As clsMyClass)
    TheArgument.FieldA = 99
    Debug.Print "The Value of FieldA is ";TheArgument.FieldA
    End Sub
```

And this is the result:

```
The Value of FieldA is 0
```

```
The Value of FieldA is 99
The Value of FieldA is 99
```

Remember, an object variable is like a nickname; it contains a reference to an object, not the object itself. When you pass an object reference **ByVal** as an argument, that argument variable becomes another nickname for the same object. One more variation of this example should clarify this behavior. We begin with the same calling procedure:

```
Dim MyObject As New clsMyClass
MyObject.FieldA = 0
Debug.Print "The Value of FieldA is ";MyObject.FieldA
Call AnyProcedure(MyObject)
Debug.Print "The Value of FieldA is ";MyObject.FieldA
```

The **AnyProcedure**() still takes an object reference as its argument, but this time it assigns it a new instance of **clsMyClass**:

```
Sub AnyProcedure(ByVal TheArgument As clsMyClass)
    TheArgument = New clsMyClass
    TheArgument.FieldA = 99
    Debug.Print "The Value of FieldA is ";TheArgument.FieldA
    End Sub
```

And here's what happens:

```
The Value of FieldA is 0
The Value of FieldA is 99
The Value of FieldA is 0
```

This time, **TheArgument** behaves like a local variable. It enters the procedure with a reference to an object, but we discard that reference by assigning it a reference to a new object.

In **SearchWeb**(), we use this last principle to manage the **Diplomat** objects. Each time the procedure recurses, it checks whether the current **Diplomat** represents the current URL's server. If not, it creates a new instance of **clsDiplomat** and assigns it to **Diplomat**, leaving intact the original object referenced by **Diplomat**. When a recursive call to **SearchWeb**() returns to the previous instance of **SearchWeb**(), that instance of the procedure still holds a reference to a diplomat object representing its **CurrentWebNode**'s server. If we didn't manage the diplomat objects in this way, we would need to create a new instance of **clsDiplomat** for every Web document we retrieved.

One more variation of object passing still deserves our attention. When you pass an object reference *by reference*—VB's default method, also made explicit with the keyword **ByRef**—you're passing a reference to the object variable, which is itself a reference to an object. In this case, if you change the object reference within the called procedure, the outer reference changes too

```
Sub AnyProcedure(ByRef TheArgument As clsMyClass)
    TheArgument = New clsMyClass
    TheArgument.FieldA = 99
    Debug.Print "The Value of FieldA is ";TheArgument.FieldA
    End Sub
```

with these results:

```
The Value of FieldA is 0
The Value of FieldA is 99
The Value of FieldA is 99
```

Take great care how you declare object parameters. Reference errors are among the most difficult bugs to identify. Ask any C programmer.

One other block of code in **SearchWeb()** deserves some attention:

```
Do Until DateDiff("s", TimeOfLastTransfer, Now) > 5
    DoEvents
    Loop
```

This delay loop keeps our Web Robot from monopolizing the servers it visits. The time delay of five seconds is rather small—before turning your own robots loose, set this delay to the maximum value you can tolerate. Yes, this will slow down your search on a server with numerous pages, but it will also permit the server to respond efficiently to other users. Voluntary delays between document requests are just one form of Web Robot etiquette. Next, let's take a closer look at how the class **clsDiplomat** manages another major courtesy issue.

Don't Let Your Robots Grow Up To Be Monsters

To prevent the Web Robot from wreaking havoc with the servers it visits, it needs to observe some rules. The first, which we discussed above, dictates that Robots should not monopolize servers with rapid-fire document requests. The second requires that it obey the access restrictions imposed by each server's system administrator.

System administrators and robot developers have agreed on a standard for managing robots. Many servers now include a text file called Robots.Txt in their root directories, which contains a list of prohibited directories. Administrators can even specify access restrictions for particular robots. As an example, here are the contents of the Robots.Txt file at http://www.microsoft.com/:

```
# robots.txt for http://www.microsoft.com/

User-agent: *
Disallow: /isapi/   # keep robots out of the executable tree
Disallow: /scripts/
```

This file contains three types of entries. Lines (or partial lines) that begin with the # sign are comments. The **User-agent** label specifies the name of a robot. An asterisk in this field means that the following restrictions apply to all robots. By the way, most of the well-known robots—those operated by the popular Web directory and search services—identify themselves in their HTTP request headers. This is how system administrators discover who is hogging their servers. Lines beginning with the **Disallow** label specify prohibited directories. You'll notice that Microsoft asks robots to stay out of their /isapi/ directory. That's because those Web documents present information stored in databases. If the robot hits the right pages, it could begin requesting every record in the database. This situation could tie up the server for hours, or even days—probably not what the robot's owner intended. The same goes for servers with directories that contain CGI-based pages; by convention, these often reside in a directory called /cgi-bin/.

In the Web Robot, the responsibility for reading and evaluating Robots.Txt files is encapsulated in the class **clsDiplomat**, whose entire contents are shown in Listing 3.20.

Listing 3.20 The complete listing of clsDiplomat.CLS.

```
Option Explicit

Public Text
Private Restrictions()
Private CurrentServerURL

Public Sub Init(URL As String, AgentAccessFile As String)
    Dim TempText As String
```

```
    Dim TempString As String
    Dim CurrentLine As String
    Dim Loc As Long

    ReDim Restrictions(0)
    CurrentServerURL = GetServerURLFrom(URL)
    Text = LCase(AgentAccessFile)
    TempText = Text
    Do While (Len(TempText) > 0)
        CurrentLine = LCase(Trim(GetNextLineFrom(TempText)))
        Debug.Print "Current Line: "; CurrentLine
        If Left(CurrentLine, 9) = "disallow:" Then
            Loc = InStr(CurrentLine, "#")
            If Loc > 10 Then
                TempString = Trim(Mid(CurrentLine, 10, Loc - 10))
              Else
                TempString = Trim(Mid(CurrentLine, 10))
              End If
            Restrictions(UBound(Restrictions)) = TempString
            Debug.Print "Restrictions: "; Restrictions( _
                UBound(Restrictions))
            ReDim Preserve Restrictions(UBound(Restrictions) + 1)
            Restrictions(UBound(Restrictions)) = ""
          End If
        Loop
    End Sub

Private Function GetNextLineFrom(TextString As String) As String
    Dim Loc As Long
    Dim TempLine As String

    Loc = InStr(TextString, vbLf)
    If Loc <> 0 Then
        TempLine = Mid(TextString, 1, Loc - 1)
        Do While (Asc(Right(TempLine, 1)) < 32) And _
            (Len(TempLine) > 1)
            TempLine = Left(TempLine, Len(TempLine) - 1)
            Loop
        GetNextLineFrom = TempLine
        TextString = Mid(TextString, Loc + 1)
      Else
        GetNextLineFrom = TextString
        TextString = ""
      End If
    End Function
```

```
Public Function NewServerURL(URL As String)
    If InStr(URL, CurrentServerURL) <> 0 Then
        NewServerURL = False
      Else
        NewServerURL = True
      End If

    End Function

Public Function Rejects(URLToExamine As String)
    Dim Loc As Long
    Dim Counter As Integer

    Loc = 0
    For Counter = 1 To UBound(Restrictions) - 1
        Loc = InStr(URLToExamine, Restrictions(Counter))
        If Loc <> 0 Then Exit For
        Next Counter
    Rejects = (Loc <> 0) Or (InStr(URLToExamine, "cgi") > 0)
    End Function
```

To ensure that the Web Robot behaves like a good Internet citizen, this implementation is especially paranoid. It obeys all restrictions, even those targeted at specific commercial robots. And just for good measure, it rejects any URL that includes "cgi".

Resources For Robot Designers

*For more information on robot ethics and mechanics, visit **http://info.webcrawler.com/mak/projects/robots/robots.html**.*

HIGH PERFORMANCE

The VB Document Analyst

CHAPTER 4

The heart of any Internet search engine or smart Internet client is a powerful text analyst. Use this compact, object-based parser to build your own intelligent search systems.

The VB Document Analyst

Text analysis is the process of evaluating the contents of a target document against a search expression that specifies words or combinations of words. To accomplish this, we need to carry out two different but simultaneous parsing operations: one to read and evaluate the search expression and one to search the document for the words specified in the search expression.

In Chapter 3, we used a collection of five class modules to analyze HTML documents retrieved by our Web Robot program. That object model consisted of five class modules, known collectively as the *Visual Basic Document Analyst.* In this chapter, we'll look closely at the inner workings of these modules and explore the techniques they incorporate to parse and evaluate a search expression.

Parser Primer

Before we go any further, let's get a grip on some of this terminology. First of all, what do we mean by a parser? *Parsing* is the process of breaking a text string down into its constituent parts—words—and optionally performing operations on (or according to) those words. All computer languages, for example, are defined by a sophisticated parser that can differentiate between statements, variables, functions, and other program elements. The expression parser in our Visual Basic Document Analyst will detect four types of elements: *operators, operands,* quotation marks, and parentheses. Operands are the words that we're searching for in the text document. Operators specify relationships between those words.

One way to figure out which words are indeed operators is to look them up in a table. However, you'll still need to determine whether the other words in the expression are in the right places in relationship to the operators before you know what to do with them. The other way to identify operators is to look for them in the places where you would expect to find them, according to the rules with which expressions are written in the first place—in other words, according to the expression *syntax.* To identify any particular element syntactically, the parser not only needs to keep track of which elements it has already encountered, but also what it expects to find next. For example, when we enter the expression

Prince and Charles

we're asking the parser to determine whether the text document contains the words "Prince" and "Charles," no matter where they appear within the text, or in what order. "Prince" and "Charles" are the operands; "and" is the operator.

The parser reads the first word from the expression and assumes that it must be an operand. It now knows that the next word must be an operator, so it reads and tries to identify it. If it can't, it raises an error and quits. If it can, it holds on to that information and reads the next word, treating it as an operand. It then applies the operator to the two operands and returns a result. In the case of the "and" operator, the Visual Basic Document Analyst searches the target document for the two operands. If it finds them both, it returns **True**.

Although the parser scans the expression from left to right, it evaluates it according to the *precedence of operators,* which is an arbitrary set of rules that determine which operators should be evaluated before other operators. This version of the Visual Basic Document Analyst supports five operators:

- not
- in_sentence_with
- near
- or
- and

Operators are evaluated in the order listed above. For example, the expression

Prince and Charles or Andrew

could specify two distinct searches. If you read the expression from left to right, it means that you wish to see documents containing either the words "Prince" and

"Charles," or documents containing the word "Andrew," but not necessarily with "Prince." But the parser evaluates "or" before "and," which means it will look for documents containing the word "Prince" and either "Charles" or "Andrew". Just as with VB's expression parser, you could force the other order of evaluation with parentheses:

(Prince and Charles) or Andrew

Operator precedence introduces a little complexity into the parser because it can't just work its way through the expression, reducing operators and operands to results. Instead, it needs to keep track of various intermediate results until they are needed.

The parser first searches for "Prince" in the target document and sets aside the results. When it detects the operator "and" it picks up "Charles" and searches for it in the target document. But before it returns that result to the "and" operator, it peeks at the next operator in the search expression. The "or" operator has higher precedence than "and". So instead of returning the previous result to the "and" operator, it grabs the next operand, "Andrew," and again searches the target document. At this point, none of the results for the individual operands have been combined by operators. With nothing remaining to read, the parser returns the result of the last search to the "or" operator, which applies itself to the two latest search results—those that tallied the occurrences of "Charles" and "Andrew". It then returns the combined result to the "and" operator, where it is analyzed against the first search results—those for "Prince".

The difficulty of this process is keeping track of all the intermediate results, especially when you consider that the search expression can have arbitrary complexity, with numerous intermixed operators. But that problem can be managed.

The VB Document Analyst

Computer language wizard Markus Roberts has developed a nifty document analysis and parsing system specifically for this book. Markus' system, implemented as a family of VB object classes, provides a modular structure that makes it easy to add new operators, so we can easily expand it to perform not just semantic analysis but syntactic analysis as well.

The main class **clsDocumentAnalyst** performs the actual evaluation of operators and encapsulates a **Document** object of class **clsDocuments** (a **PatternParser** of class

clsParsers) and a **PatternSource**, which is the string containing the search expression. The other two classes—**clsMatchLists** and **clsMatch**—represent a data structure used to record occurrences of words in the target **Document**.

Here's how it works. For each operand—or *keyword*—in the search expression, the parser calls the **Document** object's **OccurrencesOf** method, which builds a match list. A *match list* is a collection of matches, and each match records the starting and ending position of a match within the document. For most operators, the **DocumentAnalyst** contains a procedure that compares the match lists of two operands and returns a single match list as a result. Each match in this combined collection represents a region of the document within which the sub-expression is true. When the evaluation ends, it returns a single list of matches. If that list is empty, the search returns **False**. If it contains any match regions, the result is **True**.

Think of each match as an example of compliance with a *clause*, which consists of an operator and its operands. We use regions instead of simple boolean flags because we'll need that additional information to implement some of the more advanced operators such as "near" and "in_sentence_with".

Let's look at the methods in **clsDocumentAnalyst** from the top down.

Implementing The Parser

The class **clsDocumentAnalyst**, shown in Listing 4.1, exposes two methods, the **Init**() procedure and the **DocumentMatches**() function.

Listing 4.1 The complete listing of clsDocumentAnalyst.CLS.

```
Option Explicit

Private Document As clsDocuments
Public PatternSource As String
Private PatternParser As clsParsers

Public Function DocumentMatches(ByVal DocumentString As String) _
   As Boolean
    Dim MatchList As New clsMatchLists

    If Trim(PatternSource) <>"" Then
        Set Document = New clsDocuments
        Document.Init LCase(DocumentString)
```

```
      Set PatternParser = New clsParsers
      PatternParser.Init LCase(PatternSource)
      PatternMatch MatchList
      DocumentMatches = (MatchList.Matches.Count <> 0)
    Else
      DocumentMatches = False
    End If

  End Function

Private Sub PatternMatch(Result As clsMatchLists)
    AndMatch Result
    End Sub

Private Sub WordMatch(Result As clsMatchLists)
    If PatternParser.CanRead("(") Then
        PatternMatch Result
        PatternParser.Expect")"
      Else
        Document.OccurrencesOf PatternParser.NextWord, Result
        PatternParser.Advance
      End If

    End Sub

Private Sub NearMatch(Result As clsMatchLists)
    Const NearLimit = 200
    Dim MatchListA As clsMatchLists
    Dim MatchListB As clsMatchLists
    Dim MatchA As clsMatch
    Dim MatchB As clsMatch

    SentenceMatch Result
    Do While PatternParser.CanRead("near")
        Set MatchListA = New clsMatchLists
        For Each MatchA In Result.Matches
            MatchListA.AddMatch MatchA
            Next MatchA
        SentenceMatch MatchListB
        Set Result = New clsMatchLists
        For Each MatchA In MatchListA.Matches
            For Each MatchB In MatchListB.Matches
                If (Abs(MatchA.StartingPosition - _
                        MatchB.EndingPosition) < NearLimit) Or _
                   (Abs(MatchB.StartingPosition - _
                        MatchA.EndingPosition) < NearLimit) Then
```

```
                Result.AddSpread MatchA, MatchB
              End If
            Next MatchB
        Next MatchA
    Loop
End Sub

Private Sub OrMatch(Result As clsMatchLists)
    Dim MatchListA As clsMatchLists
    Dim MatchListB As clsMatchLists
    Dim MatchA As clsMatch
    Dim MatchB As clsMatch

    NearMatch Result
    Do While PatternParser.CanRead("or")
        Set MatchListA = New clsMatchLists
        For Each MatchA In Result.Matches
            MatchListA.AddMatch MatchA
            Next MatchA
        NearMatch MatchListB
        Set Result = New clsMatchLists
        For Each MatchA In MatchListA.Matches
            Result.AddMatch MatchA
            Next MatchA
        For Each MatchB In MatchListB.Matches
            Result.AddMatch MatchB
            Next MatchB
        Loop
    End Sub

Private Sub AndMatch(Result As clsMatchLists)
    Dim MatchListA As clsMatchLists
    Dim MatchListB As clsMatchLists
    Dim MatchA As clsMatch
    Dim MatchB As clsMatch

    OrMatch Result
    Do While PatternParser.CanRead("and")
        Set MatchListA = New clsMatchLists
        For Each MatchA In Result.Matches 'A = 1 To Result.Count
            MatchListA.AddMatch MatchA
            Next MatchA
        OrMatch MatchListB
        Set Result = New clsMatchLists
        For Each MatchA In MatchListA.Matches
```

```
            For Each MatchB In MatchListB.Matches
                Result.AddSpread MatchA, MatchB
                Next MatchB
            Next MatchA
        Loop

    End Sub

Public Sub Init(ByVal Pattern As String)
    PatternSource = Pattern
    End Sub

Private Sub SentenceMatch(Result As clsMatchLists)
    Const NearLimit = 200
    Dim MatchListA As clsMatchLists
    Dim MatchListB As clsMatchLists
    Dim MatchA As clsMatch
    Dim MatchB As clsMatch

    NotMatch Result
    Do While PatternParser.CanRead("in_sentence_with")
        Set MatchListA = New clsMatchLists
        For Each MatchA In Result.Matches
            MatchListA.AddMatch MatchA
            Next MatchA
        NotMatch MatchListB
        Set Result = New clsMatchLists
        For Each MatchA In MatchListA.Matches
            For Each MatchB In MatchListB.Matches
                If Document.SentenceOf(MatchA.StartingPosition) = _
                   Document.SentenceOf(MatchB.StartingPosition) Then
                    Result.AddSpread MatchA, MatchB
                  End If
                Next MatchB
            Next MatchA
        Loop

    End Sub

Private Sub NotMatch(Result As clsMatchLists)
    If PatternParser.CanRead("not") Then
        WordMatch Result
        If Result.Matches.Count = 0 Then
            Result.AddNewMatch Len(Document.Text), 1
          Else
            Set Result = New clsMatchLists
          End If
```

```
    Else
      WordMatch Result
    End If
  End Sub
```

To test a document for compliance with the search expression, you must first create an instance of **clsDocumentAnalyst** and initialize it with the search expression. You may then call the function **DocumentMatches()** repeatedly, passing it a new target document each time.

DocumentMatches() begins by creating an instance of **clsDocument** initialized to the text string passed in the **DocumentString** argument. Objects of **clsDocument** perform the actual task of searching the document for keywords and recording their locations in match lists. Next, **DocumentMatches()** creates an instance of **clsParsers**, which will perform the task of reading tokens from the search string. A *token* is any item with intrinsic meaning: an operator, an operand, or a mark of punctuation such as a quotation mark or parenthesis. Finally, **DocumentMatches()** calls the method **PatternMatch()**, shown in Listing 4.2.

Listing 4.2 The procedural method **PatternMatch()** from clsDocumentAnalyst.CLS.

```
Public Sub PatternMatch(Result As clsMatchLists)
    AndMatch Result
    End Sub
```

Notice that **DocumentMatches()** declares an instance of **clsMatchLists**, which it passes into **PatternMatch()** by reference. **PatternMatch()** then passes that same match list—now known as **Result**—on to the procedure **AndMatch()**. Before the grand finale, **Result** will have danced with several partners. Keep your eye on it.

The Parser Poseidon Adventure

The parsing and analysis begins inside **AndMatch()**, shown in Listing 4.3.

Listing 4.3 The procedure **AndMatch()** from clsDocumentAnalyst.CLS.

```
Public Sub AndMatch(Result As clsMatchLists)
    Dim MatchListA As clsMatchLists
    Dim MatchListB As clsMatchLists
```

```
Dim MatchA As clsMatch
Dim MatchB As clsMatch


OrMatch Result
Do While PatternParser.CanRead("and")
    Set MatchListA = New clsMatchLists
    For Each MatchA In Result.Matches
        MatchListA.AddMatch MatchA
        Next MatchA
    OrMatch MatchListB
    Set Result = New clsMatchLists
    For Each MatchA In MatchListA.Matches
        For Each MatchB In MatchListB.Matches
            Result.AddSpread MatchA, MatchB
            Next MatchB
        Next MatchA
    Loop

End Sub
```

AndMatch() obviously implements the "and" operator. For each operator it supports, **clsDocumentAnalyst** contains a corresponding operator procedure. Most of the operator procedures are structured similarly to **AndMatch()**, so it's worth taking a close look at how it works.

The oddest line of code in this procedure is the first:

```
OrMatch Result
```

Why do we begin an operator procedure by calling another operator procedure? The answer to that question is the key to understanding how the entire parser works. You'll need to look at the process upside down. Almost every operator procedure will begin by calling the operator procedure of next highest precedence. This will give the higher precedence operators first crack at evaluation. That logic may seem backwards, but it makes perfect sense when you remember that each method sets the **Result** argument before returning to the calling procedure. This means that any lower precedence operator can receive the result of a higher precedence operator as one or both of its operands, which is the definition of operator precedence.

The highest-precedence operator—the one hanging at the end of this daisy-chain—will call a procedure named **WordMatch()**, which will fill **Result** with the matches for the current keyword extracted from the search expression. For now, let's ignore the details of how **WordMatch**() works and treat it as a black box. The first time we call **PatternMatch**(), the parser will descend all the way down to **WordMatch**() before it does anything else, causing it to pull the first keyword off the expression and record its matches. When it returns to the calling procedure, that procedure will check whether the next token in the search expression contains the operator for which it is responsible. If so, it descends down the chain again to pick up the next operand, which then resurfaces with another match list. This pattern has the effect of alternating between operators and operands. As the calls ratchet back up through the chain, each operator procedure—beginning with the last, the highest precedence—gets a crack at the search expression. If its operator is next in the expression, it can manipulate the match list referenced by **Result**. See what I mean by looking at things upside down? All the action takes place on the way up the calling chain, not on the way down. This technique makes it easy for lower-precedence operators—those at the top of the calling chain—to hold on to intermediate results while waiting for the results of higher precedence clauses—those at the bottom of the calling chain.

When it detects an "and" operator in the search string, **AndMatch**() steals the match list in **Result** and tucks it away in its own internal **MatchListA**. It then starts the whole process again by calling **OrMatch**(). Eventually, it will receive another match list, stored in its **MatchListB**. Either resulting match list may represent either the matches belonging to a particular keyword or the combined match list produced by one or more operators further down the chain.

With two match lists in hand, **AndMatch**() is ready to perform its logic. First, it sets **Result** with a reference to a fresh instance of **clsMatchLists.** It then steps through the regions stored in **MatchListA** and **MatchListB**, building new regions that document every possible combination of the matches in the two lists, as shown in Figure 4.1. Each region in the new **Result** describes a segment of the target document in which it is true that both operands occur. You could say that each match acts as a proof for the "and" operation.

Also notice the **Do While** loop that circumscribes each operator procedure, ensuring that the parser will not exit until it has exhausted all the clauses in the search expression. For example, we could add another "and" clause to the end of the expression:

Prince and Charles or Andrew and marriage

Search String: Prince and Charles or Andrew

Princes Charles and Andrew this week sequestered themselves at Buckingham Palace to discuss personal affairs with Her Majesty the Queen. Charles has presented sibling Andrew with a proposal...

Match.StartingPosition = 1
Match.EndingPosition = 15

Princes Charles and Andrew this week sequestered themselves at Buckingham Palace to discuss personal affairs with Her Majesty the Queen. Charles has presented sibling Andrew with a proposal...

Match.StartingPosition = 1
Match.EndingPosition = 26

Princes Charles and Andrew this week sequestered themselves at Buckingham Palace to discuss personal affairs with Her Majesty the Queen. Charles has presented sibling Andrew with a proposal...

Match.StartingPosition = 1
Match.EndingPosition = 142

Princes Charles and Andrew this week sequestered themselves at Buckingham Palace to discuss personal affairs with Her Majesty the Queen. Charles has presented sibling Andrew with a proposal...

Match.StartingPosition = 1
Match.EndingPosition = 171

Figure 4.1
Recording match regions.

If that were the case, **AndMatch()** would transfer the previous result to its **MatchListA**, then descend again to build the match list for "marriage". It would then perform the "and" operation on those two match lists and return the result by way of its referential argument, **Result**.

Other Operator Procedures

The actual calling chain under **DocumentMatches**() includes seven procedures:

- **PatternMatch**()
- **AndMatch**()
- **OrMatch**()
- **NearMatch**()
- **SentenceMatch**()
- **NotMatch**()
- **WordMatch**()

Five of these represent operators: **AndMatch**(), **OrMatch**(), **NearMatch**(), **SentenceMatch**(), and **NotMatch**(). **OrMatch**(), shown in Listing 4.4, closely resembles **AndMatch**().

Listing 4.4 The procedure **OrMatch()** from clsDocumentAnalyst.CLS.

```
Public Sub OrMatch(Result As clsMatchLists)
    Dim MatchListA As clsMatchLists
    Dim MatchListB As clsMatchLists
    Dim MatchA As clsMatch
    Dim MatchB As clsMatch

    NearMatch Result
    Do While PatternParser.CanRead("or")
        Set MatchListA = New clsMatchLists
        For Each MatchA In Result.Matches
            MatchListA.AddMatch MatchA
            Next MatchA
        NearMatch MatchListB
        Set Result = New clsMatchLists
        For Each MatchA In MatchListA.Matches
            Result.AddMatch MatchA
            Next MatchA
        For Each MatchB In MatchListB.Matches
            Result.AddMatch MatchB
            Next MatchB
        Loop
    End Sub
```

Since the "or" operator must accept any occurrence of either keyword operand within the target document, this procedure adds the contents of both match lists to the new **Result** match list.

NearMatch(), shown in Listing 4.5, begins to make things a little more interesting.

Listing 4.5 The procedure **NearMatch()** from clsDocumentAnalyst.CLS.

```
Public Sub NearMatch(Result As clsMatchLists)
    Const NearLimit = 200
    Dim MatchListA As clsMatchLists
    Dim MatchListB As clsMatchLists
    Dim MatchA As clsMatch
    Dim MatchB As clsMatch

    SentenceMatch Result
    Do While PatternParser.CanRead("near")
        Set MatchListA = New clsMatchLists
        For Each MatchA In Result.Matches
            MatchListA.AddMatch MatchA
            Next MatchA
        SentenceMatch MatchListB
        Set Result = New clsMatchLists
        For Each MatchA In MatchListA.Matches
            For Each MatchB In MatchListB.Matches
                If (Abs(MatchA.StartingPosition - _
                        MatchB.EndingPosition) < NearLimit) Or _
                   (Abs(MatchB.StartingPosition -
                        MatchA.EndingPosition) < NearLimit) Then
                    Result.AddSpread MatchA, MatchB
                  End If
                Next MatchB
            Next MatchA
        Loop
    End Sub
```

The "near" operator determines whether the two operands appear together in the document within some arbitrary number of characters, as specified in the **NearLimit** constant. The "near" operator demonstrates the value of keeping positional information instead of simple boolean flags. Most document filters offer simple boolean analysis based on the "and," "or," and "not" operators. Some even support "near," or some other similar operator. The process of analyzing a document for the presence of particular keywords is called *semantic analysis.* Semantic analysis works well for most situations because so many topics are characterized by unique terminology. But sometimes we need to identify concepts, and concepts don't always identify themselves with a simple collection of words. Meaning in language also depends on the organization of words into phrases, sentences, paragraphs, and larger structures. The process of identifying how words function in context is called *syntactic analysis.* The "near" operator performs a crude kind of syntactic analysis by determining whether two words appear in close proximity. The next operator in the chain, however, refines the search even further.

The procedure **SentenceMatch**(), shown in Listing 4.6, implements the operator "in_sentence_with," which attempts to detect operands that appear within the same sentence.

Listing 4.6 The procedure **SentenceMatch()** from clsDocumentAnalyst.CLS.

```
Public Sub SentenceMatch(Result As clsMatchLists)
    Const NearLimit = 200
    Dim MatchListA As clsMatchLists
    Dim MatchListB As clsMatchLists
    Dim MatchA As clsMatch
    Dim MatchB As clsMatch

    NotMatch Result
    Do While PatternParser.CanRead("in_sentence_with")
        Set MatchListA = New clsMatchLists
        For Each MatchA In Result.Matches
            MatchListA.AddMatch MatchA
            Next MatchA
        NotMatch MatchListB
        Set Result = New clsMatchLists
        For Each MatchA In MatchListA.Matches
            For Each MatchB In MatchListB.Matches
                If Document.SentenceOf(MatchA.StartingPosition) = _
                   Document.SentenceOf(MatchB.StartingPosition) Then
                    Result.AddSpread MatchA, MatchB
                  End If
                Next MatchB
            Next MatchA
        Loop

    End Sub
```

While this procedure is cut from the same familiar pattern as the earlier listings, it contains one significant twist: a pair of calls to the **SentenceOf()** method of the **Document** object. When we first initialize the **Document** object, it builds a collection of sentence markers. This minor optimization enables the parser to handle multiple "in_sentence_with" operators without repeatedly reparsing for sentence boundaries. Later, we'll look more closely at the **clsDocuments** class.

SentenceMatch() calls one other operator procedure, **NotMatch()**, shown in Listing 4.7.

Listing 4.7 The procedure **NotMatch()** from clsDocumentAnalyst.CLS.

```
Public Sub NotMatch(Result As clsMatchLists)
    If PatternParser.CanRead("not") Then
        WordMatch Result
        If Result.Matches.Count = 0 Then
            Result.AddNewMatch Len(Document.Text), 1
          Else
            Set Result = New clsMatchLists
          End If
      Else
        WordMatch Result
      End If
    End Sub
```

"Not" is a *prefix* operator, which means that it has only one operand:

Prince and Charles and not Andrew

The parser would not expect to find an operand before the "not" operator. So before it calls the next procedure in the chain, **WordMatch()**, **NotMatch()** calls the **PatternParser.CanRead()** method. If it detects the "not" operator, it calls **WordMatch()** to pick up and search the document for its operand. But then it does something odd. When it calls the **AddNewMatch()** method, it inverts the arguments, passing the length of the document as its starting position and 1 as its ending position.

Because "not" is a negative operator, it can produce only two possible results: either it doesn't find the operand in the document, which *validates* the entire document, or it *does* find the operand, which *invalidates* the entire document. In the second case, it returns an empty **Result**. But in the first case, it must return a **Result** with a single match. Here's the catch. If you take another look at **AndMatch()**, you'll see that it records matches with a method called **AddSpread()** (shown later in the chapter in

Listing 4.1), which calculates the region occupied by each pair of matches in its **MatchListA** and **MatchListB**. **AddSpread()** uses a **Min** and a **Max** function to calculate the starting and ending positions of the new match. If one of those match lists contains a single match that describes the entire document, then all the matches in the second set would expand to those extreme boundaries, invalidating any further use of the "near" operator. By inverting the "not" match, however, we trick the **AddSpread()** method into maintaining the dimensions of the existing matches.

Picking Up The Pieces

Beneath the stack of operator procedures lies **WordMatch()**, shown in Listing 4.8.

Listing 4.8 The procedure **WordMatch()** from clsDocumentAnalyst.CLS.

```
Public Sub WordMatch(Result As clsMatchLists)
    If PatternParser.CanRead("(") Then
      PatternMatch Result
      PatternParser.Expect")"
    Else
      Document.OccurrencesOf PatternParser.NextWord, Result
      PatternParser.Advance
    End If

End Sub
```

Let's examine the two main clauses of **WordMatch()** in reverse order. The main purpose of **WordMatch()** is to search for keywords, which it does by calling the method **OccurrencesOf()** from the class module clsDocument.CLS, shown in Listing 4.9.

Listing 4.9 The complete listing of clsDocuments.CLS.

```
Option Explicit

Public Text As String
Public Sentences As New clsMatchLists
Public Paragraphs As New clsMatchLists

Public Sub OccurrencesOf(S As String, Result As clsMatchLists)
    Dim Loc As Long
    Dim EndOfMatch As Long
```

```
    Set Result = New clsMatchLists
    Loc = InStr(Me.Text, S)
    Do While Loc <> 0
        Debug.Print S;" found at pos"; Loc
        EndOfMatch = Loc + Len(S)
        Result.AddNewMatch Loc, EndOfMatch
        Loc = InStr(EndOfMatch, Me.Text, S)
        DoEvents
        Loop
    End Sub

Public Function SentenceOf(Loc As Integer) As Integer
    Dim M As clsMatch
    SentenceOf = 0
    For Each M In Sentences.Matches
        If (Loc >= M.StartingPosition) And _
           (Loc <= M.EndingPosition) Then
            SentenceOf = M.StartingPosition
            Debug.Print"SentenceOf(", Loc,") = _
                       ", M.StartingPosition
            Exit For
            End If
        Next M
    End Function
Public Function ParagraphOf(Loc As Integer) As Integer
    Dim M As clsMatch
    ParagraphOf = 0
    For Each M In Paragraphs
        If (Loc >= M.StartingPosition) And _
           (Loc <= M.EndingPosition) Then
            ParagraphOf = M.StartingPosition
            Exit For
            End If
        Next M

    End Function

Public Sub Init(Document As String)
    Dim I As Long
    Dim J As Long

    Text = Document

    'Find paragraphs and remove tags
    I = 0
```

```
    J = InStr(I + 1, Text,"<")
    Do While J <> 0
        If Mid(Text, J, 3) ="<P>" Then
            Paragraphs.AddNewMatch I, J
            End If
        I = J
        Text = Mid(Text, 1, I - 1) & _
               Mid(Text, InStr(I + 1, Text &">",">") + 1)
        J = InStr(I + 1, Text,"<")
        Loop
    Paragraphs.AddNewMatch I, Len(Text)

    'Find sentences
    I = 0
    J = InStr(I + 1, Text,".")
    Do While J <> 0
        Sentences.AddNewMatch I, J
        I = J
        J = InStr(I + 1, Text,".")
        Loop
    Sentences.AddNewMatch I, Len(Text)
    End Sub
```

The simple method **OccurrencesOf()** uses VB's **InStr()** function to search for the word specified in the **S** argument. For each occurrence, it calls **Result.AddNew Match()**, shown in Listing 4.10.

Listing 4.10 The method **AddNewMatch()** from clsMatchLists.CLS.

```
Public Sub AddNewMatch(StartPos As Long, EndPos As Long)
    Dim Match As New clsMatch

    Match.StartingPosition = StartPos
    Match.EndingPosition = EndPos
    AddMatch Match

    End Sub
```

AddNewMatch() creates a new instance of **clsMatch**, sets its **StartingPosition** and **EndingPosition** properties, and adds it to the **Result.Matches** collection.

WordMatch() also detects and handles parentheses. Just as in VB's expression parser—and most other parsers, for that matter—parentheses provide a way to override operator precedence. Think of each expression that appears within parentheses as an independent clause that returns a **Result**, which we then treat the same as any other operand. To do this, when **WordMatch()** runs into an open parenthesis, it calls **PatternMatch()** recursively, effectively spawning a whole new parsing session just for the parenthetical clause. Evaluation terminates whenever the parser fails to detect an operator. The closing parenthesis—which the parser treats as a full-fledged token—will cause that condition, and **WordMatch()** will call the **PatterParser.Expect()** method to confirm the presence of a closing parenthesis for each open parenthesis it has detected. As shown in Listing 4.11, if **Expect()** does not find the closing parenthesis, it will report an error.

Listing 4.11 The complete listing of clsParsers.CLS from the project NewsReader.VBP.

```
Option Explicit

Public NextWord As String
Public Remainder As String

Public Sub Advance()
    NextWord =""
    Do While (Remainder <>"") And (Left(Remainder, 1) ="")
        Remainder = Mid(Remainder, 2)
        Loop
    If Remainder <>"" Then
        If (Left(Remainder, 1) ="(") Or _
           (Left(Remainder, 1) =")") Then
            NextWord = Left(Remainder, 1)
            Remainder = Mid(Remainder, 2)
          ElseIf Left(Remainder, 1) ="""" Then
            Remainder = Mid(Remainder, 2)
            Do While (Remainder <>"") And _
                     (Left(Remainder, 1) <>"""")
                NextWord = NextWord + Left(Remainder, 1)
                Remainder = Mid(Remainder, 2)
                Loop
            Remainder = Mid(Remainder, 2)
          Else
            Do While (Remainder <>"") And Not _
                     ((Left(Remainder, 1) ="(") Or _
                      (Left(Remainder, 1) =")") Or _
                      (Left(Remainder, 1) =""))
                NextWord = NextWord + Left(Remainder, 1)
                Remainder = Mid(Remainder, 2)
```

```
                Loop
            End If
        End If
    End Sub

Public Sub Init(Source As String)
    Remainder = Source
    Advance
    End Sub

Public Function CanRead(S As String) As Boolean
    If NextWord = S Then
        Advance
        CanRead = True
      Else
        CanRead = False
      End If

    End Function

Public Sub Expect(S As String)
    If Not CanRead(S) Then
        MsgBox"Expected" & S & vbCrLf & _
               " but found" & NextWord &".", _
                vbOKOnly + vbCritical, _
               "Invalid Search String"
      End If
    End Sub
```

Like the operator procedures, the **Expect**() method calls the **CanRead**() method to identify and remove the next token off the front of the search expression.

Finally, we arrive at the method that actually walks through the search expression, **Advance**(), also shown in Listing 4.11.

Because we never know just when we're going to make use of the next word in the expression, we can't use a function to extract and return it. Instead, the **Advance**() method procedure places it in the parser object's **NextWord** property, where it will remain until **Advance**() replaces it. This makes it available to the function **CanRead**() no matter how many times it's queried during the process of evaluating operators.

Advance() has a simple mission: to identify the next token, store it in **NextWord,** and remove it from the expression stored in **Remainder**. To carry out that task, it must detect three types of delimiters: spaces, parentheses, and quotation marks. The simplest case is a parenthesis, because a parenthesis is a token in itself:

```
If (Left(Remainder, 1) ="(") Or (Left(Remainder, 1) =")") Then
    NextWord = Left(Remainder, 1)
    Remainder = Mid(Remainder, 2)
```

When the procedure finds a parenthesis, it copies it to **NextWord** and removes it from the string. If it doesn't detect a parenthesis, it looks for a quotation mark:

```
ElseIf Left(Remainder, 1) ="""" Then
  Remainder = Mid(Remainder, 2)
  Do While (Remainder <>"") And (Left(Remainder, 1) <>"""")
      NextWord = NextWord + Left(Remainder, 1)
      Remainder = Mid(Remainder, 2)
      Loop
  Remainder = Mid(Remainder, 2)
```

Quoted phrases act as complete keywords. You could, for example, enter the search expression:

"Prince Charles" or "Prince Andrew"

This expression will accept only documents in which either the word "Charles" or the word "Andrew" immediately follows the word "Prince". After detecting the first quotation mark, this **ElseIf** clause advances character by character through the expression until it either finds a closing quotation mark or runs out of characters.

The final **Else** clause identifies words:

```
Else
  Do While (Remainder <>"") And Not _
          ((Left(Remainder, 1) ="(") Or _
           (Left(Remainder, 1) =")") Or _
           (Left(Remainder, 1) =""))
      NextWord = NextWord + Left(Remainder, 1)
      Remainder = Mid(Remainder, 2)
      Loop
```

Any series of characters that ends with a space or parenthesis is considered a word. Notice that this procedure makes no attempt to determine whether a word represents a keyword or an operator; it simply pulls the next word or quoted clause off the front of the string and copies it to **NextWord**. The identity of any token is determined exclusively by syntax. In other words, the position of a token within the expression determines how it will be interpreted by the parser. In fact, you could write the expression

and and or

to search the target document for the words "and" and "or".

The only other method in **clsParsers** is **Init**():

```
Public Sub Init(Source As String)
    Remainder = Source
    Advance
    End Sub
```

This method copies the search expression to the property **Remainder** and calls **Advance**() to pull off the first token and copy it to **NextWord**. The only properties in **clsParsers** are **NextWord** and **Remainder**.

Other clsDocuments Methods

The class **clsDocuments** contains three other methods in addition to **OccurrencesOf**(), which we discussed earlier. The **Init**() method, shown in Listing 4.12, builds two special collections. We used the one called **Sentences**—which contains the positions of sentence boundaries—to implement the **SentenceMatch**() operator procedure. The second, called **Paragraphs**, contains paragraph boundaries identified in HTML documents. With the **Paragraphs** collection, you could implement an operator that identifies keyword matches within paragraphs of Web documents.

Listing 4.12 The **Init()** method from clsDocuments.CLS.

```
Public Sub Init(Document As String)
    Dim I As Long
    Dim J As Long

    Text = Document

    'Find paragraphs and remove tags
    I = 0
    J = InStr(I + 1, Text,"<")
    Do While J <> 0
        If Mid(Text, J, 3) ="<P>" Then
```

```
            Paragraphs.AddNewMatch I, J
            End If
        I = J
        Text = Mid(Text, 1, I - 1) & Mid(Text, InStr(I + 1, _
                                          Text &">",">") + 1)
        J = InStr(I + 1, Text,"<")
        Loop
    Paragraphs.AddNewMatch I, Len(Text)

    'Find sentences
    I = 0
    J = InStr(I + 1, Text,".")
    Do While J <> 0
        Sentences.AddNewMatch I, J
        I = J
        J = InStr(I + 1, Text,".")
        Loop
    Sentences.AddNewMatch I, Len(Text)
    End Sub
```

It doesn't take much effort to pick out the paragraphs in an HTML document. You just look for the <P> tags. Sentences, however, can be a little trickier. The method we used here is crude, because it looks only for periods without even considering whether they represent sentence terminators or decimal points. You might want to refine this code to account for question marks and exclamation points, and to ignore periods surrounded by numerals. For most Web documents, however, it works well enough as is.

The two functional methods, **SentenceOf()** and **ParagraphOf()** (both shown in Listing 4.13) return the **StartingPosition** of the sentence or paragraph that includes the position specified in the argument **Loc**.

Listing 4.13 The functional methods **SentenceOf()** and **ParagraphOf()** from clsDocuments.CLS.

```
Public Function SentenceOf(Loc As Integer) As Integer
    Dim M As clsMatch
    SentenceOf = 0
    For Each M In Sentences.Matches
        If (Loc >= M.StartingPosition) And _
           (Loc <= M.EndingPosition) Then
            SentenceOf = M.StartingPosition
            Debug.Print"SentenceOf(", Loc,") =", M.StartingPosition
            Exit For
```

```
        End If
    Next M
End Function

Public Function ParagraphOf(Loc As Integer) As Integer
    Dim M As clsMatch
    ParagraphOf = 0
    For Each M In Paragraphs
        If (Loc >= M.StartingPosition) And _
           (Loc <= M.EndingPosition) Then
            ParagraphOf = M.StartingPosition
            Exit For
            End If
        Next M

End Function
```

ParagraphOf() is not currently used by the parser.

The clsMatchLists And clsMatch Classes

clsMatchLists, shown in its entirety in Listing 4.14, contains a handful of simple functions that add new matches to its **Matches** collection.

Listing 4.14 The complete listing of clsMatchLists.CLS from the project NewsReader.VBP.

```
Option Explicit

Public Matches As New Collection

Public Sub AddMatch(AMatch As clsMatch)
    Matches.Add AMatch
    End Sub

Private Function Min(A As Integer, B As Integer) As Integer
    If A < B Then Min = A Else Min = B
    End Function

Private Function Max(A As Integer, B As Integer) As Integer
    If A > B Then Max = A Else Max = B
    End Function

Public Sub AddNewMatch(StartPos As Long, EndPos As Long)
    Dim Match As New clsMatch
```

```
    Match.StartingPosition = StartPos
    Match.EndingPosition = EndPos
    AddMatch Match

    End Sub

Public Sub AddSpread(A As clsMatch, B As clsMatch)
    AddNewMatch _
        Min(A.StartingPosition, B.StartingPosition), _
        Max(A.EndingPosition, B.EndingPosition)
    End Sub
```

clsMatch represents the data element in which we store matches. It contains no code and only two declarations, as shown below in Listing 4.15.

Listing 4.15 The complete listing of clsMatch.CLS from the project NewsReader.VBP.

```
Option Explicit

Public StartingPosition As Integer
Public EndingPosition As Integer
```

Hacking The Parser

The modular structure of the Visual Basic Document Analyst makes it easy to add new operators and optimizations. And you can easily drop the entire system into any VB project using these steps:

1. Add its five class modules to the project.
2. Declare and initialize an instance of **clsDocumentAnalyst.**
3. Call the new object's **DocumentMatches()** method.

The volume of information available instantly in electronic form is swelling at a phenomenal rate. To make good use of all that information, we need to discover new methods of filtering and manipulating it. Advanced methods, such as syntactic analysis, will provide the sensitive instrumentation we need to excavate the most valuable facts and ideas. Don't stop with the "in_sentence_with" operator. Expand the parser to include other syntactic operators such as "precedes" or "follows." With the right collection of tools, you'll soon be searching not just for words, but for ideas.

Reading The News

CHAPTER 5

You can use the Winsock control with Visual Basic to implement any of the well-known Internet protocols. Learn how by tackling the Network News Transfer Protocol (NNTP).

Reading The News

Millions of Internauts now share their thoughts over the rapidly expanding network of Internet newsgroups, Usenet. Unfortunately, not all of those thoughts are worth sharing. With so many newsgroups and so much chatter, it can be maddeningly tedious to pick out the useful tidbits. In the absence of diligent editors, the best way to filter the news for impurities is to sift it ourselves. In this chapter, we'll start by using the *Network News Transfer Protocol* (NNTP) to gather the news. Then we'll add a handy *text parser* that will turn it into a Usenet bloodhound.

The Network News Transfer Protocol

Like all other Internet data transfers, NNTP exchanges take place over a TCP/IP connection. But NNTP itself is a text-based protocol, which means that it uses text commands to make requests and sends its responses as text; no binary data changes hands. The text messages are wrapped in TCP packets—called *datagrams*—for transmission, then reopened and read as text by the receiver. By using the Winsock control, we can largely ignore the details of data transmission and concentrate on issuing and processing the results of NNTP commands.

Read The Original NNTP Specification

For detailed information on the NNTP specification and the correct syntax for all currently defined commands, visit InterNIC at ***http:/www.internic.net****. Locate the section called Information and Education Services (currently located at* ***http://rs.internic.net/nic-support/****) and request documents RFC977.TXT, RFC1036.TXT, and draft-barber-nntp-imp-05.TXT.*

A news session primarily consists of six general operations:

- Connecting to a news server
- Retrieving a list of newsgroups

- Selecting a newsgroup
- Retrieving an article from the selected newsgroup
- Posting an article to the newsgroup
- Disconnecting from the news server

To perform most of these operations, we send a simple text command to the news server. For example, to retrieve a list of new groups, we could send the word LIST, followed by a carriage return/line feed (CR/LF) sequence. To select a particular group, we would send the GROUP command, followed by the name of the group and CR/LF. In response to each command, the server sends back a line of text that begins with a *response code* and, if appropriate, additional lines containing the requested data. (See Tables 5.1 and 5.2 for a list of NNTP commands.) The NEWGROUPS command, for example, which retrieves a list of newsgroups that have appeared since a specified date, returns response code 231, followed by the list of newsgroups:

```
231 result code 27 970101 0 0 852102000
alt.binaries.pictures.sports.ocean 0 1 y
alt.fan.alan-shearer 0 1 y
alt.www.webmaster 0 1 y
alt.irc.fan.slackie 0 1 y
alt.culture.turkestan 0 1 y
alt.culture.kazakhstan 0 1 y
alt.culture.chechnya 0 1 y
alt.culture.turkmenistan 0 1 y
alt.culture.dagestan 0 1 y
alt.culture.caucasia 0 1 y
```

Each multiline response ends with a period on a line by itself—i.e., a period preceded and followed by CR/LF.

Table 5.1 NNTP commands specified in RFC 977.

ARTICLE <message-id>|[nnn]	Returns an article by number or by message-id.
BODY <message-id>|[nnn]	Returns an article body alone.
GROUP ggg	Selects the specified group; returns first and last article numbers.
HEAD <message-id>|[nnn]	Returns article headers alone.

continued

Table 5.1 NNTP commands specified in RFC 977 (continued).

HELP	Returns a summary of commands supported by the server.
IHAVE <message-id>	Informs the server that it has a specific article; used by servers to exchange messages.
LAST	Sets the current article pointer to the previous article in the current newsgroup.
LIST	Returns a list of all valid newsgroups on the server.
NEWGROUPS YYMMDD HH:MM:SS [GMT] [<distributions>]	Returns a list of new newsgroups.
NEWNEWS newsgroups YYMMDD HH:MM:SS [GMT] [<distribution>]	Returns a list of all new messages in the specified newsgroups.
NEXT	Sets the current article pointer to the next article in the current newsgroup.
POST	Requests the server to accept an article.
QUIT	Instructs the server that it may terminate the session.
SLAVE	Identifies slave servers to other news servers.
STAT <message-id>l[nnn]	Sets the current article pointer.

Since the publication of the original NNTP specification in 1986 (in RFC 977), several additional commands have been defined, as shown in Table 5.2. These commands are described in detail in an Internet Draft Document entitled *Common NNTP Extensions*, currently available under the file name draft-barber-nntp-imp-05.TXT.

Table 5.2 NNTP extended commands as specified in Internet Draft Document.

XREPLIC ggg:nnn [,ggg:nnn...]	Used by servers to duplicate newsgroups and their articles.
LIST ACTIVE [wildmat]	Lists newsgroups whose names match the wildmat pattern.
LIST ACTIVE.TIMES	Lists who created each newsgroup and when it was created.
LIST DISTRIBUTIONS	Describes contents of user-defined Distribution article header.

continued

Table 5.2 NNTP extended commands as specified in Internet Draft Document (continued).

LIST DISTRIB.PATS	Lists default values for Distribution article header.
LIST NEWSGROUPS [wildmat]	Lists newsgroups with a short description.
LIST OVERVIEW.FMT	Lists information about the storage of header information on the server.
LIST SUBSCRIPTIONS	Returns default subscription list for new users of the server.
LISTGROUP [ggg]	Lists all article numbers for the specified newsgroup.
MODE READER	Identifies a news-reading client to server.
XGTITLE [wildmat]	Returns descriptions for specified newsgroups.
XHDR header [range|<message-id>]	Lists specific header from specified articles.
XINDEX ggg	Returns a special index file for use in the TIN newsreader.
XOVER [range]	Returns article information from the server's overview database.
XPAT header range|<message-id> pat[pat...]	Returns header information based on pattern matching.
XPATH <message-id>	Returns filename of server file in which message is stored.
XROVER [range]	Returns reference information for articles specified.
XTHREAD [DBINIT|THREAD]	Returns threading information for use by the TIN newsreader.
AUTHINFO USER username	Used with AUTHINFO PASS to identify user to server.
AUTHINFO PASS password	Used with AUTHOINFO USER to identify user to server.
AUTHINFO SIMPLE...user password	Used to identify user to server.
AUTHINFO GENERIC authenticator arguments...	Used to perform server-specific user authentication.
DATE	Returns GMT time from server.

Some responses include no additional data beyond the information that immediately follows the response code on the same line. The GROUP command, for example, causes the news server to send a single line, beginning with response code 211:

```
211 23 199 222 alt.www.webmaster y
```

The 211 response code acknowledges that the requested group has been selected. The first argument indicates the estimated number of articles currently listed under that group—the article count. The second and third arguments specify the article numbers of the first and last articles currently available, and the fourth argument returns the name of the newsgroup selected. For a variety of reasons, the article count sometimes does not reconcile with the first and last article numbers. When in doubt, trust the article numbers.

The first digit of the response code indicates whether the server accepted or rejected the command, or is awaiting additional information (refer to Table 5.3). The second digit indicates which operational category the response belongs to, and the third digit identifies a specific error (see Table 5.4).

Table 5.3 NNTP server response code categories per RFC 977.

Response Code	Meaning
1xx	Informative message
2xx	Command OK
3xx	Command OK so far; send the rest of it.
4xx	Command was correct but couldn't be performed for some reason.
5xx	Command unimplemented, or incorrect, or a serious program error occurred.
x0x	Connection, setup, and miscellaneous messages
x1x	Newsgroup selection
x2x	Article selection
x3x	Distribution functions
x4x	Posting
x8x	Nonstandard (private implementation) extensions
x9x	Debugging output

Table 5.4 Some of the NNTP Response Codes

Response Code	**Meaning**
100	Help text follows.
199	Debug output.
200	Server ready—posting allowed.
201	Server ready—no posting allowed.
202	Slave status noted.
205	Closing connection—goodbye!
211	n f l s group selected.
215	List of newsgroups follows.
220	n <a> article retrieved—head and body follow.
221	n <a> article retrieved—head follows.
222	n <a> article retrieved—body follows.
223	n <a> article retrieved—request text separately.
230	List of new articles by message-id follows.
231	List of new newsgroups follows.
235	Article transferred OK.
240	Article posted OK.
281	User authorized.
335	Send article to be transferred. End with <CR/LF>.<CR/LF>.
340	Send article to be posted. End with <CR/LF>.<CR/LF>.
381	Send password.
400	Service discontinued.
411	No such newsgroup.
412	No newsgroup has been selected.
420	No current article has been selected.
421	No next article in this group.
422	No previous article in this group.
423	No such article number in this group.
430	No such article found.
435	Article not wanted—do not send it.
436	Transfer failed—try again later.
437	Article rejected—do not try again.

continued

Table 5.4 Some of the NNTP Response Codes (continued).

Response Code	Meaning
440	Posting not allowed.
441	Posting failed.
480	Authorization required.
500	Command not recognized.
501	Command syntax error.
502	Access restriction or permission denied.
503	Program fault—command not performed.

That's easy enough—send a text command, receive a text response. What we do with that text is up to us.

Internet News Experiment

Before we disguise it underneath all kinds of fancy lists, trees, and buttons, let's use the Winsock control to make a bare-bones network news reader. We'll keep the controls to a minimum and crowd the whole business into a single form where none of it can hide from view. Take a look at Figure 5.1.

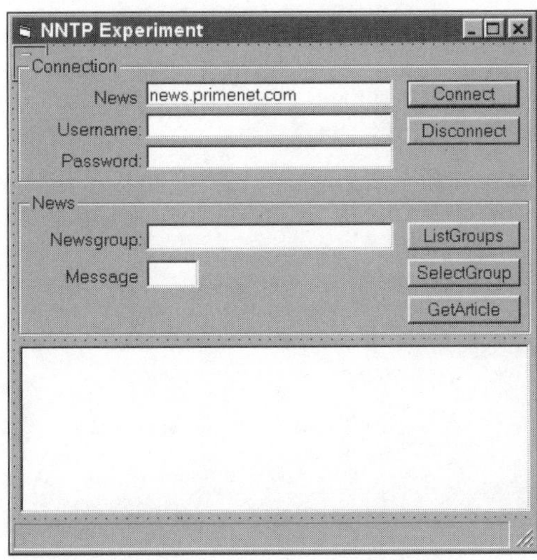

Figure 5.1
The form frmNNTPExp from the project NNTPExp at design time.

Running NNTPExp

Before you can browse the news, you have to be connected to a news server. In the top section of the program window, enter the name of a news server, as shown in Figure 5.2. Some news servers also restrict access to authorized users. If so, enter your username and password in the appropriate text boxes. When you click Connect, the Winsock control will attempt to establish a connection. If that works, it will then engage the server in the transaction state.

Before you can begin to retrieve news articles—also known as *messages*—you must know the name of a newsgroup. Click the ListGroups button to request the list of current newsgroups from the server, as shown in Figure 5.3. The number of newsgroups is growing rapidly, now including more than 20,000. Since this is just a demonstration, I have arbitrarily set the request to retrieve only those groups added since January 1, 1997, which should relieve any strain on system resources.

To select a particular group, use your mouse to highlight its name in the text box, then click SelectGroup. The contents of the text box will clear, then display a list of message headers for the selected newsgroup, as shown in Figure 5.4. The label to the right of the Message text box indicates the range of message numbers on that group. Keep in mind that these numbers aren't always accurate; sometimes articles are deleted out of sequence.

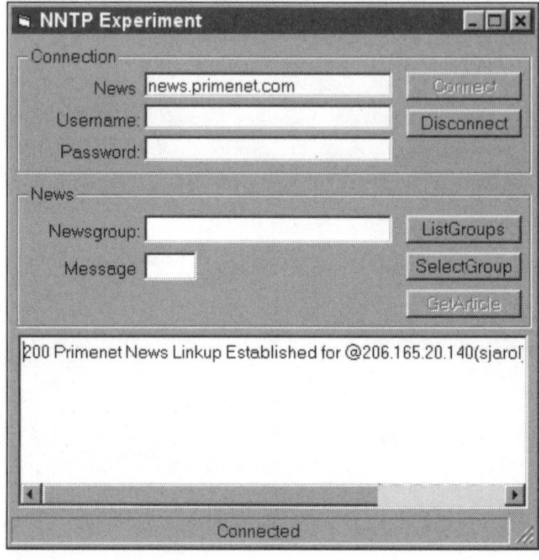

Figure 5.2
The program NNTPExp.EXE after connecting to a Usenet news server.

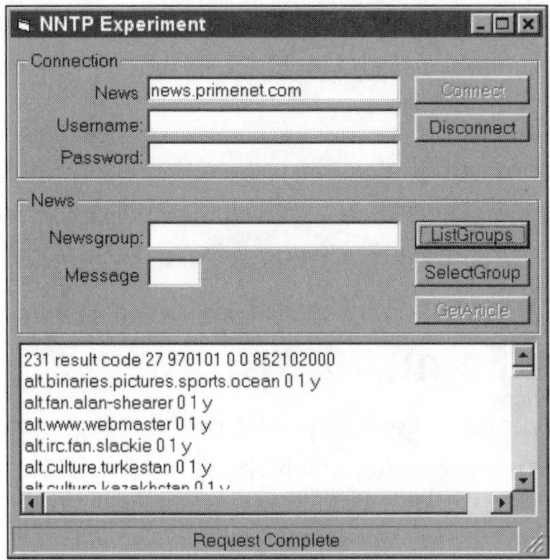

Figure 5.3
NNTPExp.EXE displays an unformatted list of newsgroups in the text box control.

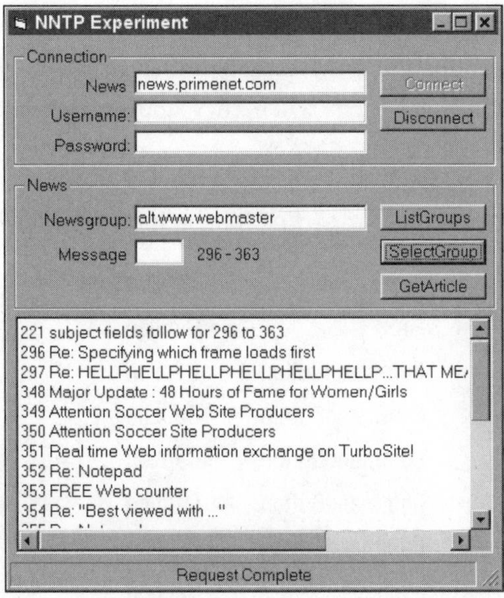

Figure 5.4
NNTPExp.EXE displays an unformatted list of message headers in the text box control.

To select an article, either highlight its number in the text box or enter the number in the Message text box, then click GetArticle. The text box will clear once again before displaying the selected message.

The program does not retain the list of newsgroups or the list of message headers. To select another message, you have to repeat the steps described above to list the groups, or reselect the group currently displayed in the Newsgroup text box.

Building The Form

The interface for this program consists primarily of six text boxes and five command buttons, the controls and properties of which are listed in Table 5.5. We'll also need one Winsock control, and an assortment of labels. I've used two frames to organize the form into three major sections. The top group of controls handles connection information. The **txtNewServer** control accepts the name of a news server. If the server requires user authorization, you may enter a username and password in **txtUsername** and **txtPassword** before requesting a connection. The second section holds the controls used to select newsgroups and articles. You may enter values directly into **txtNewsGroups** and **txtMessageNumber**, or you may select newsgroups and articles by highlighting them when they appear in the main display area, **txtOutput**.

Table 5.5 The controls and properties for the form frmNNTPExp.

Control Name	Type	Properties	Value
frmNNTPExp	Form	Caption	"NNTP Experiment"
cmdListGroups	CommandButton	Caption	"ListGroups"
cmdSelectGroup	CommandButton	Caption	"Select Group"
cmdGetArticle	CommandButton	Caption	"GetArticle"
cmdConnect	CommandButton	Caption	"Connect"
cmdDisconnect	CommandButton	Caption	"Disconnect"
frConnection	Frame	Caption	"Connection"
frNews	Frame	Caption	"News"
lblMessageNumberRange	Label	Caption	(Set at runtime)
lblNewsGroup	Label	Alignment	1 - Right Justify
		Caption	"Newsgroup:"

continued

Table 5.5 The controls and properties for the form frmNNTPExp (continued).

Control Name	Type	Properties	Value
lblMessageNumber	Label	Alignment	1 - Right Justify
		Caption	"Message Number:"
lblNewsServer	Label	Alignment	1 - Right Justify
		Caption	"News Server:"
lblPassword	Label	Alignment	1 - Right Justify
		Caption	"Password:"
lblUsername	Label	Alignment	1 - Right Justify
		Caption	"Username:"
sbNNTPStatus	StatusBar		
txtMessageNumber	TextBox		
txtNewsServer	TextBox		
txtNewsgroups	TextBox		
txtOutput	RichTextBox	Multiline	True
		ScrollBars	3 - Both
txtPassword	TextBox	PasswordChar	*
txtUsername	TextBox		
Winsock1	Winsock	Protocol	0 - sckTCPProtocol

The Winsock Control

With the Winsock control, we can connect to a server of any type, anywhere on the Internet. All you need to know to establish a connection is the server's name or IP address and the port on which it is listening. With an open connection, we can exchange data with the server. If we wish, we can even create a custom server and client that communicate on any available port number and that perform functions of our own design.

The Winsock control's **Connect()** method takes two optional arguments, **RemoteHost** and **RemotePort**. Of course, you couldn't connect to a server without these values, so they're not really optional at all. When they're omitted from the argument list, the **Connect()** method will instead use the values specified in the **RemoteHost** and **RemotePort** properties.

If the connection request succeeds, the Winsock control will fire its **Connect()** event procedure. From that point on, we can use the **SendData()** method to transmit data to the server. To receive data, we respond to the **DataArrival()** event procedure by calling the **GetData()** method to retrieve the data from the control's receive buffer. When we're finished, we call the **Close()** method to shut down the connection.

Altogether, the Winsock control supports nine methods. The methods I haven't mentioned are used primarily to implement servers. In this project, we will use six of the control's seven event procedures. The exception is **ConnectionRequest()**—which occurs only on a server—although most will do nothing more than report connection activity by displaying brief messages in the Status bar.

NNTP Operations

When the program opens, only one command button is enabled: **cmdConnect**. The **cmdConnect_Click()** event procedure, shown in Listing 5.1, calls the method **Winsock.Connect()**, passing it the server name entered in **txtNewsServer** and socket 119, the commonly known socket for Internet News. It also sets **NNTPTransactionSemaphore**, a form level variable that we'll use to keep track of the current state of the client/server transaction. I'll explain the semaphore system in greater detail later in this chapter.

Listing 5.1 The **cmdConnect_Click()** event procedure from frmNNTPExp.FRM.

```
Private Sub cmdConnect_Click()
    cmdConnect.Enabled = False
    NNTPTransactionSemaphore = tsConnect
    txtOutput.Text = ""
    Winsock1.Connect txtNewsServer.Text, 119
    End Sub
```

If the server accepts the connection request, the Winsock control will fire the **Winsock1_Connect()** event procedure, shown in Listing 5.2.

Listing 5.2 The **Winsock1_Connect()** event procedure from frmNNTPExp.FRM.

```
Private Sub Winsock1_Connect()
    Do
        sbNNTPStatus.Panels(1).Text = _
            WinsockStateString(Winsock1.State)
        DoEvents
        Loop Until (NNTPTransactionSemaphore = tsConnected) Or _
            (NNTPTransactionSemaphore = tsNone)
    If NNTPTransactionSemaphore = tsConnected Then
        sbNNTPStatus.Panels(1).Text = "Connected"
        cmdDisconnect.Enabled = True
        cmdListGroups.Enabled = True
        cmdListGroups.Default = True
        cmdSelectGroup.Enabled = True
      Else
        cmdConnect.Enabled = True
      End If
    End Sub
```

We receive all server responses in the **Winsock1_DataArrival()** event procedure, shown in Listing 5.3. The first thing this procedure does is call the Winsock control's **GetData()** method, which transfers the contents of the control's receive buffer to the string variable passed as its argument, **OutputData**. For other applications, you may wish to use this method's two optional arguments, **type** and **maxLen**. The **type** argument enables data type matching—also known as type casting—so you can assign the output to a variable of a type other than **String**. The **maxLen** argument specifies the maximum number of bytes to return and remove from the buffer. To retrieve the contents of a large receive buffer, you could call **GetData()** repeatedly with a fixed size buffer variable, processing the results in smaller chunks to conserve system resources until the receive buffer is empty.

Listing 5.3 The **Winsock1_DataArrival()** event procedure from frmNNTPExp.FRM.

```
Private Sub Winsock1_DataArrival(ByVal bytesTotal As Long)
    Dim OutputData As String
    Dim MessageCount As String
    Dim FirstMessageNumber As String
    Dim LastMessageNumber As String
    Dim ResponseString As String
    Dim ResponseCode As Integer
```

```
Winsock1.GetData OutputData
Select Case NNTPTransactionSemaphore
  Case tsConnect
    txtOutput.Text = txtOutput.Text & OutputData
    ResponseString = txtOutput.Text
    ResponseCode = CInt(GetWordFrom(ResponseString))
    If ResponseCode = 480 Then
        NNTPTransactionSemaphore = tsAuthorizing
        txtOutput.Text = ""
        Winsock1.SendData "AUTHINFO USER " & _
                          Trim(txtUsername.Text)
      ElseIf (ResponseCode = 200) Or (ResponseCode = 201) Then
        NNTPTransactionSemaphore = tsConnected
      Else
        NNTPTransactionSemaphore = tsNone
      End If
  Case tsAuthorizing
    txtOutput.Text = txtOutput.Text & OutputData
    ResponseString = txtOutput.Text
    ResponseCode = CInt(GetWordFrom(ResponseString))
    If ResponseCode = 381 Then
        NNTPTransactionSemaphore = tsAuthorizationResponse
        txtOutput.Text = ""
        Winsock1.SendData "AUTHINFO PASS " & _
                          Trim(txtPassword.Text)
      Else
        NNTPTransactionSemaphore = tsNone
      End If
  Case tsAuthorizationResponse
    txtOutput.Text = txtOutput.Text & OutputData
    ResponseString = txtOutput.Text
    ResponseCode = CInt(GetWordFrom(ResponseString))
    If ResponseCode = 281 Then
        NNTPTransactionSemaphore = tsConnected
      Else
        NNTPTransactionSemaphore = tsNone
      End If
  Case tsListGroups
    txtOutput.Text = txtOutput.Text & OutputData
  Case tsSelectGroup
    ResponseString = OutputData
    ResponseCode = CInt(GetWordFrom(ResponseString))
    If ResponseCode = 211 Then
        NNTPTransactionSemaphore = tsListArticles
        GetGroupInfo OutputData, MessageCount, _
                     FirstMessageNumber, LastMessageNumber
```

```
            txtOutput.Text = ""
            Winsock1.SendData "XHDR subject " & _
                              Trim(FirstMessageNumber) & _
                              "-" & Trim(LastMessageNumber) & _
                              vbCrLf
            lblMessageNumberRange = Trim(FirstMessageNumber) & _
                                    " - " & Trim(LastMessageNumber)
            cmdGetArticle.Enabled = True
          End If
      Case tsListArticles
        txtOutput.Text = txtOutput.Text & OutputData
      Case tsGetArticle
        txtOutput.Text = txtOutput.Text & OutputData
      Case Else
        txtOutput.Text = txtOutput.Text & OutputData
      End Select
    If Right(OutputData, 3) = "." & vbCrLf Then
        sbNNTPStatus.Panels(1).Text = "Request Complete"
      End If
    End Sub
```

In the **cmdConnect_Click()** event procedure, we raised the semaphore **tsConnect**, causing the **Winsock1_DataArrival()** event procedure to execute the first **Case** clause in its **Select** statement:

```
Case tsConnect
  txtOutput.Text = txtOutput.Text & OutputData
  ResponseString = txtOutput.Text
  ResponseCode = CInt(GetWordFrom(ResponseString))
  If ResponseCode = 480 Then
      NNTPTransactionSemaphore = tsAuthorizing
      txtOutput.Text = ""
      Winsock1.SendData "AUTHINFO USER " & Trim(txtUsername.Text)
    ElseIf (ResponseCode = 200) Or (ResponseCode = 201) Then
      NNTPTransactionSemaphore = tsConnected
    Else
      NNTPTransactionSemaphore = tsNone
    End If
```

This code uses the general function **GetWordFrom()** (shown later in the chapter in Listing 5.9) to extract the response code from the server's response string. A response code of 200 indicates that the server has accepted the connection request and that the client is free to make further requests and post articles. A code of 201 indicates that the client may request data but may not post articles. With either of these responses, we may raise the **tsConnected** semaphore. A response code of 480, however, indicates that the server will accept connection requests only from authorized users, so the procedure begins the authorization process by raising the **tsAuthorizing** semaphore. It then sends the AUTHINFO USER command, followed by the contents of **txtUsername.Text**.

After sending the AUTHINFO USER command, the program expects to receive response code 381, indicating that the server is ready to receive the user's password. If that occurs, the **Case tsAuthorizing** clause continues the authorization process by raising the **tsAuthorizationResponse** semaphore and by sending the AUTHINFO PASS command, followed by the contents of **txtPassword.Text**.

Finally, in the **Case tsAuthorizationResponse** clause, if we find that the server has sent the 281 response code—meaning that it has accepted the user's authorization request—we raise the **tsConnect** semaphore to signal completion of the connection process.

Retrieving The List Of Newsgroups

Once we've opened a connection to the server, the first thing we'll need to do is request a list of newsgroups. The **cmdListGroups_Click**() event procedure, shown in Listing 5.4, uses the Winsock control's **SendData**() method to send the command NEWGROUPS, followed by the date "970101 00:00:00" in the required format. This command will retrieve a list of all newsgroups added to the server since midnight on January 1, 1997. The alternative command, LIST, which I have remarked out, will return a list of all newsgroups on the server. Considering that the number of newsgroups carried by most news servers now exceeds 20,000, I thought the shorter version would return enough data to illustrate the rudiments of NNTP.

Listing 5.4 The **cmdListGroups_Click()** event procedure from frmNNTPExp.FRM.

```
Private Sub cmdListGroups_Click()
    NNTPTransactionSemaphore = tsListGroups
    txtOutput.Text = ""
    'Winsock1.SendData "LIST"
    Winsock1.SendData "NEWGROUPS " & _
                      Format(DateSerial(97, 1, 1), _
                      "yymmdd hh:mm:ss") & vbCrLf
    End Sub
```

The **Case tsListGroups** clause in **Winsock1_DataArrival()** collects the blocks of text transmitted by the server and displays them in the **txtOutput** text box:

```
Case tsListGroups
  txtOutput.Text = txtOutput.Text & OutputData
```

Selecting A Newsgroup

The **cmdSelectGroup_Click()** event procedure, shown in Listing 5.5, raises the **tsSelectGroup** semaphore and sends the GROUP command, followed by the contents of the **txtNewsgroup** text box.

Listing 5.5 The **cmdSelectGroup_Click()** event procedure from frmNNTPExp.FRM.

```
Private Sub cmdSelectGroup_Click()
    NNTPTransactionSemaphore = tsSelectGroup
    Winsock1.SendData "GROUP " & Trim(txtNewsgroup.Text) & vbCrLf
    End Sub
```

To make it easier to enter a newsgroup from the list displayed in **txtOutput**, I've implemented the **txtOutput_SelChange()** event procedure, as shown in Listing 5.6. This procedure uses the general procedure **GetWordFrom()** to extract the first word from the current selection. It copies the result to either **txtNewsgroup** or **txtMessageNumber**, depending on the current program state, as indicated by the **NNTPTransactionSemaphore**.

Listing 5.6 The **txtOutput_SelChange()** event procedure from frmNNTPExp.FRM.

```
Private Sub txtOutput_SelChange()
    Dim TempString As String

    TempString = txtOutput.SelText
    Select Case NNTPTransactionSemaphore
      Case tsListGroups
        txtNewsgroup.Text = Trim(GetWordFrom(TempString))
      Case tsListArticles
        txtMessageNumber.Text = Trim(GetWordFrom(TempString))
      Case Else
        ' Do nothing.
      End Select

    End Sub
```

If the GROUP command succeeds, the news server should send response code 211, followed by the message statistics for the selected group, all on the same line. In the event procedure **Winsock1_DataArrival()**, the **Case tsSelectGroup** clause raises the **tsListArticles** semaphore. Next, it uses the general procedure **GetGroupInfo()** to set **MessageCount**, **FirstMessageNumber**, and **LastMessageNumber** by parsing the response line. It then requests a list of the messages belonging to the current newsgroup by sending the XHDR command, followed by the first and last message numbers:

```
Case tsSelectGroup
  ResponseString = OutputData
  ResponseCode = CInt(GetWordFrom(ResponseString))
  If ResponseCode = 211 Then
      NNTPTransactionSemaphore = tsListArticles
      GetGroupInfo OutputData, MessageCount, _
                   FirstMessageNumber, LastMessageNumber
      txtOutput.Text = ""
      Winsock1.SendData "XHDR subject " & _
                       Trim(FirstMessageNumber) & _
                       "-" & Trim(LastMessageNumber) & _
                       vbCrLf
      lblMessageNumberRange = Trim(FirstMessageNumber) & _
                             " - " & Trim(LastMessageNumber)
      cmdGetArticle.Enabled = True
    End If
```

The server sends response 221, followed by the headers for each message in the newsgroup. The **Case tsListArticles** in **Winsock1_DataArrival()** transfers the results to **txtOutput**:

```
Case tsListArticles
  txtOutput.Text = txtOutput.Text & OutputData
```

Retrieving A Message

The **cmdGetArticle_Click()** event procedure, shown in Listing 5.7, raises the **tsGetArticle** semaphore before sending the ARTICLE command.

Listing 5.7 The **cmdGetArticle_Click()** event procedure from frmNNTPExp.FRM.

```
Private Sub cmdGetArticle_Click()
    NNTPTransactionSemaphore = tsGetArticle
    txtOutput.Text = ""
    Winsock1.SendData "ARTICLE " & Trim(txtMessageNumber) & vbCrLf
    End Sub
```

The message header and body follow response code 220. Once again, **Winsock1_DataArrival()** displays the data in **txtOutput**.

Closing The Connection

The final step in an NNTP transaction is closing the connection. We need to know whether the connection has closed successfully. Otherwise, we might attempt to open another connection prematurely and trigger a runtime error. One way to close the connection is to call the Winsock control's **Close()** *method*. But that will not cause the control to execute its **Close()** *event procedure*, which means that we won't receive any confirmation that the connection is closed. Instead of calling the **Close()** method, we'll send the server the QUIT command. Then, when the server closes the connection, the Winsock control will detect the termination and will fire the close event. We can use the **Winsock1_Close()** event procedure to tidy up, as shown in Listing 5.8.

Listing 5.8 The **Winsock1_Close()** event procedure from frmNNTPExp.FRM.

```
Private Sub Winsock1_Close()
    Winsock1.Close
    Do
        sbNNTPStatus.Panels(1).Text = _
           WinsockStateString(Winsock1.State)
        DoEvents
        Loop Until Winsock1.State = sckClosed
    cmdConnect.Enabled = True
    cmdConnect.Default = True
    cmdDisconnect.Enabled = False
    cmdListGroups.Enabled = False
    cmdSelectGroup.Enabled = False
    cmdGetArticle.Enabled = False
    End Sub
```

Complete Listing Of FrmNNTPExp.FRM

Here is the complete listing of frmNNTPExp.FRM. Take note of the simple functions **GetWordFrom()** and **WinsockStateString()**, and the event procedure **cmdDisconnect_Click()**, which do not appear separately in the text above.

Listing 5.9 The complete listing of frmNNTPExp.FRM.

```
Option Explicit

Private NNTPTransactionSemaphore As Integer

Const tsNone = 0
Const tsConnect = 1
Const tsAuthorizing = 2
Const tsAuthorizationResponse = 3
Const tsConnected = 4
Const tsListGroups = 5
Const tsSelectGroup = 6
Const tsListArticles = 7
Const tsGetArticle = 8
Const tsDisconnect = 9

Private MinimumFormWidth As Long

Private Function GetWordFrom(AnyString As String) As String
    Dim SpacePosition As Long
    Dim ReturnString As String
    Dim TempString As String

    SpacePosition = InStr(AnyString, " ")
    If SpacePosition = 0 Then
        ReturnString = AnyString
        TempString = ""
      Else
        ReturnString = Left(AnyString, SpacePosition)
        TempString = Mid(AnyString, SpacePosition + 1)
      End If
    If Right(ReturnString, 2) = vbCrLf Then
        ReturnString = Left(ReturnString, Len(ReturnString) - 2)
      End If
    AnyString = TempString
    GetWordFrom = ReturnString
    End Function
```

```
Private Sub GetGroupInfo(ByVal ResponseString As String, _
                               MessageCount As String, _
                               FirstMessageNumber As String, _
                               LastMessageNumber As String)

    Dim ResponseCode As String

    ResponseCode = GetWordFrom(ResponseString)
    MessageCount = GetWordFrom(ResponseString)
    FirstMessageNumber = GetWordFrom(ResponseString)
    LastMessageNumber = GetWordFrom(ResponseString)
    End Sub

Private Sub cmdConnect_Click()
    cmdConnect.Enabled = False
    NNTPTransactionSemaphore = tsConnect
    txtOutput.Text = ""
    Winsock1.Connect txtNewsServer.Text, 119
    End Sub


Private Sub cmdDisconnect_Click()
    NNTPTransactionSemaphore = tsDisconnect
    txtOutput.Text = ""
    Winsock1.SendData "QUIT" & vbCrLf
    End Sub

Private Sub cmdGetArticle_Click()
    NNTPTransactionSemaphore = tsGetArticle
    txtOutput.Text = ""
    Winsock1.SendData "ARTICLE " & Trim(txtMessageNumber) & vbCrLf
    End Sub

Private Sub cmdListGroups_Click()
    NNTPTransactionSemaphore = tsListGroups
    txtOutput.Text = ""
    'Winsock1.SendData "LIST"
    Winsock1.SendData "NEWGROUPS " & _
                      Format(DateSerial(97, 1, 1),
                      "yymmdd hh:mm:ss") & vbCrLf
    End Sub


Private Sub cmdSelectGroup_Click()
    NNTPTransactionSemaphore = tsSelectGroup
    Winsock1.SendData "GROUP " & Trim(txtNewsgroup.Text) & vbCrLf
    End Sub
```

```
Private Sub Form_Load()
    MinimumFormWidth = Me.Width
    End Sub

Private Sub Form_QueryUnload(Cancel As Integer, UnloadMode As Integer)
    If Winsock1.State = sckConnected Then
        cmdDisconnect_Click
      End If
    End Sub


Private Sub Form_Resize()
    If Me.WindowState = vbMinimized Then
        Exit Sub
      End If
    Me.Width = MaxLong(Me.Width, MinimumFormWidth)
    Me.Height = MaxLong(Me.Height, _
        frConnection.Height + frNews.Height + _
        sbNNTPStatus.Height + 1000)
    txtOutput.Top = frNews.Top + frNews.Height + 60
    txtOutput.Height = Me.ScaleHeight - _
        (sbNNTPStatus.Height + 60 + txtOutput.Top)
    txtOutput.Width = Me.ScaleWidth - 2 * txtOutput.Left

    End Sub

Private Sub txtOutput_SelChange()
    Dim TempString As String

    TempString = txtOutput.SelText
    Select Case NNTPTransactionSemaphore
      Case tsListGroups
        txtNewsgroup.Text = Trim(GetWordFrom(TempString))
      Case tsListArticles
        txtMessageNumber.Text = Trim(GetWordFrom(TempString))
      Case Else
        ' Do nothing.
      End Select

    End Sub

Private Sub Winsock1_Close()
    Winsock1.Close
    Do
        sbNNTPStatus.Panels(1).Text = _
           WinsockStateString(Winsock1.State)
```

```
        DoEvents
        Loop Until Winsock1.State = sckClosed
    cmdConnect.Enabled = True
    cmdConnect.Default = True
    cmdDisconnect.Enabled = False
    cmdListGroups.Enabled = False
    cmdSelectGroup.Enabled = False
    cmdGetArticle.Enabled = False
    End Sub

Private Sub Winsock1_Connect()
    Do
        sbNNTPStatus.Panels(1).Text = _
           WinsockStateString(Winsock1.State)
        DoEvents
        Loop Until (NNTPTransactionSemaphore = tsConnected) Or _
             (NNTPTransactionSemaphore = tsNone)
    If NNTPTransactionSemaphore = tsConnected Then
        sbNNTPStatus.Panels(1).Text = "Connected"
        cmdDisconnect.Enabled = True
        cmdListGroups.Enabled = True
        cmdListGroups.Default = True
        cmdSelectGroup.Enabled = True
      Else
        cmdConnect.Enabled = True
      End If
    End Sub

Private Sub Winsock1_ConnectionRequest(ByVal requestID As Long)
    sbNNTPStatus.Panels(1).Text = "Connection Request"
    End Sub

Private Sub Winsock1_DataArrival(ByVal bytesTotal As Long)
    Dim OutputData As String
    Dim MessageCount As String
    Dim FirstMessageNumber As String
    Dim LastMessageNumber As String
    Dim ResponseString As String
    Dim ResponseCode As Integer

    Winsock1.GetData OutputData
    Select Case NNTPTransactionSemaphore
      Case tsConnect
        txtOutput.Text = txtOutput.Text & OutputData
        ResponseString = txtOutput.Text
        ResponseCode = CInt(GetWordFrom(ResponseString))
```

```
    If ResponseCode = 480 Then
        NNTPTransactionSemaphore = tsAuthorizing
        txtOutput.Text = ""
        Winsock1.SendData "AUTHINFO USER " & _
                          Trim(txtUsername.Text) & vbCrLf
      ElseIf (ResponseCode = 200) Or (ResponseCode = 201) Then
        NNTPTransactionSemaphore = tsConnected
      Else
        NNTPTransactionSemaphore = tsNone
      End If
  Case tsAuthorizing
    txtOutput.Text = txtOutput.Text & OutputData
    ResponseString = txtOutput.Text
    ResponseCode = CInt(GetWordFrom(ResponseString))
    If ResponseCode = 381 Then
        NNTPTransactionSemaphore = tsAuthorizationResponse
        txtOutput.Text = ""
        Winsock1.SendData "AUTHINFO PASS " & _
                          Trim(txtPassword.Text) & vbCrLf
      Else
        NNTPTransactionSemaphore = tsNone
      End If
  Case tsAuthorizationResponse
    txtOutput.Text = txtOutput.Text & OutputData
    ResponseString = txtOutput.Text
    ResponseCode = CInt(GetWordFrom(ResponseString))
    If ResponseCode = 281 Then
        NNTPTransactionSemaphore = tsConnected
      Else
        NNTPTransactionSemaphore = tsNone
      End If
  Case tsListGroups
    txtOutput.Text = txtOutput.Text & OutputData
  Case tsSelectGroup
    ResponseString = OutputData
    ResponseCode = CInt(GetWordFrom(ResponseString))
    If ResponseCode = 211 Then
        NNTPTransactionSemaphore = tsListArticles
        GetGroupInfo OutputData, MessageCount, _
                     FirstMessageNumber, LastMessageNumber
        txtOutput.Text = ""
        Winsock1.SendData "XHDR subject " & _
                          Trim(FirstMessageNumber) & _
                          "-" & Trim(LastMessageNumber) & _
                          vbCrLf
```

```
            lblMessageNumberRange = Trim(FirstMessageNumber) & _
                                    " - " & Trim(LastMessageNumber)
            cmdGetArticle.Enabled = True
          End If
      Case tsListArticles
        txtOutput.Text = txtOutput.Text & OutputData
      Case tsGetArticle
        txtOutput.Text = txtOutput.Text & OutputData
      Case Else
        txtOutput.Text = txtOutput.Text & OutputData
      End Select
    If Right(OutputData, 3) = "." & vbCrLf Then
        sbNNTPStatus.Panels(1).Text = "Request Complete"
      End If
    End Sub

Private Sub Winsock1_Error(ByVal Number As Integer, _
                           Description As String, _
                           ByVal Scode As Long, _
                           ByVal Source As String, _
                           ByVal HelpFile As String, _
                           ByVal HelpContext As Long, _
                           CancelDisplay As Boolean)
    sbNNTPStatus.Panels(1).Text = "Error"
    End Sub

Private Sub Winsock1_SendComplete()
    sbNNTPStatus.Panels(1).Text = "Send Complete"
    End Sub

Private Sub Winsock1_SendProgress(ByVal bytesSent As Long, _
                                  ByVal bytesRemaining As Long)
    sbNNTPStatus.Panels(1).Text = CStr(bytesSent) & " Bytes Sent"
    End Sub

Public Function WinsockStateString(WinsockState As Integer) As String
    Select Case WinsockState
      Case sckClosed
        WinsockStateString = "Closed"
      Case sckClosing
        WinsockStateString = "Closing"
      Case sckConnected
        WinsockStateString = "Connected"
      Case sckConnecting
        WinsockStateString = "Connecting"
```

```
    Case sckConnectionPending
      WinsockStateString = "Connection Pending"
    Case sckHostResolved
      WinsockStateString = "Host Resolved"
    Case sckError
      WinsockStateString = "Error"
    Case sckListening
      WinsockStateString = "Listening"
    Case sckResolvingHost
      WinsockStateString = "Resolving Host"
    Case sckOpen
      WinsockStateString = "Open"
    Case Else
      WinsockStateString = "Unknown State"
    End Select
  End Function
```

NNTP Experiment Project Summary

Although this simple project performs many of the basic Internet news operations, it's pretty crude. For one thing, it doesn't retain any information. Each time you want to select another message or another newsgroup, it has to go back to the news server for the appropriate list. And on top of that, it displays all its output in a text box. In the next chapter, we'll build a better house around the basic NNTP functions—one with clearer boundaries between lists and texts, and the code that manages them.

HIGH PERFORMANCE

Cut The Junk From Internet News

CHAPTER 6

Build an Internet news reader that filters out noise and chatter so you can spot the good stuff. Let's use our NNTP expertise to build a sophisticated Internet news client, complete with message posting capability and a powerful search engine.

Cut The Junk From Internet News

In the previous chapter, we explored the techniques required to at least browse and read Internet news, but a truly useful news reader will need more features. We'll want it to hold on to the catalog of newsgroups and let us freely browse articles without repeatedly downloading the list of message headers. We'll also add features that enable us to post new messages to newsgroups and to automatically filter messages by analyzing their subject headers or their contents.

Developing A Complete Internet News Client

In this project, we'll use three separate and different controls to hold and display each type of news data: newsgroup names, message headers, and complete messages. Once we get all that working, we'll be ready to add a sophisticated filter and search function based on the same text analysis system we used for the Web Robot project in Chapter 3.

Running The Visual Basic News Reader

Locate the project NewsReader.VBP on the companion CD-ROM, and copy it to your hard drive. It will not run from the CD-ROM because it needs to open and update a database in the program's default directory. When you compile and run it, the program will open with a window split into three main regions, as shown in Figure 6.1. At the left, a TreeView control will display a directory of newsgroups. Once you've selected a newsgroup, the ListView control in the pane at the upper

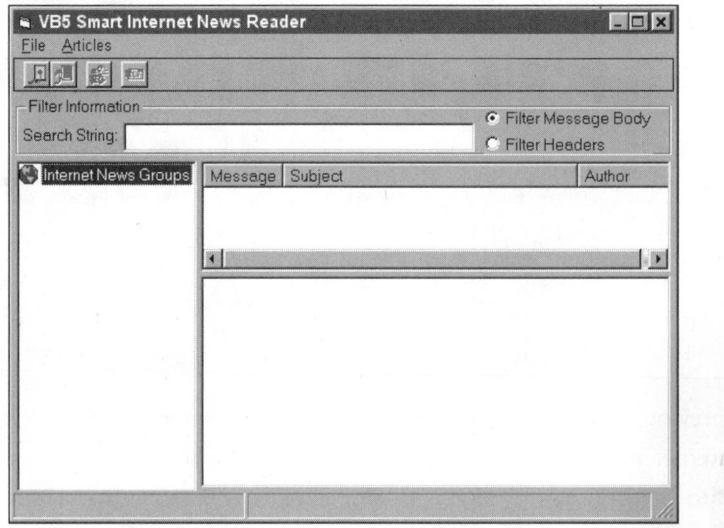

Figure 6.1
The form frmNewsReader from the project NewsReader, at runtime.

right will display its message headers. Selected messages will appear, one at a time, in the RichTextBox below the message header list.

Once again, before you can perform any news operations, you must connect to a news server. When you select File|Connect from the menu, the program will display the Connection Information dialog, as shown in Figure 6.2.

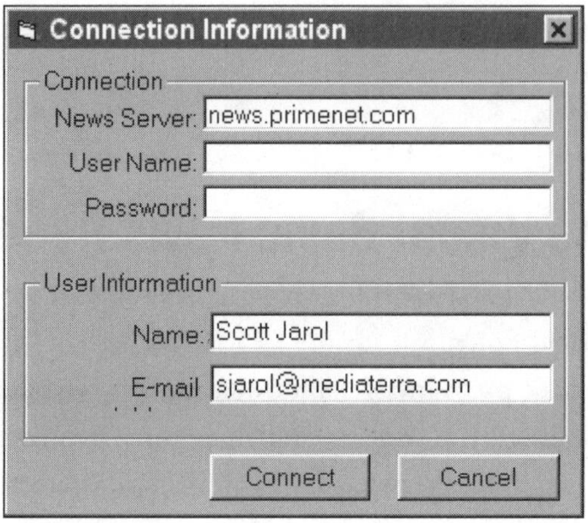

Figure 6.2
The Connection Information dialog box from the project NewsReader.

Just as in the NNTP Experiment project, the Username and Password fields are optional, depending on the requirements of the specified news server. The optional Name and E-mail Address will be used only to identify you on any messages that you might post to newsgroups.

After the program connects to the server and establishes an NNTP transaction state, you may request the directory of newsgroups. This time, however, the program will not immediately display the newsgroups on the screen. Instead, it will store them in an Access database. As you expand nodes in the Newsgroups TreeView control, the program will search the database for the appropriate subnodes and add them to the tree. When you reach a node that represents a newsgroup, as indicated by the document icon, the program will select it from the news server and download its message headers. As the headers arrive, they are parsed and added to the ListView control.

To filter the messages or their subject headers, enter a search string (see Chapter 4, *The VB Document Analyst*) into the TextBox labeled "Search String" in the section called "Filter Information." Then select either the "Filter Message Body" or "Filter Headers" OptionButton. When you click the newsgroup in the TreeView control, the program will first download all the message headers. It will then analyze the headers—or retrieve and analyze each message—before revising the list to include only matching messages.

From the ListView control, you may select a message, triggering yet another exchange with the news server. As the message arrives, it will appear in the RichTextBox control, as shown in Figure 6.3.

When you get tired of reading and feel like throwing in your own two cents, select Articles|Post. Enter an article header, and type the body of your message into the RichTextBox control, as shown in Figure 6.4.

Click Post to send the new article to the selected newsgroup.

Creating The Main Form

The real action in this project takes place within the TreeView, ListView, and RichTextBox controls that display newsgroups, message headers, and messages, respectively. We'll use a pair of PictureBox controls to create movable split bars. Most of the remaining controls—the ImageLists, StatusBar, Menus, and Toolbar—perform simple support functions. For a complete list of controls and properties in this form, see Table 6.1.

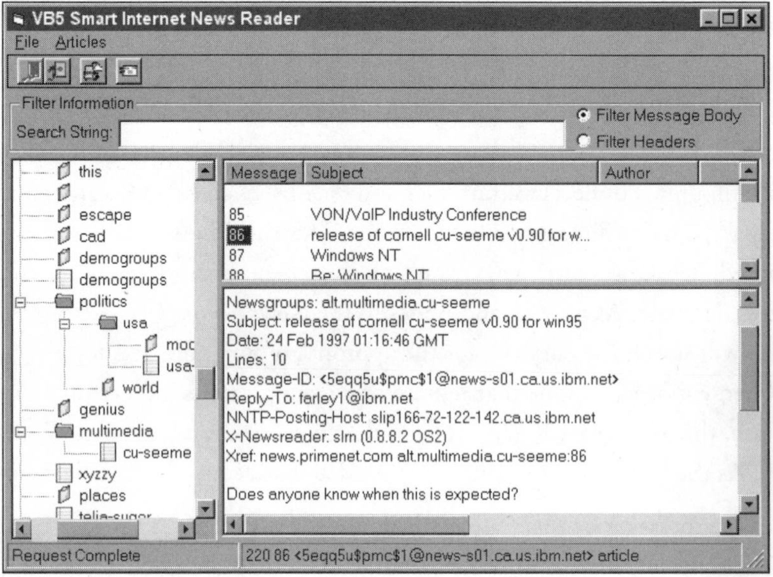

Figure 6.3
The Visual Basic News Reader in action.

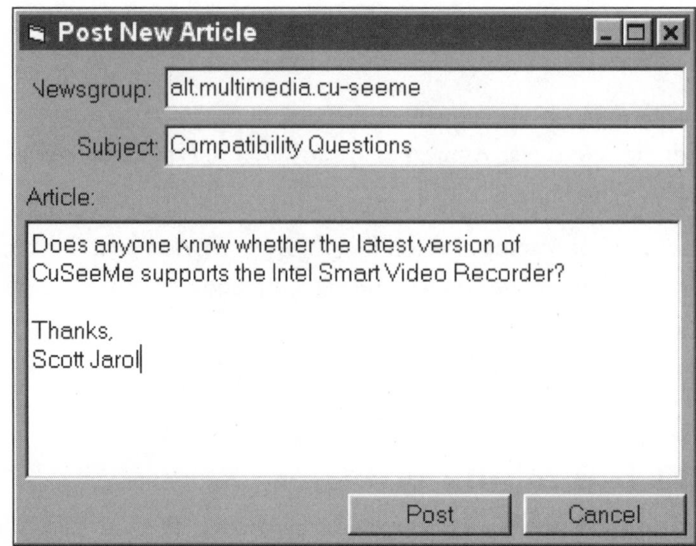

Figure 6.4
The Post New Article dialog box from the Visual Basic News Reader.

Table 6.1 The controls and properties for the form frmNewsReader in the project NewsReader.

Control Name	Type	Properties	Value
frmNewsReader	Form	Caption	"Internet News Reader"
Frame1	Frame	Caption	"Filter Information"
ilButtonIcons	ImageList	(Custom)	
ilTreeIcons	ImageList	(Custom)	
lblSearchString	Label	Alignment	1 - Right Justify
		Caption	"Search String:"
lvwMessageHeaders	ListView	LabelEdit	1 - Manual
		MultiSelect	False
		View	3 - Report
mnuArticles	Menu	Enabled	False
mnuConnect	Menu	Enabled	True
mnuDisconnect	Menu	Enabled	False
mnuExit	Menu	Enabled	True
mnuFile	Menu	Enabled	True
mnuGetNewsgroups	Menu	Enabled	False
mnuPost	Menu	Enabled	False
mnuSeparator	Menu	Enabled	True
optFilterBody	OptionButton	Caption	"Filter Message Body"
optFilterHeaders	OptionButton	Caption	"Filter Headers"
pbHorizontalDivider	PictureBox	FillStyle	Transparent
		MousePointer	7 - Size N S
pbVerticalDivider	PictureBox	FillStype	Transparent
		MousePointer	9 - Size W E
sbNNTPStatus	StatusBar	(Custom)	
tbToolbar	Toolbar	ImageList	ilButtonIcons
tmrStatus	Timer	Enabled	True
		Interval	2000

continued

Table 6.1 The controls and properties for the form frmNewsReader in the project NewsReader (continued).

Control Name	Type	Properties	Value
tvNewsGroups	TreeView	LabelEdit	1 - Manual
		LineStyle	0 - TreeLines
		Style	7 - Treelines, etc.
txtMessage	RichTextBox	MultiLine	True
		ScrollBars	3 - Both
txtSearchString	TextBox		
Winsock1	Winsock	Protocol	0 - sckTCPProtocol

Don't sweat the layout. We'll tidy up in the **Form_Resize**() event procedure, shown in Listing 6.11, the comprehensive listing of frmNewsReader.FRM.

Storing Newsgroup Names

When we request the newsgroups from any news server, we may end up with more than we bargained for. With more than 20,000 active newsgroups scattered across the Internet, the text version of the newsgroup directory now exceeds a megabyte. That's an awful lot of data to stuff into a naked TreeView control that uses system memory to hold its node objects. Not to mention that the TreeView data is transient—as soon as we exit the program, it goes away. Instead of recapturing the same data every time we want to browse or participate in newsgroup discussions, we can store each newsgroup name in a database.

What's In A Name?

By convention, newsgroup names are *hierarchical*, which means that any particular newsgroup name may consist of a series of subnames, separated by periods. For example, a newsgroup about auto racing may have the name "alt.sport.racing.auto". The names are assigned by the person who originates the newsgroup, so they don't follow any hard and fast rules. Luckily, some generally accepted categories have emerged, which keeps the rapidly expanding list of newsgroups from becoming completely unmanageable.

By breaking down newsgroup names into their constituent parts, we can organize them into a tree, where superior nodes represent categories, and leaf nodes represent actual newsgroups. For convenience, let's refer to the right most substring as the newsgroup identifier and the categories to the left of the identifer as the parent newsgroup name string (or *parent substring*, for short):

- Newsgroup name: alt.sport.racing.auto
- Newsgroup identifier: auto
- Newsgroup parent substring: alt.sport.racing.

If we wish, we could add another newsgroup to the "racing" category:

- alt.sport.racing.auto
- alt.sport.racing.horse

We could also add newsgroups to the category "sport":

- alt.sport.racing.auto
- alt.sport.racing.horse
- alt.sport.team.hockey

By breaking down each newsgroup name and storing each substring as a record in a database table, we can easily retrieve and add the children of any node in the TreeView. First, we search for the first occurrence of the clicked node's Index string in the database index. Then we step forward through the table, adding each node record to the TreeView control until we run into a node with a different parent.

To store all the information we need to construct TreeView nodes, we'll need just five fields in the database table, as shown in Table 6.2.

Table 6.2 The fields from the TableDef Newsgroups in Groups.MDB.

Field Name	Field Type	Purpose
Newsgroup	Text	Holds the complete newsgroup name. Acts as the unique, primary key for the table.
ParentPath	Text	Holds the parent path of the newsgroup. Identifies the record's parent node in the TreeView control.

continued

Table 6.2 The fields from the TableDef Newsgroups in Groups. MDB (continued).

Field Name	Field Type	Purpose
SubGroupName	Text	Identifies the rightmost substring in the newsgroup name. Becomes the text displayed in the TreeView.
Icon	Integer	Identifies the icon used to display the record in the TreeView control. This value refers to an image stored in the ilTreeIcons ImageList control.
SelectedIcon	Integer	Identifies the icon used to display the record in the TreeView control when the node is selected by the user.

The function that constructs and opens this database is shown in Listing 6.1.

Listing 6.1 The function **OpenOrGenerateGroupsDatabase()** from frmNewsReader.FRM.

```
Private Function OpenOrGenerateGroupsDatabase()
    Dim IndexField As Field
    Dim fldsNewsgroups(4) As Field
    Dim Counter As Integer

    If Len(Dir(App.Path & "\Groups.mdb")) > 0 Then
        Set dbGroupsDatabase = OpenDatabase(App.Path & "\Groups")
        OpenOrGenerateGroupsDatabase = True
      Else
        Set dbGroupsDatabase = CreateDatabase( _
            App.Path & "\Groups", dbLangGeneral)

        Set tdNewsgroups =
           dbGroupsDatabase.CreateTableDef("Newsgroups")

        Set fldsNewsgroups(0) = _
            tdNewsgroups.CreateField("Newsgroup", dbText, 255)
        Set fldsNewsgroups(1) = _
            tdNewsgroups.CreateField("ParentPath", dbText, 255)
        Set fldsNewsgroups(2) = _
            tdNewsgroups.CreateField("SubGroupName", dbText, 128)
        Set fldsNewsgroups(3) = _
            tdNewsgroups.CreateField("Icon", dbInteger)
        Set fldsNewsgroups(4) = _
            tdNewsgroups.CreateField("SelectedIcon", dbInteger)
```

```
        For Counter = 0 To 4
            tdNewsgroups.Fields.Append fldsNewsgroups(Counter)
            Next Counter

        Set idxNewsgroups = _
            tdNewsgroups.CreateIndex("NewsgroupsIndex")
        idxNewsgroups.Primary = True
        idxNewsgroups.Unique = True
        Set IndexField = idxNewsgroups.CreateField("Newsgroup")
        idxNewsgroups.Fields.Append IndexField

        Set idxParent = tdNewsgroups.CreateIndex("ParentIndex")
        idxParent.Primary = False
        idxParent.Unique = False
        Set IndexField = idxParent.CreateField("ParentPath")
        idxParent.Fields.Append IndexField

        tdNewsgroups.Indexes.Append idxNewsgroups
        tdNewsgroups.Indexes.Append idxParent

        dbGroupsDatabase.TableDefs.Append tdNewsgroups

        dbGroupsDatabase.Close
        Set dbGroupsDatabase = OpenDatabase(App.Path & "\Groups")
        OpenOrGenerateGroupsDatabase = True

      End If
    Set rsNewsgroups = dbGroupsDatabase.OpenRecordset("Newsgroups")
    End Function
```

The table would contain one—and only one—record for each unique substring. The example newsgroups mentioned earlier would decompose into seven records, as shown in Table 6.3

Table 6.3 An example of newsgroup names decomposed into database table records.

Newsgroup	ParentPath	SubGroupName
"alt"	""	"alt"
"alt.sport"	"alt"	"sport"
"alt.sport.racing"	"alt.sport"	"racing"

continued

Table 6.3 An example of newsgroup names decomposed into database table records (continued).

Newsgroup	ParentPath	SubGroupName
"alt.sport.racing.auto"	"alt.sport.racing"	"auto"
"alt.sport.racing.horse"	"alt.sport.racing"	"horse"
"alt.sport.team"	"alt.sport"	"team"
"alt.sport.team.hockey"	"alt.sport.team"	"hockey"

Converting Newsgroup Names Into Database Records

When we ask the news server for its directory of newsgroups with the "LIST" or "NEWGROUPS" command, the server will begin transmitting its response in blocks. If we were to wait for the entire transmission, we'd be back to the problem of storing all the data in system memory before we could transfer it to the database. Instead, we'll process each block as it arrives by using the general procedures **ConvertGroupsTextToDatabaseRecords()**, **TransferGroupToDatabase()**, and **AddGroupRecord()**.

The simple procedure **ConvertGroupsTextToDatabaseRecords()**, shown in Listing 6.2 takes the raw text returned by the news server and breaks it into lines. Each line may contain a group name followed by a description, separated from the name by a space. The real work begins when this procedure passes the group name to **TransferGroupToDatabase()**, shown in Listing 6.3.

Listing 6.2 The general procedure **ConvertGroupsTextToDatabase Records()** from frmNewsReader.FRM.

```
Public Sub ConvertGroupsTextToDatabaseRecords( _
   ByVal GroupsText As String)
    Dim CharPos As Long
    Dim GroupLine As String
    Dim groupName As String
    Dim GroupDesc As String
    Static OrphanedTextChunk As String

    If Len(OrphanedTextChunk) > 0 Then
        GroupsText = OrphanedTextChunk & GroupsText
      End If
```

```
Do While Len(GroupsText) > 0
    CharPos = InStr(GroupsText, vbCr)
    If CharPos > 0 Then
        GroupLine = Left(GroupsText, CharPos - 1)
        GroupsText = Mid(GroupsText, CharPos + 2)
        CharPos = InStr(GroupLine, " ")
        If CharPos > 0 Then
            groupName = Left(GroupLine, CharPos - 1)
            GroupDesc = Mid(GroupLine, CharPos + 1)
          Else
            groupName = GroupLine
          End If
        If Len(groupName) > 0 Then
            TransferGroupToDatabase groupName, "", GroupDesc
          End If
      Else
        OrphanedTextChunk = GroupsText
        GroupsText = ""
      End If

    Loop
End Sub
```

The **Static** variable **OrphanedTextChunk** enables us to process one data block at a time. The text we receive from the server will not necessarily be divided neatly at line breaks. We won't know that we have a complete line until we detect a carriage return; so when we reach the end of the current block, we need to hold on to the last piece. When we receive the next chunk, we append it to the **OrphanedTextChunk** before we begin processing the next line. This will mend any lines that are broken by the data transfer.

Listing 6.3 The general procedure **TransferGroupToDatabase()** from frmNewsReader.FRM.

```
Public Sub TransferGroupToDatabase(ByVal GroupName As String, _
                                   ByVal GroupPath As String, _
                                   GroupDesc As String)

    Dim CharPos As Long
    Dim SubGroupName As String
    Dim ParentKey As String
    Dim NodeIcon As Integer
    Dim NodeSelectedIcon As Integer
```

```
Dim BaseIcon As Integer
Dim SelectedIcon As Integer

On Error Resume Next
CharPos = InStr(groupName, ".")
If CharPos > 0 Then
    SubGroupName = Mid(groupName, 1, CharPos - 1)
    If Len(GroupPath) > 0 Then
        ParentKey = GroupPath
      Else
        ParentKey = "InternetNewsGroups"
      End If
    GroupPath = GroupPath & Mid(groupName, 1, CharPos)
    groupName = Mid(groupName, CharPos + 1)
    AddGroupRecord ParentKey, GroupPath, SubGroupName, _
                   icoClosedFolder, icoClosedFolder
    TransferGroupToDatabase groupName, _
                            GroupPath, GroupDesc
  Else
    SubGroupName = groupName
    ParentKey = GroupPath
    GroupPath = GroupPath & groupName
    groupName = ""
    AddGroupRecord ParentKey, GroupPath, SubGroupName, _
                   icoDocument, icoDocument
  End If

End Sub
```

The recursive procedure, **TransferGroupToDatabase()**, divides the **GroupName** into substrings by searching for the dot delimiters. For each substring, it prepares a **ParentKey**, a **GroupName**, a **GroupPath**, and a **SubGroupName**.

The **ParentKey** will be used to identify the parent node in the TreeView control and will be passed to **AddGroupRecord()**.

The **GroupName** will be passed recursively to **TransferGroupToDatabase()**, where it will be further split into path and name components.

The **GroupPath** will consist of the parent path, plus the portion of the group name through the first period. It will be passed to **AddGroupRecord()**, where it will be assigned to the database field **NewsGroup**. When we transfer the record to the TreeView, the contents of **NewsGroup** will become the node's **Key** value, which uniquely identifies each node. **GroupPath** will also be passed recursively to **TransferGroupToDatabase**(), where it will become the new **ParentKey**. Each time the procedure recurses, the **GroupPath** grows by one word, while the **GroupName** shrinks. When it reaches the end of the original group name string, **GroupPath** will contain the complete group name, and the recursion will terminate.

The **SubGroupName** will be the first word in the group name—up to, but excluding, the first period. It will be passed to **AddGroupRecord**(). It has only one purpose: If the record is ever used to create a TreeView node, the **SubGroupName** will appear as the text displayed by that node.

Because of the hierarchical naming system for newsgroups, the program will often attempt to add duplicate records. The procedure **AddGroupRecord**(), shown in Listing 6.4, filters the redundancy by searching the **NewsgroupsIndex** of the table **Newsgroups** for the value passed in **GroupPath** to determine whether it already exists. If not, it adds a new record; otherwise, it harmlessly ignores it.

Listing 6.4 The general procedure **AddGroupRecord()** from frmNewsReader.FRM.

```
Public Sub AddGroupRecord(ParentPath As String, GroupPath As String, _
                          SubGroupName As String, _
                          Icon As Integer, SelectedIcon As Integer)

    rsNewsgroups.Index = "NewsgroupsIndex"
    rsNewsgroups.Seek "=", GroupPath
    If rsNewsgroups.NoMatch Then
        rsNewsgroups.AddNew
        rsNewsgroups.Fields!NewsGroup = GroupPath
        rsNewsgroups.Fields!ParentPath = ParentPath
        rsNewsgroups.Fields!SubGroupName = SubGroupName
        rsNewsgroups.Fields!Icon = Icon
        rsNewsgroups.Fields!SelectedIcon = SelectedIcon
        rsNewsgroups.Update
      End If
    End Sub
```

From Database To TreeView

We've already done the hard work. The procedures **ConvertGroupsTextToDatabaseRecords**() and **TransferGroupToDatabase**() have taken apart the newsgroup names and saved them as a series of records representing families of newsgroups. To display these records as nodes in the TreeView, all we have to do is create one node for each record. We don't want to do that all at once, however. One reason we stored the newsgroup names in a database was to avoid overstuffing the TreeView control. What we really want to do is add nodes to the tree as they're needed—in other words, as the user expands the tree. The code that performs this function will reside in the **tvNewsGroups_NodeClick()** event procedure, shown in Listing 6.5.

Listing 6.5 The event procedure **tvNewsGroups_NodeClick()** from frmNewsReader.FRM.

```
Private Sub tvNewsGroups_NodeClick(ByVal Node As Node)
    Dim KeyValue As String
    Dim MatchFailed As Boolean
    Dim NewNode As Node
    Dim NewNodeKey As String
    Dim NewNodeValue As String
    Dim NewNodeIcon As Integer
    Dim NewNodeSelectedIcon As Integer

    If Not NewsGroupsEnabled Then
        Exit Sub
      End If

    If Node.Children > 0 Then
        ' Node already updated from database
        Exit Sub
      End If

    If CInt(Node.Image) = icoDocument Then
        ' SelectGroup
        OrphanedTextChunk = ""
        lvwMessageHeaders.ListItems.Clear
        NNTPTransactionSemaphore = tsSelectGroup
        Winsock1.SendData "GROUP " & Trim(Node.Key) & vbCrLf
      Else
        KeyValue = Node.Key
        rsNewsgroups.Index = "ParentIndex"
        rsNewsgroups.Seek "=", Node.Key
        MatchFailed = rsNewsgroups.NoMatch
        If Not (MatchFailed Or (Node.Key = "InternetNewsGroups")) Then
            Node.Image = icoOpenFolder
            Node.SelectedImage = icoOpenFolder
```

```
      End If
    Do Until rsNewsgroups.EOF Or MatchFailed
        NewNodeKey = rsNewsgroups.Fields!NewsGroup
        NewNodeValue = rsNewsgroups.Fields!SubGroupName
        NewNodeIcon = rsNewsgroups.Fields!Icon
        NewNodeSelectedIcon = rsNewsgroups.Fields!SelectedIcon
        Set NewNode = tvNewsGroups.Nodes.Add( _
                        KeyValue, _
                        tvwChild, _
                        NewNodeKey, _
                        NewNodeValue, _
                        NewNodeIcon, _
                        NewNodeSelectedIcon)
        If Not (NewNode Is Nothing) Then
            NewNode.Image = NewNodeIcon
            NewNode.SelectedImage = NewNodeSelectedIcon
            NewNode.EnsureVisible
          End If
        rsNewsgroups.MoveNext
        MatchFailed = Not (rsNewsgroups.Fields!ParentPath = _
                            KeyValue)
        Loop
    Node.EnsureVisible
  End If
End Sub
```

This procedure begins by trying to get out of doing anything. It calls **Exit Sub** for either of two reasons:

- The tree view control is disabled—presumably because the program is performing a conflicting operation—as indicated by **NewsGroupsEnabled**.
- The node already has its children loaded, as indicated by a non-zero value in the node's **Children** property.

If a node has children, then it's just a member of a newsgroup path, just as a Windows folder represents a subdirectory. A node with no children, however, either represents an unexpanded path member or it's a leaf node representing a full-fledged newsgroup. To identify a leaf node, we just check the node's **Image** property for the value represented by the constant **icoDocument**. When the user clicks a leaf node, we send the news server the "GROUP" command. When the user clicks a previously unexpanded path node, however, we expand the tree by searching the database for its children and converting them to new nodes. Once we expand the TreeView control, it retains those nodes only for the duration of the current session. The next time the program runs, the process of expanding the tree begins from scratch.

Selecting A Newsgroup

Just as in the NNTP Experiment project, selecting a newsgroup is a two-step process. First, we send the server the "GROUP" command, followed by the full name of the newsgroup we wish to browse. If the server locates the newsgroup, it sends response code 211, followed on the same line by the message count, and the first and last message numbers. We then use those message numbers to request a list of messsage headers. Most of this occurs within the **Winsock1_DataArrival()** event procedure in the **Case tsSelectGroup** and **Case tsListArticles** clauses, as shown in Listing 6.6.

Listing 6.6 The **Winsock1_DataArrival()** event procedure from frmNewsReader.FRM.

```
Private Sub Winsock1_DataArrival(ByVal bytesTotal As Long)
    Dim OutputData As String
    Dim CrLfPosition As Long
    Dim MessageCount As String
    Dim FirstMessageNumber As String
    Dim LastMessageNumber As String
    Dim ResponseString As String
    Dim ResponseCode As Integer

    Winsock1.GetData OutputData
    If Not ReceivingData Then
        CrLfPosition = InStr(OutputData, vbCrLf)
        If CrLfPosition > 0 Then
            ResponseString = Left(OutputData, CrLfPosition - 1)
            OutputData = Mid(OutputData, CrLfPosition + 2)
          Else
            ResponseString = OutputData
          End If
        sbNNTPStatus.Panels(2).Text = ResponseString
        ResponseCode = CInt(GetWordFrom(ResponseString))
      End If
    Select Case NNTPTransactionSemaphore
      Case tsConnect
        If ResponseCode = 480 Then
            NNTPTransactionSemaphore = tsAuthorizing
```

```
        Winsock1.SendData "AUTHINFO USER " & _
                          Trim(ConnectionInfo.Username) & _
                          vbCrLf
      ElseIf (ResponseCode = 200) Or (ResponseCode = 201) Then
        NNTPTransactionSemaphore = tsConnected
      Else
        NNTPTransactionSemaphore = tsNone
      End If
  Case tsAuthorizing
    If ResponseCode = 381 Then
        NNTPTransactionSemaphore = tsAuthorizationResponse
        Winsock1.SendData "AUTHINFO PASS " & _
                          Trim(ConnectionInfo.Password) & _
                          vbCrLf
      Else
        NNTPTransactionSemaphore = tsNone
      End If
  Case tsAuthorizationResponse
    If ResponseCode = 281 Then
        NNTPTransactionSemaphore = tsConnected
      Else
        NNTPTransactionSemaphore = tsNone
      End If
  Case tsListGroups
    ReceivingData = True
    NewsGroupsEnabled = False
    Me.MousePointer = vbHourglass
    ConvertGroupsTextToDatabaseRecords OutputData
    NewsGroupsEnabled = True
    Me.MousePointer = vbDefault
  Case tsSelectGroup
    mnuPost.Enabled = False
    tbToolbar.Buttons("btnPost").Enabled = False
    Me.MousePointer = vbHourglass
    If ResponseCode = 211 Then
        NNTPTransactionSemaphore = tsListArticles
        GetGroupInfo ResponseString, MessageCount, _
                     FirstMessageNumber, LastMessageNumber
        Winsock1.SendData "XHDR subject " & _
                          Trim(FirstMessageNumber) & _
                          "-" & Trim(LastMessageNumber) & _
                          vbCrLf
      End If
    lvwMessageHeaders.Enabled = True
    Me.MousePointer = vbDefault
```

```
        mnuPost.Enabled = True
        tbToolbar.Buttons("btnPost").Enabled = True
      Case tsListArticles
        ReceivingData = True
        MessageHeadersEnabled = False
        UpdateMessageHeaderList lvwMessageHeaders, _
            OutputData, tsGetArticleHeaderSubjects
        MessageHeadersEnabled = True
      Case tsGetArticleByNumber
        ReceivingData = True
        txtMessage.Text = txtMessage.Text & OutputData
      Case tsPostRequest
        If ResponseCode = 340 Then
            mnuPost.Enabled = False
            tbToolbar.Buttons("btnPost").Enabled = False
            NNTPTransactionSemaphore = tsSubmitArticleForPosting
            Winsock1.SendData ArticleToPost
          End If
      Case tsSubmitArticleForPosting
        mnuPost.Enabled = True
        tbToolbar.Buttons("btnPost").Enabled = True
        NNTPTransactionSemaphore = tsNone
      Case Else
        txtMessage.Text = txtMessage.Text & OutputData
      End Select
    If Right(OutputData, 3) = "." & vbCrLf Then
        sbNNTPStatus.Panels(1).Text = "Request Complete"
        NNTPTransactionSemaphore = tsDone
        ReceivingData = False
      End If
    End Sub
```

You'll notice several differences between this version of **Winsock1_DataArrival**() and the version in the previous project. First, it maintains a boolean flag variable called **ReceivingData**, enabling it to differentiate between the first block of a server response and subsequent blocks. It uses that information to help identify the server response code, which appears only at the beginning of the first data block. **ReceivingData** is modified only within this procedure, which means it could have been declared locally as **Static**. But I tend to distrust uninitialized variables, so I've declared it as a private global and initialized it to **False** in the **Form_Load**() event procedure.

The final **If** statement tests for the end of the transmission by looking for a period on a line by itself at the end of the block:

```
If Right(OutputData, 3) = "." & vbCrLf Then
    sbNNTPStatus.Panels(1).Text = "Request Complete"
    NNTPTransactionSemaphore = tsDone
    ReceivingData = False
  End If
```

If it detects the termination line, it raises the **tsDone** semaphore and resets **ReceivingData** to **False**.

Instead of dumping its data in a TextBox control, the **Case tsListArticles** clause now calls the general procedure **UpdateMessageHeaderList()**, shown in Listing 6.7, which breaks down the text file and places the data in a ListView control.

Listing 6.7 The general procedure **UpdateMessageHeaderList()** from frmNewsReader.FRM.

```
Public Sub UpdateMessageHeaderList(lvwMessageHeaders As ListView, _
                                   ByVal MessageText As String, _
                                         HeaderType As Integer)
    Dim CharPos As Long
    Dim AllDataReceived As Boolean
    Dim HeaderLine As String
    Dim MessageNumberString As String
    Dim MessageHeaderBody As String

    If Len(OrphanedTextChunk) > 0 Then
        MessageText = OrphanedTextChunk & MessageText
        OrphanedTextChunk = ""
      End If
    ' If end of transmission, then strip "."/Cr/Lf
    If Right(MessageText, 3) = "." & vbCrLf Then
        MessageText = Left(MessageText, Len(MessageText) - 3)
        AllDataReceived = True
      Else
        AllDataReceived = False
      End If
    Do While Len(MessageText) > 0
        CharPos = InStr(MessageText, vbCrLf)
        If (CharPos = 0) And (NNTPTransactionSemaphore = tsDone) Then
            CharPos = Len(MessageText) + 1
          End If
```

```
        If (CharPos > 0) Then
            HeaderLine = Left(MessageText, CharPos - 1)
            MessageText = Mid(MessageText, CharPos + 2)
            CharPos = InStr(HeaderLine, " ")
            If CharPos > 0 Then
                MessageNumberString = _
                   Trim(Left(HeaderLine, CharPos - 1))
                MessageHeaderBody = Mid(HeaderLine, CharPos + 1)
              End If
            If Len(MessageNumberString) > 0 Then
                ' Update ListView
                If HeaderType = tsGetArticleHeaderSubjects Then
                    lvwMessageHeaders.ListItems.Add _
                        , "KEY" & MessageNumberString, _
                        MessageNumberString
                    lvwMessageHeaders.ListItems.Item("KEY" & _
                        MessageNumberString). _
                        SubItems(1) = MessageHeaderBody
                  Else
                    lvwMessageHeaders.ListItems.Item("KEY" & _
                        MessageNumberString). _
                        SubItems(2) = MessageHeaderBody
                  End If
              End If
          Else
            OrphanedTextChunk = MessageText
            MessageText = ""
          End If
        Loop
    If AllDataReceived And (Len(txtSearchString.Text) > 0) Then
        PerformSearchStringAnalysis
      End If
    End Sub
```

Like **ConvertGroupsTextToDatabaseRecords**(), the procedure **UpdateMessage HeaderList**() looks for CR/LF sequences and holds any residual text found after the final CR/LF in **OrphanedTextChunk**. It then prepends this fragment to the subsequent block before it begins parsing the lines, which mends the lines split during the blocked data transmission.

Next, **UpdateMessageHeaderList**() looks for the end-of-transmission marker—a period on a line by itself—and sets the local boolean variable, **AllDataReceived**. We'll need this at the end of the procedure.

The main loop steps through the text line by line. In each line, it searches for the first space, separating the message number from the subject string and storing their values in **MessageNumberString** and **MessageHeaderBody**, respectively. It calls the **Add**() method to insert the message into the ListView control's **ListItems** collection, placing the message number in the first display field and building an **Item** key from the message number by appending it to the string "KEY". With this key value, we can then use the **Item** property of the **ListItems** collection to update the newly added element. In this case, we add a second report column to the list by setting **SubItems**(2) to the contents of **MessageHeaderBody**.

Using DoEvents During Asynchronous Data Transfers

When I first wrote the procedure ***UpdateMessage HeaderList()****, I decided to make it more Windows-friendly by calling* ***DoEvents*** *within the main loop. This, I reasoned, would keep the time-consuming parsing process from stalling the entire system. But when I ran the program and tried to retrieve message headers from a newsgroup with numerous messages, the list became scrambled—messages were listed out of numerical order—and I began to parse invalid message numbers.*

It dawned on me that I was processing the data blocks out of sequence, which was mixing up the message numbers and randomly attaching the contents of ***OrphanedTextChunk****. To process the data block by block, I needed to be sure that* ***UpdateMessageHeaderList()*** *would only be called one block at a time, and in the order the blocks arrived from the server. By removing* ***DoEvents****, I prevented the Winsock control from triggering its* ***DataArrival()*** *event procedure for the next block until the current block had been parsed. As each block arrives, Winsock adds it to its receive buffer, where it remains until the current instance of* ***UpdateMessageHeaderList()*** *terminates.*

Do not repeat my mistake. Don't call ***DoEvents*** *during an asynchronous data transfer when you are processing the data blocks as they arrive.*

The last step in the procedure checks **AllDataReceived** to determine whether to activate the search string parser. We'll cover that process later.

Retrieving A News Article

The simple process of retrieving a news article is handled entirely within two event procedures. The first, **lvwMessageHeaders_ItemClick()**, shown in Listing 6.8, raises the **tsGetArticleByNumber** transaction semaphore. It then sends the "ARTICLE" command to the server, followed by the article number.

Listing 6.8 The **lvwMessageHeaders_ItemClick()** event procedure from frmNewsReader.FRM.

```
Private Sub lvwMessageHeaders_ItemClick(ByVal Item As ListItem)
    If MessageHeadersEnabled Then
        NNTPTransactionSemaphore = tsGetArticleByNumber
        txtMessage.Text = ""
        Winsock1.SendData "ARTICLE " & Trim(Item.Text) & vbCrLf
      End If
    End Sub
```

When the article arrives, the **Case tsGetArticleByNumber** clause in **Winsock1_DataArrival**() transfers it to the **txtMessages** RichTextBox control:

```
Case tsGetArticleByNumber
  ReceivingData = True
  txtMessage.Text = txtMessage.Text & OutputData
```

Posting A News Article

The final major operation performed by an NNTP client application is the posting of new messages to newsgroups. Somewhat like selecting a newsgroup, the NNTP procedure for posting requires a three-step dialog:

1. Send the "POST" command to the news server.
2. Await a 340 response code from the server.
3. Send the message headers and body text, followed by a period on a line by itself.

If the server accepts the message, it will respond with code 240. If the posting fails, it will send response code 441.

Of course, before we can post a message, we need to compose it. The form **frmPostNewArticle**, shown in Figure 6.5, accepts three values: a newsgroups name, a subject header, and the article body text. We'll discuss the workings of this form module later.

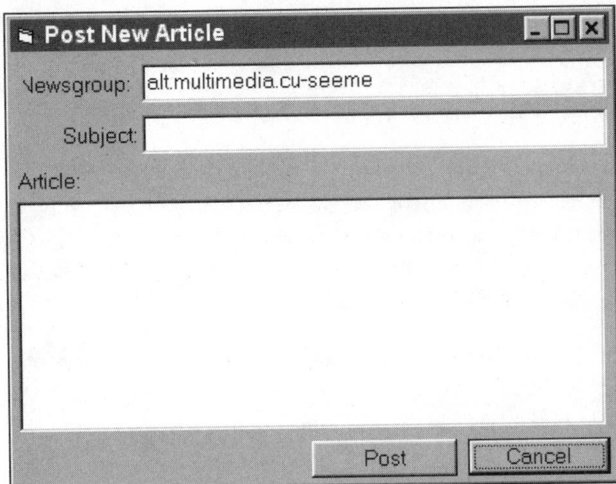

Figure 6.5
The form frmPostNewArticle.FRM at runtime.

The **mnuPost_Click()** event procedure calls the general procedure **PostNewArticle()**, shown in Listing 6.9, which activates the form **frmPostNewArticle. PostNewArticle()** then uses the data entered there and in the form **frmConnectionInfo** to construct the six required headers (according to RFC 1036). It then assembles the headers and body text into a single form-level string variable, **ArticleToPost**. It also raises the **tsPostRequest** semaphore before sending the "POST" command, which takes no arguments.

Listing 6.9 The general procedure **PostNewArticle()** from frmNewsGroup.FRM.

```
Private Sub PostNewArticle()
    Dim Header As String 'New DocHeadersCls
    Dim FieldName As String
    Dim FieldValue As String
    Dim TargetNewsGroup As String
    Dim ArticleSubject As String
    Dim ArticleBodyText As String

    ' Open and display article posting form:
    Load frmPostNewArticle
    frmPostNewArticle.txtNewsGroup.Text = _
        tvNewsGroups.SelectedItem.Key
```

```
frmPostNewArticle.txtSubject.Text = ""
frmPostNewArticle.txtArticleBody.Text = ""

frmPostNewArticle.Show vbModal

' Retrieve fields from article posting form:
TargetNewsGroup = frmPostNewArticle.txtNewsGroup.Text
ArticleSubject = frmPostNewArticle.txtSubject.Text
ArticleBodyText = frmPostNewArticle.txtArticleBody.Text & _
                  vbCrLf & "." & vbCrLf

If (Len(TargetNewsGroup) > 0) And _
   (Len(ArticleSubject) > 0) And _
   (Len(ArticleBodyText) > 0) Then
    Header = ""

    ' Set minimum required header fields, per RFC 1036:
    FieldName = "From: "
    FieldValue = ConnectionInfo.Name & _
        " <" & ConnectionInfo.EMail & ">"
    Header = FieldName & FieldValue & vbCrLf

    FieldName = "Date: "
    FieldValue = Format(Date, "ddd, dd-mmm-yyyy") & _
        " " & Format(Time, "hh:mm:ss") & " MST"
    Header = Header & FieldName & FieldValue & vbCrLf

    FieldName = "Newsgroups: "
    FieldValue = TargetNewsGroup
    Header = Header & FieldName & FieldValue & vbCrLf

    FieldName = "Subject: "
    FieldValue = ArticleSubject
    Header = Header & FieldName & FieldValue & vbCrLf

    FieldName = "Message-ID: "
    FieldValue = "<" & Trim(Format(Date, "mmddyyyy")) & _
                 Trim(Format(Time, "hhmmss")) & _
                 ConnectionInfo.EMail & ">"
    Header = Header & FieldName & FieldValue & vbCrLf

    FieldName = "Path: "
    FieldValue = Winsock1.RemoteHost
    Header = Header & FieldName & FieldValue & vbCrLf

    Header = Header & vbCrLf
```

```
        ' Send article to news server:
        NNTPTransactionSemaphore = tsPostRequest
        ArticleToPost = Header & vbCrLf & ArticleBodyText
        Winsock1.SendData "POST" & vbCrLf
      End If

    End Sub
```

The rest of the posting operation takes place within the **Case tsPostRequest** and **Case tsSubmitArticleForPosting** clauses within the **Winsock1_DataArrival**() event procedure:

```
Case tsPostRequest
  If ResponseCode = 340 Then
      mnuPost.Enabled = False
      tbToolbar.Buttons("btnPost").Enabled = False
      NNTPTransactionSemaphore = tsSubmitArticleForPosting
      Winsock1.SendData ArticleToPost
    End If
Case tsSubmitArticleForPosting
  mnuPost.Enabled = True
  tbToolbar.Buttons("btnPost").Enabled = True
  NNTPTransactionSemaphore = tsNone
```

When the program receives the 340 response code from the server, it raises the **tsSubmitArticleForPosting** semaphore and transmits the article headers and body text. Whether the posting succeeds or fails, the **Case tsSubmitArticleForPosting** clause re-enables the Post menu option and toolbar button and resets **NNTP TransactionSemaphore** to **tsNone**. If you wish, you may check the response code and raise a message box to report whether the posting was accepted by the server. Beware, however, that response code 240 means only that the server accepted the uploaded text—it does not necessarily mean that it will post the message on the newsgroup. Typically, the server will not analyze the message headers until its posting daemon gets around to updating the newsgroups. If the daemon finds one or more of the headers unacceptable, it will simply ignore the posting. Although some news server software may scrutinize the headers before sending the 240 response code, NNTP does not specify a mechanism to verify the posting. The only way you will know that a message has reached its newsgroup is by waiting for it to appear.

Filtering The News

The final function in the VB Smart News Reader is its filtering system. In Chapter 3, we used the Visual Basic Document Analyst—a collection of object classes—to build a Web Robot. (For a detailed explanation of how the Document Analyst works, see Chapter 4, *The VB Document Analyst*). Now let's use the same code to build some intelligence into our News Reader program.

As you may recall, when the procedure **UpdateMessageHeaderList()** reached the end of the header response text (as identified by its period terminator), it responded to a non-null **txtSearchString** by calling the general procedure **PerformSearch StringAnalysis()**. That procedure, shown in Listing 6.10, searches either the retrieved subject headers or the complete header and body text of each message to determine whether they match the criteria specified in the search string.

Listing 6.10 The general procedure **PerformSearchString Analysis()** from frmNewsReader.FRM.

```
Public Sub PerformSearchStringAnalysis()
    Dim ListItem As ListItem
    Dim DocumentAnalyst As clsDocumentAnalyst
    Dim FailsMatch As Boolean
    Dim ItemsToRemove As New Collection

    NewsGroupsEnabled = False
    MessageHeadersEnabled = False
    mnuDisconnect.Enabled = False
    mnuGetNewsgroups.Enabled = False
    mnuPost.Enabled = False
    tbToolbar.Buttons("btnDisconnect").Enabled = False
    tbToolbar.Buttons("btnGetGroups").Enabled = False
    tbToolbar.Buttons("btnPost").Enabled = False
    Me.MousePointer = vbHourglass

    Set DocumentAnalyst = New clsDocumentAnalyst
    DocumentAnalyst.Init txtSearchString.Text
    For Each ListItem In lvwMessageHeaders.ListItems
        If optFilterBody Then
            NNTPTransactionSemaphore = tsGetArticleByNumber
            txtMessage.Text = ""
            Winsock1.SendData "ARTICLE " & Trim(ListItem.Text) & _
                vbCrLf
```

```
            Do
                DoEvents
                Loop Until NNTPTransactionSemaphore = tsDone
            FailsMatch = _
                Not DocumentAnalyst.DocumentMatches(txtMessage.Text)
          Else
            FailsMatch = _
                Not DocumentAnalyst.DocumentMatches( _
                ListItem.SubItems(1))
          End If
        If FailsMatch Then
           ItemsToRemove.Add ListItem
          End If
        Next ListItem
    For Each ListItem In ItemsToRemove
        lvwMessageHeaders.ListItems.Remove ListItem.Key
        Next ListItem
    txtMessage.Text = ""

    NewsGroupsEnabled = True
    MessageHeadersEnabled = True
    mnuDisconnect.Enabled = True
    mnuGetNewsgroups.Enabled = True
    mnuPost.Enabled = True
    tbToolbar.Buttons("btnDisconnect").Enabled = True
    tbToolbar.Buttons("btnGetGroups").Enabled = True
    tbToolbar.Buttons("btnPost").Enabled = True
    Me.MousePointer = vbDefault
    End Sub
```

The procedure begins by creating an instance of **clsDocumentAnalyst** and initializing it with the contents of **txtSearchString**:

```
Set DocumentAnalyst = New clsDocumentAnalyst
DocumentAnalyst.Init txtSearchString.Text
```

Next, it must step through the message headers and submit either the headers themselves or the messages they represent to the Document Analyst. The lines that appear in the ListView control are stored in a collection property called **ListItems**. With a **For Each** loop, we can retrieve each header from the collection. To analyze the headers, we just pass the contents of their **SubItems(1)** property to the method function **DocumentAnalyst.DocumentMatches()**. To analyze the message bodies, we must retrieve each message from the server, one by one, passing its entire contents to **DocumentMatches()**.

We need to remove the message headers from the list whose contents or whose message contents fail the analysis. But because we're executing a **For Each** loop, we can't immediately remove them from the collection. Instead, we build a second collection, **ItemsToRemove**, to keep track of those we wish to remove. When the analysis is complete, we step through **ItemsToRemove** with another **For Each** loop, passing the **ListItem.Key** to the **Remove()** method of the original collection. As we modify the original **ListItems** collection, the ListView control will refresh its displayed list of message headers, leaving only those that have passed the scrutiny of the Document Analyst.

Filtering With NNTP WILDMAT

The NNTP revised specifications (described in Internet Draft draft-barber-nntp-imp-05.TXT) describe a wild card system known as WILDMAT. WILDMAT may be used with certain NNTP commands to perform character-based filtering on newsgroup names and headers (see Table 4.2).

For the complete listing of the form module frmNewsReader.FRM, including all declarations and support procedures, see Listing 6.11.

Listing 6.11 The complete listing of frmNewsReader.FRM from the project NewsReader.VBP.

```
Option Explicit

Const FormSpace = 30

Private NNTPTransactionSemaphore As Integer

Const tsNone = 0
Const tsConnect = 1
Const tsAuthorizing = 2
Const tsAuthorizationResponse = 3
Const tsConnected = 4
Const tsListGroups = 5
Const tsSelectGroup = 6
Const tsListArticles = 7
Const tsGetArticleByNumber = 8
```

```
Const tsGetArticleHeaderSubjects = 9
Const tsGetArticleHeaderAuthors = 10
Const tsPostRequest = 11
Const tsSubmitArticleForPosting = 12
Const tsDisconnect = 13
Const tsDone = 14

Private ReceivingData As Boolean
Private dbGroupsDatabase As Database
Private tdNewsgroups As TableDef
Private idxNewsgroups As Index
Private idxParent As Index
Private rsNewsgroups As Recordset
Private NewsGroupsEnabled As Boolean
Private MessageHeadersEnabled As Boolean

Private Type tConnectionInfo
    NewsServer As String
    Username As String
    Password As String
    Name As String
    EMail As String
    End Type

Private ConnectionInfo As tConnectionInfo
Private OrphanedTextChunk As String
Private ArticleToPost As String

Const icoClosedFolder = 1
Const icoOpenFolder = 2
Const icoDocument = 3
Const icoRoot = 4

Private Function GetWordFrom(AnyString As String) As String
    Dim SpacePosition As Long
    Dim ReturnString As String
    Dim TempString As String

    SpacePosition = InStr(AnyString, " ")
    If SpacePosition = 0 Then
        ReturnString = AnyString
        TempString = ""
      Else
        ReturnString = Left(AnyString, SpacePosition)
        TempString = Mid(AnyString, SpacePosition + 1)
      End If
```

```
    If Right(ReturnString, 2) = vbCrLf Then
        ReturnString = Left(ReturnString, Len(ReturnString) - 2)
      End If
    AnyString = TempString
    GetWordFrom = ReturnString
    End Function

Private Sub GetGroupInfo(ByVal ResponseString As String, _
                               MessageCount As String, _
                               FirstMessageNumber As String, _
                               LastMessageNumber As String)

    MessageCount = GetWordFrom(ResponseString)
    FirstMessageNumber = GetWordFrom(ResponseString)
    LastMessageNumber = GetWordFrom(ResponseString)
    End Sub

Private Sub Form_Load()
    Dim DatabaseOpen As Boolean

    tvNewsGroups.Nodes.Add , , "InternetNewsGroups", _
       "Internet Newsgroups", icoRoot, icoRoot
    DatabaseOpen = OpenOrGenerateGroupsDatabase

    Me.Width = 0.8 * Screen.Width
    Me.Height = 0.8 * Screen.Height
    Me.Top = (Screen.Height - Me.Height) \ 2
    Me.Left = (Screen.Width - Me.Width) \ 2

    ReceivingData = False
    End Sub

Private Sub Form_QueryUnload(Cancel As Integer, _
                             UnloadMode As Integer)
    If Winsock1.State = sckConnected Then
        Winsock1.Close
      End If
    dbGroupsDatabase.Close
    End Sub


Private Sub Form_Resize()
    Dim VerticalScalar As Single
    Dim HorizontalScalar As Single
    Static OldFormWidth As Long
    Static OldFormHeight As Long
```

```
If Me.WindowState = vbMinimized Then
    Exit Sub
  End If

Me.Width = MaxLong(Me.Width, (5000 + (Me.Width - Me.ScaleWidth)))
Me.Height = MaxLong(Me.Height, _
    (tbToolbar.Height + Frame1.Height + sbNNTPStatus.Height + _
     3 * FormSpace + 1500 + (Me.Height - Me.ScaleHeight)))

If OldFormWidth > 0 Then
    HorizontalScalar = Me.ScaleWidth / OldFormWidth
    VerticalScalar = Me.ScaleHeight / OldFormHeight
  Else
    HorizontalScalar = 1
    VerticalScalar = 1
  End If

OldFormWidth = Me.ScaleWidth
OldFormHeight = Me.ScaleHeight

Frame1.Left = FormSpace
Frame1.Width = Me.ScaleWidth - 2 * FormSpace
optFilterBody.Left = Frame1.Width - (optFilterBody.Width + _
                                     FormSpace)
optFilterHeaders.Left = optFilterBody.Left
txtSearchString.Width = optFilterBody.Left - _
     (txtSearchString.Left + FormSpace * 4)
optFilterBody.Value = True

tvNewsGroups.Left = FormSpace
tvNewsGroups.Top = tbToolbar.Top + tbToolbar.Height + _
     Frame1.Height + FormSpace * 4
tvNewsGroups.Height = Me.ScaleHeight - _
    (tbToolbar.Height + Frame1.Height + _
     sbNNTPStatus.Height + FormSpace * 3)
tvNewsGroups.Width = MinLong( _
    Me.ScaleWidth - (tvNewsGroups.Left + FormSpace * 5), _
    tvNewsGroups.Width * HorizontalScalar)

pbVerticalDivider.Top = tvNewsGroups.Top
pbVerticalDivider.Left = tvNewsGroups.Left + tvNewsGroups.Width
pbVerticalDivider.Height = tvNewsGroups.Height
pbVerticalDivider.Width = FormSpace
```

```
    lvwMessageHeaders.Top = tvNewsGroups.Top
    lvwMessageHeaders.Left = _
        pbVerticalDivider.Left + pbVerticalDivider.Width
    lvwMessageHeaders.Width = Me.ScaleWidth - _
        (lvwMessageHeaders.Left + FormSpace)
    lvwMessageHeaders.Height = MinLong( _
         Me.ScaleHeight - (lvwMessageHeaders.Top + _
             sbNNTPStatus.Height + FormSpace * 5), _
         lvwMessageHeaders.Height * VerticalScalar)

    pbHorizontalDivider.Left = lvwMessageHeaders.Left
    pbHorizontalDivider.Top = _
        lvwMessageHeaders.Top + lvwMessageHeaders.Height
    pbHorizontalDivider.Width = lvwMessageHeaders.Width
    pbHorizontalDivider.Height = FormSpace

    txtMessage.Top = _
        pbHorizontalDivider.Top + pbHorizontalDivider.Height
    txtMessage.Left = lvwMessageHeaders.Left
    txtMessage.Height = Me.ScaleHeight - _
        (txtMessage.Top + sbNNTPStatus.Height + FormSpace)
    txtMessage.Width = lvwMessageHeaders.Width

    End Sub

Private Sub lvwMessageHeaders_ItemClick(ByVal Item As ListItem)
    If MessageHeadersEnabled Then
        NNTPTransactionSemaphore = tsGetArticleByNumber
        txtMessage.Text = ""
        Winsock1.SendData "ARTICLE " & Trim(Item.Text) & vbCrLf
      End If
    End Sub


Private Sub mnuConnect_Click()
    ConnectToNewsServer
    End Sub


Private Sub mnuDisconnect_Click()
    NNTPTransactionSemaphore = tsDisconnect
    Winsock1.SendData "QUIT" & vbCrLf
    End Sub
```

```
Private Sub mnuExit_Click()
    Unload Me
    End Sub

Private Sub mnuGetNewsgroups_Click()
    NNTPTransactionSemaphore = tsListGroups
    OrphanedTextChunk = ""
    'Winsock1.SendData "LIST" & vbCrLf
    Winsock1.SendData "NEWGROUPS " & _
                      Format(DateSerial(97, 1, 1), _
                      "yymmdd hh:mm:ss") & _
                      vbCrLf
    End Sub

Private Sub mnuPost_Click()
    PostNewArticle
    End Sub

Private Function OpenOrGenerateGroupsDatabase()
    Dim IndexField As Field
    Dim fldsNewsgroups(4) As Field
    Dim Counter As Integer

    If Len(Dir(App.Path & "\Groups.mdb")) > 0 Then
        Set dbGroupsDatabase = OpenDatabase(App.Path & "\Groups")
        OpenOrGenerateGroupsDatabase = True
      Else
        Set dbGroupsDatabase = CreateDatabase( _
            App.Path & "\Groups", dbLangGeneral)

        Set tdNewsgroups = _
            dbGroupsDatabase.CreateTableDef("Newsgroups")

        Set fldsNewsgroups(0) = _
            tdNewsgroups.CreateField("Newsgroup", dbText, 255)
        Set fldsNewsgroups(1) = _
            tdNewsgroups.CreateField("ParentPath", dbText, 255)
        Set fldsNewsgroups(2) = _
            tdNewsgroups.CreateField("SubGroupName", dbText, 128)
        Set fldsNewsgroups(3) = _
            tdNewsgroups.CreateField("Icon", dbInteger)
        Set fldsNewsgroups(4) = _
            tdNewsgroups.CreateField("SelectedIcon", dbInteger)
```

```
        For Counter = 0 To 4
            tdNewsgroups.Fields.Append fldsNewsgroups(Counter)
            Next Counter

        Set idxNewsgroups = _
            tdNewsgroups.CreateIndex("NewsgroupsIndex")
        idxNewsgroups.Primary = True
        idxNewsgroups.Unique = True
        Set IndexField = idxNewsgroups.CreateField("Newsgroup")
        idxNewsgroups.Fields.Append IndexField

        Set idxParent = tdNewsgroups.CreateIndex("ParentIndex")
        idxParent.Primary = False
        idxParent.Unique = False
        Set IndexField = idxParent.CreateField("ParentPath")
        idxParent.Fields.Append IndexField

        tdNewsgroups.Indexes.Append idxNewsgroups
        tdNewsgroups.Indexes.Append idxParent

        dbGroupsDatabase.TableDefs.Append tdNewsgroups

        dbGroupsDatabase.Close
        Set dbGroupsDatabase = OpenDatabase(App.Path & "\Groups")
        OpenOrGenerateGroupsDatabase = True

      End If
    Set rsNewsgroups = dbGroupsDatabase.OpenRecordset("Newsgroups")
    End Function

Public Sub TransferGroupToDatabase(ByVal groupName As String, _
                                  ByVal GroupPath As String, _
                                  GroupDesc As String)

    Dim CharPos As Long
    Dim SubGroupName As String
    Dim ParentKey As String
    Dim NodeIcon As Integer
    Dim NodeSelectedIcon As Integer
    Dim BaseIcon As Integer
    Dim SelectedIcon As Integer

    On Error Resume Next
    CharPos = InStr(groupName, ".")
    If CharPos > 0 Then
        SubGroupName = Mid(groupName, 1, CharPos - 1)
```

```
        If Len(GroupPath) > 0 Then
            ParentKey = GroupPath
          Else
            ParentKey = "InternetNewsGroups"
          End If
        GroupPath = GroupPath & Mid(groupName, 1, CharPos)
        groupName = Mid(groupName, CharPos + 1)
        AddGroupRecord ParentKey, GroupPath, SubGroupName, _
                       icoClosedFolder, icoClosedFolder
        TransferGroupToDatabase groupName, _
                                GroupPath, GroupDesc
      Else
        SubGroupName = groupName
        ParentKey = GroupPath
        GroupPath = GroupPath & groupName
        groupName = ""
        AddGroupRecord ParentKey, GroupPath, SubGroupName, _
                       icoDocument, icoDocument
      End If

    End Sub

Public Sub ConvertGroupsTextToDatabaseRecords(ByVal _
                                              GroupsText As String)
    Dim CharPos As Long
    Dim GroupLine As String
    Dim groupName As String
    Dim GroupDesc As String
    'Static OrphanedTextChunk As String

    If Len(OrphanedTextChunk) > 0 Then
        GroupsText = OrphanedTextChunk & GroupsText
        OrphanedTextChunk = ""
      End If
    Do While Len(GroupsText) > 0
        CharPos = InStr(GroupsText, vbCr)
        If CharPos > 0 Then
            GroupLine = Left(GroupsText, CharPos - 1)
            GroupsText = Mid(GroupsText, CharPos + 2)
            CharPos = InStr(GroupLine, " ")
            If CharPos > 0 Then
                groupName = Left(GroupLine, CharPos - 1)
                  GroupDesc = Mid(GroupLine, CharPos + 1)
              Else
                groupName = GroupLine
              End If
```

```
            If Len(groupName) > 0 Then
                TransferGroupToDatabase groupName, "", GroupDesc
              End If
          Else
            OrphanedTextChunk = GroupsText
            GroupsText = ""
          End If

        Loop
    End Sub

Public Sub AddGroupRecord(ParentPath As String, GroupPath As String, _
                          SubGroupName As String, _
                          Icon As Integer, SelectedIcon As Integer)

    rsNewsgroups.Index = "NewsgroupsIndex"
    rsNewsgroups.Seek "=", GroupPath
    If rsNewsgroups.NoMatch Then
        rsNewsgroups.AddNew
        rsNewsgroups.Fields!NewsGroup = GroupPath
        rsNewsgroups.Fields!ParentPath = ParentPath
        rsNewsgroups.Fields!SubGroupName = SubGroupName
        rsNewsgroups.Fields!Icon = Icon
        rsNewsgroups.Fields!SelectedIcon = SelectedIcon
        rsNewsgroups.Update
      End If
    End Sub

Private Sub optFilterBody_Click()

End Sub

Private Sub pbHorizontalDivider_MouseMove(Button As Integer, _
    Shift As Integer, X As Single, Y As Single)
    If Button = vbLeftButton Then
        pbHorizontalDivider.Top = _
            MaxLong(tbToolbar.Height + sbNNTPStatus.Height + 200 + _
                    3 * FormSpace, _
                    MinLong((pbHorizontalDivider.Top + Y), _
                            (Me.ScaleHeight - (sbNNTPStatus.Height + _
                             FormSpace + 200))))
      End If

    End Sub
```

```
Private Sub pbHorizontalDivider_MouseUp(Button As Integer, _
    Shift As Integer, X As Single, Y As Single)
    lvwMessageHeaders.Height = _
        pbHorizontalDivider.Top - lvwMessageHeaders.Top
    txtMessage.Top = _
        pbHorizontalDivider.Top + pbHorizontalDivider.Height
    txtMessage.Height = _
        Me.ScaleHeight - (txtMessage.Top + sbNNTPStatus.Height + _
                          FormSpace)
    End Sub

Private Sub pbVerticalDivider_MouseMove(Button As Integer, _
    Shift As Integer, X As Single, Y As Single)
    If Button = vbLeftButton Then
        pbVerticalDivider.Left = _
            MaxLong(200, _
                    MinLong((pbVerticalDivider.Left + X), _
                            (Me.ScaleWidth - 260)))
      End If

    End Sub


Private Sub pbVerticalDivider_MouseUp(Button As Integer, _
    Shift As Integer, X As Single, Y As Single)
    tvNewsGroups.Width = pbVerticalDivider.Left - tvNewsGroups.Left
    lvwMessageHeaders.Left = _
        pbVerticalDivider.Left + pbVerticalDivider.Width
    lvwMessageHeaders.Width = _
        Me.ScaleWidth - (lvwMessageHeaders.Left + FormSpace)
    pbHorizontalDivider.Left = lvwMessageHeaders.Left
    pbHorizontalDivider.Width = lvwMessageHeaders.Width
    txtMessage.Left = lvwMessageHeaders.Left
    txtMessage.Width = lvwMessageHeaders.Width

    End Sub

Private Sub tbToolbar_ButtonClick(ByVal Button As ComctlLib.Button)
    Select Case Button.Key
      Case "btnConnect"
        ConnectToNewsServer
      Case "btnDisconnect"
        NNTPTransactionSemaphore = tsDisconnect
        Winsock1.SendData "QUIT" & vbCrLf
      Case "btnGetGroups"
        NNTPTransactionSemaphore = tsListGroups
```

```
        'Winsock1.SendData "LIST" & vbCrLf
        Winsock1.SendData "NEWGROUPS " & _
                          Format(DateSerial(97, 1, 1), _
                          "yymmdd hh:mm:ss") & _
                          vbCrLf
      Case "btnPost"
        PostNewArticle
      End Select
    End Sub

Private Sub tvNewsGroups_NodeClick(ByVal Node As Node)
    Dim KeyValue As String
    Dim MatchFailed As Boolean
    Dim NewNode As Node
    Dim NewNodeKey As String
    Dim NewNodeValue As String
    Dim NewNodeIcon As Integer
    Dim NewNodeSelectedIcon As Integer

    If Not NewsGroupsEnabled Then
        Exit Sub
      End If

    If Node.Children > 0 Then
        ' Node already updated from database
        Exit Sub
      End If

    If CInt(Node.Image) = icoDocument Then
        ' SelectGroup
        OrphanedTextChunk = ""
        lvwMessageHeaders.ListItems.Clear
        NNTPTransactionSemaphore = tsSelectGroup
        Winsock1.SendData "GROUP " & Trim(Node.Key) & vbCrLf
      Else
        KeyValue = Node.Key
        rsNewsgroups.Index = "ParentIndex"
        rsNewsgroups.Seek "=", Node.Key
        MatchFailed = rsNewsgroups.NoMatch
        If Not (MatchFailed Or (Node.Key = "InternetNewsGroups")) Then
            Node.Image = icoOpenFolder
            Node.SelectedImage = icoOpenFolder
          End If
        Do Until rsNewsgroups.EOF Or MatchFailed
            NewNodeKey = rsNewsgroups.Fields!NewsGroup
            NewNodeValue = rsNewsgroups.Fields!SubGroupName
```

```
                NewNodeIcon = rsNewsgroups.Fields!Icon
                NewNodeSelectedIcon = rsNewsgroups.Fields!SelectedIcon
                Set NewNode = tvNewsGroups.Nodes.Add( _
                               KeyValue, _
                               tvwChild, _
                               NewNodeKey, _
                               NewNodeValue, _
                               NewNodeIcon, _
                               NewNodeSelectedIcon)
                If Not (NewNode Is Nothing) Then
                    NewNode.Image = NewNodeIcon
                    NewNode.SelectedImage = NewNodeSelectedIcon
                    NewNode.EnsureVisible
                  End If
                rsNewsgroups.MoveNext
                MatchFailed = Not (rsNewsgroups.Fields!ParentPath = _
                                   KeyValue)
                Loop
            Node.EnsureVisible
          End If
        End Sub
    Public Sub UpdateMessageHeaderList(lvwMessageHeaders As ListView, _
                                 ByVal MessageText As String, _
                                       HeaderType As Integer)
        Dim CharPos As Long
        Dim AllDataReceived As Boolean
        Dim HeaderLine As String
        Dim MessageNumberString As String
        Dim MessageHeaderBody As String

        If Len(OrphanedTextChunk) > 0 Then
            MessageText = OrphanedTextChunk & MessageText
            OrphanedTextChunk = ""
          End If
        ' If end of transmission, then strip "."/Cr/Lf
        If Right(MessageText, 3) = "." & vbCrLf Then
            MessageText = Left(MessageText, Len(MessageText) - 3)
            AllDataReceived = True
          Else
            AllDataReceived = False
          End If
        Do While Len(MessageText) > 0
            CharPos = InStr(MessageText, vbCrLf)
            If CharPos > 0 Then
                Debug.Print "Yes"; " ";
```

```
        Else
          Debug.Print "No"; " ";
        End If
      If (CharPos = 0) And (NNTPTransactionSemaphore = tsDone) Then
          CharPos = Len(MessageText) + 1
        End If
      If (CharPos > 0) Then
          HeaderLine = Left(MessageText, CharPos - 1)
          Debug.Print HeaderLine
          MessageText = Mid(MessageText, CharPos + 2)
          CharPos = InStr(HeaderLine, " ")
          If CharPos > 0 Then
              MessageNumberString = Trim(Left(HeaderLine, _
                                                 CharPos - 1))
              MessageHeaderBody = Mid(HeaderLine, CharPos + 1)
            End If
          If Len(MessageNumberString) > 0 Then
              ' Update ListView
              If HeaderType = tsGetArticleHeaderSubjects Then
                  lvwMessageHeaders.ListItems.Add _
                      , "KEY" & MessageNumberString, _
                      MessageNumberString
                  lvwMessageHeaders.ListItems.Item("KEY" & _
                      MessageNumberString). _
                      SubItems(1) = MessageHeaderBody
                Else
                  lvwMessageHeaders.ListItems.Item("KEY" & _
                      MessageNumberString). _
                      SubItems(2) = MessageHeaderBody
                End If
            End If
        Else
          OrphanedTextChunk = MessageText
          MessageText = ""
        End If
      Loop
    If AllDataReceived And (Len(txtSearchString.Text) > 0) Then
        PerformSearchStringAnalysis
      End If
    End Sub

Private Sub ConnectToNewsServer()
    Load frmConnectionInfo
    'frmConnectionInfo.txtServer.Text = ConnectionInfo.NewsServer
    frmConnectionInfo.txtUsername.Text = ConnectionInfo.Username
```

```
    frmConnectionInfo.txtPassword.Text = ConnectionInfo.Password
    'frmConnectionInfo.txtName.Text = ConnectionInfo.Name
    'frmConnectionInfo.txtEmail.Text = ConnectionInfo.EMail
    frmConnectionInfo.Show vbModal
    If Len(frmConnectionInfo.txtServer.Text) > 0 Then
        If Winsock1.State = sckConnected Then
            Winsock1.SendData "QUIT" & vbCrLf
            Do
                DoEvents
                Loop Until Winsock1.State = sckClosed
          End If
        ConnectionInfo.NewsServer = frmConnectionInfo.txtServer.Text
        ConnectionInfo.Username = frmConnectionInfo.txtUsername.Text
        ConnectionInfo.Password = frmConnectionInfo.txtPassword.Text
        ConnectionInfo.Name = frmConnectionInfo.txtName.Text
        ConnectionInfo.EMail = frmConnectionInfo.txtEmail.Text
        mnuConnect.Enabled = False
        tbToolbar.Buttons("btnConnect").Enabled = False
        NNTPTransactionSemaphore = tsConnect
        Winsock1.Connect ConnectionInfo.NewsServer, 119
      End If
    Unload frmConnectionInfo
    End Sub

Private Sub PostNewArticle()
    Dim Header As String 'New DocHeadersCls
    Dim FieldName As String
    Dim FieldValue As String
    Dim TargetNewsGroup As String
    Dim ArticleSubject As String
    Dim ArticleBodyText As String

    ' Open and display article posting form:
    Load frmPostNewArticle
    frmPostNewArticle.txtNewsGroup.Text = _
        tvNewsGroups.SelectedItem.Key
    frmPostNewArticle.txtSubject.Text = ""
    frmPostNewArticle.txtArticleBody.Text = ""

    frmPostNewArticle.Show vbModal

    ' Retrieve fields from article posting form:
    TargetNewsGroup = frmPostNewArticle.txtNewsGroup.Text
    ArticleSubject = frmPostNewArticle.txtSubject.Text
    ArticleBodyText = frmPostNewArticle.txtArticleBody.Text & _
                      vbCrLf & "." & vbCrLf
```

```
If (Len(TargetNewsGroup) > 0) And _
   (Len(ArticleSubject) > 0) And _
   (Len(ArticleBodyText) > 0) Then
    Header = ""

    ' Set minimum required header fields, per RFC 1036:
    FieldName = "From: "
    FieldValue = ConnectionInfo.Name & _
        " <" & ConnectionInfo.EMail & ">"
    Header = FieldName & FieldValue & vbCrLf

    FieldName = "Date: "
    FieldValue = Format(Date, "ddd, dd-mmm-yyyy") & _
        " " & Format(Time, "hh:mm:ss") & " MST"
    Header = Header & FieldName & FieldValue & vbCrLf

    FieldName = "Newsgroups: "
    FieldValue = TargetNewsGroup
    Header = Header & FieldName & FieldValue & vbCrLf

    FieldName = "Subject: "
    FieldValue = ArticleSubject
    Header = Header & FieldName & FieldValue & vbCrLf

    FieldName = "Message-ID: "
    FieldValue = "<" & Trim(Format(Date, "mmddyyyy")) & _
                 Trim(Format(Time, "hhmmss")) & _
                 ConnectionInfo.EMail & ">"
    Header = Header & FieldName & FieldValue & vbCrLf

    FieldName = "Path: "
    FieldValue = Winsock1.RemoteHost
    Header = Header & FieldName & FieldValue & vbCrLf

    Header = Header & vbCrLf

    ' Send article to news server:
    NNTPTransactionSemaphore = tsPostRequest
    ArticleToPost = Header & vbCrLf & ArticleBodyText
    Winsock1.SendData "POST" & vbCrLf
  End If

End Sub
```

```
Private Sub Winsock1_Close()
    Winsock1.Close
    NewsGroupsEnabled = False
    MessageHeadersEnabled = False
    mnuDisconnect.Enabled = False
    mnuGetNewsgroups.Enabled = False
    mnuPost.Enabled = False
    tbToolbar.Buttons("btnDisconnect").Enabled = False
    tbToolbar.Buttons("btnGetGroups").Enabled = False
    tbToolbar.Buttons("btnPost").Enabled = False
    Do
        sbNNTPStatus.Panels(1).Text = _
            WinsockStateString(Winsock1.State)
        DoEvents
        Loop Until Winsock1.State = sckClosed
    mnuConnect.Enabled = True
    tbToolbar.Buttons("btnConnect").Enabled = True
    End Sub

Private Sub Winsock1_Connect()
    Do
        sbNNTPStatus.Panels(1).Text = _
            WinsockStateString(Winsock1.State)
        DoEvents
        Loop Until (NNTPTransactionSemaphore = tsConnected) Or _
                   (NNTPTransactionSemaphore = tsNone)
    If NNTPTransactionSemaphore = tsConnected Then
        sbNNTPStatus.Panels(1).Text = "Connected"
        NewsGroupsEnabled = True
        mnuConnect.Enabled = False
        mnuDisconnect.Enabled = True
        mnuGetNewsgroups.Enabled = True
        tbToolbar.Buttons("btnConnect").Enabled = False
        tbToolbar.Buttons("btnDisconnect").Enabled = True
        tbToolbar.Buttons("btnGetGroups").Enabled = True
      Else
        mnuConnect.Enabled = True
        tbToolbar.Buttons("btnConnect").Enabled = True
      End If
    End Sub

Private Sub Winsock1_ConnectionRequest(ByVal requestID As Long)
    sbNNTPStatus.Panels(1).Text = "Connection Request"
    End Sub
```

```
Private Sub Winsock1_DataArrival(ByVal bytesTotal As Long)
    Dim OutputData As String
    Dim CrLfPosition As Long
    Dim MessageCount As String
    Dim FirstMessageNumber As String
    Dim LastMessageNumber As String
    Dim ResponseString As String
    Dim ResponseCode As Integer

    Winsock1.GetData OutputData
    If Not ReceivingData Then
        CrLfPosition = InStr(OutputData, vbCrLf)
        If CrLfPosition > 0 Then
            ResponseString = Left(OutputData, CrLfPosition - 1)
            OutputData = Mid(OutputData, CrLfPosition + 2)
          Else
            ResponseString = OutputData
          End If
        sbNNTPStatus.Panels(2).Text = ResponseString
        ResponseCode = CInt(GetWordFrom(ResponseString))
      End If
    Select Case NNTPTransactionSemaphore
      Case tsConnect
        If ResponseCode = 480 Then
            NNTPTransactionSemaphore = tsAuthorizing
            Winsock1.SendData "AUTHINFO USER " & _
                              Trim(ConnectionInfo.Username) & _
                              vbCrLf
          ElseIf (ResponseCode = 200) Or (ResponseCode = 201) Then
            NNTPTransactionSemaphore = tsConnected
          Else
            NNTPTransactionSemaphore = tsNone
          End If
      Case tsAuthorizing
        If ResponseCode = 381 Then
            NNTPTransactionSemaphore = tsAuthorizationResponse
            Winsock1.SendData "AUTHINFO PASS " & _
                              Trim(ConnectionInfo.Password) & _
                              vbCrLf
          Else
            NNTPTransactionSemaphore = tsNone
          End If
      Case tsAuthorizationResponse
        If ResponseCode = 281 Then
            NNTPTransactionSemaphore = tsConnected
```

```
        Else
          NNTPTransactionSemaphore = tsNone
        End If
    Case tsListGroups
      ReceivingData = True
      NewsGroupsEnabled = False
      Me.MousePointer = vbHourglass
      ConvertGroupsTextToDatabaseRecords OutputData
      NewsGroupsEnabled = True
      Me.MousePointer = vbDefault
    Case tsSelectGroup
      mnuPost.Enabled = False
      tbToolbar.Buttons("btnPost").Enabled = False
      Me.MousePointer = vbHourglass
      If ResponseCode = 211 Then
          NNTPTransactionSemaphore = tsListArticles
          GetGroupInfo ResponseString, MessageCount, _
                       FirstMessageNumber, LastMessageNumber
          Winsock1.SendData "XHDR subject " & _
                            Trim(FirstMessageNumber) & _
                            "-" & Trim(LastMessageNumber) & _
                            vbCrLf
        End If
      lvwMessageHeaders.Enabled = True
      Me.MousePointer = vbDefault
      mnuPost.Enabled = True
      tbToolbar.Buttons("btnPost").Enabled = True
    Case tsListArticles
      ReceivingData = True
      MessageHeadersEnabled = False
      UpdateMessageHeaderList lvwMessageHeaders, _
          OutputData, tsGetArticleHeaderSubjects
      MessageHeadersEnabled = True
    Case tsGetArticleByNumber
      ReceivingData = True
      txtMessage.Text = txtMessage.Text & OutputData
    Case tsPostRequest
      If ResponseCode = 340 Then
          mnuPost.Enabled = False
          tbToolbar.Buttons("btnPost").Enabled = False
          NNTPTransactionSemaphore = tsSubmitArticleForPosting
          Winsock1.SendData ArticleToPost
        End If
    Case tsSubmitArticleForPosting
      mnuPost.Enabled = True
```

```
        tbToolbar.Buttons("btnPost").Enabled = True
        NNTPTransactionSemaphore = tsNone
      Case Else
        txtMessage.Text = txtMessage.Text & OutputData
      End Select
    If Right(OutputData, 3) = "." & vbCrLf Then
        sbNNTPStatus.Panels(1).Text = "Request Complete"
        NNTPTransactionSemaphore = tsDone
        ReceivingData = False
      End If
    End Sub

Private Sub Winsock1_Error(ByVal Number As Integer, _
     Description As String, ByVal Scode As Long, _
     ByVal Source As String, ByVal HelpFile As String, _
     ByVal HelpContext As Long, CancelDisplay As Boolean)
    sbNNTPStatus.Panels(1).Text = "Error"
    End Sub

Private Sub Winsock1_SendComplete()
    sbNNTPStatus.Panels(1).Text = "Send Complete"
    End Sub

Private Sub Winsock1_SendProgress(ByVal bytesSent As Long, _
     ByVal bytesRemaining As Long)
    sbNNTPStatus.Panels(1).Text = CStr(bytesSent) & " Bytes Sent"
    End Sub

Public Function WinsockStateString(WinsockState As Integer) As String
    Select Case WinsockState
      Case sckClosed
        WinsockStateString = "Closed"
      Case sckClosing
        WinsockStateString = "Closing"
      Case sckConnected
        WinsockStateString = "Connected"
      Case sckConnecting
        WinsockStateString = "Connecting"
      Case sckConnectionPending
        WinsockStateString = "Connection Pending"
      Case sckHostResolved
        WinsockStateString = "Host Resolved"
      Case sckError
        WinsockStateString = "Error"
```

```
    Case sckListening
      WinsockStateString = "Listening"
    Case sckResolvingHost
      WinsockStateString = "Resolving Host"
    Case sckOpen
      WinsockStateString = "Open"
    Case Else
      WinsockStateString = "Unknown State"
    End Select
  End Function


Public Sub PerformSearchStringAnalysis()
    Dim ListItem As ListItem
    Dim DocumentAnalyst As clsDocumentAnalyst
    Dim FailsMatch As Boolean
    Dim ItemsToRemove As New Collection

    NewsGroupsEnabled = False
    MessageHeadersEnabled = False
    mnuDisconnect.Enabled = False
    mnuGetNewsgroups.Enabled = False
    mnuPost.Enabled = False
    tbToolbar.Buttons("btnDisconnect").Enabled = False
    tbToolbar.Buttons("btnGetGroups").Enabled = False
    tbToolbar.Buttons("btnPost").Enabled = False
    Me.MousePointer = vbHourglass

    Set DocumentAnalyst = New clsDocumentAnalyst
    DocumentAnalyst.Init txtSearchString.Text
    For Each ListItem In lvwMessageHeaders.ListItems
        If optFilterBody Then
            NNTPTransactionSemaphore = tsGetArticleByNumber
            txtMessage.Text = ""
            Winsock1.SendData "ARTICLE " & Trim(ListItem.Text) & _
                 vbCrLf
            Do
                DoEvents
                Loop Until NNTPTransactionSemaphore = tsDone
            FailsMatch = _
                Not DocumentAnalyst.DocumentMatches(txtMessage.Text)
          Else
            FailsMatch = Not DocumentAnalyst.DocumentMatches( _
                       ListItem.SubItems(1))
          End If
```

```
        If FailsMatch Then
            ItemsToRemove.Add ListItem
          End If
        Next ListItem
    For Each ListItem In ItemsToRemove
        lvwMessageHeaders.ListItems.Remove ListItem.Key
        Next ListItem
    txtMessage.Text = ""

    NewsGroupsEnabled = True
    MessageHeadersEnabled = True
    mnuDisconnect.Enabled = True
    mnuGetNewsgroups.Enabled = True
    mnuPost.Enabled = True
    tbToolbar.Buttons("btnDisconnect").Enabled = True
    tbToolbar.Buttons("btnGetGroups").Enabled = True
    tbToolbar.Buttons("btnPost").Enabled = True
    Me.MousePointer = vbDefault
    End Sub
```

The Connection Information Form

The general procedure **ConnectToNewsServer()** in the form module frmNews Reader.FRM opens and displays a modal form called frmConnectionInfo.FRM (shown in Figure 6.2). The code for **frmConnectionInfo**, shown in Listing 6.12, is simple. Since the form does nothing but gather information for the main form module, **frmConnectionInfo** does nothing but manage its own disappearance.

Listing 6.12 The complete listing of frmConnectionInfo.FRM from the project NewsReader.VBP.

```
Option Explicit

Private Sub cmdCancel_Click()
    txtServer.Text = ""
    Me.Hide
    End Sub

Private Sub cmdConnect_Click()
    Me.Hide
    End Sub

Private Sub Form_QueryUnload(Cancel As Integer, _
                             UnloadMode As Integer)
```

```
    If (UnloadMode = vbFormControlMenu) Then
        Cancel = True
        Call cmdCancel_Click
      End If

    End Sub
```

The Article Posting Form

Similar to **frmConnectionInfo**, the code for the form **frmPostNewArticle**, shown in Listing 6.13, deals primarily with closing the form, with one exception: This form is resizable, which means that it needs code in the **Form_Resize()** event procedure to properly arrange and scale its controls.

Listing 6.13 The complete listing of frmPostNewArticle.FRM from the project NewsReader.VBP.

```
Option Explicit

Const FormSpace = 30

Private Sub cmdCancel_Click()
    txtNewsGroup.Text = ""
    Me.Hide
    End Sub

Private Sub cmdPost_Click()
    Me.Hide
    End Sub

Private Sub Form_QueryUnload(Cancel As Integer, _
                            UnloadMode As Integer)
    If (UnloadMode = vbFormControlMenu) Then
        Cancel = True
        Call cmdCancel_Click
      End If
    End Sub

Private Sub Form_Resize()

    If Me.WindowState = vbMinimized Then
        Exit Sub
      End If
```

```
    If Me.ScaleWidth < (txtNewsGroup.Left + 500) Then
        Me.Width = txtNewsGroup.Left + 500 + _
            (Me.Width - Me.ScaleWidth)
      End If
    If (Me.ScaleHeight < (txtArticleBody.Top + 500 + _
          cmdPost.Height + 2 * FormSpace)) Then
        Me.Height = txtArticleBody.Top + 500 + _
            cmdPost.Height + 2 * FormSpace + _
            (Me.Height - Me.ScaleHeight)
      End If

    txtNewsGroup.Width = Me.ScaleWidth - _
        (txtNewsGroup.Left + FormSpace)
    txtSubject.Left = txtNewsGroup.Left
    txtSubject.Width = txtNewsGroup.Width
    txtArticleBody.Left = FormSpace
    txtArticleBody.Width = Me.ScaleWidth - _
        (txtArticleBody.Left + 2 * FormSpace)
    txtArticleBody.Height = Me.ScaleHeight - _
        (txtArticleBody.Top + cmdPost.Height + 100 + FormSpace)
    cmdPost.Left = Me.ScaleWidth - _
        (cmdPost.Width + cmdCancel.Width + 100 + FormSpace)
    cmdPost.Top = Me.ScaleHeight - (cmdPost.Height + FormSpace)
    cmdCancel.Left = cmdPost.Left + cmdPost.Width + 100
    cmdCancel.Top = cmdPost.Top
    End Sub
```

Utility Functions

This project uses a simple code module called HandyStuff.BAS, shown in Listing 6.14, that contains only two minor functions: **MinLong()** and **MaxLong()**.

Listing 6.14 The complete listing of HandyStuff.BAS from the project NewsReader.VBP.

```
Option Explicit


Public Function MinLong(A As Long, B As Long) As Long
    If A < B Then
        MinLong = A
      Else
        MinLong = B
      End If
    End Function
```

```
Public Function MaxLong(A As Long, B As Long) As Long
    If A > B Then
        MaxLong = A
      Else
        MaxLong = B
      End If
    End Function
```

Tame The Internet Document Jungle

Although the Internet doesn't quite live up to one huge corporation's characterization (no, not Microsoft) as "the sum total of all human knowledge," it is becoming a formidable repository. Unfortunately, while the promise of online information is accessibility, the curse is chaotic abundance. In the projects in this chapter, and in Chapters 3, 4, and 5, we've explored technologies that can help us cope with the enormous amount of information pouring onto the Internet. Now you can combine your knowledge of Internet protocols with your own custom version of the Visual Basic Document Analyst to create new utilities that harvest valuable crops from the information jungle.

HIGH PERFORMANCE

No-Fear CGI

CHAPTER 7

What? You say you've got megabytes of valuable data just snoozing on your hard drive? Turn bits into bucks by using VB to build database-driven Web sites that dynamically format and display information on demand.

No-Fear CGI

Publishing on the Web is about more than cool graphics and hot HTML. It's about providing information, and a lot of that information lives in organized collections known as databases. Some databases are large, making it impractical to just pour their contents into pre-formatted HTML documents. It makes more sense to enable users to request information directly from the database, displaying the results in their browsers.

In its original form, the Web was designed as a hyperlinked publishing medium with no information exchange between servers and users other than requests for documents in the form of URLs. But many Web publishers, especially those with commercial interests or those serving action committees or other organizations, realized that they needed a way to gather information from visitors to their sites. The *Common Gateway Interface*, or *CGI*, was created to provide a way for Web users to exchange information with Web servers.

CGI Fundamentals

A CGI application has three parts: a Web page that includes *form* tags, a Web server that implements CGI, and a CGI *script* or program that performs the processing requested by the Web page.

Most Web servers—whether freeware, shareware, or way-expensive-ware—implement a CGI interface, and many now include a Windows-specific CGI that makes it simple to write VB programs that can dig into all kinds of other Windows goodies. The server's CGI performs two vital functions. First, it accepts data submitted from a Web form and passes it on to another external program for processing. It then accepts the results generated by that external process—usually some kind of HTML output—and transmits them back to the browser. The details of how the server accomplishes these tasks are irrelevant. If your server software implements Windows CGI, you can use it. If not—it's time to find another Web server. The rest is up to you.

Let's begin with HTML forms.

HTML Forms

Any Web page may contain a form. A Web form consists of a special series of tags that display one or more input fields and at least one *submit* button in the browser window. The user fills in the fields, then clicks the button to transmit the data to the server. The HTML document in Listing 7.1 contains a minimal form, consisting of a single data **<INPUT>** tag and a single submit **<INPUT>** tag. Figure 7.1 shows this form as it appears in Microsoft Internet Explorer 3.0.

Listing 7.1 A simple HTML form.

```
<HTML>
<HEAD>
<TITLE>Testing Windows CGI</TITLE>

</HEAD>
<BODY>
<H1>Testing Windows CGI</H1>
<HR>
<FORM ACTION="http://localhost/cgi-win/cgiexperiment2.exe" METHOD="POST">
<PRE>
Enter your name, please: <INPUT SIZE=35 NAME="visitorname">

<INPUT TYPE="submit" VALUE="Submit It">
</PRE>
</FORM>
</BODY>
</HTML>
```

The most important ingredients between the **<FORM>** tags are the **<INPUT>** tags, which gather data from the user. Any text placed between the **<FORM>** tags appears within the browser just as it would appear outside the form section. The text within a form section typically labels the various input fields.

The **<FORM>** tag in this example has two attributes, **ACTION** and **METHOD**. **ACTION** specifies the URL of the script or application program that will process the data once it has been transmitted to the server. The URL you see here specifies a VB program called CGIExperiment2.EXE, which is stored in the /CGI-WIN/ or /CGI-BIN/ subdirectory under the Web server's base directory. **METHOD** specifies the means by which the data transfer will take place, either **GET** or **POST**. The **GET** method causes the browser to transmit the field values to the server by appending them to a URL. The server then passes the data on to the CGI program as a

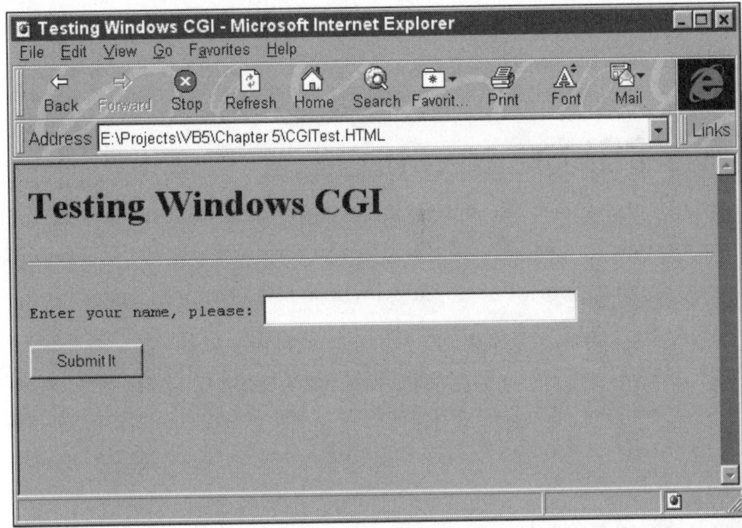

Figure 7.1

A simple HTML form in Microsoft Internet Explorer 3.0.

command line argument, which the CGI program must parse and interpret. The **POST** method, on the other hand, places the data in a separate file. The server then passes only the filename to the CGI program, which reads data from the file as needed. One popular site that uses the **GET** method is Digital's AltaVista Search service. When I entered the relatively short search string of "CGI and Windows" on AltaVista, the form constructed the following URL:

```
http://www.altavista.digital.com/cgi-bin/
query?pg=q&what=web&fmt=.&q=Windows+and+CGI
```

This URL instructs the AltaVista Web server to run the query script (which could be either a CGI macro script or a CGI program), with the remainder of the URL as its command line argument. The question mark separates the data section from the script or program name. Notice that the remainder of the string consists of *name=value* pairs, separated by ampersands (&). Each input field on the form—except for the submit button—generates a *name=value* pair. For data transmissions of any significant size, these URLs can become pretty long—so long, in fact, that some Web servers will choke on them. CGI requests sent with the **POST** method, however, do not modify the URL at all. A typical **POST** URL will end with the name of the CGI program:

```
http://localhost/cgi-win/cgiexperiment2.exe
```

For most purposes, the **POST** method is easier to deal with in the CGI program and less likely to overwhelm the server.

Windows CGI Programming

When a server that supports Windows CGI receives data with the **POST** method, it writes a temporary Windows INI file and places most of the name=value pairs in a section called [Form Literal]. For any field whose contents are larger than 255 characters, it stores the data in an external file, placing the filename in a section of the INI file called [Form External]. CGI also returns a number of standard variables that provide information about the client, the server, and the CGI request. These appear in the section [CGI] in the same INI file. Four other sections handle such things as extra headers, uploaded files, and huge fields (fields containing data that exceeds 65,536 characters). The name=value pairs are pulled from the INI file with the standard Windows API function **GetPrivateProfileString**(). With just a little effort, we could write a VB code module that acts as a framework for any VB CGI program. Our module would need to provide functions that retrieved field information and CGI standard variables and a procedure that enabled us to send responses back through the server to the client browser. Fortunately, programmer Robert Denny has already written a module that encapsulates all this functionality: CGI32.BAS, which is available as part of O'Reilly & Associates WebSite Web server software package. There's plenty of information about CGI32.BAS on the Web: by searching on "CGI32.BAS", you can download a copy of the code module and read articles about how to use it.

Let's implement a simple program called CGIExperiment2.EXE, to perform the processing for the CGI request made in the HTML document shown in Listing 7.1.

A Simple CGI Program

A VB program that serves as a CGI script includes no forms, and it must be compiled to an EXE, either native or p-code. The need to compile complicates the debugging process, but the Web server cannot run a VB program in the VB development environment.

Since formless VB projects must have a **Sub Main**() procedure, you might expect that to be the first thing we would need to implement. However, CGI32.BAS already contains a **Sub Main**(), which in turn calls a procedure called **CGI_Main**().

That's where we come in. The **Main()** procedure in CGI32.BAS performs all the initialization tasks such as retrieving the CGI standard variables, after which it turns control over to **CGI_Main()** for the program's main business.

Excluding CGI32.BAS—which is somewhat lengthy and complex—the entire program CGIExperiment2 appears in Listing 7.2.

Listing 7.2 CGIExperiment2.BAS.

```
Option Explicit

Public Sub CGI_Main()
    Send "Content-type: text/html"
    Send ""
    Send "<TITLE>Welcome to VB5 CGI!</TITLE>"
    Send "<H1>Welcome to VB5 CGI, " & GetSmallField("visitorname") & _
        "!</H1>"
    End Sub

Public Sub Inter_Main()
    MsgBox "This CGI program must be run within a Web browser."
    End Sub
```

It's almost embarrassingly simple. This program calls one procedure and one function from CGI32.BAS, **Sub Send()** and **Function GetSmallField()**. The **Send()** procedure works like a Print statement that sends its output to the browser, effectively spitting out HTML on the fly. The function **GetSmallField()** reads the value from the specified name=value pair in the [Form Literal] section of the temporary CGI INI file. If you look at the HTML document in Listing 7.1, you'll see that the **NAME** attribute in the first **<INPUT>** tag is set to "visitorname," which is the name of the field. **GetSmallField()** will return whatever the user typed into that input field on the form.

Besides **CGI_Main()**, CGI32.BAS expects to find one other standard procedure, **Inter_Main()**. It calls this procedure whenever the program is invoked directly (from the Windows Explorer, for example), without any command-line arguments. Usually, this procedure just displays a message box that reminds the user that the program is a CGI application and should be activated by a Web server. However, you may wish to provide an interactive front-end to your CGI application to perform routine database updates and content management. You'll soon see how you can build a VB application that manages and delivers an entire Web site without external HTML document files.

To run this program, compile and save it into the /CGI-WIN/ or /CGI-BIN/ subdirectory of your Web server. Then, with the server running, activate your Web browser and open the document file shown in Listing 7.1. You may need to modify the URL assigned to the **ACTION** attribute in the **<FORM>** tag to specify the correct subdirectory for the EXE file. When you click the Submit It button, the server will load the program. If all goes well, it will return a Web page that looks something like the one shown in Figure 7.2.

Who Needs Document Files?

By sticking with the **POST** method, we can take advantage of a little trick that will enable us to do away with HTML document files entirely. Instead, we'll embed the entire Web form and its response within a single VB executable file.

The default form method is **GET**, so the CGI standard variable **CGI_RequestMethod** will contain the value "**GET**" when you activate a CGI program from outside a form, with a direct HTTP query. If you always use the **POST** method to submit form data to the server (by setting the **<FORM>** tag's **METHOD** attribute to **POST**), you can check the contents of **CGI_RequestMethod** to determine whether the program was called from within a form (**POST**) or by a direct request to its URL (**GET**).

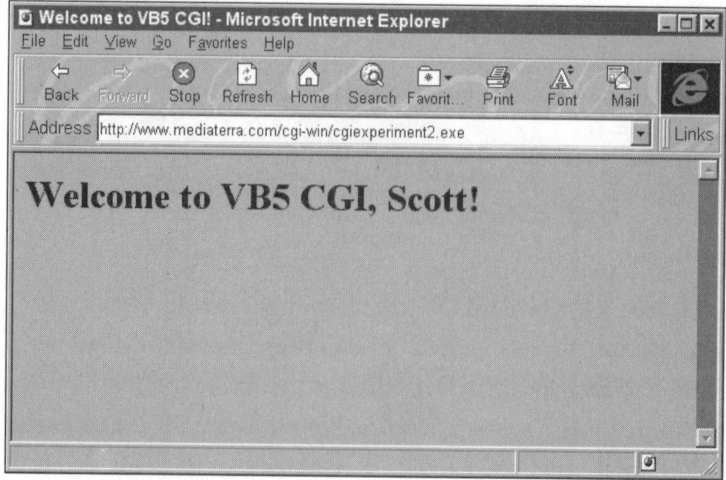

Figure 7.2
The Web page returned by CGIExperiment2.EXE.

The program shown in Listing 7.2 uses this technique to generate either the original Web page with its form or to provide the response to the form.

Listing 7.2 CGIExperiment3.BAS.

```
Option Explicit

Public Sub CGI_Main()
    Dim sName As String

    If Not (CGI_RequestMethod = "GET") Then
        sName = GetSmallField("visitorname")
        Send "Content-type: text/html"
        Send ""
        Send "<HTML>"
        Send "<HEAD>"
        Send "<TITLE>A VB5, CGI Experiment</TITLE>"
        Send "</HEAD>"
        Send "<BODY>"
        Send "<H1>A VB5, CGI Experiment</H1>"
        Send "Hey " & sName & "!"
        Send "</BODY>"
        Send "</HTML>"
      Else
        Send "Content-type: text/html"
        Send ""
        Send "<HTML>"
        Send "<HEAD>"
        Send "<TITLE>A Simple Test Form</TITLE>"
        Send "</HEAD>"
        Send "<BODY>"
        Send "<H1>Forms Processing With Visual Basic 5.0</H1>"
        Send "<HR>"
        Send "This is a test application, which will submit"
        Send "data to a Visual Basic application running on"
        Send "the server. We will begin with an out-of-process"
        Send "executable (.EXE), which will be a VB program with"
        Send "no forms."
        Send "<FORM ACTION=""CGIExperiment3.exe"" METHOD=""POST"">"
        Send "<PRE>"
        Send "Name: <INPUT SIZE=25 NAME=""visitorname"">"
        Send ""
        Send "</PRE>"
        Send "<INPUT TYPE=""submit"" VALUE=""Go Ahead"">"
        Send "<HR>"
        Send "</FORM>"
```

```
        Send "</BODY>"
        Send "</HTML>"

      End If
    End Sub

Public Sub Inter_Main()
    MsgBox "This is a CGI program."
    End Sub
```

When you activate this CGI program by entering its URL into your Web browser, you should see the page shown in Figure 7.3.

After you enter your name into the **INPUT** field and click Go Ahead, the browser should display the page shown in Figure 7.4.

Building Web Forms

Web forms are simply Web pages that include a pair of **<FORM>** tags and one or more <INPUT>, <SELECT>, or <TEXTAREA> tags. We've already discussed the

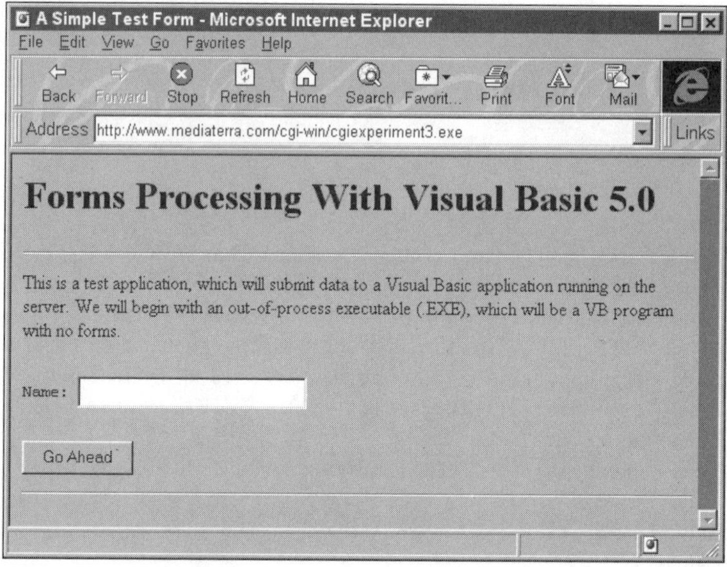

Figure 7.3
The default Web page displayed by CGIExperiment3.EXE.

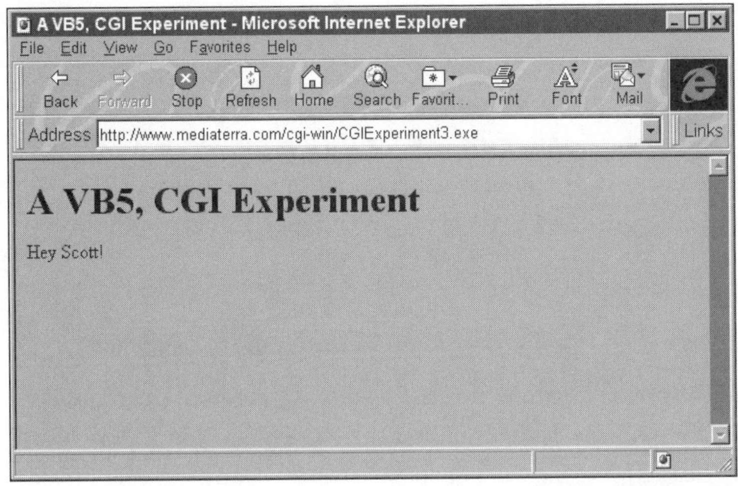

Figure 7.4
The Web page displayed after a form request.

two attributes of the <FORM> tag, **ACTION** and **METHOD**. Now let's look more closely at the tags that create data entry fields.

The <INPUT> Tag

The <INPUT> tag supports eight attributes:

- **ALIGN**
- **CHECKED**
- **MAXLENGTH**
- **NAME**
- **SIZE**
- **SRC**
- **TYPE**
- **VALUE**

The TYPE attribute specifies which type of input field to display: **TEXT, PASSWORD**, **CHECKBOX**, **RADIO**, **HIDDEN**, **IMAGE**, **SUBMIT**, or **RESET**. If you omit the **TYPE** attribute, the input type defaults to **TEXT**, as shown in Listing 7.1

and Figure 7.1. The only required attribute is **NAME**, which supplies the only means by which CGI can identify the data collected in the input fields. The value of the NAME attribute may be any string, but it's best to avoid spaces and most punctuation marks—they can confuse the server when it parses the fields. Using underscore characters is one way to represent spaces (*e.g.,* "my_data_field"). The functions of most of the other attributes depend on which input **TYPE** is specified.

Input Type TEXT

The **TEXT** input type supports just four of the input tag's attributes.

The **NAME** attribute identifies the field to the CGI script or program. For example, if you specifiy **NAME="lastname"** and the user enters "Jones", the [Form Literal] section of the CGI INI file will contain the name=value pair lastname=Jones.

The **SIZE** attribute specifies the width of the input field in characters as it should appear in the user's Web browser. If **SIZE** is omitted, the field defaults to the width of the browser window.

The **MAXLENGTH** attribute specifies the maximum number of characters that the field should accept as input from the user. If you omit **MAXLENGTH**, the field will accept an unlimited number of characters. It's usually a good idea to set both the **SIZE** and **MAXLENGTH** attributes to meaningful values, according to the data element represented by the text input field. It wouldn't make sense, for example, to allow a screen-width field of indefinite input length for a state abbreviation or a zip code. Users often receive visual cues from the graphical appearance of data entry fields. We tend to see addresses in a few common forms, with longer lines for names and street information, followed by shorter lines for city, state, and zip code. When these fields are sized and arranged aribitrarily, it's easy for the user to become confused and enter information into the wrong spaces. Use the **SIZE** and **MAXLENGTH** attributes—along with sensible layout—to develop comfortable and familiar form designs.

If you wish to provide an initial value—also known as a *default* value—in the input field, assign it to the **VALUE** attribute. Whatever **VALUE** you supply will appear in the text input field when the form is displayed in the browser. The user may then override that value by typing a replacement entry, or skip the field to accept the default.

Input Type PASSWORD

The **PASSWORD** input type works just like the **TEXT** input type, with one exception: Instead of displaying the user's actual entry, it substitutes an asterisk for each character. The string supplied to the CGI program will contain the actual value typed by the user. The asterisks just provide a minimal form of security against over-the-shoulder snoops. Beware, however, that **PASSWORD** fields are not encrypted. Once the data leaves the browser—unless the browser and server are engaged in a secure connection—the contents of the **PASSWORD** field travel in undisguised form across the Internet and through the destination server to the CGI program.

Input Type CHECKBOX

Like yes-or-no questions, checkboxes enable users to select individual items. The **CHECKBOX** input type displays nothing other than the checkbox itself—literally a small square box—either empty or containing an X. Like all other **INPUT** fields, checkboxes only become meaningful to the user when they are properly labeled. Along with **NAME**, the **CHECKBOX** input type accepts two other attributes.

The simplest type of **CHECKBOX** includes no attributes. If the box is checked, the form will submit a name=value pair to the server containing the value "on." If unchecked, the server will receive no name=value pair for the field.

To change the value in the name=value pair for a selected **CHECKBOX**, set the VALUE attribute to the string you want submitted to the server.

If you wish the **CHECKBOX** to be checked by default—that is, when the form is first activated in the browser—include the **CHECKED** attribute in its <INPUT> tag.

Checkboxes are useful when you want to enable the user to select several items from a list of choices. For example, you may wish to ask the user to identify his or her favorite types of music, as shown in Listing 7.3 and Figure 7.5.

Listing 7.3 Using the CHECKBOX type of the form <INPUT> tag.

```
<FORM>
What kinds of music do you listen to regularly?
<P>
<INPUT TYPE=CHECKBOX NAME="musical_preferences" VALUE="rock"> Rock
<BR>
<INPUT TYPE=CHECKBOX NAME="musical_preferences" VALUE="pop"> Pop
<BR>
```

```
<INPUT TYPE=CHECKBOX NAME="musical_preferences" VALUE="country">
   Country
<BR>
<INPUT TYPE=CHECKBOX NAME="musical_preferences" VALUE="jazz"> Jazz
<BR>
<INPUT TYPE=CHECKBOX NAME="musical_preferences" VALUE="blues"> Blues
<BR>
<INPUT TYPE=CHECKBOX NAME="musical_preferences" VALUE="bluegrass">
   Bluegrass
<BR>
<INPUT TYPE=CHECKBOX NAME="musical_preferences" VALUE="folk"> Folk
<BR>
<INPUT TYPE=CHECKBOX NAME="musical_preferences" VALUE="worldbeat">
   World Beat
</FORM>
```

Input Type RADIO

While radio buttons may superficially resemble checkboxes, they perform a distinctly different function. Within any group of radio buttons, the user may select only one at a time. Like **CHECKBOX**, **RADIO** supports the three attributes **NAME**, **VALUE**, and **CHECKED**, as shown in Listing 7.4 and Figure 7.6.

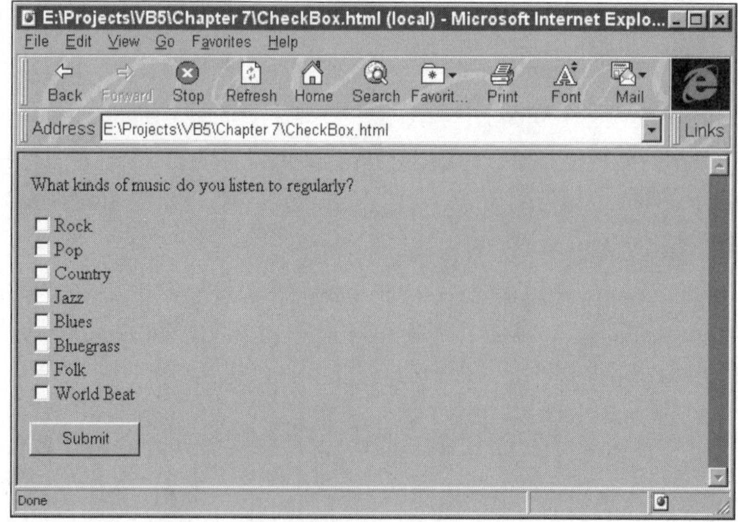

Figure 7.5
Checkboxes in action.

Listing 7.4 Using the **RADIO** type of the form **<INPUT>** tag.

```
<FORM>
<PRE>
What is your approximate age?

Under 16 years <INPUT TYPE=RADIO NAME="age" VALUE="16">
   16-24 years <INPUT TYPE=RADIO NAME="age" VALUE="24">
   25-34 years <INPUT TYPE=RADIO NAME="age" VALUE="34">
   35-44 years <INPUT TYPE=RADIO NAME="age" VALUE="44">
 Over 44 years <INPUT TYPE=RADIO NAME="age" VALUE="45">

<INPUT TYPE=SUBMIT>
</FORM>
```

Input Type SUBMIT

When clicked by the user, a button defined with the **SUBMIT** input type causes the form to send all of its fields to the Web server. Every form must have a **SUBMIT** button, and **SUBMIT** supports two optional attributes.

The **VALUE** attribute specifies the caption of the **SUBMIT** button. The default caption is "Submit." You may also specify a **NAME** for the button. When you do so,

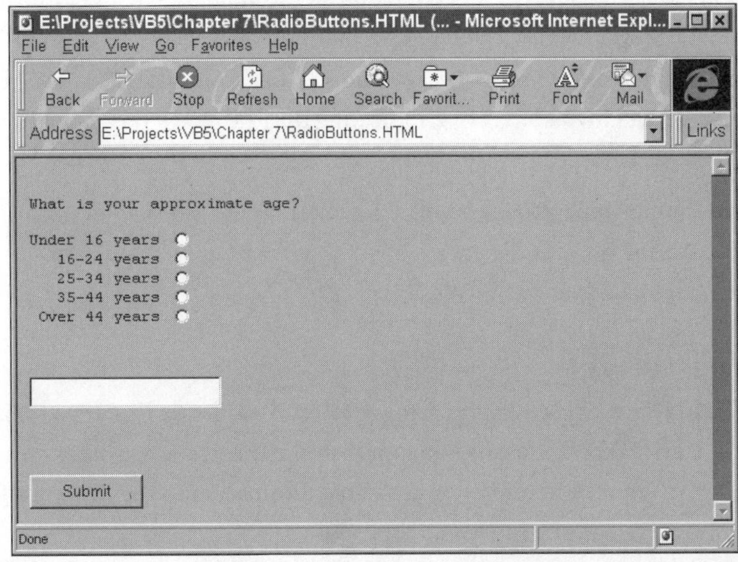

Figure 7.6
The **RADIO** type of the **<INPUT>** tag as it appears in Internet Explorer 3.0.

the form will transmit the caption specified in the **VALUE** attribute to the server. This can come in handy when you want to write a single CGI program that can process the contents of more than one form. The **SUBMIT** button can provide a unique identifier for each form.

Input Type RESET

The **RESET** button enables the user to clear the current form and start over. It never sends anything to the server and supports only the **VALUE** attribute, which simply defines an alternative caption to the default caption "Reset."

Input Type IMAGE

IMAGE buttons enable in-line images to act like **SUBMIT** buttons. **IMAGE** supports three attributes: **SRC**, **ALIGN**, and **NAME.** The **SRC** attribute specifies the URL of the image file that is to be displayed in the browser. The **ALIGN** attribute determines how the image should be aligned with adjacent text—just like any other in-line image—accepting any one of three values: **TOP**, **MIDDLE**, or **BOTTOM**. The **NAME** attribute can be used in the CGI program to identify which image has been clicked.The form will also send the mouse position as an offset from the top and left edges of the image. If a **NAME** has been specified, the name=value pairs for these coordinates will be identified in dotted notations. For example, if the **NAME** attribute is set to "mypicture", the coordinates might appear in the INI file as mypicture.x=25 and mypicture.y=73, indicating that the image was clicked at a point 25 pixels from its left edge and 73 pixels from its top.

The **IMAGE** input type provides a way for CGI applications to perform tasks as directed by clicking on various regions of an image, just as an in-line image with an image map can link to various URLs.

Input Type HIDDEN

The **HIDDEN** input type enables a form to send embedded information to the server. While **HIDDEN** fields do not appear to the user, they provide a convenient way to identify a form or to provide other static information to the server. **HIDDEN** fields can also serve an even more useful purpose.

Conventional CGI applications provide no sustained interaction between the user and the server. Each time the user submits a form, the browser connects to the server, sends its information, accepts a reply, and disconnects. If the application needs to carry on a dialog with the user, it needs some way to accumulate responses. One solution is to include **HIDDEN** fields in the response forms. If the user chooses to continue the interaction, the information gathered up to that point will be retransmitted with the next form submission. The server-side CGI application doesn't have to worry about retaining any information until the interaction has been completed, which prevents it from cluttering its database with fragments of numerous aborted sessions.

The <SELECT> Tag

When the number of items in your list of checkboxes or radio buttons gets out of hand, you may want to consider a selection list, which you can add to any CGI form with the <SELECT> tag. Figure 7.7 shows the <SELECT> tag in action.

The <SELECT> tag itself takes three attributes: **NAME**, **SIZE**, and **MULTIPLE**. Just as in any <INPUT> tag, you must specify a **NAME** for the field, identifying the data to the CGI program on the server. The optional **SIZE** attribute determines how many lines of the list will be visible, and defaults to one line. The **MULTIPLE** attribute enables the user to select two or more options simultaneously, like a series

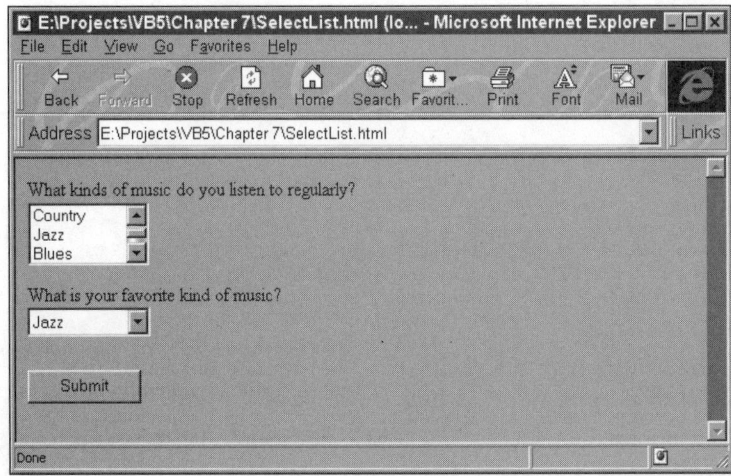

Figure 7.7
The **<SELECT>** tag builds a menu of options in a handy, compact drop-down list.

of checkboxes. Without the **MULTIPLE** attribute, the selection list acts like a group of radio buttons where only one option may be selected at a time. Listing 7.5 shows an example of how to use the **<SELECT>** and **<OPTION>** tags.

Listing 7.5 Using the **<SELECT>** and **<OPTION>** tags to build selection lists.

```
<FORM>
What kinds of music do you listen to regularly?
<BR>
<SELECT NAME="musical_preferences" MULTIPLE SIZE=3>
<OPTION>Rock
<OPTION>Pop
<OPTION>Country
<OPTION>Jazz
<OPTION>Blues
<OPTION>Bluegrass
<OPTION>Folk
<OPTION>World Beat
</SELECT>
<BR>
<BR>
What is your favorite kind of music?
<BR>
<SELECT NAME="musical_favorite">
<OPTION>Rock
<OPTION>Pop
<OPTION>Country
<OPTION>Jazz
<OPTION>Blues
<OPTION>Bluegrass
<OPTION>Folk
<OPTION>World Beat
</SELECT>
</FORM>
```

The only tag that may appear between the **<SELECT>** tags is the **<OPTION>** tag. Each **<OPTION>** tag adds a new item to the selection list. The **<OPTION>** tag supports two optional attributes. The **VALUE** attribute permits you to specify an alternative value to be returned to the server when the option is selected. If **VALUE** is omitted, the form returns the option text as its value. The **SELECTED** attribute permits you to specify a default selection, or multiple default selections if the **MULTIPLE** attribute is included in the **<SELECT>** tag.

The behavior and appearance of a selection list depends on the combination of attributes you have included in the <SELECT> tag. Without the **MULTIPLE** attribute—and with a **SIZE** of one (the default)—the list will appear as a popup menu. When **SIZE** is set to a value greater than one, or when the **MULTIPLE** attribute is present, the options will appear in a scrollable list.

Selection lists offer features similar to checkboxes and radio buttons, but require less space in the browser window, simplifying the HTML implementation.

The <TEXTAREA> Tag

While the input type **TEXT** accepts all text entry on a single line, the special tag <TEXTAREA> defines a rectangular text entry area that will accept multi-line text of virtually unlimited length—with vertical and horizontal scrollbars if necessary.

Along with the required **NAME** attribute, the <TEXTAREA> tag supports three additional attributes: **COLS**, **ROWS**, and **WRAP**. The supposedly optional **COLS** and **ROWS** attributes specify the height and width of the input field, as measured in characters. Beware! If you choose to omit these dimensions, be prepared for unpredictable results from the browser.

The optional **WRAP** attribute—which defaults to **OFF**—determines whether the text area field will perform automatic line breaks. Without **WRAP**, the text is broken into new lines only where the user enters a hard carriage return. The server will receive the text with embedded carriage return/line feed sequences (%0D%0A) at each hard line break. With **WRAP** set to **VIRTUAL**, the text will wrap automatically within the displayed area of the text entry field, but will be sent to the server with no line breaks except those entered explicitly by the user with the enter key. Virtual wrapping keeps the text from running off the right side of the text area but maintains its logical organization into contiguous paragraphs, just as in almost every word processing program. Finally, with **WRAP** set to **PHYSICAL**, the text wraps automatically to fit the displayed area and will be sent to the server with carriage return/line feed sequences after each wrapped line.

The <TEXTAREA> tag requires a closing tag. Any text placed between the tags becomes the default text and is displayed when the form first appears in the browser, as shown in Listing 7.6 and Figure 7.8. The user may modify or replace the default text before submitting the form to the server.

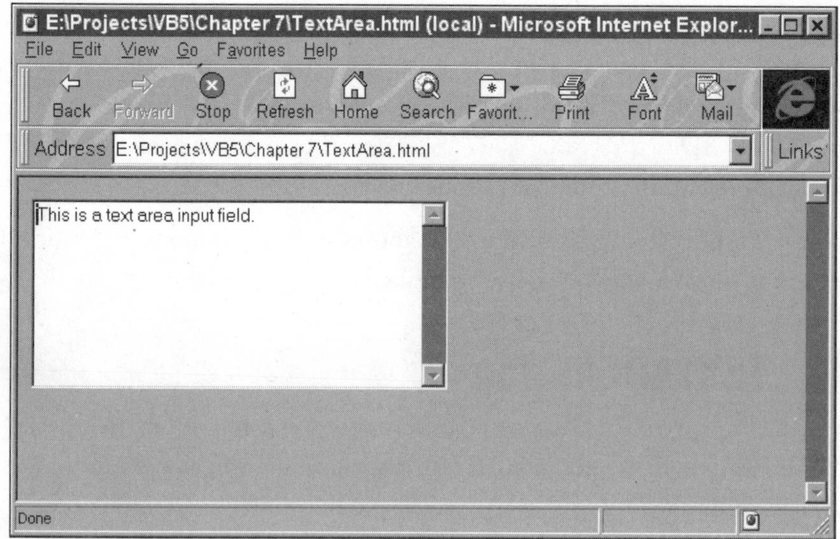

Figure 7.8
A multiple-line text entry field.

Listing 7.6 Defining a multiple-line text entry field.

```
<FORM>
<TEXTAREA COLS=45 ROWS=7 WRAP=VIRTUAL>This is a text area input field.
</TEXTAREA>
</FORM>
```

Testing Your Form

CGI32.BAS does such a fine job of retrieving and decoding CGI form fields and variables, we can use it to write a simple VB program that will help us test our forms. This program will send back an HTML document listing all of a form's data fields and their contents, along with all the standard CGI variables.

The procedure **CGI_Main()** in CGIFormTest.BAS begins by checking the request method. If the form used the **POST** method, the Web server will have translated its fields into an INI file. This allows CGI32.BAS to retrieve and store them in its arrays **CGI_FormTuples()**, **CGI_FileTuples()**, and **CGI_HugeTuples()**. To display them in the browser, we just step through the arrays, adding a few useful HTML formatting codes along the way. In particular, note the **<UL>** and **<LI>** tags, which format

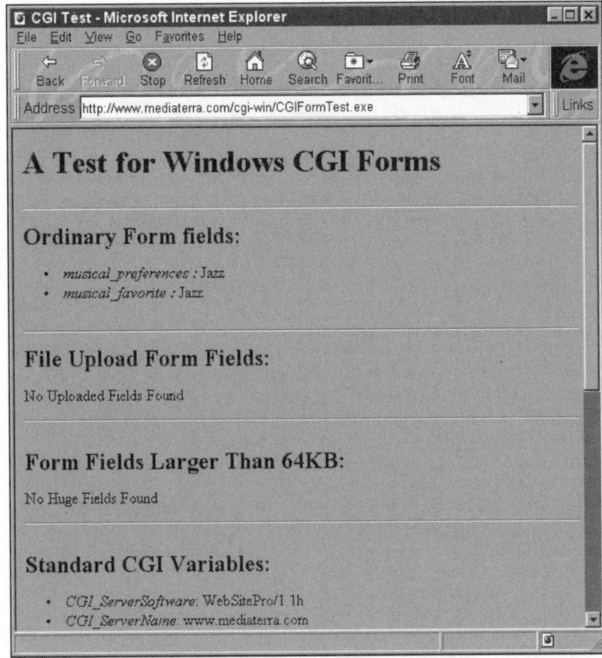

Figure 7.9

Displaying fields and CGI standard variables from a CGI form.

the output into an *unordered list*, as shown in Figure 7.9. The complete listing of CGIFormTest.BAS is shown in Listing 7.7.

To use this program, change the **ACTION** attribute of any <FORM> tag to "CGIFormTest.EXE." When you click the submission button, the browser will display a list of all the data fields received from the form.

Listing 7.7 The complete listing of CGIFormTest.BAS from the project CGIFormTest.VBP.

```
Option Explicit

Public Sub CGI_Main()
    Dim Counter As Integer

    If CGI_RequestMethod = "POST" Then
        Send "Content-type: text/html"
        Send ""
        Send "<HTML>"
        Send "<HEAD>"
```

```
Send "<TITLE>CGI Test</TITLE>"
Send "</HEAD>"
Send "<BODY>"
Send "<H1>A Test for Windows CGI Forms</H1>"
Send "<HR>"
Send "<H2>Ordinary Form fields:</H2>"
If CGI_NumFormTuples > 0 Then
    Send "<UL>"
    For Counter = 1 To CGI_NumFormTuples
        Send "<LI>"
        Send "<I>"
        Send CGI_FormTuples(Counter - 1).key
        Send ": </I>"
        Send CGI_FormTuples(Counter - 1).value
        Next Counter
    Send "</UL>"
  Else
    Send "No Fields Found"
  End If

Send "<HR>"
Send "<H2>File Upload Form Fields:</H2>"
If CGI_NumFileTuples > 0 Then
    Send "<UL>"
    For Counter = 1 To CGI_NumFileTuples
        Send "<LI>"
        Send "<I>"
        Send CGI_FileTuples(Counter - 1).key
        Send ": </I>"
        If CGI_FileTuples(Counter - 1).name <> "" Then
            Send "<code>"
            Send CGI_FileTuples(Counter - 1).name
            Send "</code>"
          Else
            Send "Filename Missing"
          End If
        Send "<UL>"
        Send "<LI>Tempfile: <code>" & CGI_FileTuples(Counter - _
              1).file & "</code>"
        Send "<LI>Content-length: " & CGI_FileTuples(Counter - _
              1).length
        Send "<LI>Content-type: " & CGI_FileTuples(Counter - _
              1).type
        Send "<LI>Content-transfer-encoding: " & _
          CGI_FileTuples(Counter - 1).encoding
        Send "</UL>"
        Next Counter
```

```
    Send "</UL>"
  Else
    Send "No Uploaded Fields Found"
  End If

Send "<HR>"
Send "<H2>Form Fields Larger Than 64KB:</H2>"
If CGI_NumHugeTuples > 0 Then
    Send "<UL>"
    For Counter = 1 To CGI_NumHugeTuples
        Send "<LI><I>"
        Send CGI_HugeTuples(Counter - 1).key
        Send ": </I>"
        Send "Offset="
        Send CStr(CGI_HugeTuples(Counter - 1).offset)
        Send ", Length="
        Send CStr(CGI_HugeTuples(Counter - 1).length)
    Next Counter
    Send "</UL>"
  Else
    Send "No Huge Fields Found"
  End If

Send "<HR>"
Send "<H2>Standard CGI Variables:</H2>"
Send "<UL>"
Send "<LI><I>CGI_ServerSoftware</I>: " & CGI_ServerSoftware
Send "<LI><I>CGI_ServerName</I>: " & CGI_ServerName
Send "<LI><I>CGI_ServerPort</I>: " & CStr(CGI_ServerPort)
Send "<LI><I>CGI_RequestProtocol</I>: " & CGI_RequestProtocol
Send "<LI><I>CGI_ServerAdmin</I>: " & CGI_ServerAdmin
Send "<LI><I>CGI_Version</I>: " & CGI_Version
Send "<LI><I>CGI_RequestMethod</I>: " & CGI_RequestMethod
Send "<LI><I>CGI_RequestKeepAlive</I>: " & _
       CStr(CGI_RequestKeepAlive)
Send "<LI><I>CGI_LogicalPath</I>: " & CGI_LogicalPath
Send "<LI><I>CGI_PhysicalPath</I>: " & CGI_PhysicalPath
Send "<LI><I>CGI_ExecutablePath</I>: " & CGI_ExecutablePath
Send "<LI><I>CGI_QueryString</I>: " & CGI_QueryString
Send "<LI><I>CGI_RequestRange</I>: " & CGI_RequestRange
Send "<LI><I>CGI_Referer</I>: " & CGI_Referer
Send "<LI><I>CGI_From</I>: " & CGI_From
Send "<LI><I>CGI_UserAgent</I>: " & CGI_UserAgent
Send "<LI><I>CGI_RemoteHost</I>: " & CGI_RemoteHost
Send "<LI><I>CGI_RemoteAddr</I>: " & CGI_RemoteAddr
Send "<LI><I>CGI_AuthUser</I>: " & CGI_AuthUser
Send "<LI><I>CGI_AuthPass</I>: " & CGI_AuthPass
```

```
        Send "<LI><I>CGI_AuthType</I>: " & CGI_AuthType
        Send "<LI><I>CGI_AuthRealm</I>: " & CGI_AuthRealm
        Send "<LI><I>CGI_ContentType</I>: " & CGI_ContentType
        Send "<LI><I>CGI_ContentLength</I>: " & CStr(CGI_ContentLength)
        Send "</BODY>"
        Send "</HTML>"
      Else
        Send "Content-type: text/html"
        Send ""
        Send "<HTML>"
        Send "<HEAD>"
        Send "<TITLE>CGI Test</TITLE>"
        Send "</HEAD>"
        Send "<BODY>"
        Send "<H1>This CGI Test Requires the POST Request Method</H1>"
        Send "</BODY>"
        Send "</HTML>"
      End If

    End Sub

Public Sub Inter_Main()
    MsgBox "This is a CGI application."
    End Sub
```

VB And The CGI Database Connection

CGI forms really become valuable when you hook them up to a database. After all, that's the whole point of CGI. And wouldn't you know, VB includes all kinds of support for database manipulation, including two complete database connectivity models: *Data Access Objects (DAO)* and *Remote Data Objects (RDO).*

RDO provides a uniform, object-based interface to a variety of database engines—including Microsoft SQL Server—in a *client/server* environment. Client/server technology permits an application running on a workstation to request data from a database engine running on a separate database server. With RDO, database-intense VB applications can offload some of their work onto the database server, which can often reduce network traffic, improve performance, and increase reliability.

DAO, on the other hand, provides an object interface to Microsoft's Access Database engine, also known as JET. The major disadvantage of the JET engine is that it does not support the client/server model. Although a JET database residing on a central file server may be accessed by multiple clients on the same local area network, each client must perform its own processing of the data—including index updates and searches. However, the DAO model does support features not found in most of the popular client/server database engines, including the ability to modify an existing data table on the fly. The other advantage of DAO is having the Access Database engine effectively built right into VB, making it possible to assemble CGI database applications with VB right out of the box. Since all the clients that need to access your database through the Web must pass through the Web server anyway, you could say that the Access database engine behaves in a client/server fashion: The Web browers are the clients, and the Web server with its Access-based CGI applications becomes the database server.

In the next project, we'll use the DAO to create, update, and search a simple database through a CGI front-end.

A Simple Database-Driven CGI Application

As in the previous project, this CGI application will contain both the user entry form and the document that displays the results in a single executable called CGIExperiment4.EXE. Once again, we'll use the request method to differentiate between the initial URL access to our Web page (shown in Figure 7.10) and the form submission.

Once it processes the form data, the program will return a document (shown in Figure 7.11) that acknowledges the person who has submitted his/her name on the greeting page.

Coding The CGI Database Experiment

The **CGI_Main()** procedure in CGIExperiment.BAS begins by calling the general procedure **OpenOrGenerateVisitorsDatabase()**, as shown in Listing 7.8. This procedure first checks whether the database already exists by calling the VB **Dir()** function:

```
If Len(Dir(App.Path & "\Visitors.mdb")) > 0 Then
```

If it does exist, it sets the global object variable **dbVisitorsDatabase** with a reference to the open database object:

```
Set dbVisitorsDatabase = OpenDatabase(App.Path & "\Visitors.mdb")
```

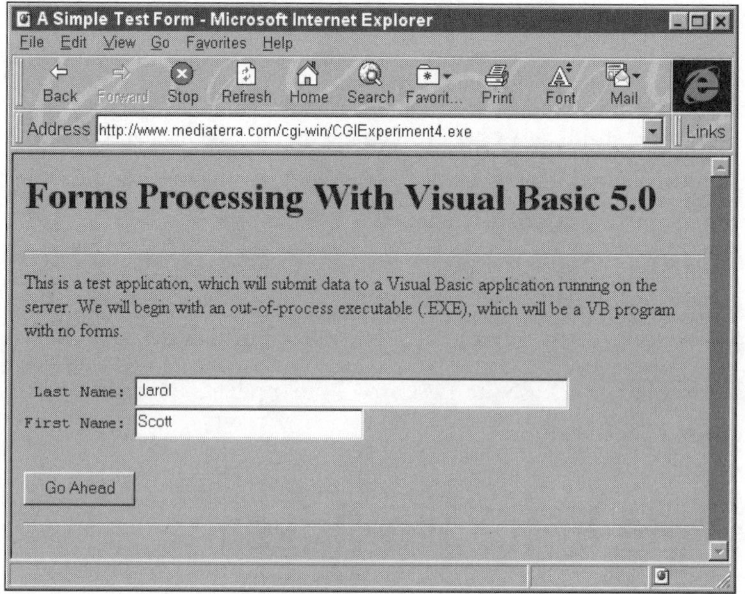

Figure 7.10

The form document associated with CGIExperiment4.EXE.

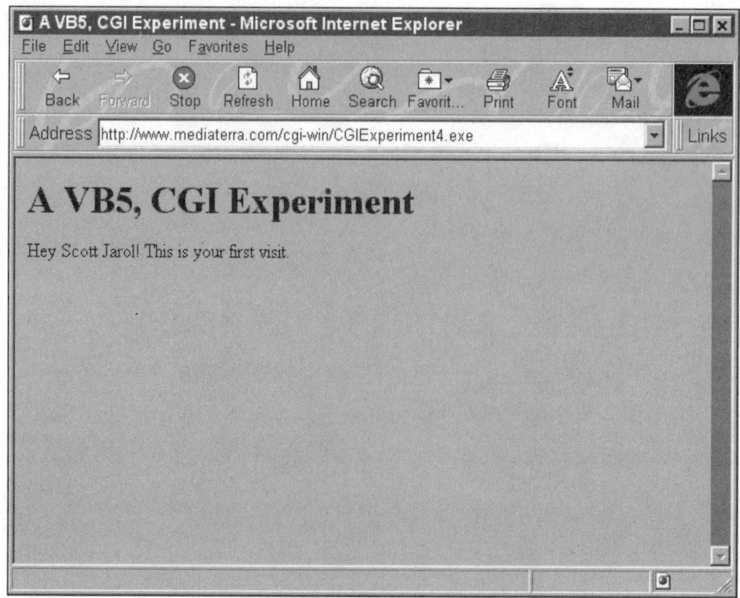

Figure 7.11

Users are recognized as new visitors or as previous visitors.

If it fails to detect the database file Visitors.MDB, it builds the database from DAO objects.

Constructing The Database

For most practical purposes, an Access database consists of a database file containing one or more table objects and their corresponding table definition objects. Each of these contains one or more fields, and one or more indexes. A database may also contain a few other types of objects such as query definitions and relations—which aren't relevant to our example.

To create a new Access database from within VB, we declare instances of the various objects, which we then assemble by appending them to their approriate parent objects. In **OpenOrGenerateVisitorsDatabase()**, we first declare an instance of a database residing in a file called Visitors.MDB. Then, using the database object's **CreateTableDef()** method, we declare an instance of the **TableDef** object called "Visitors." Once we've established a **TableDef** object, we can define and append its fields. In this example, I've declared a small array of field object references called **fldsVisitors()**. This enables us to use the **CreateField()** method of the **TableDef** object to instantiate each of three fields before adding them to the **TableDef's Fields** collection with its **Append()** method:

```
Set fldsVisitors(0) = tdVisitors.CreateField("LastName", dbText, 50)
Set fldsVisitors(1) = tdVisitors.CreateField("FirstName", dbText, 25)
Set fldsVisitors(2) = tdVisitors.CreateField("LastVisit", dbDate)
For Counter = 0 To 2
    tdVisitors.Fields.Append fldsVisitors(Counter)
    Next Counter
```

You could accomplish the same task with a single **Field** object variable by calling the **Fields.Append()** method after each call to the **CreateField()** method. For **TableDefs** with numerous fields, however, the technique of building an array of **Field** objects enables you to **Append()** all the fields to the **TableDef** in a compact **For** loop. This allows us to avoid a whole series of separate calls, one for each field. The **Visitors** table will have three fields: **LastName**, **FirstName**, and a date field called **LastVisit**.

Indexes enable us to traverse, display, and search the table in a particular order, based on the collating sequence of any combination of fields. We build an index much as we build the table itself, by declaring an instance of an **Index** object and appending fields to the index's **Fields** collection. But in this case, all the fields we append to an index object's **Fields** collection must already exist in the **TableDef**. We may also need to set certain properties for each index we declare. In this project, the **Primary** and **Unique** properties of **VisitorsIndex** are set to **True**. This designates the index as the default index for the table and indicates that the fields shared by the index must—for each entry in the table—combine to produce a unique *key*, or index value. In other words, if the index comprises more than one field—as in the **VisitorsIndex**—then two or more records may share common values for any individual field, as long as the combined values within each record result in a unique key. For example, the **Visitors** table may contain entries for two or more people with **LastName** "Smith," as long as each has a different **FirstName**. To create index fields, we call the Index object's **CreateField**() method, followed by the **Append**() method of the **Index.Fields** collection.

To finish the database definition, we need to complete two more assembly steps. First, we call the **Append**() method of the **TableDef's Indexes** collection, which adds the index **VisitorsIndex** to the **Visitors TableDef**. Finally, we call the **Append**() method of the database object's **TableDefs** collection to add the **Visitors TableDef** to the database object.

Here is a summary of the basic DAO database creation steps:

1. Declare an instance of a Database object.
2. Declare an instance of at least one **TableDef** object.
3. Declare instances of **Field** objects.
4. Append **Field** objects to the **TableDef**'s **Fields** collection.
5. Declare an instance of an **Index** object.
6. Declare instances of **Field** objects.
7. Append index **Field** objects to the **Index**'s **Fields** collection.
8. Append **Index** object to **Index**'s collection of the **TableDef** object.
9. Append **TableDef** object to **Database** object's **TableDefs** collection.
10. Close and reopen database before using it.

You could use Microsoft Access to build your databases, then just open them from within your VB programs. However, the practice of writing a procedure that builds the database from scratch assists in documenting your project by including a complete database definition within the application code. This technique also ensures that you can create a new, empty database whenever you wish—just delete the existing database and run the program, or install the program in a new directory.

Using The Database

The form section of the greeting document includes three **<INPUT>** tags. The first two accept input into two fields—Last Name and First Name—which are transferred to the CGI program under the names **lastname** and **firstname**, respectively. The third **<INPUT>** tag creates a submit button labeled "Go Ahead":

```
Send "<FORM ACTION=""CGIExperiment4.exe"" METHOD=""POST"">"
Send "<PRE>"
Send " Last Name: <INPUT SIZE=50 NAME=""lastname"">"
Send "First Name: <INPUT SIZE=25 NAME=""firstname"">"
Send ""
Send "</PRE>"
Send "<INPUT TYPE=""submit"" VALUE=""Go Ahead"">"
Send "<HR>"
Send "</FORM>"
```

When the user submits this form back to the server, it will use the **POST** method, causing the CGI program to execute the code in the **Else** clause that generates the response document.

Before it can do anything else, the program must open and prepare the database. We've already seen how **OpenOrGenerateVisitorsDatabase()** opens an existing database or creates a new one. The last part of this procedure uses the **OpenRecordset()** method of the Database object to set the global **RecordSet** object variable **rsVisitors** with a reference to the **Visitors** table. It then sets the **Index** property of **rsVisitors** to **VisitorsIndex**, making it the current index for all **Seek** operations:

```
Set rsVisitors = dbVisitorsDatabase.OpenRecordset("Visitors")
rsVisitors.Index = "VisitorsIndex"
```

With the database open and **rsVisitors** instantiated, we can begin processing updates and inquiries. This couldn't get much easier. We just call the **Seek()** method of the **Recordset** object:

```
rsVisitors.Seek "=", sLastName, sFirstName
```

VisitorsIndex is a two-field index consisting of **LastName** followed by **FirstName**. To search the **Recordset** for any given username, we just submit the two field values to the **Seek()** method in the order defined by the index.

After it sends back the header information and the opening HTML tags, the program outputs either of two possible responses. If the **Seek()** has failed to locate the username in **rsVisitors**—as reported by a value of **True** in the recordset's **NoMatch** property—the program sends back an appropriate reply and adds the new user to the database:

```
Send "This is your first visit."
rsVisitors.AddNew
rsVisitors!LastName = sLastName
rsVisitors!FirstName = sFirstName
rsVisitors!LastVisit = Now
rsVisitors.Update
```

To add a new record to a table through DAO, you must first call the **AddNew()** method of the **Recordset** object to establish a new record buffer. Next, you assign values to whichever fields you wish. When the fields are set, you must call the **Update()** method to add the new record to the recordset. If you change your position in the recordset (with another **Seek()**, for example) before you call **Update()**, the new record will not be added.

If **NoMatch** returns a value of **False**—meaning that the current user has been previously recorded in the database—the program retrieves the date and time of the last visit, sends a greeting, and updates the **LastVisit** field to the current time and date:

```
vtDateAndTime = rsVisitors!LastVisit
sDate = Format(vtDateAndTime, "Long Date")
sTime = Format(vtDateAndTime, "Medium Time")
Send "Welcome back."
Send "<BR>"
Send "Your last visit was on " & sDate & " at " & sTime & "."
rsVisitors.Edit
rsVisitors!LastVisit = Now
rsVisitors.Update
```

To modify an exisiting record, instead of beginning the field updates with the **AddNew()** method, we begin with a call to the **Recordset** object's **Edit()** method. Once again, we must call the **Update()** method to complete the operation.

Once the program, shown in Listing 7.8, has sent its reply, it terminates automatically and unloads itself from memory. Each CGI transaction takes place autonomously. When you use a standard VB executable as the CGI script, each user session causes the server to load and execute a separate instance of the program. Because HTTP does not establish a *persistent client state*, a CGI program does not remember its interaction with the user from one request to the next. In the next chapter, we'll see how to create CGI scripts that maintain a user context throughout your Web site by simulating persistence.

Listing 7.8 The complete listing of CGIExperiment4.VBP.

```
Option Explicit

Private dbVisitorsDatabase As Database
Private tdVisitors As TableDef
Private idxVisitors As Index
Private rsVisitors As Recordset

Public Sub CGI_Main()
    Dim sLastName As String
    Dim sFirstName As String
    Dim vtDateAndTime As Date
    Dim sDate As String
    Dim sTime As String

    If (CGI_RequestMethod = "GET") Then
        Send "Content-type: text/html"
        Send ""
        Send "<HTML>"
        Send "<HEAD>"
        Send "<TITLE>A Simple Test Form</TITLE>"
        Send "</HEAD>"
        Send "<BODY>"
        Send "<H1>Forms Processing With Visual Basic 5.0</H1>"
        Send "<HR>"
        Send "This is a test application, which will submit"
        Send "data to a Visual Basic application running on"
        Send "the server. We will begin with an out-of-process"
        Send "executable (.EXE), which will be a VB program with"
        Send "no forms."
        Send "<FORM ACTION=""CGIExperiment4.exe"" METHOD=""POST"">"
        Send "<PRE>"
        Send " Last Name: <INPUT SIZE=50 NAME=""lastname"">"
        Send "First Name: <INPUT SIZE=25 NAME=""firstname"">"
        Send ""
```

```
    Send "</PRE>"
    Send "<INPUT TYPE=""submit"" VALUE=""Go Ahead"">"
    Send "<HR>"
    Send "</FORM>"
    Send "</BODY>"
    Send "</HTML>"
  Else
    OpenOrGenerateVisitorsDatabase
    sLastName = GetSmallField("lastname")
    sFirstName = GetSmallField("firstname")
    rsVisitors.Index = "VisitorsIndex"
    rsVisitors.Seek "=", sLastName, sFirstName

    Send "Content-type: text/html"
    Send ""
    Send "<HTML>"
    Send "<HEAD>"
    Send "<TITLE>A VB5, CGI Experiment</TITLE>"
    Send "</HEAD>"
    Send "<BODY>"
    Send "<H1>A VB5, CGI Experiment</H1>"
    Send "<P>"
    Send "Hey " & sFirstName & " " & sLastName & "!"
    If rsVisitors.NoMatch Then
        Send "This is your first visit."
        rsVisitors.AddNew
        rsVisitors!LastName = sLastName
        rsVisitors!FirstName = sFirstName
        rsVisitors!LastVisit = Now
        rsVisitors.Update
      Else
        vtDateAndTime = rsVisitors!LastVisit
        sDate = Format(vtDateAndTime, "Long Date")
        sTime = Format(vtDateAndTime, "Medium Time")
        Send "Welcome back."
        Send "<BR>"
        Send "Your last visit was on " & sDate & " at " & _
            sTime & "."
        rsVisitors.Edit
        rsVisitors!LastVisit = Now
        rsVisitors.Update
      End If
    Send "</BODY>"
    Send "</HTML>"
  End If
End Sub
```

```
Public Sub Inter_Main()
    MsgBox "This is a CGI program." & Format(Now, "General Date")
    End Sub

Public Function OpenOrGenerateVisitorsDatabase() As Boolean

    Dim IndexField As Field
    Dim fldsVisitors(2) As Field
    Dim Counter As Integer

    If Len(Dir(App.Path & "\Visitors.mdb")) > 0 Then
        Set dbVisitorsDatabase = OpenDatabase(App.Path & _
            "\Visitors.mdb")
        OpenOrGenerateVisitorsDatabase = True
      Else
        Set dbVisitorsDatabase = CreateDatabase( _
            App.Path & "\Visitors.mdb", dbLangGeneral)

        Set tdVisitors = dbVisitorsDatabase.CreateTableDef( _
            "Visitors")

        Set fldsVisitors(0) = tdVisitors.CreateField("LastName", _
            dbText, 50)
        Set fldsVisitors(1) = tdVisitors.CreateField("FirstName", _
            dbText, 25)
        Set fldsVisitors(2) = tdVisitors.CreateField("LastVisit", _
            dbDate)
        For Counter = 0 To 2
            tdVisitors.Fields.Append fldsVisitors(Counter)
            Next Counter

        Set idxVisitors = tdVisitors.CreateIndex("VisitorsIndex")
        idxVisitors.Primary = True
        idxVisitors.Unique = True
        Set IndexField = idxVisitors.CreateField("LastName")
        idxVisitors.Fields.Append IndexField
        Set IndexField = idxVisitors.CreateField("FirstName")
        idxVisitors.Fields.Append IndexField

        tdVisitors.Indexes.Append idxVisitors

        dbVisitorsDatabase.TableDefs.Append tdVisitors

        dbVisitorsDatabase.Close
        Set dbVisitorsDatabase = OpenDatabase(App.Path & _
            "\Visitors.mdb")
```

```
        OpenOrGenerateVisitorsDatabase = True
      End If
    Set rsVisitors = dbVisitorsDatabase.OpenRecordset("Visitors")
    rsVisitors.Index = "VisitorsIndex"
    End Function
```

Returning CGI Query Results In An HTML Table

In the previous project, we wrote a simple VB program that acted as a complete mini Web site, supplying its own form document and appropriate response. Now let's take advantage of one of HTML's more advanced features to generate formatted output from a database.

With the HTML **<TABLE>** tag and its subordinate tags, **<CAPTION>**, **<TR>**, **<TD>**, and **<TH>**, we can format data into neatly aligned columns and rows—perfect for displaying lists of records from database tables. In this project, we'll look at the first of two distinct ways to construct an HTML table. First, we'll implement a simple procedure that outputs the data and HTML tags as it walks through the database recordset. In the next version of this project, we'll look at a more complex—but ultimately more flexible—approach based on a VB object model.

HTML Tables

HTML tables are based on a few simple tags, allowing you to organize otherwise unwieldy information into some remarkably useful and attractive page designs. All tables begin with the tag **<TABLE>**, and end with the corresponding end tag **</TABLE>**. Between the **<TABLE>** tags, you can place any number of rows, defined by the **<TR>** and **</TR>** tags. Within rows, you can specify any number of data or header cells, defined with the **<TR>** and **<TH>** tags and their optional end tags. You may also use the **<CAPTION>** tags to place a single caption above or below the table. The HTML for a typical table might look something like this:

```
<TABLE BORDER=3 CELLPADDING=3 CELLSPACING=1>
    <CAPTION VALIGN=TOP>Sales by Quarter</CAPTION>
    <TR>
        <TH></TH>
        <TH>1st Qtr</TH>
```

```
        <TH>2nd Qtr</TH>
        <TH>3rd Qtr</TH>
        <TH>4th Qtr</TH>
    </TR>
    <TR>
        <TH>Bob</TH>
        <TD>12,000</TD>
        <TD>11,350</TD>
        <TD>17,635</TD>
        <TD>22,110</TD>
    </TR>
    <TR>
        <TH>Denise</TH>
        <TD>35,000</TD>
        <TD>42,430</TD>
        <TD>47,725</TD>
        <TD>50,200</TD>
    </TR>
    <TR>
        <TH>Malcolm</TH>
        <TD>1,340</TD>
        <TD>2,200</TD>
        <TD>1,800</TD>
        <TD>3,750</TD>
    </TR>
</TABLE>
```

This HTML code will produce the table shown in Figure 7.12.

HTML Table Tags

Each of the five table tags supports several attributes that control everything from border widths to background colors and alignment of data within cells. Tables are among the most remarkable of HTML features. With a little "wizardry," you can use tables to accomplish an amazing variety of page layout effects.

<TABLE>

This tag and its corresponding end tag declare a table within your Web page. The **<TABLE>** tag currently supports twelve attributes.

The **ALIGN** attribute controls the alignment of the table within the surrounding text, accepting a value of either **LEFT** or **RIGHT**.

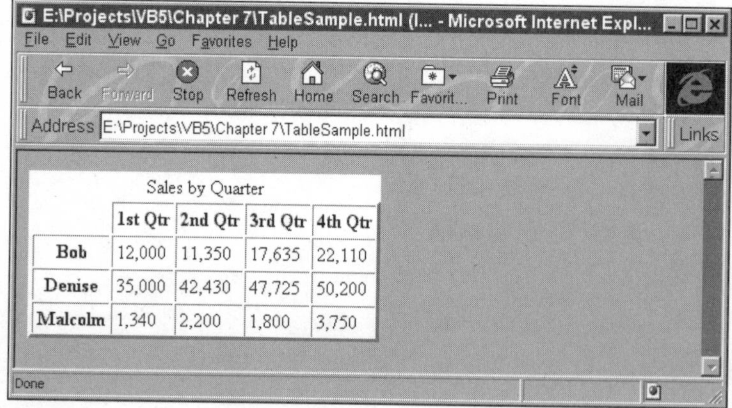

Sales by Quarter

	1st Qtr	2nd Qtr	3rd Qtr	4th Qtr
Bob	12,000	11,350	17,635	22,110
Denise	35,000	42,430	47,725	50,200
Malcolm	1,340	2,200	1,800	3,750

Figure 7.12
A simple HTML table.

BGCOLOR sets the background color of the entire table. Colors in HTML tags are specified either with a six-digit hexadecimal value or with one of the handful of predefined color names (**BGCOLOR=FUCHSIA**). In hexadecimal color values, the two most significant digits specify the intensity of the red color component (**BGCOLOR=FF0000** for pure red), the least significant digits specify blue (**BGCOLOR=0000FF** for pure blue), and the middle digits specify green (**BGCOLOR=00FF00** for pure green). Internet Explorer 3.0 supports 16 predefined colors:

AQUA	BLACK	BLUE	FUCHSIA
GRAY	GREEN	LIME	MAROON
NAVY	OLIVE	PURPLE	RED
SILVER	TEAL	WHITE	YELLOW

By default, tables have no borders, which for some applications can make attractive lists without all the boxy clutter. With the **BORDER** attribute, however, you may add borders to the table and its cells. The integer value assigned to **BORDER** determines the border width in pixels. If you include **BORDER** with no assigned value, the border width defaults to one pixel.

Table borders in Netscape Navigator and Microsoft Internet Explorer are drawn with beveled edges for a three-dimensional look. To draw a 3D border, you need three colors: one for the main flat portion, one for the highlighted edges, and one for the shaded edges. The three attributes of **BORDERCOLOR**, **BORDERCOLORLIGHT**, and **BORDERCOLORDARK** set the colors used to draw the border. Border colors default to shades of gray, which may look odd if you've applied a different background color.

CELLPADDING, like a margin setting, controls the amount of space between the cell's contents and its borders. **CELLSPACING** controls the amount of space between cells within the table. Just as the **BORDER** attribute controls the width of the border around the outside of the table, **CELLSPACING** controls the width of the borders between cells. The presence or absence of the **BORDER** attribute, however, determines whether any of the borders show at all.

HSPACE and **VSPACE** determine how much space—in pixels—to place between the table and the surrounding text.

With the **VALIGN** attribute, you may set the vertical alignment of data within the cells. By default, most browsers vertically center all text or images within each cell. You may also set **VALIGN** to **TOP** or **BOTTOM**.When used within the <TABLE> tag, this attribute specifies the global alignment for all cells within the table. It may be overriden with alternative settings at the row and cell levels.

The final <TABLE> attribute, **WIDTH**, specifies an explicit width for the table. Without the WIDTH attribute, the browser will automatically size the table to the dimensions of the data. You may set the WIDTH either to a specific number of pixels (**WIDTH=250**) or to a percentage of the width of the browser's display area (**WIDTH=60%**).

<CAPTION>

Within each table you may specify one <CAPTION>. You may use the **ALIGN** attribute to set the horizontal position of the caption to **LEFT**, **CENTER**, or **RIGHT**. The **VALIGN** attribute sets its position to **TOP** or **BOTTOM**, meaning above or below the table, respectively.

<TR>

The data in a table is stored in cells that are arranged into rows. The <TABLE> tags enclose one or more sets of <TR> tags, which in turn enclose one or more <TD> or <TH> tags. The <TR> tag supports six attributes.

The **BGCOLOR**, **BORDERCOLOR**, **BORDERCOLORLIGHT**, and **BORDER COLORDARK** attributes perform the same functions as described above in the section on the <TABLE> tag. Their effects, however, are restricted to the cells within the current row.

ALIGN and **VALIGN** control the alignment of data within all cells in the current row. **ALIGN** accepts values of **LEFT**, **CENTER**, or **RIGHT**; while **VALIGN** accepts values of **TOP**, **CENTER**, or **BOTTOM**.

<TD> And <TH>

The <TD> and <TH> tags (whose names stand for table data and table header, respectively) perform nearly identical functions. The only difference is that Internet Explorer 3.0 and some other browsers will apply different default display attributes to the contents of header cells than they apply to ordinary data cells—specifically, bold and centered text.

When added to <TD> or <TH> tags, the **ALIGN** and **VALIGN** attributes control alignment of data within an individual cell. And the **BGCOLOR**, **BORDERCOLOR**, **BORDERCOLORLIGHT**, and **BORDERCOLORDARK** can be used within these tags to control a cell's background and border colors, overriding the alignment and color values specified at the row or table level.

The **COLSPAN** tag sets the width of a cell to the total width of more than one column. Since you never explicitly specify the number of columns in a table, this attribute can be a little confusing. The browser sets the total number of columns in a table to the number of columns it detects in the table's longest row—long in terms of the number of cells, not actual pixel width. The **COLSPAN** attribute allows an individual cell to bridge multiple columns, which can come in especially handy for headings. The **ROWSPAN** attribute performs a similar function—but in the vertical dimension—enabling one cell to bridge two or more rows.

With the **WIDTH** attribute, you can override the default width on any column in the table. Although this attribute goes in a <TD> or <TH> tag, it affects the entire column to which that cell belongs. **WIDTH** accepts values either in pixels (**WIDTH=140**) or as a percentage of the table's total width (**WIDTH=25%**).

Sending A Table

In this example program, when you enter the last name "everyone" or "all", the CGI program will return the reply page shown in Figure 7.13: a list of all visitors who have registered on the site to date.

In the procedure **CGI_Main()**, we'll modify the main **Else** clause to test for a **lastname** of "all" or "everyone":

```
Else
  OpenOrGenerateVisitorsDatabase
  Send "Content-type: text/html"
  Send ""
  Send "<HTML>"
  Send "<HEAD>"
  Send "<TITLE>A VB5, CGI Experiment</TITLE>"
  Send "</HEAD>"
  Send "<BODY>"
  Send "<H1>A VB5, CGI Experiment</H1>"
  sLastName = GetSmallField("lastname")
  sFirstName = GetSmallField("firstname")
  If UCase(sLastName) = "EVERYONE" Or UCase(sLastName) = "ALL" Then
      Set VisitorTable = BuildTableData
      OutputHTMLText VisitorTable.HTMLText
      'DisplayTableData
```

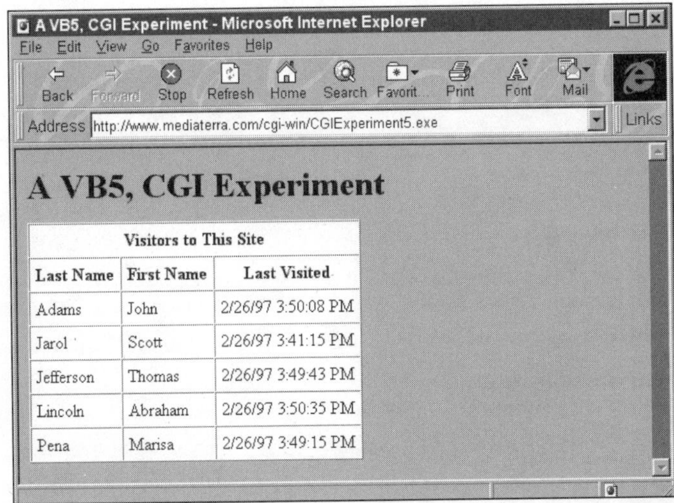

Figure 7.13

An HTML table listing all visitors to the site.

The general procedure **DisplayTableData()** uses the **MoveFirst()** and **MoveNext()** methods of the **RecordSet** object class to step through **rsVisitors.** It sends to the browser all the text and HTML tags necessary to display a table of three columns: one each for "Last Name," "First Name," and the time and date "Last Visited." **MoveFirst()** positions the **RecordSet** *cursor* at the first record, according to the current index. **MoveNext()** advances the cursor to the next record in the index until it passes the last record, at which point the **EOF** property will return **True**. The entire procedure is shown in Listing 7.9.

Listing 7.9 The general procedure **DisplayTableData()**.

```
Public Sub DisplayTableData()
    Send "<TABLE BORDER CELLSPACING=0 CELLPADDING=5>"
    Send "<TR>"
    Send "<TH COLSPAN=3>Visitors to This Site</TH>"
    Send "</TR>"
    Send "<TR>"
    Send "<TH>Last Name</TH>"
    Send "<TH>First Name</TH>"
    Send "<TH>Last Visited</TH>"
    Send "</TR>"
    rsVisitors.MoveFirst
    Do While Not rsVisitors.EOF
        Send "<TR>"
        Send "<TD>" & rsVisitors!LastName & "</TD>"
        Send "<TD>" & rsVisitors!FirstName & "</TD>"
        Send "<TD>" & Format(rsVisitors!LastVisit, _
            "General Date") & "</TD>"
        Send "</TR>"
        rsVisitors.MoveNext
        Loop
    Send "</TABLE>"
    End Sub
```

That's really all it takes to store and retrieve data in an Access database, as well as to dress your data in an HTML table. Listing 7.10 shows the entire CGIExperiment5.BAS program

Listing 7.10 CGIExperiment5.BAS.

```
Option Explicit

Private dbVisitorsDatabase As Database
Private tdVisitors As TableDef
```

```
Private idxVisitors As Index
Private rsVisitors As Recordset


Public Sub CGI_Main()
    Dim sLastName As String
    Dim sFirstName As String
    Dim vtDateAndTime As Date
    Dim sDate As String
    Dim sTime As String
    Dim VisitorTable As clsTables

    If (CGI_RequestMethod = "GET") Then
        Send "Content-type: text/html"
        Send ""
        Send "<HTML>"
        Send "<HEAD>"
        Send "<TITLE>A Simple Test Form</TITLE>"
        Send "</HEAD>"
        Send "<BODY>"
        Send "<H1>Forms Processing With Visual Basic 5.0</H1>"
        Send "<HR>"
        Send "This is a test application, which will submit"
        Send "data to a Visual Basic application running on"
        Send "the server. We will begin with an out-of-process"
        Send "executable (.EXE), which will be a VB program with"
        Send "no forms."
        Send "<FORM ACTION=""CGIExperiment5.exe"" METHOD=""POST"">"
        Send "<PRE>"
        Send " Last Name: <INPUT SIZE=50 NAME=""lastname"">"
        Send "First Name: <INPUT SIZE=25 NAME=""firstname"">"
        Send ""
        Send "</PRE>"
        Send "<INPUT TYPE=""submit"" VALUE=""Go Ahead"">"
        Send "<HR>"
        Send "</FORM>"
        Send "</BODY>"
        Send "</HTML>"
      Else
        OpenOrGenerateVisitorsDatabase
        Send "Content-type: text/html"
        Send ""
        Send "<HTML>"
        Send "<HEAD>"
        Send "<TITLE>A VB5, CGI Experiment</TITLE>"
        Send "</HEAD>"
        Send "<BODY>"
```

```
        Send "<H1>A VB5, CGI Experiment</H1>"
        sLastName = GetSmallField("lastname")
        sFirstName = GetSmallField("firstname")
        If UCase(sLastName) = "EVERYONE" Or UCase(sLastName) = _
            "ALL" Then
            DisplayTableData
          Else
            rsVisitors.Index = "VisitorsIndex"
            rsVisitors.Seek "=", sLastName, sFirstName
            Send "<P>"
            Send "Hey " & sFirstName & " " & sLastName & "!"
            If rsVisitors.NoMatch Then
                Send "This is your first visit."
                rsVisitors.AddNew
                rsVisitors!LastName = sLastName
                rsVisitors!FirstName = sFirstName
                rsVisitors!LastVisit = Now
                rsVisitors.Update
              Else
                vtDateAndTime = rsVisitors!LastVisit
                sDate = Format(vtDateAndTime, "Long Date")
                sTime = Format(vtDateAndTime, "Medium Time")
                Send "Welcome back."
                Send "<BR>"
                Send "Your last visit was on " & sDate & _
                    " at " & sTime & "."
                rsVisitors.Edit
                rsVisitors!LastVisit = Now
                rsVisitors.Update
              End If
          End If
        Send "</BODY>"
        Send "</HTML>"

      End If
    End Sub

Public Sub Inter_Main()
    MsgBox "This is a CGI program." & Format(Now, "General Date")
    End Sub

Public Function OpenOrGenerateVisitorsDatabase() As Boolean

    Dim IndexField As Field
    Dim fldsVisitors(2) As Field
    Dim Counter As Integer
```

```
    If Len(Dir(App.Path & "\Visitors.mdb")) > 0 Then
        Set dbVisitorsDatabase = OpenDatabase(App.Path & _
            "\Visitors.mdb")
        OpenOrGenerateVisitorsDatabase = True
      Else
        Set dbVisitorsDatabase = CreateDatabase( _
            App.Path & "\Visitors.mdb", dbLangGeneral)

        Set tdVisitors = dbVisitorsDatabase.CreateTableDef( _
            "Visitors")

        Set fldsVisitors(0) = tdVisitors.CreateField("LastName", _
            dbText, 50)
        Set fldsVisitors(1) = tdVisitors.CreateField("FirstName", _
            dbText, 25)
        fldsVisitors(1).AllowZeroLength = True
        Set fldsVisitors(2) = tdVisitors.CreateField("LastVisit", _
            dbDate)
        For Counter = 0 To 2
            tdVisitors.Fields.Append fldsVisitors(Counter)
            Next Counter

        Set idxVisitors = tdVisitors.CreateIndex("VisitorsIndex")
        idxVisitors.Primary = True
        idxVisitors.Unique = True
        idxVisitors.Required = False
        Set IndexField = idxVisitors.CreateField("LastName")
        idxVisitors.Fields.Append IndexField
        Set IndexField = idxVisitors.CreateField("FirstName")
        idxVisitors.Fields.Append IndexField

        tdVisitors.Indexes.Append idxVisitors

        dbVisitorsDatabase.TableDefs.Append tdVisitors

        dbVisitorsDatabase.Close
        Set dbVisitorsDatabase = OpenDatabase(App.Path & _
            "\Visitors.mdb")
        OpenOrGenerateVisitorsDatabase = True
      End If
    Set rsVisitors = dbVisitorsDatabase.OpenRecordset("Visitors")
    rsVisitors.Index = "VisitorsIndex"
    End Function

Public Sub DisplayTableData()
    Send "<TABLE BORDER CELLSPACING=0 CELLPADDING=5>"
```

```
Send "<TR>"
Send "<TH COLSPAN=3>Visitors to This Site</TH>"
Send "</TR>"
Send "<TR>"
Send "<TH>Last Name</TH>"
Send "<TH>First Name</TH>"
Send "<TH>Last Visited</TH>"
Send "</TR>"
rsVisitors.MoveFirst
Do While Not rsVisitors.EOF
    Send "<TR>"
    Send "<TD>" & rsVisitors!LastName & "</TD>"
    Send "<TD>" & rsVisitors!FirstName & "</TD>"
    Send "<TD>" & Format(rsVisitors!LastVisit, _
        "General Date") & "</TD>"
    Send "</TR>"
    rsVisitors.MoveNext
    Loop
Send "</TABLE>"
End Sub
```

A Database-Driven Event Calendar

The combination of VB's extensive database capabilites, Web CGI, and some clever HTML can pack a powerful punch. To see how useful these tools can be, let's build something—well, *useful.* In this project, we'll create a CGI-based calendar that allows visitors to add their own event listings.

Running The CGI Event Calendar

To run this program, compile and save it into the /CGI-WIN/ or /CGI-BIN/ subdirectory of your Web server. Then, with the server running, activate your Web browser and open the following URL:

```
http://localhost/cgi-bin/CGICalendar.exe
```

Change /CGI-BIN/ to /CGI-WIN/ if you're using the WebSite Web server. Your browser should display a document similar to the one shown in Figure 7.14. The calendar will default to the current month.

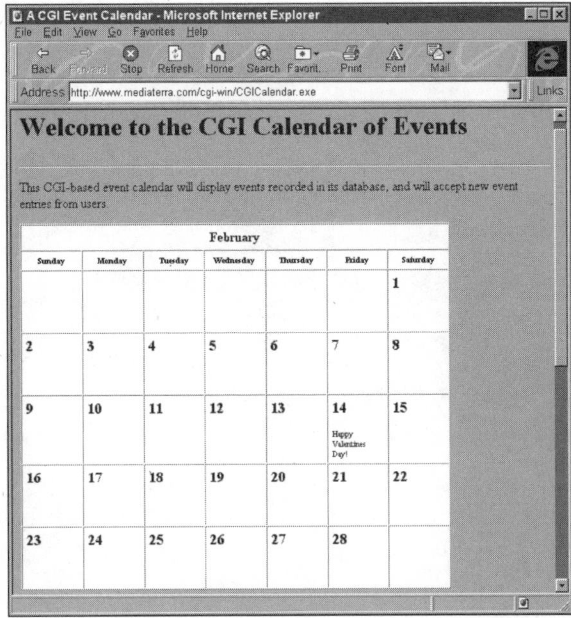

Figure 7.14
The default document displayed by CGICalendar.EXE.

To display the calendar for a different month, select the month name from the list that appears below the calendar and click "Open Calendar." To add a new event to the calendar, scroll down to the last section of the document, shown in Figure 7.15. Select a date from the popup list box, type your announcement into the text area input field and click "Add Event."

The program will update the database and redisplay the calendar with the new event listing.

Table Trials And Tribulations

To construct the calendars for this application, we'll once again use the HTML table model. But this time, we'll use VB's object capabilities to build classes that will enable us to prefabricate and manipulate tables before we transmit them back to the client browser.

HTML tables can be challenging. The ultimate structure of a table is defined implicitly, rather than explicitly. For example, rather than specifying the number of

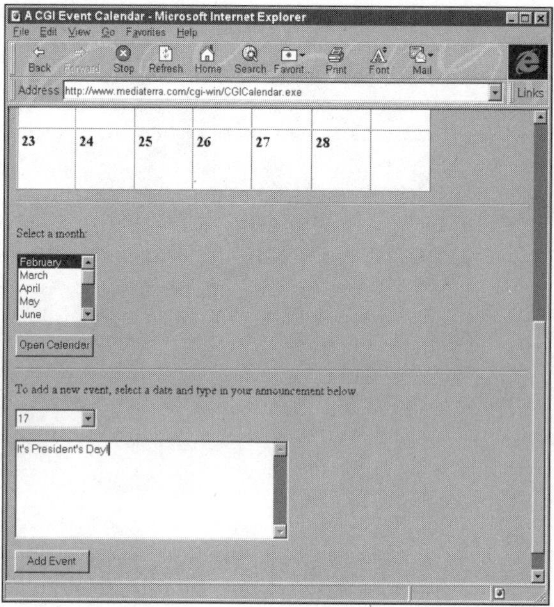

Figure 7.15
Adding a new event listing to a calendar.

columns you want in your table, you allow the browser to analyze the contents of the <TR> tags, determining the number of columns required to display the row with the largest number of cells. Even if you set various explicit attributes, the browser proportions the table according to its own interpretation of the data. For database applications, you often generate the various table tags in sequence as you step through the data. This works well for many types of tables—particularly when you just want to spit out the data in uniform rows and let the browser worry about making it look nice. In some cases, however, you'll want to begin with a more complex determinant structure, fill in the details as you process the data, and transmit the table's tags and text only after it's fully assembled.

For the CGI Event Calendar project, we'll want to create a table that represents a monthly calendar. We'll use headings for the name of the month and days of the week, followed by a seven-column matrix of cells to display the days themselves. The number of rows will depend on the particular month, varying from four to six.

Calendar assembly requires three steps:

1. Create a grid of appropriate dimensions for the current month selected.

2. Fill in the headings and number the dated cells.

3. Add the event announcements to the appropriate date cells.

Unfortunately, HTML does not dynamically update existing page elements—we can't just toss out an empty grid, then go back and fill it in. Instead of trying to braid all three tasks together—spitting out table tags, dates, and text all at the same time—we'll create a data structure that represents an HTML table. In this way, we can assemble the calendar before we send it to the client.

A Table Object Model

If HTML contains any natural candidate for object modeling, it would have to be tables. A table consists of a simple structure containing one optional caption and one or more rows, which in turn contain one or more cells (data or header). With a few simple object classes that are equipped themselves with the appropriate object references, we can build a dynamic data structure capable of representing any HTML table. Then, with just a little more effort, we can build a special-purpose class that manipulates the table classes to build our monthly calendars.

The first class, **clsTables** (which is contained in the file clsTables.CLS), is shown in Listing 7.11.

Listing 7.11 The object class clsTables.

```
Option Explicit

Public ALIGN As Variant
Public BGCOLOR As Variant
Public BORDER As Variant
Public BORDERCOLOR As Variant
Public BORDERCOLORLIGHT As Variant
Public BORDERCOLORDARK As Variant
Public CELLPADDING As Variant
Public CELLSPACING As Variant
Public HSPACE As Variant
Public VSPACE As Variant
Public VALIGN As Variant
Public WIDTH As Variant

Public TableCaption As clsTableCaptions
Private TableRows As clsTableRows
```

```
Public Sub AddRow(NewRow As clsTableRows)
    If TableRows Is Nothing Then
        Set TableRows = NewRow
      Else
        Set TableRows.LastRow.NextTableRow = NewRow
      End If
    End Sub

Public Function HTMLText() As String
    Dim TempText As String

    TempText = "<TABLE"
    If Not IsNull(ALIGN) Then
        TempText = TempText & " ALIGN=" & ALIGN
      End If
    If Not IsNull(BGCOLOR) Then
        TempText = TempText & " BGCOLOR=" & BGCOLOR
      End If
    If Not IsNull(BORDER) Then
        TempText = TempText & " BORDER=" & BORDER
      End If
    If Not IsNull(BORDERCOLOR) Then
        TempText = TempText & " BORDERCOLOR=" & BORDERCOLOR
      End If
    If Not IsNull(BORDERCOLORLIGHT) Then
        TempText = TempText & " BORDERCOLORLIGHT=" _
          & BORDERCOLORLIGHT
      End If
    If Not IsNull(BORDERCOLORDARK) Then
        TempText = TempText & " BORDERCOLORDARK=" _
          & BORDERCOLORDARK
      End If
    If Not IsNull(CELLPADDING) Then
        TempText = TempText & " CELLPADDING=" & CELLPADDING
      End If
    If Not IsNull(CELLSPACING) Then
        TempText = TempText & " CELLSPACING=" & CELLSPACING
      End If
    If Not IsNull(HSPACE) Then
        TempText = TempText & " HSPACE=" & HSPACE
      End If
    If Not IsNull(VSPACE) Then
        TempText = TempText & " VSPACE=" & VSPACE
      End If
    If Not IsNull(VALIGN) Then
        TempText = TempText & " VALIGN=" & VALIGN
```

```
        End If
      If Not IsNull(WIDTH) Then
          TempText = TempText & " WIDTH=" & WIDTH
        End If

      TempText = TempText & ">" & vbCrLf
      If Not (TableCaption Is Nothing) Then
          TempText = TempText & TableCaption.HTMLText & vbCrLf
        End If
      If Not (TableRows Is Nothing) Then
          TempText = TempText & TableRows.HTMLText
        End If
      TempText = TempText & "</TABLE>"
      HTMLText = TempText
      End Function

Private Sub Class_Initialize()
      ALIGN = Null
      BGCOLOR = Null
      BORDER = Null
      BORDERCOLOR = Null
      BORDERCOLORLIGHT = Null
      BORDERCOLORDARK = Null
      CELLPADDING = Null
      CELLSPACING = Null
      HSPACE = Null
      VSPACE = Null
      VALIGN = Null
      WIDTH = Null
      End Sub

Public Function GetDataCellReferenceAt(Column As Integer, _
                    Row As Integer) As clsTableDataCells

      If TableRows Is Nothing Then
          Set GetDataCellReferenceAt = Nothing
        Else
          Set GetDataCellReferenceAt = _
              TableRows.GetDataCellReferenceAt(Column, Row, 1)
        End If
      End Function
```

This class defines a table as an object possessing two object references and twelve HTML attributes. The **<TABLE>** tag may directly contain only two types of tags, **<TR>** and **<CAPTION>**. Thus, the two object references, **TableRows** and

TableCaption, will refer to objects that represent table rows and captions, respectively. Although it looks odd, **clsTables** references only one row object. The actual rows will be linked into a list, each row referencing the next. We could have declared a collection of row objects, but the linked list will explicitly preserve the order of the rows, enabling us to implement recursive searches and updates. As for the caption object, each table may contain only one optional caption, so this property may contain a reference to a single caption object.

Sacrificing good programming style in the name of consistency, I've declared all of the twelve attributes as variants. Many HTML attributes can accept values of various data types. For example, color attributes such as **BGCOLOR** will accept either a hexadecimal RGB value or the name of a predefined color. VB's handy variant data type makes it a snap to deal with HTML's loose data typing.

The class **clsTables** contains just three methods and an initialization procedure. The **AddRow()** method accepts a single argument—a reference to a row object—and appends it to the current list of rows. If **TableRows** already contains a reference to the first row in the table, **AddRow()** calls the row object's **LastRow()** method to retrieve a reference to the last row object in the linked list. We'll take a closer look at **LastRow()** when we cover the row object class.

The function method **HTMLText()** gathers the information contained in the object-based table data structure and returns a text string containing a valid HTML representation of a table. It begins by building the <TABLE> tag itself, which may include any or all of the tag's twelve attributes. To determine whether to include an attribute, it uses VB's **IsNull()** function to check each attribute property variable for a value of **NULL**. The **NULL** value enables us to differentiate between attributes set explicitly to zero (or an empty string) versus attributes that are not needed at all. The procedure **Class_Initialize**, which executes once for each new instance of the class, initializes the twelve attribute properties to **NULL**. As we build a table, each attribute property we set will become non-**NULL** and will therefore be included in the <TABLE> tag.

After it checks all the attribute properties and closes the <TABLE> tag, **HTMLText()** checks the **TableCaption** property for a valid reference. If the table contains a caption object, it calls that object's own **HTMLText()** method to generate the <CAPTION> tag—along with its contents, attributes, and end tag. It then performs the same operation on the **TableRows** property, once again invoking the **HTMLText()** method for the referenced object—in this case, the first row object. Finally, it completes the table by appending the end tag, **</TABLE>**, and returns the result.

The last method in **clsTables**, **GetDataCellReferenceAt()**, enables us to retrieve a reference to any cell object within the table. This gives us the capability to update its contents or attributes—which is the whole point of building this object model in the first place.

The class **clsTableRows** (shown in Listing 7.12) comprises six attribute properties and three object references. The object reference **NextTableRow** contains the link that allows us to daisy-chain the rows, while **TableDataCells** and **TableHeaderCells** contain references to the first data and header cells in their own respective daisy-chains.

Listing 7.12 The class module clsTableRows.CLS.

```
Option Explicit

Public ALIGN As Variant
Public BGCOLOR As Variant
Public BORDERCOLOR As Variant
Public BORDERCOLORLIGHT As Variant
Public BORDERCOLORDARK As Variant
Public VALIGN As Variant

Public NextTableRow As clsTableRows

Private TableDataCells As clsTableDataCells
Private TableHeaderCells As clsTableHeaderCells


Public Sub AddDataCell(NewTableDataCell As clsTableDataCells, _
                             Column As Integer)

    If TableDataCells Is Nothing Then
        Set TableDataCells = NewTableDataCell
      Else
        Set TableDataCells = _
            TableDataCells.InsertCell(NewTableDataCell, Column, 1)
      End If
    End Sub
```

```
Public Function HTMLText() As String
    Dim TempText As String
    'Dim TempDataCell As clsTableDataCells

    TempText = "<TR"
    If Not IsNull(ALIGN) Then
        TempText = TempText & " ALIGN=" & ALIGN
      End If
    If Not IsNull(BGCOLOR) Then
        TempText = TempText & " BGCOLOR=" & BGCOLOR
      End If
    If Not IsNull(BORDERCOLOR) Then
        TempText = TempText & " BORDERCOLOR=" & BORDERCOLOR
      End If
    If Not IsNull(BORDERCOLORLIGHT) Then
        TempText = TempText & " BORDERCOLORLIGHT=" & BORDERCOLORLIGHT
      End If
    If Not IsNull(BORDERCOLORDARK) Then
        TempText = TempText & " BORDERCOLORDARK=" & BORDERCOLORDARK
      End If
    If Not IsNull(VALIGN) Then
        TempText = TempText & " VALIGN=" & """" & VALIGN & """"
      End If
    TempText = TempText & ">" & vbCrLf
    If Not (TableHeaderCells Is Nothing) Then
        TempText = TempText & TableHeaderCells.HTMLText
      End If
    If Not (TableDataCells Is Nothing) Then
        TempText = TempText & TableDataCells.HTMLText
      End If
    TempText = TempText & "</TR>" & vbCrLf
    If Not (NextTableRow Is Nothing) Then
        TempText = TempText & NextTableRow.HTMLText
      End If
    HTMLText = TempText
    End Function


Public Function LastRow() As clsTableRows
    If NextTableRow Is Nothing Then
        Set LastRow = Me
      Else
        Set LastRow = NextTableRow.LastRow
      End If
    End Function
```

```
Private Sub Class_Initialize()
    ALIGN = Null
    BGCOLOR = Null
    BORDERCOLOR = Null
    BORDERCOLORLIGHT = Null
    BORDERCOLORDARK = Null
    VALIGN = Null
    End Sub

Public Sub AddHeaderCell(NewTableHeaderCell As clsTableHeaderCells, _
                            Column As Integer)

    If TableHeaderCells Is Nothing Then
        Set TableHeaderCells = NewTableHeaderCell
      Else
        Set TableHeaderCells = _
            TableHeaderCells.InsertCell(NewTableHeaderCell, Column, 1)
      End If

    End Sub

Public Function GetDataCellReferenceAt(Column As Integer, _
    Row As Integer, _
    ByVal CurrentRow As Integer) As clsTableDataCells

    If CurrentRow = Row Then
        If TableDataCells Is Nothing Then
            Set GetDataCellReferenceAt = Nothing
          Else
            Set GetDataCellReferenceAt = _
                TableDataCells.GetDataCellReferenceAt(Column, Row, 1)
          End If
      ElseIf (NextTableRow Is Nothing) Then
        Set GetDataCellReferenceAt = Nothing
      Else
        Set GetDataCellReferenceAt = _
            NextTableRow.GetDataCellReferenceAt(Column, Row, _
                CurrentRow + 1)
      End If
    End Function
```

The **AddDataCell()** method resembles the **AddRow()** method in **clsTables**, except that it supports the insertion of cells at arbitrary positions within the existing list. For example, to insert a new cell in the first column, pass the value 1 as the second argument of **AddDataCell()**. The existing cell at the given position—and all cells to the right of that cell—will shift to the right one position. If you specify a column number that is too high, the method will just append the new cell to the end of the row.

This implementation does not generate blank cells to fill the row out to an arbitrary length, although you could easily modify it to do so. A glance at the **AddHeaderCell()** method will reveal another shortcoming of my design. Notice that you can specify column positions for either data cells or for header cells, but the two lists are created independently. The **HTMLText()** method will automatically generate header cells before data cells, which means that header cells will bump the data cells to the right. This problem could be fixed by making a single list, although it would be necessary to declare the **TableDataCells** property more generically (and therefore less rigorously) **As Object**. You would also need to change the declarations of the links in the classes **clsTableDataCells** and **clsTableHeaderCells** so that an instance of either class could reference an instance of the other, allowing you to intermix header and data cells freely.

The **LastRow()** function method demonstrates once again the economy of recursion. With this method, each instance of **clsTableRows** looks at its own **NextTableRow** property to determine whether it contains a valid object reference. If not, it knows that it is the last row object in the list and returns a reference to itself. Otherwise, it recursively calls the **LastRow()** method on the instance referenced by **NextTableRow**.

The **GetDataCellReferenceAt()** function method performs the second of three portions of the recursive search for a specific data cell, identified by its column and row position.

HTMLText() returns the HTML text representing a complete table row, including all its header cells and data cells as well as its opening and closing **<TR>** tags. Notice, once again, that just as the **HTMLText()** method of **clsTables** calls the **HTMLText()** method of **clsTableRows**, this method now calls **HTMLText()** on instances of its subordinate classes, **clsTableDataCells** and **clsTableHeaderCells**.

The class **clsTableDataCells** (shown in Listing 7.13) defines eleven attribute properties, a **CellData** property, and one object reference property, which links each cell in a row to the next.

Listing 7.13 The class module clsTableDataCells.CLS.

```
Option Explicit

Public ALIGN As Variant
Public BGCOLOR As Variant
Public BORDERCOLOR As Variant
Public BORDERCOLORLIGHT As Variant
Public BORDERCOLORDARK As Variant
Public COLSPAN As Variant
Public NOWRAP As Variant
Public ROWSPAN As Variant
Public VALIGN As Variant
Public WIDTH As Variant
Public HEIGHT As Variant

Public NextCell As clsTableDataCells

' A cell may contain a complete HTML document,
' but it does not require all the bracketing codes
' that are needed for a free-standing document, such
' as <HTML></HTML> and <BODY></BODY>, so
' we will declare the CellData property with the
' more general-purpose data type String.
Public CellData As String

Public Function GetDataCellReferenceAt(Column As Integer, _
    Row As Integer, _
    ByVal CurrentColumn As Integer) _
    As clsTableDataCells
    If CurrentColumn = Column Then
        Set GetDataCellReferenceAt = Me
      ElseIf NextCell Is Nothing Then
        Set GetDataCellReferenceAt = Nothing
      Else
        Set GetDataCellReferenceAt = _
            NextCell.GetDataCellReferenceAt(Column, Row, _
                CurrentColumn + 1)
      End If
    End Function

Public Function InsertCell(NewTableDataCell As clsTableDataCells, _
                           Column As Integer, _
                           ByVal CurrentColumn As Integer) _
                           As clsTableDataCells
```

```
    If (Column = CurrentColumn) Then
        Set NewTableDataCell.NextCell = Me
        Set InsertCell = NewTableDataCell
      ElseIf NextCell Is Nothing Then
        Set NextCell = NewTableDataCell
        Set InsertCell = Me
      Else
        Set NextCell = NextCell.InsertCell(NewTableDataCell, _
            Column, CurrentColumn + 1)
        Set InsertCell = Me
      End If
    End Function

Public Function HTMLText() As String
    Dim TempText As String

    TempText = TempText & "<TD"
    If Not IsNull(ALIGN) Then
        TempText = TempText & " ALIGN=" & ALIGN
      End If
    If Not IsNull(BGCOLOR) Then
        TempText = TempText & " BGCOLOR=" & BGCOLOR
      End If
    If Not IsNull(BORDERCOLOR) Then
        TempText = TempText & " BORDERCOLOR=" & BORDERCOLOR
      End If
    If Not IsNull(BORDERCOLORLIGHT) Then
        TempText = TempText & " BORDERCOLORLIGHT=" & BORDERCOLORLIGHT
      End If
    If Not IsNull(BORDERCOLORDARK) Then
        TempText = TempText & " BORDERCOLORDARK=" & BORDERCOLORDARK
      End If
    If Not IsNull(COLSPAN) Then
        TempText = TempText & " COLSPAN=" & COLSPAN
      End If
    If Not IsNull(NOWRAP) Then
        TempText = TempText & " NOWRAP=" & NOWRAP
      End If
    If Not IsNull(ROWSPAN) Then
        TempText = TempText & " ROWSPAN=" & ROWSPAN
      End If
    If Not IsNull(VALIGN) Then
        TempText = TempText & " VALIGN=" & """" & VALIGN & """"
      End If
```

```
    If Not IsNull(WIDTH) Then
        TempText = TempText & " WIDTH=" & WIDTH
      End If
    If Not IsNull(HEIGHT) Then
        TempText = TempText & " HEIGHT=" & HEIGHT
      End If

    TempText = TempText & ">"
    TempText = TempText & CellData
    TempText = TempText & "</TD>" & vbCrLf
    If Not (NextCell Is Nothing) Then
        TempText = TempText & NextCell.HTMLText
      End If
    HTMLText = TempText
    End Function

Private Sub Class_Initialize()
    ALIGN = Null
    BGCOLOR = Null
    BORDERCOLOR = Null
    BORDERCOLORLIGHT = Null
    BORDERCOLORDARK = Null
    COLSPAN = Null
    NOWRAP = Null
    ROWSPAN = Null
    VALIGN = Null
    WIDTH = Null
    End Sub
```

With the third and final function in the **GetDataCellReferenceAt()** trilogy, an instance of **clsTableDataCells** considers three possibilities before returning a result. First, it looks to see if it lies at the specified column position. If so, it returns a reference to itself and ends the search. If not, it examines its **NextCell** property to determine whether it points to another cell. If so, the list continues. It then invokes the **GetDataCellReferenceAt()** method of the next cell object in the list, incrementing the **CurrentColumn** argument, which it passes **ByVal**. If not, it returns the object reference **Nothing**, indicating that no cell exists at the specified column position.

The **InsertCell()** method works similarly to **GetDataCellReferenceAt()**. If the cell needs to be inserted into the list, it must first locate the correct position for the new cell. Then it sets the **NextCell** property of the new cell to reference the cell that currently occupies the specified position. In the **ElseIf** clause, the function handles cells that need to be appended to the end of the linked list. If neither one of the first two conditions has been satisfied, the **Else** clause continues the search for the correct insertion point. This function is a little unusual: It sets the **NextCell** property for every cell in the list, regardless of whether or not its position changes. The **ElseIf** and **Else** clauses cause the object to return a reference to itself, leaving the list unchanged. However, the **Then** clause returns a reference to the new data cell object, completing the insertion of the new cell into the list.

The **HTMLText()** method also uses recursion to traverse the list of data cells:

```
If Not (NextCell Is Nothing) Then
        TempText = TempText & NextCell.HTMLText
      End If
```

The other class that represents cells, **clsTableHeaderCells** (shown in Listing 7.14), nearly matches the data cell class with the following exception: I have omitted a method to return references to existing header cells, and its link properties and method calls refer to **clsTableHeaderCells.**

Listing 7.14 ClsTableHeaderCells.CLS.

```
Option Explicit

Public ALIGN As Variant
Public BGCOLOR As Variant
Public BORDERCOLOR As Variant
Public BORDERCOLORLIGHT As Variant
Public BORDERCOLORDARK As Variant
Public COLSPAN As Variant
Public NOWRAP As Variant
Public ROWSPAN As Variant
Public VALIGN As Variant
Public WIDTH As Variant

Public NextCell As clsTableHeaderCells

' A cell may contain a complete HTML document,
' but it does not require all the bracketing codes
' that are needed for a free-standing document, such
' as <HTML></HTML> and <BODY></BODY>, so
' we will declare the CellData property with the
' more general-purpose data type String.
Public CellData As String
```

```
Public Function InsertCell(NewTableHeaderCell As _
    clsTableHeaderCells, _
    Column As Integer, _
    ByVal CurrentColumn As Integer) _
    As clsTableHeaderCells

    If (Column = CurrentColumn) Then
        Set NewTableHeaderCell.NextCell = Me
        Set InsertCell = NewTableHeaderCell
      ElseIf NextCell Is Nothing Then
        Set NextCell = NewTableHeaderCell
        Set InsertCell = Me
      Else
        Set NextCell = NextCell.InsertCell(NewTableHeaderCell, _
            Column, CurrentColumn + 1)
        Set InsertCell = Me
      End If
    End Function

Public Function HTMLText() As String
    Dim TempText As String

    TempText = TempText & "<TH"
    If Not IsNull(ALIGN) Then
        TempText = TempText & " ALIGN=" & ALIGN
      End If
    If Not IsNull(BGCOLOR) Then
        TempText = TempText & " BGCOLOR=" & BGCOLOR
      End If
    If Not IsNull(BORDERCOLOR) Then
        TempText = TempText & " BORDERCOLOR=" & BORDERCOLOR
      End If
    If Not IsNull(BORDERCOLORLIGHT) Then
        TempText = TempText & " BORDERCOLORLIGHT=" & BORDERCOLORLIGHT
      End If
    If Not IsNull(BORDERCOLORDARK) Then
        TempText = TempText & " BORDERCOLORDARK=" & BORDERCOLORDARK
      End If
    If Not IsNull(COLSPAN) Then
        TempText = TempText & " COLSPAN=" & COLSPAN
      End If
    If Not IsNull(NOWRAP) Then
        TempText = TempText & " NOWRAP=" & NOWRAP
      End If
    If Not IsNull(ROWSPAN) Then
        TempText = TempText & " ROWSPAN=" & ROWSPAN
```

```
        End If
      If Not IsNull(VALIGN) Then
          TempText = TempText & " VALIGN=" & VALIGN
        End If
      If Not IsNull(WIDTH) Then
          TempText = TempText & " WIDTH=" & WIDTH
        End If

      TempText = TempText & ">"
      TempText = TempText & CellData
      TempText = TempText & "</TH>" & vbCrLf
      If Not (NextCell Is Nothing) Then
          TempText = TempText & NextCell.HTMLText
        End If
      HTMLText = TempText
      End Function

Private Sub Class_Initialize()
    ALIGN = Null
    BGCOLOR = Null
    BORDERCOLOR = Null
    BORDERCOLORLIGHT = Null
    BORDERCOLORDARK = Null
    COLSPAN = Null
    NOWRAP = Null
    ROWSPAN = Null
    VALIGN = Null
    WIDTH = Null
    End Sub
```

To complete our basic HTML table object model, we need one more class, **clsTableCaptions** (shown in Listing 7.15).

Listing 7.15 ClsTableCaptions.CLS.

```
Option Explicit

Public CaptionText As String
Public ALIGN As Variant
Public VALIGN As Variant

Public Function HTMLText() As String
    Dim TempText As String

    TempText = "<CAPTION"
```

```
    If Not IsNull(ALIGN) Then
        TempText = TempText & " ALIGN=" & ALIGN
      End If
    If Not IsNull(VALIGN) Then
        TempText = TempText & "VALIGN=" & VALIGN
      End If
    TempText = TempText & ">"
    TempText = TempText & CaptionText
    TempText = TempText & "</CAPTION>"
    HTMLText = TempText
    End Function

Private Sub Class_Initialize()
    ALIGN = Null
    VALIGN = Null
    End Sub
```

Since each table may have only one caption, this class doesn't require any of the list manipulation methods required for rows and cells. The **<CAPTION>** tag supports only two attributes, which means that even the **Class_Initialize**() and **HTMLText**() methods are much shorter than their counterparts in the other classes in the table object model.

Like the classes in the DAO model, the table classes form a hierarchy. To build a table, you need to create the cells, assembling them into rows and then assembling the rows into a table:

1. Declare an instance of **clsTables** and optionally set its attributes.
2. Declare an instance of **clsTableRows** and optionally set its attributes.
3. Declare an instance of **clsTableDataCells** or **clsTableHeaderCells**, set its **CellData** property, and optionally set its attributes.
4. Add the cell to the row with either the row class' **AddDataCell**() or **AddHeaderCell**() methods.
5. Repeat steps 3 and 4 as necessary to complete a row.
6. Add the row to the table with the table class' **AddRow**() method.
7. Repeat steps 2 through 6 as necessary to complete the table.

Calendars From Tables

So far, the table object model just organizes the HTML table model into a VB object model. But the real value of such a model is the ability to build specialty classes that help us construct and manipulate particular kinds of tables. For the CGI Event Calendar project, we'll create a wrapper class that uses the HTML table object model to define and fill in a monthly calendar.

At the beginning of this project, we reviewed the requirements of a monthly calendar, including appropriate headings and a grid to display the days with their event listings. The new class, **clsCalendars** (shown in Listing 7.16), will encapsulate an HTML table, referenced by the property **HTMLTable**. The only other property, **FirstDayOfMonth**, is a date field containing a complete date that represents the first day of the month represented by **HTMLTable**.

Listing 7.16 The class module clsCalendars.CLS.

```
Option Explicit

Public FirstDayOfMonth As Date
Private HTMLTable As clsTables

Public Sub AddToCell(NewContents As String, Column As Integer, _
    Row As Integer)

    Dim CellToUpdate As clsTableDataCells

    Set CellToUpdate = HTMLTable.GetDataCellReferenceAt(Column, _
        Row + 2)
    If Not (CellToUpdate Is Nothing) Then
        If CellToUpdate.CellData = "<BR>" Then
            CellToUpdate.CellData = ""
          End If
        CellToUpdate.CellData = CellToUpdate.CellData & NewContents
      End If
    End Sub


Public Sub AddEvent(EventDate As Date, EventDescription As String)
    Dim MonthOffset As Integer

    MonthOffset = WeekDay(FirstDayOfMonth) - 1
    AddToCell "<BR><BR><FONT SIZE=-4>" & EventDescription & _
```

```
        "</FONT>", ((Day(EventDate) + MonthOffset - 1) Mod 7 + 1), _
        ((Day(EventDate) + MonthOffset - 1) \ 7 + 1)
    End Sub

Public Function HTMLText() As String
    HTMLText = HTMLTable.HTMLText
    End Function

Public Sub Init()
    Dim MonthOffset As Integer
    Dim FirstDayOfNextMonth As Date
    Dim TotalCellsRequired As Integer
    Dim RowsRequired As Integer
    Dim RowCounter As Integer
    Dim ColumnCounter As Integer
    Dim TableCell As clsTableDataCells
    Dim TableHeaderCell As clsTableHeaderCells
    Dim TableRow As clsTableRows
    Dim Column As Integer
    Dim Row As Integer
    Dim DateCounter As Integer
    Dim Counter As Integer

    MonthOffset = WeekDay(FirstDayOfMonth) - 1
    FirstDayOfNextMonth = DateSerial(Year(FirstDayOfMonth) + _
        (Month(FirstDayOfMonth) \ 12), _
        (Month(FirstDayOfMonth) Mod 12) + 1, 1)
    TotalCellsRequired = DaysInMonth(FirstDayOfMonth) + MonthOffset
    RowsRequired = (TotalCellsRequired + 6) \ 7
    Set HTMLTable = New clsTables
    HTMLTable.BORDER = 1
    HTMLTable.CELLSPACING = 0
    HTMLTable.CELLPADDING = 5
    HTMLTable.BGCOLOR = "WHITE" '&H88CC88
    ' Add header to display name of month.
    Set TableRow = New clsTableRows
    Set TableHeaderCell = New clsTableHeaderCells
    TableHeaderCell.CellData = Format(FirstDayOfMonth, "mmmm")
    TableHeaderCell.COLSPAN = 7
    TableRow.AddHeaderCell TableHeaderCell, 1
    HTMLTable.AddRow TableRow
    ' Add row of headers to display days of week.
    Set TableRow = New clsTableRows
    Set TableHeaderCell = New clsTableHeaderCells
    TableHeaderCell.CellData = "<FONT SIZE=-2>Sunday</FONT>"
```

```
    TableRow.AddHeaderCell TableHeaderCell, 1
    Set TableHeaderCell = New clsTableHeaderCells
    TableHeaderCell.CellData = "<FONT SIZE=-2>Monday</FONT>"
    TableRow.AddHeaderCell TableHeaderCell, 2
    Set TableHeaderCell = New clsTableHeaderCells
    TableHeaderCell.CellData = "<FONT SIZE=-2>Tuesday</FONT>"
    TableRow.AddHeaderCell TableHeaderCell, 3
    Set TableHeaderCell = New clsTableHeaderCells
    TableHeaderCell.CellData = "<FONT SIZE=-2>Wednesday</FONT>"
    TableRow.AddHeaderCell TableHeaderCell, 4
    Set TableHeaderCell = New clsTableHeaderCells
    TableHeaderCell.CellData = "<FONT SIZE=-2>Thursday</FONT>"
    TableRow.AddHeaderCell TableHeaderCell, 5
    Set TableHeaderCell = New clsTableHeaderCells
    TableHeaderCell.CellData = "<FONT SIZE=-2>Friday</FONT>"
    TableRow.AddHeaderCell TableHeaderCell, 6
    Set TableHeaderCell = New clsTableHeaderCells
    TableHeaderCell.CellData = "<FONT SIZE=-2>Saturday</FONT>"
    TableRow.AddHeaderCell TableHeaderCell, 7
    HTMLTable.AddRow TableRow
    ' Create empty cells for calendar days.
    For RowCounter = 1 To RowsRequired
        Set TableRow = New clsTableRows
        For ColumnCounter = 1 To 7
            Set TableCell = New clsTableDataCells
            TableCell.CellData = "<BR>"
            TableCell.VALIGN = "TOP"
            TableCell.WIDTH = "75"
            TableCell.HEIGHT = "75"
            TableRow.AddDataCell TableCell, ColumnCounter
            Next ColumnCounter
        TableRow.VALIGN = "TOP"
        HTMLTable.AddRow TableRow
        Next RowCounter
    For DateCounter = 1 To (FirstDayOfNextMonth - FirstDayOfMonth)
        Column = (MonthOffset + DateCounter - 1) Mod 7 + 1
        Row = (MonthOffset + DateCounter - 1) \ 7 + 1
        AddToCell "<B><FONT SIZE=+1>" & _
            CStr(DateCounter) & "</FONT></B>", Column, Row
        Next DateCounter
    End Sub
```

We need to set the **FirstDayOfMonth** property before we build the table, and we can't pass an argument to the **Class_Initialize**() procedure. Therefore, we'll need a special **Init**() method that we can call explicitly after we instantiate a calendar object.

Init() begins by calculating the total number of cells it needs to display the specified month. The VB function **WeekDay()** returns an integer from 1 to 7, representing the day of the week for any given serial date. If we want to stick to the convention of a seven-column calendar—with the first column representing Sundays—we need to add **MonthOffset** to the length of the month, as returned by the **DaysInMonth()** function (shown in Listing 7.17). This determines the **TotalCellsRequired**, a number we can then use to calculate the number of **RowRequired.**

After we add the headers to display the name of the month and the days of the week, we use **RowsRequired** to create a grid of empty cells large enough to hold the calendar. Actually, we can't leave them entirely empty. Many browsers will just ignore empty cells, leaving us with nothing but the header rows. So we insert a single **
** tag into each cell as a place marker.

The last section of **Init()** uses the calendar class' **AddToCell()** method to insert the date numbers into the appropriate cells. **AddToCell()** uses the table's **GetDataCellReferenceAt()** method to locate the cells and update their contents. If a cell contains nothing but the **
** tag, it removes the unnecessary placemarker before appending the new contents.

The calendar class' **AddEvent()** method enables us to ignore the details of the table layout as we update the calendar with event announcements. To add an event, we just pass in the **EventDate** and **EventDescription**, allowing **AddEvent()** to perform the translation between the date and the actual column and row required by **AddToCell()**.

Listing 7.17 The **DaysInMonth()** function.

```
Public Function DaysInMonth(AnyMonth As Date) As Long
    Dim FirstDayOfAnyMonth As Date
    Dim FirstDayOfNextMonth As Date

    FirstDayOfAnyMonth = DateSerial(Year(AnyMonth), _
        Month(AnyMonth), 1)
    FirstDayOfNextMonth = DateSerial(Year(FirstDayOfAnyMonth) _
        + (Month(FirstDayOfAnyMonth) \ 12), _
        (Month(FirstDayOfAnyMonth) Mod 12) + 1, 1)
    DaysInMonth = DateDiff("d", FirstDayOfAnyMonth,
        FirstDayOfNextMonth)
    End Function
```

Completing The CGI Event Calendar Program

The main program module, CGICalendar.BAS (shown in Listing 7.18), follows a similar structure to those in the previous projects in this chapter. The procedure **CGI_Main()** checks **CGI_RequestMethod** to determine whether the program was activated by a form submission (**POST**) or directly through a URL request (**GET**).

Listing 7.18 CGICalendar.BAS.

```
Option Explicit

Private dbCalendarDatabase As Database
Private tdEvents As TableDef
Private idxEvents As Index
Private rsEvents As Recordset


Public Sub CGI_Main()
    Dim MonthSelected As Integer
    Dim DateSelected As Date
    Dim FirstOfCurrentMonth As Date
    Dim FirstOfMonthSelected As Date
    Dim Counter As Integer
    Dim DefaultMonth As Integer
    Dim MonthNumber As Integer

    OpenOrGenerateEventCalendarDatabase
    FirstOfCurrentMonth = DateSerial(Year(Now), Month(Now), 1)
    If CGI_RequestMethod = "POST" Then
        MonthSelected = CInt(GetSmallField("month"))
        FirstOfMonthSelected = DateSerial(Year(Now), MonthSelected, 1)
        If FirstOfMonthSelected < FirstOfCurrentMonth Then
            FirstOfMonthSelected = DateSerial(Year(Now) + 1,
MonthSelected, 1)
          End If
        If (GetSmallField("operation") = "Add Event") Then
            ' Add new event listing to calendar table.
            DateSelected = DateSerial(Year(FirstOfMonthSelected), _
                                      MonthSelected, _
                                      CInt(GetSmallField("date")))
            AddEventToCalendar DateSelected, _
                GetSmallField("event_description")
          End If
      End If
```

```
Send "Content-type: text/html"
Send ""
Send "<HTML>"
Send "<HEAD>"
Send "<TITLE>A CGI Event Calendar</TITLE>"
Send "</HEAD>"
Send "<BODY>"
Send "<H1>Welcome to the CGI Calendar of Events</H1>"
Send "<HR>"
Send "This CGI-based event calendar will display events"
Send "recorded in its database and will accept new event"
Send "entries from users."
Send "<BR><BR>"
If (CGI_RequestMethod = "GET") Then
    FirstOfMonthSelected = FirstOfCurrentMonth
  End If
DisplayCalendarFor FirstOfMonthSelected
DefaultMonth = Month(FirstOfMonthSelected)

Send "<HR>"
Send "<FORM ACTION=""CGICalendar.exe"" METHOD=""POST"">"
Send "Select a month:"
Send "<BR><BR>"
Send "<SELECT NAME=""month"" SIZE=5>"
For Counter = Month(FirstOfCurrentMonth) To _
    Month(FirstOfCurrentMonth) + 11
    MonthNumber = (Counter - 1) Mod 12 + 1
    Send "<OPTION VALUE=" & CStr(MonthNumber)
    If MonthNumber = DefaultMonth Then
        Send " SELECTED "
      End If
    Send ">" & Format(DateSerial(1997, MonthNumber, 1), "mmmm")
    Next Counter
Send "</SELECT>"
Send "<BR><BR>"
Send "<INPUT TYPE=""submit"" NAME=""operation"" " & _
    "VALUE=""Open Calendar""> "
Send "<HR>"
Send "To add a new event, select a date and " & _
    "type in your announcement below."
Send "<BR><BR>"
Send "<SELECT NAME=""date"">"
For Counter = 1 To DaysInMonth(FirstOfMonthSelected)
    Send "<OPTION>" & CStr(Counter)
    Next Counter
```

```
    Send "</SELECT>"
    Send "<BR><BR>"
    Send "<TEXTAREA NAME=""event_description"" COLS=50 Rows=6>"
    Send "</TEXTAREA>"
    Send "<BR><BR>"
    Send "<INPUT TYPE=""submit"" NAME=""operation"" " & _
        "VALUE=""Add Event"">"
    Send "<HR>"
    Send "</FORM>"
    Send "</BODY>"
    Send "</HTML>"
    End Sub

Public Sub Inter_Main()
    MsgBox "This is a CGI program." & Format(Now, "General Date")
    End Sub

Public Function OpenOrGenerateEventCalendarDatabase() As Boolean

    Dim IndexField As Field
    Dim fldsEvents(2) As Field
    Dim Counter As Integer

    If Len(Dir(App.Path & "\Calendar.mdb")) > 0 Then
        Set dbCalendarDatabase = _
            OpenDatabase(App.Path & "\Calendar.mdb")
        OpenOrGenerateEventCalendarDatabase = True
      Else
        Set dbCalendarDatabase = CreateDatabase( _
            App.Path & "\Calendar.mdb", dbLangGeneral)

        Set tdEvents = dbCalendarDatabase.CreateTableDef("Events")

        Set fldsEvents(0) = tdEvents.CreateField("EventDate", dbDate)
        Set fldsEvents(1) = _
            tdEvents.CreateField("Description", dbMemo)
        Set fldsEvents(2) = tdEvents.CreateField("Counter", dbLong)
        fldsEvents(2).Attributes = dbAutoIncrField
        For Counter = 0 To 2
            tdEvents.Fields.Append fldsEvents(Counter)
            Next Counter

        Set idxEvents = tdEvents.CreateIndex("EventsIndex")
        idxEvents.Primary = True
        idxEvents.Unique = True
```

```
        idxEvents.Required = True
        Set IndexField = idxEvents.CreateField("EventDate")
        idxEvents.Fields.Append IndexField
        Set IndexField = idxEvents.CreateField("Counter")
        idxEvents.Fields.Append IndexField

        tdEvents.Indexes.Append idxEvents

        dbCalendarDatabase.TableDefs.Append tdEvents

        dbCalendarDatabase.Close
        Set dbCalendarDatabase = _
            OpenDatabase(App.Path & "\Calendar.mdb")
        OpenOrGenerateEventCalendarDatabase = True
      End If
    Set rsEvents = dbCalendarDatabase.OpenRecordset("Events")
    rsEvents.Index = "EventsIndex"
    End Function

Public Sub OutputHTMLText(HTMLText As String)
    Dim LinePos As Integer
    Dim LineEndPos As Integer

    LinePos = 1
    Do While (LinePos <= Len(HTMLText))
        LineEndPos = InStr(LinePos, HTMLText, vbCrLf)
        If LineEndPos <= 0 Then
            LineEndPos = Len(HTMLText) + 1
          End If
        Send Mid(HTMLText, LinePos, LineEndPos - LinePos)
        LinePos = LineEndPos + 2
        Loop
    End Sub

Public Sub DisplayCalendarFor(AnyDate As Date)
    Dim Calendar As New clsCalendars

    Calendar.FirstDayOfMonth = DateSerial(Year(AnyDate), _
        Month(AnyDate), 1)
    Calendar.Init
    rsEvents.Seek ">=", Calendar.FirstDayOfMonth, 1
    If Not rsEvents.NoMatch Then
        Do While (Not rsEvents.EOF)
            If (Month(rsEvents!EventDate) = _
                Month(Calendar.FirstDayOfMonth)) Then
```

```
                Calendar.AddEvent rsEvents!EventDate, _
                    rsEvents!Description
              Else
                rsEvents.MoveLast
              End If
            rsEvents.MoveNext
            Loop
      End If
    OutputHTMLText Calendar.HTMLText
    End Sub

Public Sub AddEventToCalendar(EventDate As Date, _
    EventDescription As String)
    rsEvents.AddNew
    rsEvents!EventDate = EventDate
    rsEvents!Description = EventDescription
    rsEvents.Update
    End Sub
```

Each time it's called, this program displays a calendar. If it detects a **GET** request method, it knows that the user has made a direct request—no month has been selected, so it displays the current month. If it detects a **POST** request, it checks whether the form was submitted with the "Add Event" button. If so, it adds the new event to the database before it redisplays the calendar.

The procedure **AddEventToCalendar**() performs a simple update to the Events table in the Calendar database. The procedure **DisplayCalendarFor**() steps through the database table, locating event announcement records that belong on the current calendar and adding them to the table object model with the calendar object's **AddEvent**() method. Once it has finished updating the table object model with the event announcements, it passes the result of **Calendar.HTMLText**() to the procedure **OutputHTMLText**(), which transmits the text line-by-line to the client browser.

No-Fear CGI With VB5

Combining VB's flexible database capabilities with the Windows CGI makes it possible to create some amazing Web sites that feature programmed layout and rich interactivity. In this chapter, we've seen how easy it is to bring together all the pieces of a database-driven Web site:

- CGI form design
- The Windows CGI
- Visual Basic's Data Access Object Model
- HTML tables
- Object-oriented document construction

With VB and a Web server that supports Windows CGI, you can construct an entire Web site within a single program, storing all your data in an Access database and providing custom responses to users with documents that generate themselves on the fly. VB may be the ultimate online database publishing system.

Advanced CGI

CHAPTER 8

Ready to pump up your Web site with low-doze, code-driven pages? Or how about cashing in on the online buying craze? Then you'll need to keep in touch with your customers with some secrets from the CGI masters.

Advanced CGI

In Chapter 7, we talked about the Common Gateway Interface (CGI), the standard means by which Web pages can gather information from users and provide custom responses to their inquiries. A CGI application, also known as a script, depends on three elements: an HTML form, a CGI-compatible Web server, and a script program that can process the submitted data and send back an appropriate response. We used Visual Basic to write a CGI script that supplied both the form and its response. In this chapter, we'll see how we can actually build an entire Web site within a VB CGI script, featuring any number of distinct pages.

Building A Web Site In Visual Basic

In the CGI example applications we developed in Chapter 7, we saw how we can use the CGI request method to differentiate between a form submission event and a direct call to our CGI script. This enables us to embed the form itself within its own script. When the user calls our CGI script, either by linking to it from another document or by typing its URL directly into his or her browser, the script receives a **GET** request and responds by sending the text of the input form. When the user clicks the submit button on that form, the form uses the **POST** method to send its data to the same script program. The script program then processes the information and assembles a meaningful response.

That works great if your site has only two pages. But how can we use this technique to build a programmed Web site with a more realistically varied selection of pages and forms? Let's take a few steps backward and construct a simple CGI-based Web site that will serve up multiple documents and forms.

Differentiating Pages With The CGI Logical Path

While we can use the request method to tell the difference between a form submission and a direct link, we'll need some other kind of identifier to select a particular page or form. The easiest way to do this is to add some information to the end of the URLs that we assign to our **HREF** and form **ACTION** attributes. The standard CGI variable **CGI_LogicalPath** will contain any part of the URL that follows the CGI program name. Given the following URL:

```
http://localhost/cgi-bin/MyCGIProgram.exe/HOME_PAGE
```

CGI_LogicalPath will contain the string "/HOME_PAGE". That handy little piece of information will identify specific links among our programmed pages and forms, whether they're triggered by ordinary hyperlinks or by form submit events.

Running The CGI Web Site Experiment

Compile the project CGIWebSiteExp.VBP and place the file CGIWebSiteExp.EXE in your Web server's CGI subdirectory (for example, \CGI-BIN). Start your Web browser and enter the following URL:

```
http://LocalHost/cgi-bin/CGIWebSiteExp.EXE
```

Substitute the name of your server's CGI directory as appropriate.

When the application loads, it will display the document shown in Figure 8.1.

Click on the first of the three hyperlinks in the list of options, "User Login". The program responds by displaying a simple form with a single input field and a submit button, as shown in Figure 8.2.

Enter your name in the text field, then click the submit button labeled "Login". The program will receive the value you entered into the text field, incorporating it into the response page shown in Figure 8.3.

To return to the main document—also the default document—click the *Home* link on any of the pages. The second link on that page will also display a form, and the third link in the list will display a simple HTML document without a **<FORM>** section.

Coding The CGI Web Site Experiment

Each of the links in this simple Web site demonstration activates the same CGI program, CGIWebSiteExp.EXE. The only difference between their URLs is their appended extensions.

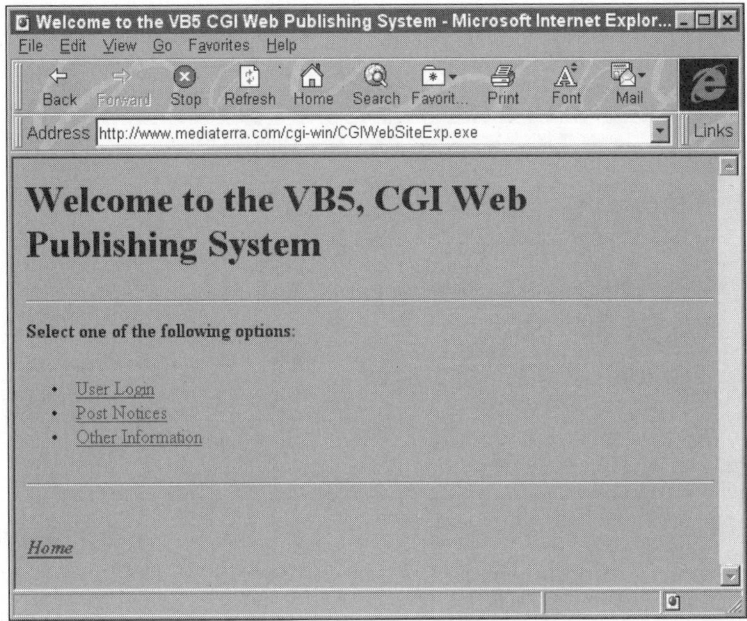

Figure 8.1

The opening document shown by CGIWebSiteExp.EXE.

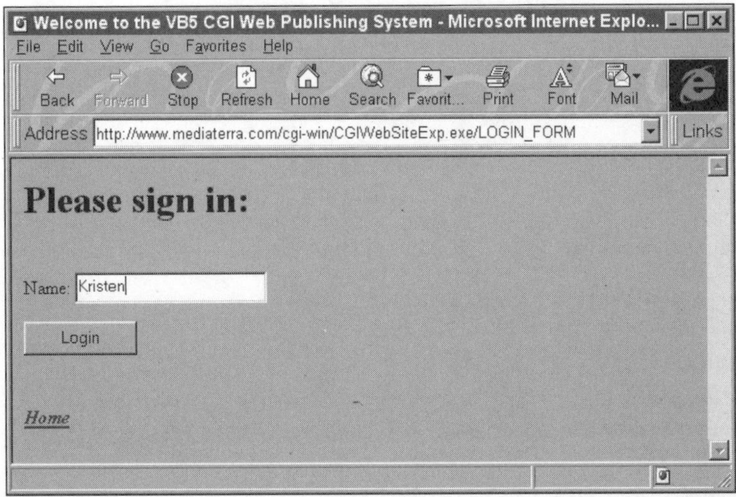

Figure 8.2

The User Login form returned by CGIWebSiteExp.EXE.

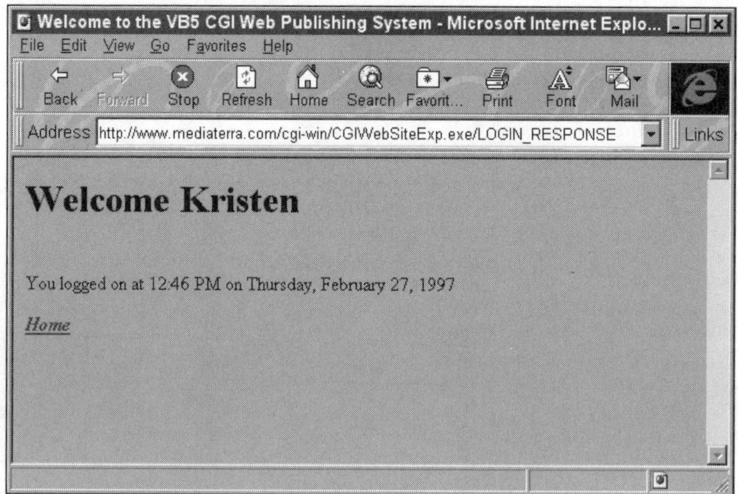

Figure 8.3
The document displayed by CGIWebSiteExp.EXE in response to the Login form.

Just as in the previous CGI projects, this program contains two main procedures, **Inter_Main**() and **CGI_Main**(), as shown in Listing 8.1.

Listing 8.1 The code for modCGIWebSiteExp.BAS.

```
Option Explicit

Public Sub CGI_Main()
  Dim PageRequested As String

  PageRequested = UCase$(CGI_LogicalPath)

  Send "Content-type: text/html"
  Send ""
  Send "<HTML>"
  Send "<HEAD>"
  Send "<TITLE>Welcome to the VB5 CGI Web Publishing System</TITLE>"
  Send "</HEAD>"
  Send "<BODY>"
  If CGI_RequestMethod = "GET" Then
    Select Case PageRequested
     Case ""
      Send "<H1>Welcome to the VB5, CGI Web Publishing System</H1>"
      Send "<HR>"
```

```
 Send "<B>Select one of the following options:</B>"
 Send "<BR><BR>"
 Send "<UL>"
 Send "<LI><A HREF=""" & CGI_ExecutablePath & _
    "/LOGIN_FORM"">User Login</A>"
 Send "<LI><A HREF=""" & CGI_ExecutablePath & _
    "/NOTICE_FORM"">Post Notices</A>"
 Send "<LI><A HREF=""" & CGI_ExecutablePath & _
    "/OTHER_INFO_FORM"">Other Information</A>"
 Send "</UL>"
 Send "<HR>"
Case "/LOGIN_FORM"
 Send "<H1>Please sign in:</H1>"
 Send "<BR><BR>"
 Send "<FORM ACTION=""" & CGI_ExecutablePath & _
    "/LOGIN_RESPONSE"" METHOD=POST>"
 Send "Name: <INPUT NAME=""name"">"
 Send "<BR><BR>"
 Send "<INPUT TYPE=SUBMIT VALUE=""Login"">"
 Send "</FORM>"
Case "/NOTICE_FORM"
 Send "<H1>Post your notice:</H1>"
 Send "<BR><BR>"
 Send "<FORM ACTION=""" & CGI_ExecutablePath & _
    "/NOTICE_RESPONSE"" METHOD=POST>"
 Send "Enter your message below:"
 Send "<BR><BR>"
 Send "<TEXTAREA NAME=""noticetext"" COLS=60 ROWS=6 WRAP=VIRTUAL>"
 Send "</TEXTAREA>"
 Send "<BR><BR>"
 Send "<INPUT TYPE=SUBMIT VALUE=""Post Notice"">"
 Send "</FORM>"
Case "/OTHER_INFO_FORM"
 Send "<H1>Here's the latest news:</H1>"
 Send "<HR>"
 Send "You can build an entire Web Site within a Visual Basic "
 Send "CGI application. "
 Send "By responding to the CGI Request Method and by " & _
     "interpreting "
 Send "the logical path, you can direct users to any " & _
     "page or form "
 Send "within your site."
 Send "<BR><BR>"
 Send "Any page in your site may then contain information "
 Send "extracted from database records, or assembled " & _
     "from other "
```

```
        Send "data sources. In other words, you can build an " & _
            "interactive "
        Send "Web Site that provides custom information and " & _
            "layouts to "
        Send "each visitor."
        Send "<HR>"
      End Select
    ElseIf CGI_RequestMethod = "POST" Then
     Select Case PageRequested
      Case "/LOGIN_RESPONSE"
        Send "<H1>Welcome " & GetSmallField("name") & "</H1>"
        Send "<BR><BR>"
        Send "You logged on at " & Format(Now, "Medium Time") & _
           " on " & Format(Now, "Long Date")
      Case "/NOTICE_RESPONSE"
        Send "<H1>Notice Posted</H1>"
        Send "<HR>"
        Send GetSmallField("noticetext")
        Send "<HR>"
      End Select
    Else
     Send "<H1>This CGI application does not support the " & _
        CGI_RequestMethod & _
        " Request Method</H1>"
    End If

  Send "<BR><BR>"
  Send "<I><B><A HREF=""" & CGI_ExecutablePath & """>Home</A></B></I>"
  Send "</BODY>"
  Send "</HTML>"

  End Sub

Public Sub Inter_Main()
  MsgBox "This CGI program must be run within a Web browser."
  End Sub
```

Inter_Main() is called when the program is invoked directly, rather than through CGI. This program does not have any "offline" features, so its **Inter_Main**() procedure just displays a message box that reminds the user that the program must be run from a Web browser.

The somewhat unwieldy **CGI_Main**() procedure does all the work of displaying documents and forms. It begins by copying an all-uppercase version of

CGI_LogicalPath into the variable **PageRequested.** It then sends an HTTP header and a common block of tags that represent the opening of an HTML document:

```
Send "Content-type: text/html"
Send ""
Send "<HTML>"
Send "<HEAD>"
Send "<TITLE>Welcome to the VB5 CGI Web Publishing System</TITLE>"
Send "</HEAD>"
Send "<BODY>"
```

If you look at the end of the procedure, you'll see that it closes by sending the corresponding end tags, preceded by a common *Home* page link:

```
Send "<BR><BR>"
Send "<I><B><A HREF=""" & CGI_ExecutablePath & """>Home</A></B></I>"
Send "</BODY>"
Send "</HTML>"
```

You aren't required to supply common opening and closing sections for your CGI-embedded documents. I just wanted to minimize repetition in this example. Between these two blocks of common HTML, you'll find an **If...Then...ElseIf... Else... End If** statement that handles the branching based on the CGI request method, as reported by the variable **CGI_RequestMethod**. The final **Else** clause handles requests other than **POST** and **GET**—such as **HEAD**, which instructs the server to return only headers for the file specified by the given URL. As we saw in Chapter 3, some Web client utilities query the server to identify the Content-type before requesting an actual transfer of the data. If you wish, you may create a **HEAD** clause that will return a set of headers with no further document data. Keep in mind that you'll need to remove the common HTML sections and incorporate them into the **GET** and **POST** clauses, or into the **Case** clauses that generate the individual documents.

The **Select Case** statement that appears within the **Then** clause handles documents that need to be returned in response to ordinary HTTP requests: those that come from direct links to our virtual Web site—not from form submit events. The first **Case**, the one with a selector value of "", responds to a naked URL, such as:

```
http://HostName/cgi-bin/CGIWebSiteExp.exe
```

This **Case** represents the site's "home page" and generates the document that users will see if they request your site by its commonly known URL. For any CGI-based Web site, you'll want to use this **Case** clause, under the conditional code that responds to the **GET** method, to send your home page. It's also possible to generate the document by calling a separate procedure.

Each of the other **Case** clauses—in both this **Select Case** statement and in the one under the **POST** method—responds to an extended URL. Look at the **Case** for the selector "/LOGIN_FORM":

```
Case "/LOGIN_FORM"
 Send "<H1>Please sign in:</H1>"
 Send "<BR><BR>"
 Send "<FORM ACTION=""" & CGI_ExecutablePath & _
    "/LOGIN_RESPONSE"" METHOD=POST>"
 Send "Name: <INPUT NAME=""name"">"
 Send "<BR><BR>"
 Send "<INPUT TYPE=SUBMIT VALUE=""Login"">"
 Send "</FORM>"
```

When the user clicks the option "User Login" on the home page, the program will execute this code, as specified by a URL such as:

```
http://HostName/cgi-bin/CGIWebSiteExp.exe/LOGIN_FORM
```

The **ACTION** attribute of the **<FORM>** tag in this **Case** clause specifies a URL such as:

```
http://HostName/cgi-bin/CGIWebSiteExp.exe/LOGIN_RESPONSE
```

and the **METHOD** attribute specifies **POST**. When the user clicks the submit button, which is labeled "Login". the program will execute the code in the **Case** clause for the selector value "/LOGIN_RESPONSE":

```
Case "/LOGIN_RESPONSE"
 Send "<H1>Welcome " & GetSmallField("name") & "</H1>"
 Send "<BR><BR>"
 Send "You logged on at " & Format(Now, "Medium Time") & _
    " on " & Format(Now, "Long Date")
```

That's all there is to it. You can add as many documents as you wish. Just assign a separate URL extension for each document and add a **Case** clause to handle it in the appropriate **Select Case** statement. For a real Web site, you would probably want to break out the code that generates the actual documents into more manageable procedures. In fact, a little later in this chapter, we'll modify this framework to do away with the **Select Case** statements and respond to each request with a document retrieved from a database.

Who's Who On Your Web Site

One of the toughest Web publishing problems to solve right now is how to identify users/visitors. In a couple of our sample programs—including the one in Listing 8.1—we incorporated a login form that asks the user to submit his or her name to the server. Using this information as a record of visitors to our site is no problem; but it's another matter entirely to use it as identification for further operations that the user might perform while "logged in" to our site.

Let's say, for example, that you're running a mailorder business from your Web site, and you want to provide a shopping cart feature. Shopping carts would enable each of your users to accumulate a list of items to purchase as they browse your online catalog. When they're done shopping, they click a button to submit their order. This is a common function used by many commercial Web sites.

The Web, however, does not support *persistent* connections, which means that each time the user requests a document or data file from the server, the server sends its response and forgets that the user ever existed. Each request submitted by the browser to the server is autonomous, or *stateless*, making it pretty difficult to carry on any kind of dialog with the user. Since we can't depend on the Web server and browser to maintain an open session, we need to implement a virtual connection by tracking users as they contact our site and browse our pages. Unfortunately, no perfect solution to this problem exists.

Let's look at three different ways to identify users and maintain a persistent client state as they browse our Web sites:

- IP addresses
- Logical path identifiers
- Cookies

As you'll see in the next few projects, each approach has its advantages and shortcomings. The method you use or devise for yourself will depend on several factors, including the number of visitors you expect to handle at any given time, and the amount of work you want to invest in the tracking scheme.

Identifying Clients By Their IP Addresses

Each time it receives a CGI request, the server will set the standard CGI variable, Remote Address—which appears in CGI32.BAS as **CGI_RemoteAddr**—to the IP address of the client. Theoretically, every node on the Internet has a unique IP address, which means that each user could be identified temporarily by the IP address of the computer from which he has logged on to your site. When users contact your URL, you prompt them for their user name—or better yet, their email address, which is unique to every Internet user—and associate that name with their current IP address. Users that connect through an ISP using PPP or SLIP often have their IP addresses assigned dynamically at the time of connection, but that doesn't really matter. You only need to maintain the relationship between user name and IP address for the duration of the current session. As users log in, you record their names and IP addresses in a database table. Each time someone requests another page from your site, you look up her IP address in the table to determine whether she has logged in. You can also use this information to associate a working profile with that user, such as an open shopping cart. All in all, it seems like a good plan. And it would be, except for a large monkey-wrench known as the *proxy server*.

Proxy servers act as intermediaries between the Internet and clients who are not directly connected to the Internet. For example, a company with its own local area network (LAN) might have dozens or hundreds of users connected to a central server. Instead of assigning every workstation its own global IP address, the server handles all Internet traffic on behalf of the other workstations, passing their requests through to the Internet and handing them back the responses. To other servers on the Internet, all requests coming from the proxy server originate from the same IP address, regardless of the number of users hidden behind that proxy server.

An enormous number of users now connect to the Web through online services—especially through America Online—and online services connect their users to the Internet through proxies. Thanks to proxies, at any particular moment, hundreds or thousands of Internet users may share the same IP address. If you're reasonably certain, however, that no more than one user from any given proxy server will contact your Web server at any one time, or if your application needs to serve only the users of a corporate Intranet on which every workstation has a unique IP address, then IP addresses offer the simplest way to build a CGI application that mimics a client/server environment.

Project: Establishing A User Context By IP Address

While IP addresses may change from session to session, you may want to hold on to information voluntarily provided by individual users, such as their names, their email addresses, and their preferences regarding the information you offer on your site. In the case of certain commerce sites, this could also include a history of their purchases and an open purchase order, commonly known as a shopping cart or shopping basket.

In this project, we'll modify the CGI Web Site Experiment so that logging in to the site will associate the user's current IP address with his user name. To accomplish this, we'll need to add a database with a table to store user information.

Managing The Shortcomings Of IP Address Identification

Since we can't count on unique IP addresses for each user, we'll need to make a couple of assumptions. First, we'll declare that we can unlog any user who hasn't hit our site for some arbitrarily defined time period. Unlogging does not prevent a user from hitting the site again. It's just an assumption that they will probably not do so and therefore will not likely conflict with another user at the same IP address. This is a poor but necessary assumption, since we have no way of knowing when a user has "left" our site. Secondly, we'll say that when two or more users log into the site from the same IP address, we will treat them all as unlogged. We really have no choice about this. Once we recognize more than one user at a particular IP address, we have no way to differentiate between them. This means that we would pass user-specific information—perhaps even personal information—to anyone with the same address. When duplicate addresses occur, we need to either restrict all conflicting users from access to information that would be specific to any of them, or we need to provide a form-by-form logging mechanism.

Unique IP Addresses On Corporate Intranets

If you're writing a CGI application for your corporate intranet, and all your workstations have unique IP addresses, you can dispense with most of this complexity. Just record the users' IP addresses in the **Users** *table as they log in, and use them as identification. You'll still need to use an expiration period to unlog them, but you won't need to worry about conflicts. If two users log in from the same IP address, it probably means that one user has taken over another's physical workstation, so you can safely unlog the previous user before logging in the new user.*

Building A User Database For The CGI Web Site

The first change you'll notice in **CGI_Main()**, shown in Listing 8.2, is the call to the function **OpenOrGenerateCGIWebSiteDatabase()**, shown later in the same listing.

Listing 8.2 The code for modCGIWebSiteExp.BAS.

```
Option Explicit

Private dbWebSiteDatabase As Database
Private tdUsers As TableDef
Private idxUsers As Index
Private idxIPAddress As Index
Private rsUsers As Recordset
Private Const TimeThreshold = 30 'minutes

Public Sub CGI_Main()
  Dim ErrorMessage As String
  Dim PageRequested As String
  Dim UserID As String

  If Not OpenOrGenerateCGIWebSiteDatabase Then
    ErrorMessage = "Unable to open site database. "
    ErrorMessage = ErrorMessage & "Please contact the " & _
        "site administrator "
    ErrorMessage = ErrorMessage & _
        "at <A HREF=""mailto:admin@CGIWebSite.com"">"
    ErrorMessage = ErrorMessage & "admin@CGIWebSite</A>."
    SendMessageDocument ErrorMessage
    Exit Sub
  End If

  UnlogExpiredUsers
```

```
UserID = IdentifyUserAtCurrentIPAddress(CGI_RemoteAddr)
PageRequested = UCase$(CGI_LogicalPath)

Send "Content-type: text/html"
Send ""
Send "<HTML>"
Send "<HEAD>"
Send "<TITLE>Welcome to the VB5 CGI Web Publishing System</TITLE>"
Send "</HEAD>"
Send "<BODY>"
If CGI_RequestMethod = "GET" Then
  Select Case PageRequested
   Case "/HOME"
    Send "<H1>Welcome to the VB5, CGI Web Publishing System</H1>"
    Send "<HR>"
    Send "<B>Select one of the following options:</B>"
    Send "<BR><BR>"
    Send "<UL>"
    Send "<LI><A HREF=""" & CGI_ExecutablePath & _
       "/LOGIN_FORM"">User Login</A>"
    Send "<LI><A HREF=""" & CGI_ExecutablePath & _
       "/NOTICE_FORM" & """>Post Notices</A>"
    Send "<LI><A HREF=""" & CGI_ExecutablePath & _
       "/OTHER_INFO_FORM" & """>Other Information</A>"
    Send "</UL>"
    Send "<HR>"
   Case "", "/LOGIN_FORM"
    Send "<H1>Welcome to the VB5, CGI Web Publishing System</H1>"
    Send "<HR>"
    Send "<H2>Please sign in:</H2>"
    Send "<BR><BR>"
    Send "<FORM ACTION=""" & CGI_ExecutablePath & _
       "/LOGIN_RESPONSE" & """ METHOD=POST>"
    Send "<PRE>"
    Send "  Name: <INPUT NAME=""username"" SIZE=50, MAXLENGTH=50>"
    Send "<BR>"
    Send "Password: <INPUT TYPE=PASSWORD NAME = ""password"""
    Send "SIZE=15 MAXLENGTH=15>"
    Send "<BR><BR>"
    Send "</PRE>"
    Send "<INPUT TYPE=SUBMIT VALUE=""Login"">"
    Send "</FORM>"
   Case "/NOTICE_FORM"
    Send "<H1>Post your notice:</H1>"
    Send "<BR><BR>"
```

```
    Send "<FORM ACTION=""" & CGI_ExecutablePath & _
      "/NOTICE_RESPONSE" & """ METHOD=POST>"
    Send "Enter your message below:"
    Send "<BR><BR>"
    Send "<TEXTAREA NAME=""noticetext"" COLS=60 ROWS=6 WRAP=VIRTUAL>"
    Send "</TEXTAREA>"
    Send "<BR><BR>"
    Send "<INPUT TYPE=SUBMIT VALUE=""Post Notice"">"
    Send "</FORM>"
   Case "/OTHER_INFO_FORM"
    Send "<H1>Here's the latest news:</H1>"
    Send "<HR>"
    Send "You can build an entire Web Site within a Visual Basic "
    Send "CGI application. "
    Send "By responding to the CGI Request Method and by " & _
       "interpreting "
    Send "the logical path, you can direct users to any page " & _
       "or form "
    Send "within your site."
    Send "<BR><BR>"
    Send "Any page in your site may then contain information "
    Send "extracted from database records, or assembled " & _
       "from other "
    Send "data sources. In other words, you can build " & _
       "an interactive "
    Send "Web Site that provides custom information and " & _
       "layouts to "
    Send "each visitor."
    Send "<HR>"
   End Select
 ElseIf CGI_RequestMethod = "POST" Then
  Select Case PageRequested
   Case "/LOGIN_RESPONSE"
    UserID = GenerateLoginResponse()
   Case "/NOTICE_RESPONSE"
    Send "<H1>Notice Posted by " & UserID & "</H1>"
    Send "<HR>"
    Send GetSmallField("noticetext")
    Send "<HR>"
   End Select
 Else
  ' If you wish, rearrange the code so that this
  ' section sends just the reply headers in
  ' response to the HEAD request method:
  '
```

```
    ' Send "Content-type: text/HTML"
    ' Send ""
    '
    Send "<H1>This CGI application does not support the " & _
       CGI_RequestMethod & _
       " Request Method</H1>"
   End If

  If (Len(UserID) > 0) And (PageRequested <> "/LOGIN_FORM") Then
    Send "<BR><BR>"
    Send "You are user: " & UserID
    Send "<BR><BR>"
    Send "<I><B><A HREF=""" & CGI_ExecutablePath & "/HOME" & _
       """>Home</A></B></I>"
   End If
  Send "</BODY>"
  Send "</HTML>"

  End Sub

Public Sub Inter_Main()
  MsgBox "This CGI program must be run within a Web browser."
  End Sub

Public Function OpenOrGenerateCGIWebSiteDatabase() As Boolean

  Dim IndexField As Field
  Dim fldsUsers(4) As Field
  Dim Counter As Integer

  If Len(Dir(App.Path & "\CGIWebSite.mdb")) > 0 Then
    Set dbWebSiteDatabase = OpenDatabase(App.Path & "\CGIWebSite.mdb")
    OpenOrGenerateCGIWebSiteDatabase = True
   Else
    Set dbWebSiteDatabase = CreateDatabase( _
      App.Path & "\CGIWebSite.mdb", dbLangGeneral)

    Set tdUsers = dbWebSiteDatabase.CreateTableDef("Users")

    Set fldsUsers(0) = tdUsers.CreateField("Username", dbText, 50)
    Set fldsUsers(1) = tdUsers.CreateField("Password", dbText, 15)
    fldsUsers(1).AllowZeroLength = True
    fldsUsers(1).Required = False
    Set fldsUsers(2) = tdUsers.CreateField("IPAddress", dbText, 15)
    fldsUsers(2).AllowZeroLength = True
```

```
        fldsUsers(2).Required = False
        Set fldsUsers(3) = tdUsers.CreateField("LastSeen", dbDate)
        Set fldsUsers(4) = tdUsers.CreateField("Counter", dbLong)
        fldsUsers(4).Attributes = dbAutoIncrField
        For Counter = 0 To 4
          tdUsers.Fields.Append fldsUsers(Counter)
          Next Counter

        Set idxUsers = tdUsers.CreateIndex("UsersIndex")
        idxUsers.Primary = True
        idxUsers.Unique = True
        idxUsers.Required = True
        Set IndexField = idxUsers.CreateField("Username")
        idxUsers.Fields.Append IndexField

        tdUsers.Indexes.Append idxUsers

        Set idxIPAddress = tdUsers.CreateIndex("IPAddressIndex")
        idxIPAddress.Unique = False
        idxIPAddress.Required = False
        Set IndexField = idxIPAddress.CreateField("IPAddress")
        idxIPAddress.Fields.Append IndexField
        Set IndexField = idxIPAddress.CreateField("LastSeen")
        idxIPAddress.Fields.Append IndexField

        tdUsers.Indexes.Append idxIPAddress

        dbWebSiteDatabase.TableDefs.Append tdUsers

        dbWebSiteDatabase.Close
        Set dbWebSiteDatabase = OpenDatabase(App.Path & _
            "\CGIWebSite.mdb")
        OpenOrGenerateCGIWebSiteDatabase = True
      End If
    Set rsUsers = dbWebSiteDatabase.OpenRecordset("Users")
    rsUsers.Index = "UsersIndex"
    End Function

Public Sub SendMessageDocument(MessageText As String)
  Send "Content-type: text/HTML"
  Send ""
  Send "<HTML>"
  Send "<HEAD>"
  Send "<TITLE>CGIWebSite Error</TITLE>"
  Send "</HEAD>"
```

```
  Send "<BODY>"
  Send "<H1>CGI Web Site Error</H1>"
  Send "<BR><BR>"
  Send MessageText
  Send "</BODY>"
  Send "</HTML>"

  End Sub

Public Sub UnlogExpiredUsers()
  Dim Done As Boolean

  rsUsers.Index = "IPAddressIndex"
  rsUsers.Seek ">=", CGI_RemoteAddr ',0?
  Done = False
  Do Until rsUsers.NoMatch Or Done
    If (DateDiff("n", rsUsers!LastSeen, Now) > TimeThreshold) Then
      rsUsers.Edit
      rsUsers!IPAddress = " "
      rsUsers.Update
      rsUsers.Seek ">=", CGI_RemoteAddr
     Else
      Done = True
     End If
    Loop

  End Sub

Public Function IdentifyUserAtCurrentIPAddress( _
    IPAddress As String) As String
  Dim UserBookmark As String

  rsUsers.Seek ">=", IPAddress
  UserBookmark = ""
  If rsUsers.NoMatch Then
    IdentifyUserAtCurrentIPAddress = ""
   Else
    UserBookmark = rsUsers.Bookmark
    rsUsers.MoveNext
    If rsUsers.EOF Then
      rsUsers.Bookmark = UserBookmark
      IdentifyUserAtCurrentIPAddress = Trim(rsUsers!UserName)
     Else
      If Trim(rsUsers!IPAddress) = IPAddress Then
        IdentifyUserAtCurrentIPAddress = "Unresolvable IP Conflict"
```

```
      Else
       rsUsers.Bookmark = UserBookmark
       IdentifyUserAtCurrentIPAddress = Trim(rsUsers!UserName)
      End If
    End If
  End If
 ' Reset time of last visit - LastSeen
 rsUsers.Seek ">=", IPAddress
 Do While Not rsUsers.EOF
   If rsUsers!IPAddress = IPAddress Then
     rsUsers.Edit
     rsUsers!LastSeen = Now
     rsUsers.Update
    Else
     rsUsers.MoveLast
    End If
   rsUsers.MoveNext
   Loop
 End Function

Public Function GenerateLoginResponse() As String
  Dim UserID As String

  If Len(Trim(GetSmallField("username"))) = 0 Then
    UserID = ""
    Send "<H1>You must enter a user name.</H1>"
    Send "<BR><BR>"
    Send "Click <A HREF=""" & CGI_ExecutablePath & _
       "/LOGIN_FORM" & """>here</A> to login again."
    GenerateLoginResponse = ""
    Exit Function
   End If

  ' Update database with user information:
  rsUsers.Index = "UsersIndex"
  rsUsers.Seek "=", UCase(Trim(GetSmallField("username")))
  If rsUsers.NoMatch Then
    rsUsers.AddNew
    rsUsers!UserName = UCase(GetSmallField("username"))
    rsUsers!Password = UCase(GetSmallField("password"))
    rsUsers!IPAddress = CGI_RemoteAddr
    rsUsers!LastSeen = Now
    rsUsers.Update
    rsUsers.Bookmark = rsUsers.LastModified
    UserID = Trim(rsUsers!UserName)
```

```
   Send "<H1>Welcome " & UserID & "</H1>"
   Send "<BR><BR>"
   Send "You logged on for the first time at " & _
      Format(Now, "Medium Time") & _
      " on " & Format(Now, "Long Date")
  ElseIf UCase(GetSmallField("password")) = rsUsers!Password Then
   rsUsers.Edit
   rsUsers!IPAddress = CGI_RemoteAddr
   rsUsers!LastSeen = Now
   rsUsers.Update
   rsUsers.Bookmark = rsUsers.LastModified
   UserID = Trim(rsUsers!UserName)
   Send "<H1>Welcome back " & UserID & "</H1>"
   Send "<BR><BR>"
   Send "You logged on at " & Format(rsUsers!LastSeen, _
       "Medium Time") & _
      " on " & Format(rsUsers!LastSeen, "Long Date")
  Else
   UserID = ""
   Send "<H1>Your password did not match.</H1>"
   Send "<BR><BR>"
   Send "Click <A HREF=""" & CGI_ExecutablePath & _
      "/LOGIN_FORM" & """>here</A> to login again."
  End If
 GenerateLoginResponse = UserID
 End Function
```

This function resembles similarly named functions in projects in earlier chapters. In a nutshell, it uses the VB Data Access Object model to build an Access database named CGWebSite.MDB. This database contains just one table, called **Users**, which contains five fields: **Username**, **Password**, **IPAddress**, **LastSeen**, and **Counter**. I've also defined two indexes for the table. The index **UsersIndex** enables us to search the database by Username, which we'll need to log in new or existing users.

With the index **IPAddressIndex**, we'll check each document request to determine whether the user making the request has logged in to the site. If **OpenOrGenerate CGIWebSiteDatabase**() fails, it will return **False**. This causes **CGI_Main**() to call the simple general procedure **SendMessageDocument**(), passing it an error message instructing the user to contact the site administrator. This guarantees that the user will receive some kind of message from the server, even when the database cannot be opened. In fact, the error trapping built in to CGI32.BAS will probably trap the VB runtime error that prevented the database from opening before **CGI_Main**() gets the opportunity to respond. However, it never hurts to be thorough.

Unlogging Expired Users

After it opens the database, **CGI_Main()** calls the general procedure **UnlogExpiredUsers()**, shown in Listing 8.3. This procedure searches the **Users** table for any users logged in at the current IP address whose **LastSeen** time is older than the number of minutes specified by the constant **TimeThreshold.** On each expired user, it removes the **IPAddress**, effectively unlogging them.

Listing 8.3 The general procedure **UnlogExpiredUsers()**.

```
Public Sub UnlogExpiredUsers()
  Dim Done As Boolean

  rsUsers.Index = "IPAddressIndex"
  rsUsers.Seek ">=", CGI_RemoteAddr ',0?
  Done = False
  Do Until rsUsers.NoMatch Or Done
    If (DateDiff("n", rsUsers!LastSeen, Now) > TimeThreshold) Then
      rsUsers.Edit
      rsUsers!IPAddress = " "
      rsUsers.Update
      rsUsers.Seek ">=", CGI_RemoteAddr
     Else
      Done = True
     End If
    Loop

  End Sub
```

Identifying Users After Each HTTP Request

The general function **IdentifyUserAtCurrentIPAddress()**, shown in Listing 8.4, takes a single argument, **IPAddress**, for which it then searches the **Users** table. If it finds no record that contains that address, it returns a null string, which is assigned to the variable **UserID**. If it finds only one instance of that address, it returns the name of the associated user. If it finds just one more entry with the same address, it returns the string "Unresolvable IP Conflict." After it identifies the user, it calls the **Seek()** method again to locate the first record that contains **IPAddress.** It then steps through all the users logged at that address, resetting their **LastSeen** fields to the current time with the VB built-in function **Now()**.

Listing 8.4 The general function **IdentifyUserAtCurrentIPAddress()**.

```
Public Function IdentifyUserAtCurrentIPAddress( _
    IPAddress As String) As String
  Dim UserBookmark As String

  rsUsers.Seek ">=", IPAddress
  UserBookmark = ""
  If rsUsers.NoMatch Then
    IdentifyUserAtCurrentIPAddress = ""
   Else
    UserBookmark = rsUsers.Bookmark
    rsUsers.MoveNext
    If rsUsers.EOF Then
      rsUsers.Bookmark = UserBookmark
      IdentifyUserAtCurrentIPAddress = Trim(rsUsers!UserName)
     Else
      If Trim(rsUsers!IPAddress) = IPAddress Then
        IdentifyUserAtCurrentIPAddress = "Unresolvable IP Conflict"
       Else
        rsUsers.Bookmark = UserBookmark
        IdentifyUserAtCurrentIPAddress = Trim(rsUsers!UserName)
       End If
     End If
   End If
  ' Reset time of last visit - LastSeen
  rsUsers.Seek ">=", IPAddress
  Do While Not rsUsers.EOF
    If rsUsers!IPAddress = IPAddress Then
      rsUsers.Edit
      rsUsers!LastSeen = Now
      rsUsers.Update
     Else
      rsUsers.MoveLast
     End If
    rsUsers.MoveNext
    Loop
  End Function
```

Logging In New Or Existing Users

The other major difference between this program and the last is in the **Case "/LOGIN_RESPONSE"** clause, under the section that handles **POST** method requests. To keep the size of **CGI_Main()** a little more under control, I've removed the code from this section and placed it in a new general function called **GenerateLoginResponse()**, shown in Listing 8.5.

Listing 8.5 The general function **GenerateLoginResponse()**.

```
Public Function GenerateLoginResponse() As String
  Dim UserID As String

  If Len(Trim(GetSmallField("username"))) = 0 Then
    UserID = ""
    Send "<H1>You must enter a user name.</H1>"
    Send "<BR><BR>"
    Send "Click <A HREF=""" & CGI_ExecutablePath & _
       "/LOGIN_FORM" & """>here</A> to login again."
    GenerateLoginResponse = ""
    Exit Function
   End If

  ' Update database with user information:
  rsUsers.Index = "UsersIndex"
  rsUsers.Seek "=", UCase(Trim(GetSmallField("username")))
  If rsUsers.NoMatch Then
    rsUsers.AddNew
    rsUsers!UserName = UCase(GetSmallField("username"))
    rsUsers!Password = UCase(GetSmallField("password"))
    rsUsers!IPAddress = CGI_RemoteAddr
    rsUsers!LastSeen = Now
    rsUsers.Update
    rsUsers.Bookmark = rsUsers.LastModified
    UserID = Trim(rsUsers!UserName)
    Send "<H1>Welcome " & UserID & "</H1>"
    Send "<BR><BR>"
    Send "You logged on for the first time at " & _
       Format(Now, "Medium Time") & _
       " on " & Format(Now, "Long Date")
   ElseIf UCase(GetSmallField("password")) = rsUsers!Password Then
    rsUsers.Edit
    rsUsers!IPAddress = CGI_RemoteAddr
    rsUsers!LastSeen = Now
    rsUsers.Update
    rsUsers.Bookmark = rsUsers.LastModified
    UserID = Trim(rsUsers!UserName)
    Send "<H1>Welcome back " & UserID & "</H1>"
    Send "<BR><BR>"
    Send "You logged on at " & Format(rsUsers!LastSeen, _
        "Medium Time") & _
        " on " & Format(rsUsers!LastSeen, "Long Date")
   Else
    UserID = ""
```

```
    Send "<H1>Your password did not match.</H1>"
    Send "<BR><BR>"
    Send "Click <A HREF=""" & CGI_ExecutablePath & _
       "/LOGIN_FORM" & """>here</A> to login again."
  End If
GenerateLoginResponse = UserID
End Function
```

GenerateLoginResponse() begins by verifying that the user has actually entered some sort of **username** on the CGI form (shown in Figure 8.4). If not, it instructs them to try again and displays a link back to the login form. If so, it considers one of three possibilites. If it cannot locate **username** in the **Users** table, it adds the new user. If it identifies the user as someone who has logged in previously, it verifies his password. On failure, it sends a message indicating a password mismatch and instructs the user to try again, as shown in Figure 8.5.

I've made another, more subtle change to this program that also affects the way in which users log in to the site. The **Case "/HOME"** clause—under the section that handles the **GET** request method—no longer responds to the site's commonly known URL, the URL with no extended path. Instead, the **Case** clause for the login form

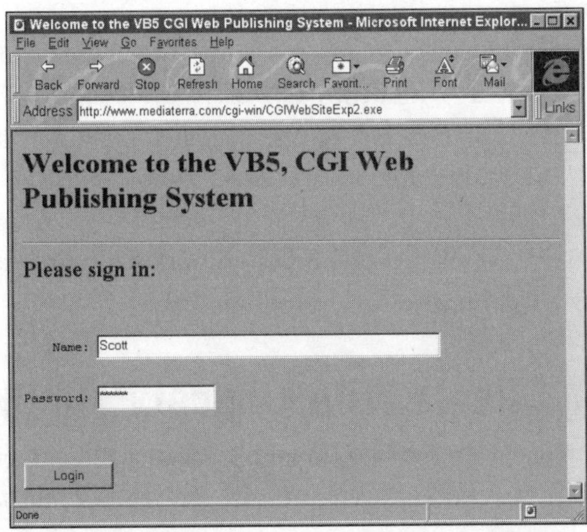

Figure 8.4
The login form displayed by CGIWebSiteExp2.EXE.

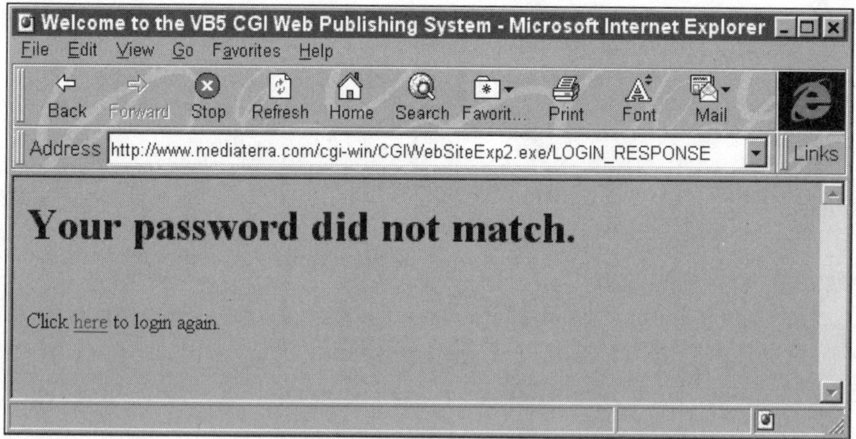

Figure 8.5
The password-mismatch message displayed by **GenerateLoginResponse()**.

now includes the two selector values, "" and "**/LOGIN_FORM**", which will cause visitors to enter the site through the login page (shown in Figure 8.4). This doesn't protect the site against users who know—or have bookmarked—URLs within the site, but it does encourage most users to log in before proceeding. We're already making substantial compromises by using IP addresses to identify users, which means that throughout the site we would need to restrict the activities of unidentified or unidentifiable users. We could simply declare that anyone who skips the login page will be treated as an unidentified user. That won't work, though—unless they log in, we won't know about any users logged in with duplicate IP addresses. In the end, a user identification scheme based solely on IP addresses—at least for sites other than corporate Intranets or Internet sites with low activity—would prove feeble and unreliable.

Identifying Clients With Logical Path Identifiers

A more reliable, though far more labor-intensive, way to identify users is to pin their identification on them as they navigate your site. As we saw in the previous experiments, you can append any information you wish to the end of your site's URL. In those programs, we added a document identifier that enabled a single CGI program to respond to user requests with any number of documents and forms. After the document identifier, we could also tack on a unique user ID.

To propagate it, however, every hyperlink on every document and form within the site would need to include that extra piece of information. So each time the user requests a new document by clicking a link or a submit button, we would need to extract the user's ID code from the logical path and append it to all the links on the requested document before feeding it to the browser.

Project: Establishing A User Context With Logical Path Identifiers

The next version of the CGI Web Site Experiment, shown in Listing 8.6, incorporates logical path identifiers as a means of tracking requests from a specific user.

Listing 8.6 The complete listing of modCGIWebSiteExp3.BAS.

```
Option Explicit

Public Sub CGI_Main()
  Dim PageRequested As String
  Dim UserID As String
  Dim UserIDPosition As Integer

  UserIDPosition = InStr(2, CGI_LogicalPath, "/")
  If UserIDPosition > 0 Then
    PageRequested = UCase$(Left(CGI_LogicalPath, UserIDPosition - 1))
    UserID = UCase$(Mid(CGI_LogicalPath, UserIDPosition))
   Else
    PageRequested = UCase$(CGI_LogicalPath)
    UserID = ""
   End If

  Send "Content-type: text/html"
  Send ""
  Send "<HTML>"
  Send "<HEAD>"
  Send "<TITLE>Welcome to the VB5 CGI Web Publishing System</TITLE>"
  Send "</HEAD>"
  Send "<BODY>"
  If CGI_RequestMethod = "GET" Then
    Select Case PageRequested
     Case "", "/HOME"
      Send "<H1>Welcome to the VB5, CGI Web Publishing System</H1>"
      Send "<HR>"
```

```
    Send "<B>Select one of the following options:</B>"
    Send "<BR><BR>"
    Send "<UL>"
    Send "<LI><A HREF=""" & CGI_ExecutablePath & _
       "/LOGIN_FORM"">User Login</A>"
    Send "<LI><A HREF=""" & CGI_ExecutablePath & _
       "/NOTICE_FORM" & UserID & """>Post Notices</A>"
    Send "<LI><A HREF=""" & CGI_ExecutablePath & _
       "/OTHER_INFO_FORM" & UserID & """>Other Information</A>"
    Send "</UL>"
    Send "<HR>"
  Case "/LOGIN_FORM"
    Send "<H1>Please sign in:</H1>"
    Send "<BR><BR>"
    Send "<FORM ACTION=""" & CGI_ExecutablePath & _
       "/LOGIN_RESPONSE" & UserID & """ METHOD=POST>"
    Send "Name: <INPUT NAME=""name"">"
    Send "<BR><BR>"
    Send "<INPUT TYPE=SUBMIT VALUE=""Login"">"
    Send "</FORM>"
  Case "/NOTICE_FORM"
    Send "<H1>Post your notice:</H1>"
    Send "<BR><BR>"
    Send "<FORM ACTION=""" & CGI_ExecutablePath & _
       "/NOTICE_RESPONSE" & UserID & """ METHOD=POST>"
    Send "Enter your message below:"
    Send "<BR><BR>"
    Send "<TEXTAREA NAME=""noticetext"" COLS=60 ROWS=6 " & _
       "WRAP=VIRTUAL>"
    Send "</TEXTAREA>"
    Send "<BR><BR>"
    Send "<INPUT TYPE=SUBMIT VALUE=""Post Notice"">"
    Send "</FORM>"
  Case "/OTHER_INFO_FORM"
    Send "<H1>Here's the latest news:</H1>"
    Send "<HR>"
    Send "You can build an entire Web Site within a Visual Basic "
    Send "CGI application. "
    Send "By responding to the CGI Request Method and by interpreting "
    Send "the logical path, you can direct users to any page or form "
    Send "within your site."
    Send "<BR><BR>"
    Send "Any page in your site may then contain information "
    Send "extracted from database records, or assembled from other "
    Send "data sources. In other words, you can build an interactive "
```

```
      Send "Web Site that provides custom information and layouts to "
      Send "each visitor."
      Send "<HR>"
     End Select
   ElseIf CGI_RequestMethod = "POST" Then
    Select Case PageRequested
     Case "/LOGIN_RESPONSE"
      UserID = "/" & UCase(GetSmallField("name"))
      Send "<H1>Welcome " & GetSmallField("name") & "</H1>"
      Send "<BR><BR>"
      Send "You logged on at " & Format(Now, "Medium Time") & _
         " on " & Format(Now, "Long Date")
     Case "/NOTICE_RESPONSE"
      Send "<H1>Notice Posted by " & Mid(UserID, 2) & "</H1>"
      Send "<HR>"
      Send GetSmallField("noticetext")
      Send "<HR>"
     End Select
   Else
    Send "<H1>This CGI application does not support the " & _
       CGI_RequestMethod & _
       " Request Method</H1>"
   End If

  Send "<BR><BR>"
  If Len(UserID) > 0 Then
    Send "You are user: " & Mid(UserID, 2)
    Send "<BR>"
   End If
  Send "<I><B><A HREF=""" & CGI_ExecutablePath & "/HOME" & _
     UserID & """>Home</A></B></I>"
  Send "</BODY>"
  Send "</HTML>"

  End Sub

Public Sub Inter_Main()
  MsgBox "This CGI program must be run within a Web browser."
  End Sub
```

The procedure **CGI_Main()** begins by dividing the logical path into two components: the user name, stored in **UserID**; and the document identifier, stored in **PageRequested.** When a user first requests the home page, he will specify its base URL, which will pass a null logical path to the CGI program. Once they "enter" the site, the embedded links will pass extended URLs with identifiers for each page. After the user logs in to the site, however, the logical path will contain two identifiers: the page identifier and the user name, separated by a forward slash character. After searching the logical path for a second forward slash character—the first slash always appears at the front of the string—**UserIDPosition** will contain either a zero to indicate that no second slash exists, or the position of the first slash found:

```
UserIDPosition = InStr(2, CGI_LogicalPath, "/")
If UserIDPosition > 0 Then
  PageRequested = UCase$(Left(CGI_LogicalPath, UserIDPosition - 1))
  UserID = UCase$(Mid(CGI_LogicalPath, UserIDPosition))
 Else
  PageRequested = UCase$(CGI_LogicalPath)
  UserID = ""
 End If
```

The presence of a forward slash indicates that the logical path contains a user name. If no slash is found, the logical path contains either a page identifier or nothing at all, which incidentally identifies the home page. But how does the user name get into the logical path in the first place?

After users request and submit the "User Login" page, the CGI program will run the code in the **Case "/LOGIN_RESPONSE"** clause:

```
Case "/LOGIN_RESPONSE"
 UserID = "/" & UCase(GetSmallField("name"))
 Send "<H1>Welcome " & GetSmallField("name") & "</H1>"
 Send "<BR><BR>"
 Send "You logged on at " & Format(Now, "Medium Time") & _
    " on " & Format(Now, "Long Date")
```

The first line of this code segment assigns the name to the variable **UserID**. Next, the procedure must incorporate that string into any **<A>** tag on the current page that will link to another page within the site. The only link on this page will be *Home*, which is created in the statements that wrap up the page, near the end of the procedure:

```
Send "<BR><BR>"
If Len(UserID) > 0 Then
  Send "You are user: " & Mid(UserID, 2)
```

```
  Send "<BR>"
 End If
Send "<I><B><A HREF=""" & CGI_ExecutablePath & "/HOME" & _
  UserID & """>Home</A></B></I>"
Send "</BODY>"
Send "</HTML>"
```

Case "/LOGIN_RESPONSE" produces HTML source similar to the document shown in Figure 8.6.

The combination of **CGI_ExecutablePath**, "/HOME", and **UserID** create a custom URL that links back to the home page, complete with a user identifier. Every URL specifier constructed throughout the rest of the procedure appends **UserID**, which causes its value to be passed back and forth between the CGI application and the documents returned to the Web browser. Although the server and browser maintain no persistent connection, the custom URLs generated by the CGI application create a kind of virtual connection. With the user name—or some more reliably unique identifier—we can perform all kinds of user-specific tasks, including updates to customer records in a database.

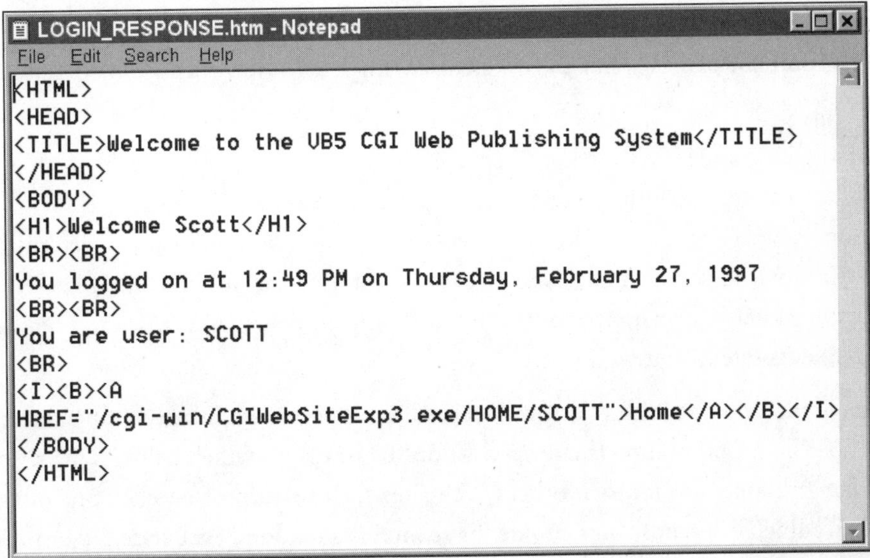


```
<HTML>
<HEAD>
<TITLE>Welcome to the VB5 CGI Web Publishing System</TITLE>
</HEAD>
<BODY>
<H1>Welcome Scott</H1>
<BR><BR>
You logged on at 12:49 PM on Thursday, February 27, 1997
<BR><BR>
You are user: SCOTT
<BR>
<I><B><A
HREF="/cgi-win/CGIWebSiteExp3.exe/HOME/SCOTT">Home</A></B></I>
</BODY>
</HTML>
```

Figure 8.6
The HTML code of a typical "/LOGIN_RESPONSE".

Identifying Clients With Cookies

The latest and most reliable way to establish a user context on the Web is with a cookie. *Cookies*, as defined by Netscape Corporation (see the Online Cookie Resources that follow) are snippets of data that a Web server or CGI application can ask the browser to store on the client computer. With cookies, we can write Web applications that can store and retrieve all kinds of user-specific information such as site preferences, or the contents of the user's open shopping cart, or a user identification code.

Cookies are advantageous because they're easy to implement and provide a reliable mechanism for user identification. Their disadvantage is being browser-dependent. Although the most popular browsers—including Microsoft Internet Explorer 3.0 and most versions of Netscape Navigator—now support cookies, several others do not, including earlier versions of Internet Explorer.

Are Cookies Safe?

Cookies contain only non-executable data. They cannot spread viruses or harm the client computer system in any way, and they return data only to the Web server that created them—cookie information is never shared between Web sites at different domain names. They have, however, triggered a few disputes over subtler privacy issues.

Although a cookie can't store any more information about a specific client than a CGI application can either detect or create, it does become a mechanism of identification. A Web site that has dropped a cookie on your computer cannot determine specifically who you are unless you give it that information voluntarily. However, it can still gather information about you, based on your behavior, that it can then use to refine its interaction with you.

One of the biggest cookie controversies has been their use by an advertising agency, DoubleClick Corporation (**http://www.doubleclick.net**), which helps its members exchange banner ads for each other's Web sites. The first time you click one of the ads, DoubleClick sends you a cookie that contains a randomly generated identification code. From that point on, whenever you click one of their members' ads, DoubleClick receives your ID number, which enables them to build a profile of your advertising preferences. To some people, this sort of targeting constitutes an invasion of privacy—it does, after all, permit a third party to choose for you which information you will see, at least as far as advertising. It's important to remember, however, that DoubleClick has no way to determine who owns the assigned identification number. It knows you only as some anonymous Internet user, which means that the information it gathers can't be used, for example, to place you on a postal or email mailing list.

Peeking At Your Cookies

If you use Internet Explorer 3.0, you will find your cookies in the subdirectory \COOKIES, under your \WINDOWS directory, each stored as a separate text file. If you use Netscape Navigator, you'll find all your cookies in a single file called cookies.txt, in your main Navigator directory. Tinkering is highly discouraged!

How Cookies Work

Servers and browsers exchange cookies by sending each other special cookie headers. When the server wants to send you a cookie, it includes a "Set-cookie" header in its HTTP response:

```
Set-cookie: <name>=<value>; expires=<Weekday, DD-Mon-YYYY HH:MM:SS GMT>;
path=</path>; domain=<domain name>; secure
```

From then on (or until the cookie expires), whenever the browser sends a request to that server—or more specifically, to that domain name—it will send a "Cookie" header that includes the name/value pairs from all cookies belonging to that domain:

```
Cookie: name1=value1; name2=value2Ö
```

To set a cookie, you must specify at least a **name** and its corresponding **value**. The **name** and **value** consist of an arbitrary pair of strings. To replace a cookie, send a "Set-cookie" header with the same **name** but a new **value**. To remove a cookie, you may send a "Set-cookie" header with an existing **name** and a new **expires** attibute value.

The optional **path** and **domain** attributes of the "Set-cookie" header default to the path and server of the document described by the response header. Although you may specify an alternative **domain** and **path**, the host setting the cookie must belong to the specified domain.

The **expires** attribute—also optional—will set a time and date on which the browser may remove the cookie. You must follow the prototype format for the time and date rather closely. Browsers may vary, but in one test that I ran, one browser accepted an **expires** attribute value of "Saturday, 01-Feb-1997 23:00:00," but rejected "Saturday, 01-02-97 23:00:00." If you omit this attibute, the cookie will expire when the browser session ends.

The final optional attibute, **secure**, will prevent the browser from sending the cookie unless it has established a secure connection with the server.

Your CGI application can store whatever information you wish in the name/value pair, with some limitations:

- The length of the name/value pair in each cookie may not exceed 4,096 bytes.
- No client is required to store more than 300 cookies for all domains combined.
- No server or domain may store more than 20 cookies on each client.

These limits were set arbitrarily to protect client systems from becoming flooded with uninvited data. When the client browser reaches either of the count limits, it is supposed make room for new cookies by disposing of the oldest.

Online Cookie Resources

For more information on cookies, see Netscape's preliminary cookie specification (already widely adopted), Persistent Client State: HTTP Cookies, at ***http://www.netscape.com/newsref/std/cookie_spec.html****; or the Bell Laboratories' (now Lucent Technologies) Cookie Internet Draft at* ***http://portal.research.bell-labs.com/~dmk/cookie.html****. For additional links related to cookies and their application, visit Malcolm's Guide to Persistent Cookies resources at* ***http://www.emf.net/~mal/cookiesinfo.html****.*

Project: A Cookie Experiment

To run this experiment, you must have a server running with a valid domain name. Cookies will not be accepted by a host named "LocalHost." In fact, browsers are supposed to accept cookies only for domain names that include at least two dots. Otherwise you could write a cookie with such broad scope, it would be sent to any server belonging to one of the top-level domains, such as "com" or "edu."

Place the compiled EXE into your server's \CGI-BIN or \CGI-WIN directory. When you enter its URL into your browser, the program should return the simple form shown in Figure 8.7.

The input field in this form is just a dummy, placed there to make it a legitimate form. Some servers will not accept a submit event from a form with no data fields. You don't have to enter anything into the field—just click the "Show Cookie" button. Your browser should display a document similar to the one shown in Figure 8.8.

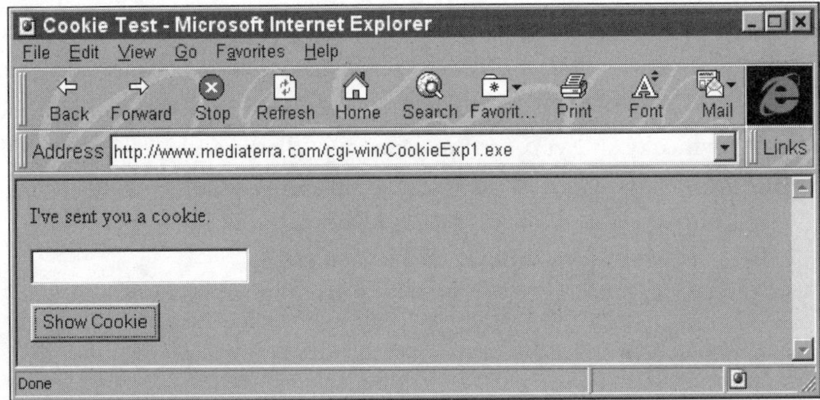

Figure 8.7
The form returned by CookieExp1.EXE.

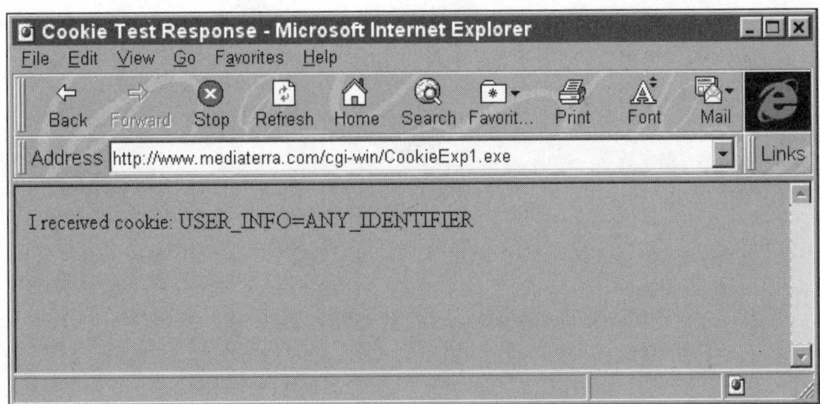

Figure 8.8
The document returned by CookieExp1.EXE.

As you can see in the brief but complete listing of modCookieExp.BAS, shown in Listing 8.7, it doesn't take much to add support for cookies to a CGI program. Although I've added the "Set-cookie" header to the form sent in response to the **GET** request method, you could add a similar header to create or update a cookie from any document in your site. You can see that the action performed by the form has no meaning in this example at all; the response header causes the browser to create the cookie before the user even has a chance to touch the form.

In the document returned in response to the **POST** method, I've used the function **FindExtraHeader()**, from the module CGI32.BAS, to locate the "Cookie" header and retrieve its contents. Even if the browser held several cookies for the current domain, it would send all the name/value pairs in a single "Cookie" request header, delimited by semicolons. If you need to send your clients multiple cookies, you'll need to pull apart the contents of the "Cookie" header yourself.

Listing 8.7 The code for modCookieExp.BAS.

```
Option Explicit

Public Sub CGI_Main()
  Dim CookieValue As String

  If CGI_RequestMethod = "GET" Then
    CookieValue = FindExtraHeader("Cookie")
    Send "Set-cookie: USER_INFO=ANY_IDENTIFIER; " & _
       "expires=Saturday, 01-Feb-1997 23:00:00"
    Send "Content-type: text/HTML"
    Send ""
    Send "<HTML>"
    Send "<HEAD>"
    Send "<TITLE>Cookie Test</TITLE>"
    Send "</HEAD>"
    Send "<BODY>"
    Send "I've sent you a cookie."
    Send "<BR><BR>"
    Send "<FORM ACTION=CookieExp1.exe METHOD=POST>"
    Send "<INPUT NAME=""anytext"">"
    Send "<BR><BR>"
    Send "<INPUT TYPE=SUBMIT VALUE=""Show Cookie"">"
    Send "</FORM>"
    Send "</BODY>"
    Send "</HTML>"
  Else
```

```
    CookieValue = FindExtraHeader("Cookie")
    Send "Content-type: text/HTML"
    Send ""
    Send "<HTML>"
    Send "<HEAD>"
    Send "<TITLE>Cookie Test Response</TITLE>"
    Send "</HEAD>"
    Send "<BODY>"
    Send "I received cookie: " & CookieValue
    Send "</BODY>"
    Send "</HTML>"
  End If
  End Sub

Public Sub Inter_Main()
  MsgBox "This is a CGI program."
  End Sub
```

Project: Establishing A User Context With Cookies

With hardly any effort at all, we can adapt the CGI Web Site Experiment to maintain a user context by exchanging cookies with the client browser. In this project, we'll use some of the database features we developed back in CGIWebSiteExp2.VBP. But instead of playing guessing games with IP addresses, we'll generate a unique identification number for each user who logs in to our site, storing that number in a cookie. Each time the user requests a document from—or submits a form to—our site, we'll look for the cookie and use it to look up their name in the database.

Running CGIWebSiteExp4.EXE

As in the previous experiment, this project will not work if you run it from a local host. You must install it on a Web server with a registered domain name. Contact it from your browser with a URL such as:

```
http://www.myserver.com/cgi-bin/CGIWebSiteExp4.exe
```

The program should respond by sending you the home page, as shown in Figure 8.9.

Notice the line that says "You are user: unknown," near the bottom of the page. Now select the option "User Login." When the browser displays the form, enter a username

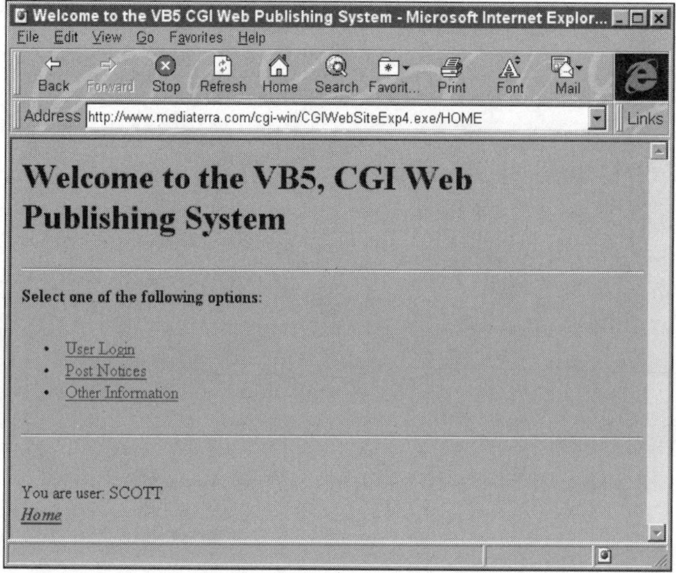

Figure 8.9
The home page displayed by CGIWebSiteExp4.EXE.

and a password, and click the "Login" button. The program should then display a welcome message, and your username should appear at the bottom of each page you select within the site. You may change to another user identity at any time by selecting the login page and entering a different name and password. If you enter an existing name with the incorrect password, the program will display a warning and ask you to try again.

If you leave the site by navigating to a different domain and then return to CGIWebSiteExp4.EXE, you will find that the program still recognizes you. If you close your browser, however, then re-open it and navigate back to CGIWebSiteExp4.EXE, you will see that the username has reverted to "unknown." The cookies created by this project include no expiration date, which means that your browser retains them only until you end your current session.

Modifications To The User Database

The project CGIWebSiteExp2.VBP had a database with one table, **Users**. We'll use that same general structure in this project, but we'll rename the **Counter** field to **UserID** and replace the index called **IPAddressIndex** with **UserIDIndex**. The program again includes a function, called **OpenOrGenerateCGIWebSiteDatabase()**, shown in Listing 8.8, that will either open an existing database or create a new one.

Listing 8.8 The code for modCGIWebSiteExp.BAS.

```
Option Explicit

Private dbWebSiteDatabase As Database
Private tdUsers As TableDef
Private idxUsers As Index
Private idxUserID As Index
Private rsUsers As Recordset


Public Sub CGI_Main()
  Dim ErrorMessage As String
  Dim CookieValueString As String
  Dim PageRequested As String
  Dim UserIDNumber As String
  Dim UserIDPosition As Integer
  Dim UserName As String

  If Not OpenOrGenerateCGIWebSiteDatabase Then
    ErrorMessage = "Unable to open site database. "
    ErrorMessage = ErrorMessage & _
        "Please contact the site administrator "
    ErrorMessage = ErrorMessage & _
        "at <A HREF=""mailto:admin@CGIWebSite.com"">"
    ErrorMessage = ErrorMessage & "admin@CGIWebSite</A>."
    SendMessageDocument ErrorMessage
    Exit Sub
   End If

  CookieValueString = FindExtraHeader("Cookie")
  UserIDNumber = Trim(GetCookieField(CookieValueString, "UserID"))
  UserName = GetUserNameFrom(UserIDNumber)
  PageRequested = UCase$(CGI_LogicalPath)

  If CGI_RequestMethod = "GET" Then
    Select Case PageRequested
     Case "", "/HOME"
      SendDocumentHead
      Send "<H1>Welcome to the VB5, CGI Web Publishing System</H1>"
      Send "<HR>"
```

```
 Send "<B>Select one of the following options:</B>"
 Send "<BR><BR>"
 Send "<UL>"
 Send "<LI><A HREF=""" & CGI_ExecutablePath & _
    "/LOGIN_FORM"">User Login</A>"
 Send "<LI><A HREF=""" & CGI_ExecutablePath & _
    "/NOTICE_FORM" & """>Post Notices</A>"
 Send "<LI><A HREF=""" & CGI_ExecutablePath & _
    "/OTHER_INFO_FORM" & """>Other Information</A>"
 Send "</UL>"
 Send "<HR>"
Case "/LOGIN_FORM"
 SendDocumentHead
 Send "<H1>Welcome to the VB5, CGI Web Publishing System</H1>"
 Send "<HR>"
 Send "<H2>Please sign in:</H2>"
 Send "<BR><BR>"
 Send "<FORM ACTION=""" & CGI_ExecutablePath & _
    "/LOGIN_RESPONSE" & """ METHOD=POST>"
 Send "<PRE>"
 Send "  Name: <INPUT NAME=""username"" SIZE=50, MAXLENGTH=50>"
 Send "<BR>"
 Send "Password: <INPUT TYPE=PASSWORD NAME = ""password"""
 Send "SIZE=15 MAXLENGTH=15>"
 Send "<BR><BR>"
 Send "</PRE>"
 Send "<INPUT TYPE=SUBMIT VALUE=""Login"">"
 Send "</FORM>"
Case "/NOTICE_FORM"
 SendDocumentHead
 Send "<H1>Post your notice:</H1>"
 Send "<BR><BR>"
 Send "<FORM ACTION=""" & CGI_ExecutablePath & _
    "/NOTICE_RESPONSE" & """ METHOD=POST>"
 Send "Enter your message below:"
 Send "<BR><BR>"
 Send "<TEXTAREA NAME=""noticetext"" COLS=60 ROWS=6 WRAP=VIRTUAL>"
 Send "</TEXTAREA>"
 Send "<BR><BR>"
 Send "<INPUT TYPE=SUBMIT VALUE=""Post Notice"">"
 Send "</FORM>"
Case "/OTHER_INFO_FORM"
 SendDocumentHead
 Send "<H1>Here's the latest news:</H1>"
 Send "<HR>"
```

```
    Send "You can build an entire Web Site within a Visual Basic "
    Send "CGI application. "
    Send "By responding to the CGI Request Method and by interpreting "
    Send "the logical path, you can direct users to any page or form "
    Send "within your site."
    Send "<BR><BR>"
    Send "Any page in your site may then contain information "
    Send "extracted from database records, or assembled from other "
    Send "data sources. In other words, you can build an interactive "
    Send "Web Site that provides custom information and layouts to "
    Send "each visitor."
    Send "<HR>"
   Case Else
    SendDocumentHead
    Send "<H1>Unknown Document Requested</H1>"
   End Select
 ElseIf CGI_RequestMethod = "POST" Then
  Select Case PageRequested
   Case "/LOGIN_RESPONSE"
    UserName = GenerateLoginResponse()
   Case "/NOTICE_RESPONSE"
    SendDocumentHead
    Send "<H1>Notice Posted by " & UserName & "</H1>"
    Send "<HR>"
    Send GetSmallField("noticetext")
    Send "<HR>"
   Case Else
    SendDocumentHead
    Send "<H1>Unknown Document Requested</H1>"
   End Select
 Else
  Send "<H1>This CGI application does not support the " & _
     CGI_RequestMethod & _
     " Request Method</H1>"
 End If

Send "<BR><BR>"
If Len(UserName) > 0 Then
  Send "You are user: " & UserName
 Else
  Send "You are user: unknown"
 End If
Send "<BR>"
Send "<I><B><A HREF=""" & CGI_ExecutablePath & "/HOME" & _
   """>Home</A></B></I>"
```

```
  Send "</BODY>"
  Send "</HTML>"

  End Sub

Public Sub Inter_Main()
  MsgBox "This CGI program must be run within a Web browser."
  End Sub

Public Function OpenOrGenerateCGIWebSiteDatabase() As Boolean

  Dim IndexField As Field
  Dim fldsUsers(4) As Field
  Dim Counter As Integer

  If Len(Dir(App.Path & "\CGIWebSite4.mdb")) > 0 Then
    Set dbWebSiteDatabase = OpenDatabase(App.Path & "\CGIWebSite4.mdb")
    OpenOrGenerateCGIWebSiteDatabase = True
   Else
    Set dbWebSiteDatabase = CreateDatabase( _
      App.Path & "\CGIWebSite4.mdb", dbLangGeneral)

    Set tdUsers = dbWebSiteDatabase.CreateTableDef("Users")

    Set fldsUsers(0) = tdUsers.CreateField("Username", dbText, 50)
    Set fldsUsers(1) = tdUsers.CreateField("Password", dbText, 15)
    Set fldsUsers(2) = tdUsers.CreateField("IPAddress", dbText, 15)
    Set fldsUsers(3) = tdUsers.CreateField("LastSeen", dbDate)
    Set fldsUsers(4) = tdUsers.CreateField("UserID", dbLong)
    fldsUsers(4).Attributes = dbAutoIncrField
    For Counter = 0 To 4
      tdUsers.Fields.Append fldsUsers(Counter)
      Next Counter

    Set idxUsers = tdUsers.CreateIndex("UsersIndex")
    idxUsers.Primary = True
    idxUsers.Unique = True
    idxUsers.Required = True
    Set IndexField = idxUsers.CreateField("Username")
    idxUsers.Fields.Append IndexField

    tdUsers.Indexes.Append idxUsers

    Set idxUserID = tdUsers.CreateIndex("UserIDIndex")
    idxUserID.Unique = True
```

```
    idxUserID.Required = True
    Set IndexField = idxUserID.CreateField("UserID")
    idxUserID.Fields.Append IndexField

    tdUsers.Indexes.Append idxUserID

    dbWebSiteDatabase.TableDefs.Append tdUsers

    dbWebSiteDatabase.Close
    Set dbWebSiteDatabase = OpenDatabase(App.Path & "\CGIWebSite4.mdb")
    OpenOrGenerateCGIWebSiteDatabase = True
   End If
  Set rsUsers = dbWebSiteDatabase.OpenRecordset("Users")
  rsUsers.Index = "UsersIndex"
  End Function

Public Sub SendMessageDocument(MessageText As String)
  Send "Content-type: text/HTML"
  Send ""
  Send "<HTML>"
  Send "<HEAD>"
  Send "<TITLE>CGIWebSite Error</TITLE>"
  Send "</HEAD>"
  Send "<BODY>"
  Send "<H1>CGI Web Site Error</H1>"
  Send "<BR><BR>"
  Send MessageText
  Send "</BODY>"
  Send "</HTML>"
  End Sub

Public Function GetCookieField(CookieValueString As String, _
                FieldName As String) As String
  Dim FieldPos As Integer
  Dim Char As String
  Dim Done As Boolean
  Dim Result As String

  FieldPos = InStr(UCase(CookieValueString), UCase(FieldName))
  If FieldPos > 0 Then
    FieldPos = InStr(FieldPos, CookieValueString, "=")
    If FieldPos > 0 Then
      FieldPos = FieldPos + 1
      Done = False
      Result = ""
```

```
      Do Until Done Or (FieldPos > Len(CookieValueString))
        Char = Mid(CookieValueString, FieldPos, 1)
        Done = (Char = ";") Or (Char = " ")
        If Not Done Then
          Result = Result & Char
         End If
        FieldPos = FieldPos + 1
        Loop
     Else
      Result = ""
     End If
   Else
    Result = ""
   End If
  GetCookieField = Result
  End Function

Public Function GenerateLoginResponse() As String
  Dim CurrentUserName As String

  If Len(Trim(GetSmallField("username"))) = 0 Then
    SendDocumentHead
    Send "<H1>You must enter a user name.</H1>"
    Send "<BR><BR>"
    Send "Click <A HREF=""" & CGI_ExecutablePath & _
       "/LOGIN_FORM" & """>here</A> to login again."
    CurrentUserName = ""
    GenerateLoginResponse = ""
    Exit Function
   End If

  ' Update database with user information:
  rsUsers.Index = "UsersIndex"
  rsUsers.Seek "=", UCase(Trim(GetSmallField("username")))
  If rsUsers.NoMatch Then
    rsUsers.AddNew
    rsUsers!UserName = UCase(GetSmallField("username"))
    rsUsers!Password = UCase(GetSmallField("password"))
    rsUsers!IPAddress = CGI_RemoteAddr
    rsUsers!LastSeen = Now
    rsUsers.Update
    rsUsers.Bookmark = rsUsers.LastModified
    CurrentUserName = Trim(rsUsers!UserName)
    Send "Set-cookie: USERID=" & Trim(UCase(CStr(rsUsers!UserID)))
    SendDocumentHead
```

```
        Send "<H1>Welcome " & Trim(rsUsers!UserName) & "</H1>"
        Send "<BR><BR>"
        Send "You logged on for the first time at " & _
           Format(Now, "Medium Time") & _
           " on " & Format(Now, "Long Date")
      ElseIf UCase(GetSmallField("password")) = rsUsers!Password Then
        rsUsers.Edit
        rsUsers!IPAddress = CGI_RemoteAddr
        rsUsers!LastSeen = Now
        rsUsers.Update
        rsUsers.Bookmark = rsUsers.LastModified
        CurrentUserName = Trim(rsUsers!UserName)
        Send "Set-cookie: USERID=" & Trim(UCase(CStr(rsUsers!UserID)))
        SendDocumentHead
        Send "<H1>Welcome back " & Trim(rsUsers!UserName) & "</H1>"
        Send "<BR><BR>"
        Send "You logged on at " & _
           Format(rsUsers!LastSeen, "Medium Time") & _
           " on " & Format(rsUsers!LastSeen, "Long Date")
      Else
        CurrentUserName = ""
        ' Remove USERID cookie by forcing expiration:
        Send "Set-cookie: USERID=0 expires=01-Jan-90 24:00:00"
        SendDocumentHead
        Send "<H1>Your password did not match.</H1>"
        Send "<BR><BR>"
        Send "Click <A HREF=""" & CGI_ExecutablePath & _
           "/LOGIN_FORM" & """>here</A> to login again."
      End If
    GenerateLoginResponse = CurrentUserName
    End Function

Public Sub SendDocumentHead()
  Send "Content-type: text/html"
  Send ""
  Send "<HTML>"
  Send "<HEAD>"
  Send "<TITLE>Welcome to the VB5 CGI Web Publishing System</TITLE>"
  Send "</HEAD>"
  Send "<BODY>"
  End Sub

Public Function GetUserNameFrom(UserNumberString As String) As String
  Dim UserNumber As Long
```

```
  GetUserNameFrom = ""
  If Len(UserNumberString) > 0 Then
    UserNumber = CLng(UserNumberString)
    rsUsers.Index = "UserIDIndex"
    rsUsers.Seek "=", UserNumber
    If Not rsUsers.NoMatch Then
      GetUserNameFrom = rsUsers!UserName
     End If
   End If
  End Function
```

Give Me A Cookie

Let's look at the cookie operations in reverse order. Shortly, I'll explain how the program creates a cookie. First, let me explain how the program reads and interprets an existing cookie.

After it opens the database, **CGI_Main**() calls the function **FindExtraHeader**() in CGI32.BAS to retrieve the contents of the cookie, which, once it has been created, the browser will send as a header with every document request:

```
CookieValueString = FindExtraHeader("Cookie")
UserIDNumber = Trim(GetCookieField(CookieValueString, "UserID"))
UserName = GetUserNameFrom(UserIDNumber)
```

If the cookie does not yet exist, **FindExtraHeader**() will return an empty string. The function **GetCookieField**(), shown in Listing 8.9, will search the cookie's contents string for a specified cookie name and, if it finds it, will return its associated value.

Listing 8.9 The general function **GetCookieField()**.

```
Public Function GetCookieField(CookieValueString As String, _
                FieldName As String) As String
  Dim FieldPos As Integer
  Dim Char As String
  Dim Done As Boolean
  Dim Result As String

  FieldPos = InStr(UCase(CookieValueString), UCase(FieldName))
  If FieldPos > 0 Then
    FieldPos = InStr(FieldPos, CookieValueString, "=")
    If FieldPos > 0 Then
      FieldPos = FieldPos + 1
      Done = False
```

```
    Result = ""
    Do Until Done Or (FieldPos > Len(CookieValueString))
      Char = Mid(CookieValueString, FieldPos, 1)
      Done = (Char = ";") Or (Char = " ")
      If Not Done Then
        Result = Result & Char
       End If
      FieldPos = FieldPos + 1
      Loop
   Else
    Result = ""
   End If
 Else
  Result = ""
 End If
GetCookieField = Result
End Function
```

GetCookieField() uses the VB function **InStr**() to determine the position of the field name within the cookie's content string. If no such field exists, it returns an empty string. If it does find the field name and the equal sign that should appear between the name and value parts, it extracts the value by copying one character at a time until it encounters either a semicolon—which separates multiple fields from each other—a space, or the end of the string. If present, the **UserID** field will contain an integer value, which will match the **UserID** field of a record listed in the **Users** database table.

The simple function **GetUserNameFrom**(), shown in Listing 8.10, will search the index **UserIDIndex** for the **UserID** and return the **UserName** string.

Listing 8.10 The general function **GetUserNameFrom()**.

```
Public Function GetUserNameFrom(UserNumberString As String) As String
  Dim UserNumber As Long

  GetUserNameFrom = ""
  If Len(UserNumberString) > 0 Then
    UserNumber = CLng(UserNumberString)
    rsUsers.Index = "UserIDIndex"
    rsUsers.Seek "=", UserNumber
    If Not rsUsers.NoMatch Then
      GetUserNameFrom = rsUsers!UserName
     End If
  End If
End Function
```

Make Me A Cookie

The code in Listing 8.10 reads and interprets the cookie. Now let's look at how the cookie comes into existence. The function **GenerateLoginResponse**(), shown earlier in Listing 8.5, works nearly identically to its counterpart in CGIWebSiteExp2.VBP with one exception: after it accepts a user login, it sends the "Set-cookie" header to create the cookie on the client. If the user enters an existing username with an invalid password, the function sends the header with a stale expiration date to delete any existing cookie on the client:

```
Send "Set-cookie: USERID=0 expires=01-Jan-90 24:00:00"
```

To send the "Set-cookie" header from within **GenerateLoginResponse**(), I had to rearrange things a little. Instead of sending the opening tags at the top of **CGI_Main**() every time the program runs, I moved them into a procedure called **SendDocumentHead**(), shown earlier in Listing 8.8. That way, I could slip in the "Set-cookie" header whenever I needed it. Now each of the **Case** clauses—which send the CGI program's documents and forms—must call **SendDocumentHead**() before it sends its own body text and tags.

Security Alert

Keep in mind that maintaining a user context does not constitute a security scheme. Even if we maintain a user database and perform password verification, the identification key we append to each intra-site URL can be viewed by anyone with the skill and the tools to monitor Internet traffic. For commerce sites, where security is essential, you will need to provide your users with additional protection, such as a server that supports secure HTTP.

One site that uses a combination of logical paths and secure HTTP is Amazon.com Books. The Amazon site uses a combination of methods to maintain a user context for its "shopping baskets." When you contact the site, it assigns you a shopping basket identification number, which it tries to store in a cookie on your computer. It also passes that ID number in the logical path of every page link. On any page, you may choose to "Buy Items Now," which leads to a page that asks whether you wish to use the secure server or the standard server. If you select the secure server, you may safely enter your credit card information into the form. Otherwise, you may call Amazon's order department and provide credit card information by telephone. In this system, only the final purchase process is protected. Since the shopping basket contains nothing more than a list of books you intend to purchase, and since your name and that basket have no association anywhere in the system, visitors to the Amazon.com Books Web site accept this as an adequate level of security.

Designing Sites With User Contexts

Although cookies provide an apparently ideal way to establish user contexts, they don't work unless the browser supports them. Estimates vary considerably, but it's safe to assume that several million users still use browsers that lack cookie support. The logical path scheme, which we implemented in CGIWebSite3.VBP, establishes a completely reliable user context. It doesn't require a database, but it also doesn't carry information from session to session.

To accommodate all users, you may want to combine logical paths with cookies. You could, for example, drop a cookie on the client to keep track of an open shopping cart. Users who lack cookie support would lose their shopping cart if they leave the site before comitting to their purchases, while users who accept cookies could leave the site and return later to continue shopping. This, however, raises another issue.

Users don't always visit your Web site while seated at the same PC. But cookies document a relationship between two computers—not between a user and a server. If you choose to write persistent cookies, keep in mind that the next time you hear from that client, there may be another operator in the driver seat. The project CGIWebSiteExp4.VBP doesn't assume there's a permanent and exclusive relationship between a user and her computer. Amazon.com, on the other hand, creates a persistent cookie on the client computer. Although this cookie doesn't represent a user, but a "shopping basket," and although the cookie doesn't lead directly to the user who created the shopping cart, it is possible for one user to spy on the book selections of another just by sitting down at the same workstation and contacting Amazon.com. Even if you consider it a frivolous security concern, information that carries over from one user to another can at least cause some confusion. To prevent such situations, either avoid persistent cookies or use a login scheme to bind users to their data.

Whatever system you devise to track users, always consider your users' privacy concerns and never imply that your site offers reliable and comprehensive protection unless you truly use secure HTTP.

HIGH PERFORMANCE

Building ActiveX Controls For The Web

CHAPTER 9

Visual Basic has come of age—you can now write your own custom controls without ever leaving the Visual Basic development environment. But that's not all. Not only will your controls work within other major programming systems such as Visual C++, FoxPro, and Delphi, they'll even be ready for life on the World Wide Web.

Building ActiveX Controls For The Web

Just when "Websters" were beginning to fall all over themselves with chatter about Java applets, Microsoft crashed the party with *ActiveX*, a whole new specification for active Web content. "ActiveX," complained the skeptics, "will threaten freedom and equality on the Web!" But Microsoft persisted, and ActiveX is rapidly emerging as the standard specification for interactive Web design, whether you program in C++, Java, Delphi, or Visual Basic.

The Road To ActiveX

Ever since the introduction of Windows 3.0, Microsoft has been working on ways to bring object technology out of the programmer's inner sanctum into the full light of the desktop. The original specification for object sharing by applications was called *Object Linking and Embedding*, or OLE. OLE is the technology that enables us to drop an Excel spreadsheet directly into a Word document, or to link two documents together so that changes made to one automatically update the other. About the same time that OLE was really beginning to become useful, Microsoft introduced Visual Basic, a programming system that lets programmers assemble applications from pre-existing components, known as *intrinsic controls* and *custom controls*, or VBXs. With the fourth version of Visual Basic, Microsoft merged the two technologies, tossing out the old VBX model and replacing it with OLE control objects, or OCXs. OLE proved that it was possible to build components that could be shared among applications written in diverse programming languages. In fact, most of the thousands of OCXs used by Visual Basic programmers were written in C++. Each new OLE component effectively extended the operating system with its own new functions. New applications could then call either on Windows 95's intrinsic capabilities or on functions provided by any number of installed component objects, including simple code modules, graphical visual controls, or complete applications. Then came the Web.

The World Wide Web was originally designed as a hypertext system. With the Web, authors throughout the world could publish their own papers and cite each other's work simply by embedding links within their documents. This proved a godsend, especially for scientists, who otherwise had to wait months for each other's papers to appear in academic journals. It wasn't long, however, before a few clever programmers at the University of Illinois figured out a way to incorporate graphics into those documents. And once the Web met multimedia, the race was on to extend its capabilities in every way imaginable. Web development swept the computer industry, and Microsoft's fearless leaders recognized that they would have to adapt or die.

To adapt OLE to the constraints of the Internet, where data transfer rates for modem users are typically hundreds of times slower than the slowest hard disk drives, Microsoft's engineers needed to pare OLE down to the essentials. By reducing the requirements for an OLE-compliant component, they made it possible to create binary objects that could transfer from Web servers to browsers in seconds instead of minutes. At the same time, Microsoft recognized the need for a whole family of technologies that would increase the power and utility of the Web, along with the Windows 95 and Windows NT operating systems. To mark the occasion, they renamed OLE to the more market-savvy ActiveX. With ActiveX technologies, Microsoft has consolidated and extended several key technologies, including not only the *Component Object Model* (COM) that originated with OLE and that serves as ActiveX's foundation, but also *Distributed COM* (DCOM), Web-compatible controls, server- and client-based scripting languages, and a special class of applications called *Active Documents.*

Visual Basic 5 And ActiveX

Visual Basic supports ActiveX in several ways. The most obvious and straightforward is that we can add ActiveX controls to Visual Basic forms. We use Visual Basic code to tie these controls together into functional programs. But controls are just one type of ActiveX component. Others include ActiveX servers, ActiveX documents, and ActiveX containers.

In addition to using the various types of ActiveX components in our Visual Basic projects, we can now use Visual Basic to create most of them. In fact, Visual Basic supplies a template for each type of ActiveX project. Just as a conventional Visual Basic program—now called a *Standard EXE*—begins with a Form module, each ActiveX project type begins with a particular type of visual or code module. ActiveX controls, for example, begin with a UserControl *designer*—similar to the familiar Form designer. To build a control, you can either place existing controls on the designer, or you can skip directly to the code module and write graphics procedures that draw the control from scratch. Unlike controls, ActiveX servers have no visual elements, so an ActiveX server project (known either as an *ActiveX EXE* or *ActiveX DLL*) begins with a blank class module.

The inner workings of the various ActiveX components can get pretty complex. And to understand them fully, you would need to study COM. Fortunately, for many applications, Visual Basic handles the intricate details of negotiating with the operating system so we can concentrate on our components' functional elements.

In this chapter, we'll build a simple ActiveX control component. First, we'll see how to design and program a new control. Then, we'll compile the control and package it for distribution on the Web. Finally, we'll incorporate it into a simple Web page and test it in Internet Explorer 3.0.

ActiveX Controls

ActiveX controls take any of three basic forms:

- A control based on a single existing control.
- A control based on two or more existing controls.
- A control drawn from scratch using graphical methods or API functions.

The most difficult controls to create are usually those in the third category, described by Microsoft as *user-drawn controls*. In a control of this type, the programmer is responsible for everything about that control's appearance, including myriad details such as what it looks like when it's disabled, or when to draw a border to indicate that the control has focus. The graphic design of such controls can easily become the most challenging part of the project. On the other hand, user-drawn controls are the ideal way to author the most unique and original designs.

Controls based on existing controls are easier to design graphically, but come with their own special problems. Above all, you need to watch out for licensing issues. Microsoft permits the incorporation of any intrinsic Visual Basic control into new, derivative controls—whether distributed freely or for profit. But controls based on other vendors' controls can only be distributed with permission, and that will usually require payment of royalties.

The creation of an ActiveX control requires several steps:

1. Design and assemble the visual elements of the control.
2. Define and implement the control's properties and methods.
3. Define and implement the control's event procedures.
4. Fill in the appropriate initialization procedures.
5. Fill in the **ReadProperties** and **WriteProperties** event procedures to store and retrieve property settings.
6. If necessary, implement property pages.

The control can be tested as it's developed by adding it to a Standard EXE project added to the current project group. Once the control has been programmed and tested, it must then be compiled into an OCX file before it can be used in a project outside the current project group.

To incorporate the new control into a Web page, we can use the Visual Basic Setup Wizard to package it into a Microsoft CAB file, which can then be referenced from within an HTML **<OBJECT>** tag. Web-based controls also need to be digitally signed for safety and marked as either safe or unsafe for scripting and initialization (we'll discuss these safety issues later).

Project: A Rollover Menu ActiveX Web Control

Theoretically, you should be able to use any ActiveX control in a Web page, but a few differences between the container applications may affect particular controls.

In this project we'll develop a relatively simple Web control, designing the properties so they work either in a conventional Visual Basic application or in an HTML document.

This control, shown in Figure 9.1, will display a menu of clickable options. When the cursor passes over any of the options, a short descriptive passage will appear above the list—hence the name "Rollover." Clicking any of the options will trigger a Click event, which can be scripted to navigate to other Web documents.

The actual code for this project will not be particularly complex. You'll soon see, however, that programming an ActiveX control—even in Visual Basic—requires attention to myriad details.

Running The RolloverMenu Control

To run this demonstration, open Internet Explorer 3.0. The RolloverMenu control has no safety certification, so you must temporarily suppress Internet Explorer's most zealous security protection:

1. Select the View menu.
2. Select Options.

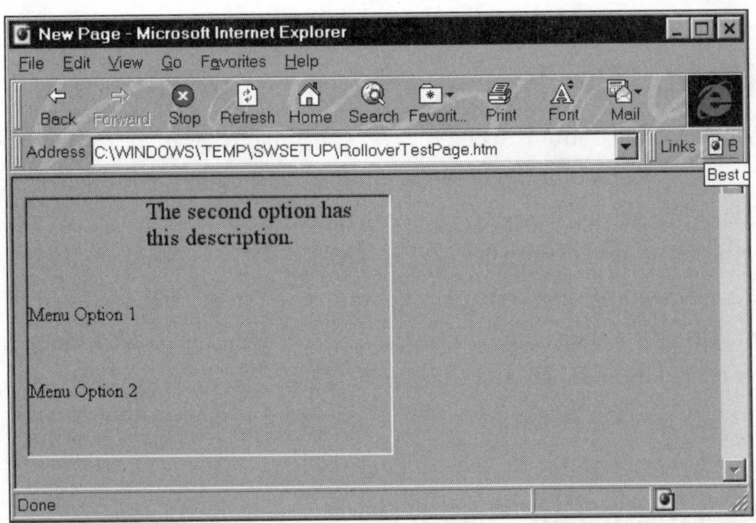

Figure 9.1
The RolloverMenu ActiveX control as it appears in Internet Explorer 3.0.

3. In the Options dialog box, choose the Security tab.
4. Locate and click the button labeled "Safety Level".
5. Choose the Medium security method.
6. Click OK in the Safety Level dialog.
7. Click OK in the Options dialog.

Watch Your Internet Explorer Security Settings

If you plan to do a lot of control development, you may want to leave Internet Explorer's Safety Level at Medium. The lowest level is not recommended because it allows any ActiveX control to install itself on your system without warning, whether or not it has been digitally signed and certified by its creators as safe.

To test the control, use Internet Explorer's File|Open menu option to locate the RolloverMenu project on the companion CD-ROM, and open the file RolloverTestPage.HTM. When the document loads, Internet Explorer will warn you of a "Potential safety violation." This means that the control has not been digitally signed, which will be the case for all controls under development. Click Yes to accept the control. Internet Explorer will copy the control and install it on your system automatically as it displays the page.

Designing The RolloverMenu Control

The RolloverMenu control is based on two constituent Label controls, as shown in Figure 9.2. To construct the list of menu options, we'll build a control array based on **lblOptions**. The second constituent control, **lblTargetDescription**, will display a lengthier description of each menu option, which will appear only while the cursor is over the corresponding menu option. The control will raise a **Click()** event whenever the user clicks one of the menu options displayed in the array of **lblOptions** controls, passing a related **TargetURL** as an argument. The value in **TargetURL** can then be used in a client script—JavaScript or VBScript—to navigate to other Web documents.

Name Those Classes Now!

Before you begin saving your new ActiveX control project, you should make sure you have the principle objects properly named. The naming of objects in an ActiveX

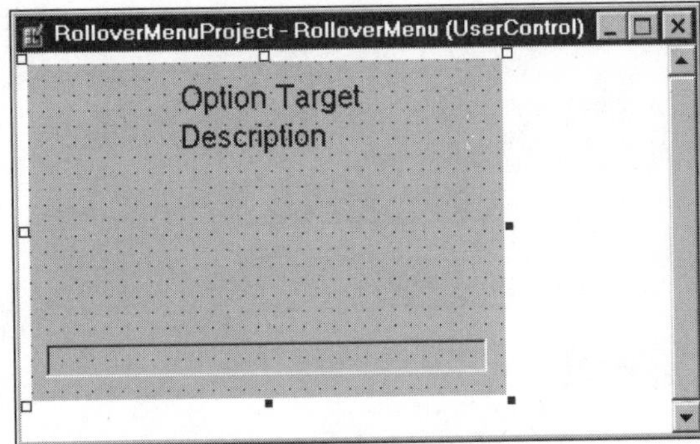

Figure 9.2

The control designer for the RolloverMenu ActiveX control.

component project is particularly important. A single ActiveX component project can include several controls. This project will contain just one, but we still need to name everything carefully. The *Project Name*, as displayed in the Project Properties dialog, will become part of the control's *fully qualified class name*, which will appear in the Object Browser and in the system Registry. When anyone tries to use your control, this is the name by which they will identify it. Do not confuse the Project Name with the file name you assign to the VBP file. Although the root of the file name may match the Project Name, saving the file under a particular name does not automatically set the Project Name. If you fail to set the Project Name before you begin compiling the project into an OCX file, it will be registered with a fully qualified class name like Project1.RolloverMenu. To change the component class name to something more sensible, you'll need to hunt down and eliminate every reference to the component in the Registry. Trust me—it's best to get it right the first time. For this project, open the Project Properties dialog and enter "RolloverMenuProject" as the Project Name, and "Rollover Menu ActiveX Control" as the Project Description, as shown in Figure 9.3. The Project Description will appear in the Visual Basic Components dialog.

You'll also need to assign a name to the **UserControl** object. To do so, make sure the control designer is open (right-click the **UserControl** object in the Project Explorer and select View Object). Then, in the Properties Window, set the **UserControl**'s **Name** property to RolloverMenu. The fully qualified name of our control will become RolloverMenuProject.RolloverMenu. The file names for the project files do not affect the control in any meaningful way. I've saved the project under the names

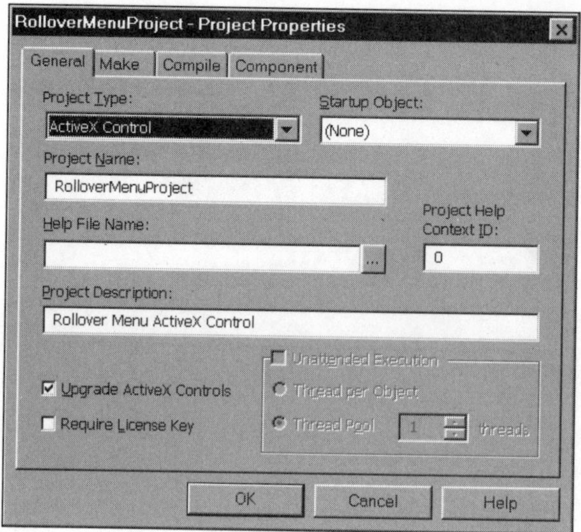

Figure 9.3
The Project Properties dialog box with settings for the RolloverMenuProject.

RolloverMenuProject.VBP and RolloverMenu.CTL. We'll be adding a few more files to the project, but we'll discuss those later.

Declaring The Control's Properties

As we begin discussing the properties of the RolloverMenu control, keep in mind that we need to think about two distinct layers of properties. The **UserControl** object itself has properties that we use to design the control, including the properties of the constituent controls. That's one layer. As we create the control, we implement properties that the control's user will use to incorporate the control into programs or Web pages. That's the second layer. To view the properties of the **UserControl** object, we open the control's designer window and use the Properties Window. To view the properties we've created for our control, we need to add the newly created control to a programming project, then select it.

If you look at the declarations section for the RolloverMenu module, shown in Listing 9.1, you'll see that it contains only one **Public** variable, **MenuOptions**. This control will certainly need more than one property. And before I explain how we're going to create the other 27 properties, let me first tell you that **MenuOptions** isn't even a real property at all—more on that later.

Listing 9.1 The declarations section from RolloverMenu.CTL.

```
Option Explicit

Public Enum RolloverMenuBackStyleConstants
    rmbsTransparent
    rmbsOpaque
    End Enum

Public Enum RolloverMenuBorderStyleConstants
    rmbdNone
    rmbdSingle
    End Enum

Public MenuOptions As Variant

'Default Property Values:
Const m_def_NumberOfOptions = 1
Const m_def_BackColor = 0 ' Not Used
Const m_def_ForeColor = 0 ' Not Used
Const m_def_Enabled = True
Const m_def_BackStyle = rmbsOpaque
Const m_def_BorderStyle = rmbdSingle
Const m_def_DescriptionProportion = 40

' Private Member Declarations
'     These values are exposed, when necessary,
'     with Get/Let/Set property procedures.
Private m_NumberOfOptions As Integer
Private m_TargetURLs() As String
Private m_Captions() As String
Private m_Descriptions() As String

Private m_BackColor As Long
Private m_ForeColor As Long
Private m_Enabled As Boolean
Private m_BackStyle As Integer
Private m_BorderStyle As Integer
Private m_DescriptionProportion As Integer

' Event Declarations
Event Click(ByVal TargetURL As String)
'Event DblClick()
'Event KeyDown(KeyCode As Integer, Shift As Integer)
```

```
'Event KeyPress(KeyAscii As Integer)
'Event KeyUp(KeyCode As Integer, Shift As Integer)
'Event MouseDown(Button As Integer, Shift As Integer, _
                X As Single, Y As Single)
Event MouseMove(MenuOption As Integer, Shift As Integer, _
                X As Single, Y As Single)
'Event MouseUp(Button As Integer, Shift As Integer, _
                X As Single, Y As Single)
```

In previous projects in this book, I have added properties to my classes by declaring public variables. That's the simplest way to add properties, but not the only way. For better control over access to properties, and to perform validation or other processes when properties change, Visual Basic—like many other object-oriented programming languages—provides a group of special procedure types called **Property Get**, **Property Let**, and **Property Set**.

Property procedures are an alternative way to add properties to an object class. Instead of declaring a public variable, we declare procedures that behave as if they were variables. In fact, the **Property Get** procedure pretty closely resembles any other type of function method. When you want the value of the property, you just use the property's **Property Get** procedure to retrieve it, passing any required arguments—such as array subscripts. The difference between a function method and a procedural property becomes clear, however, when you learn that you can also assign a value *to* the element represented by the property procedures. In that case, the property's **Property Let** procedure—or **Property Set** for object properties—takes over, performing whatever processing you choose on the assigned value, then storing it wherever you choose.

For example, consider the RolloverMenu control's **BorderStyle** property. To implement this property, we must declare two property procedures, as shown in Listing 9.2.

Listing 9.2 The property procedures for the **BorderStyle** property.

```
Public Property Get BorderStyle() As _
                    RolloverMenuBorderStyleConstants
   BorderStyle = m_BorderStyle
   End Property

Public Property Let BorderStyle(ByVal New_BorderStyle As _
                                RolloverMenuBorderStyleConstants)
```

```
m_BorderStyle = New_BorderStyle
UserControl.BorderStyle = m_BorderStyle
PropertyChanged "BorderStyle"
End Property
```

The value of the **BorderStyle** property is stored in the **Private** variable **m_BorderStyle**. When the user of the control—you or any other programmer—requests the value of **BorderStyle**, the **Property Get BorderStyle()** procedure handles the request. In this case, it simply returns the current value of **m_BorderStyle**—nothing surprising there. However, when the programmer sets **BorderStyle**, the **Property Let BorderStyle()** procedure takes over. In this example, three things take place in the **Property Let** procedure. First, it copies the newly assigned value to **m_BorderStyle**. It needs to store the value somewhere so that it can be used later, or retrieved by future calls to the **Property Get** procedure. In other words, the **Private** variable is used to *persist* the value of the property. Secondly, this sample **Property Let** procedure updates the **UserControl**'s intrinsic **BorderStyle** property. Finally, the procedure calls the **PropertyChanged** procedure, which notifies the control's host application that the property has changed so that it may refresh any relevant display—such as Visual Basic's Properties Window—and so it knows that it will need to save the updated properties. For each read/write property, we need to implement a pair of property procedures: one to set the value and one to retrieve it. To create a read-only property, we could just omit the **Property Let** (or **Property Set**) procedure. We could also include it, but use it only to raise an error.

Sixteen of the RolloverMenu control's properties are defined with property procedures. Some are more complex than others. The **BorderStyle** property is representative of a family of properties that *delegate* to properties of the **UserControl** object. In other words, the **BorderStyle** property just exposes a property that is already implemented for us in the **UserControl** object. When we set **UserControl.BorderStyle**, the **UserControl** object handles all the details of drawing the appropriate border around our control. That's why it's called delegation; instead of performing the task associated with the property, our control delegates responsibility to the **UserControl** object. The **UserControl** object supports more than 40 properties, including many of the common properties we expect to find in controls (see Table 9.1). To activate any of these properties, we declare **Property Get** and **Property Let** or **Set** procedures that expose them to the users of our control by retrieving and setting their values.

Table 9.1 Properties of the UserControl object.

Name	Type	Description
Name	**String**	Names the control—should be unique.
AccessKeys	**String**	Allows use of hot keys to shift focus to control.
Alignable	**Boolean**	Allows control to align to edge of certain containers.
Ambient	**AmbientProperties** object	Allows access to container's ambient properties.
Appearance	**Enum Integer**	Determines whether the control looks 3D.
AutoRedraw	**Boolean**	Set to True to let VB handle repainting of the control.
BackColor	**Color**	Background color.
BackStyle	**Enum Integer**	Set for opaque or transparent background.
BorderStyle	**Enum Integer**	Determines type of border around control.
CanGetFocus	**Boolean**	True if control can receive focus.
ClipControls	**Boolean**	Determines if control can draw over child controls.
ControlContainer	**Boolean**	True if control can act as a container that developers can place other controls inside.
Controls	**Collection**	List of controls that make up the ActiveX control.
CurrentX	**Long**	Current horizontal position for next graphical operation.
CurrentY	**Long**	Current vertical position for next graphical operation.
DefaultCancel	**Boolean**	True to allow control to simulate a standard button.
DrawMode	**Enum Integer**	Determines how drawings interact with existing window contents.
DrawStyle	**Enum Integer**	Affects line style for graphics output calls.
DrawWidth	**Integer**	Sets line width for graphics output calls.
EditAtDesignTime	**Boolean**	True if designers must use Edit menu.
Enabled	**Boolean**	True if control is able to be active.

continued

Table 9.1 Properties of the UserControl object (continued).

Name	Type	Description
EventsFrozen	**Boolean**	True if control is ignoring events raised by the control.
Extender	**Extender** object	Allows access to container-managed (extended) properties.
FillColor	**Color**	Color used to fill graphics interiors.
FillStyle	**Enum Integer**	Determines how graphics use **FillColor**.
Font	**Font**	Current font.
FontTransparent	**Boolean**	True if text has transparent background.
ForeColor	**Color**	Color used for foreground graphics.
ForwardFocus	**Boolean**	True if control should forward focus events to next control.
Hyperlink	**Hyperlink** object	Defines navigation for Web controls.
Image	**Handle**	Handle to the Image used for **AutoRedraw**.
InvisibleAtRuntime	**Boolean**	Determines if control is visible at runtime.
KeyPreview	**Boolean**	True if control wants to process keys before child controls.
MaskColor	**Color**	Sets the color that determines transparency for **MaskPicture.**
MaskPicture	**Picture**	Defines the opaque and transparent regions of the control.
MouseIcon	**Picture**	Icon used for mouse pointer when **MousePointer** is 99.
MousePointer	**Enum Integer**	Pointer used when mouse is over control.
Palette	**String**	Path to a bitmap containing a palette.
PaletteMode	**Enum Integer**	Specifies which object's palette to use.
Parent	**Object**	Reference to the container object.
ParentControls	**Collection**	Other controls belonging to the container.
Picture	**Picture**	Picture to display as the control's background.
PropertyPages	**String Array**	Names of ActiveX Property Pages.

continued

Table 9.1 Properties of the UserControl object (continued).

Name	Type	Description
Public	Long	Determines origin X for user-defined **ScaleMode**.
ScaleHeight	Long	Height of interior of control.
ScaleMode	Enum Integer	Sets units of measure used for **ScaleHeight**, **ScaleWidth**, etc.
ScaleTop	Long	Determines origin Y for user-defined **ScaleMode**.
ScaleWidth	Long	Width of interior of control.
ToolboxBitmap	Picture	Picture used to represent the control.

Some of the property procedures are more complex. The **Captions()** property, for example, maintains an array of menu option captions. The **Private m_Captions()** array is dynamic, meaning that it needs to be resized as items are added to it. This task is handled by the **Property Let Captions()** procedure, shown in Listing 9.3.

Listing 9.3 The **Property Get** and **Let Captions()** procedures from RolloverMenu.CTL.

```
Public Property Get Caption(ByVal Index As Integer) As String
    Caption = m_Captions(Index)
    End Property

Public Property Let Caption(ByVal Index As Integer, _
                           ByVal New_Caption As String)
    If (UBound(m_Captions) < Index) And _
       (m_NumberOfOptions <= Index) Then
        ReDim Preserve m_Captions(Index)
      End If
    m_Captions(Index) = New_Caption
    If Index <= (lblOptions.UBound + 1) Then
        lblOptions(Index - 1).Caption = m_Captions(Index)
      End If
    PropertyChanged "Caption"
    End Property
```

The **Property Get Caption()** procedure differs from its **BorderStyle** counterpart primarily by taking an argument, **Index**, which specifies which element in the array to return. From the user's perspective, the **Caption** property looks like a simple array. The **Property Let Caption()** procedure has a little more work to do. To hide the fact that the **Caption** property is actually stored in a dynamic array, the **Property Let** procedure handles all the re-allocation details internally. If the **Index** value passed in its first argument exceeds the current upper bound of the array, and the value of **Index** does not exceed the current number of options on the menu, then the **Property Let** procedure expands the array to accommodate the new entry. Notice that the **Property Let** procedure always has one more argument than its corresponding **Property Get** procedure. The last argument defined in the declaration of the **Property Let** procedure receives the new property value, and its data type must match the return data type of the **Property Get** procedure. This is true for property procedures in any kind of class module, not just for ActiveX controls.

We've seen that the **BorderStyle** property delegates to the **UserControl.BorderStyle** property. Now let's look at a property that delegates to an entire committee. To prevent the control from becoming a patchwork of mismatched colors, the **BackColor** property not only needs to update the **UserControl** object, but all the constituent controls as well. The **Property Get** and **Let BackColor()** procedures shown in Listing 9.4 update everything.

Listing 9.4 The **Property Get** and **Let BackColor()** procedures from RolloverMenu.CTL.

```
Public Property Get BackColor() As OLE_COLOR
    BackColor = m_BackColor
    End Property

Public Property Let BackColor(ByVal New_BackColor As OLE_COLOR)
    Dim Counter As Integer

    m_BackColor = New_BackColor
    UserControl.BackColor = m_BackColor
    For Counter = 0 To (NumberOfOptions - 1)
        lblOptions(Counter).BackColor = m_BackColor
        Next Counter
    lblTargetDescription.BackColor = m_BackColor
    PropertyChanged "BackColor"
    End Property
```

The most complex property procedure in the RolloverMenu control represents the **NumberOfOptions** property, shown in Listing 9.5.

Listing 9.5 The **Property Get** and **Let NumberOfOptions()** procedures from RolloverMenu.CTL.

```
Public Property Get NumberOfOptions() As Integer
    NumberOfOptions = m_NumberOfOptions
    End Property

Public Property Let NumberOfOptions( _
    ByVal New_NumberOfOptions As Integer)
    Dim Counter As Integer

    ' Remove all but the first option label control.
    If lblOptions().UBound > 0 Then
        For Counter = 1 To m_NumberOfOptions - 1
            Unload lblOptions(Counter)
            Next Counter
      End If
    m_NumberOfOptions = New_NumberOfOptions
    lblOptions(0).Caption = m_Captions(1)
    lblOptions(0).BackStyle = 0
    lblOptions(0).BorderStyle = 0
    lblOptions(0).Visible = True
    If m_NumberOfOptions > 1 Then
        ' Expand the label control array to the current
        ' number of options. The control array is zero-based,
        ' while the three property arrays are treated as
        ' if they are one-based; i.e., each array element
        ' corresponds to the position of a menu option.
        For Counter = 1 To New_NumberOfOptions - 1
            Load lblOptions(Counter)
            lblOptions(Counter).Top = _
                lblOptions(Counter - 1).Top + _
                lblOptions(Counter - 1).Height + 10
            lblOptions(Counter).BackStyle = 0
            lblOptions(Counter).BorderStyle = 0
            lblOptions(Counter).Visible = True
            Set lblOptions(Counter).Font = lblOptions(0).Font
            lblOptions(Counter).Caption = _
                m_Captions(Counter + 1)
            Next Counter
        UserControl_Resize
```

```
    End If
  PropertyChanged "NumberOfOptions"
  End Property
```

The **Property Let NumberOfOptions()** procedure does a little more than just setting **Private m_NumberOfOptions.** The RolloverMenu control uses an array of Label controls to display its menu options. The basic control design begins with just a single **lblCaptions** control. To support multiple menu options, the **Property Let NumberOfOptions()** procedure must propagate that original control. But there is a catch. The **NumberOfOptions** can go up or down, which means that the procedure may need to either add new Label controls or eliminate existing controls from the array. For simplicity's sake, I've chosen to collapse the array back to a single Label control each time the **NumberOfOptions** changes:

```
' Remove all but the first option label control.
If lblOptions().UBound > 0 Then
    For Counter = 1 To m_NumberOfOptions - 1
        Unload lblOptions(Counter)
        Next Counter
  End If
```

The **Property Let** procedure then reconstructs the control array according to the new **NumberOfOptions**, setting some basic properties on each element as it goes.

Setting Procedure IDs

The ActiveX control model defines a standard set of properties, events, and methods. By identifying your property procedures to the operating system as standard procedures, you enable the host application to call your code more efficiently. Also, many ActiveX containers will know that certain properties belong to particular data types; when the host application can identify your standard properties, it may offer special property dialog boxes such as Color and Font.

To set the Procedure IDs for your property procedures, open the Visual Basic Tools menu, select Procedure Attributes, then click the Advanced button to display the complete dialog box, which is shown in Figure 9.4.

Select the **BorderStyle** property from the Name drop-down list at the top of the dialog. Locate the Procedure ID list—it's about halfway down the box—and select

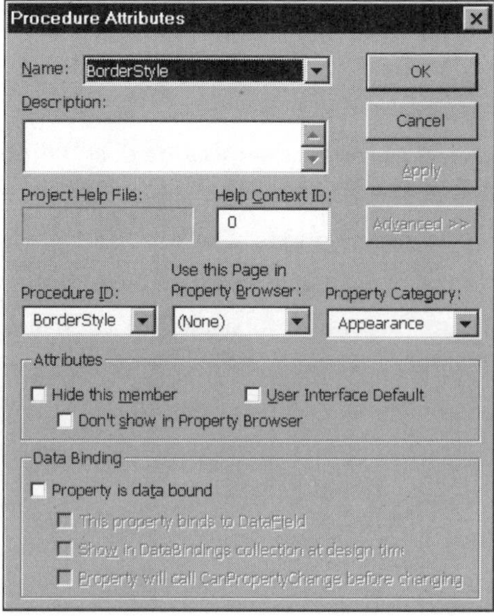

Figure 9.4
The Procedure Attributes dialog.

the procedure called **BorderStyle.** This entry refers to the standard property procedure defined by ActiveX. You may also wish to set the optional Property Category in the list shown on the right side of the dialog.

Repeat this process for all properties that implement standard control properties. Do not set Procedure IDs for properties that share names but not functionality with standard properties, such as the RolloverMenu's **Caption** property.

Properties Supplied By The Container

Ten of the RolloverMenu control's properties are not defined anywhere in the control module itself. If you examine the Properties Window for a design time instance of the control, you'll see many familiar properties listed: **Name**, **Visible**, **Left**, **Width**, and so on. These properties are contributed by the container itself. Think about it—how could the control itself determine its **Left** and **Top** positions without the cooperation of the container? Container properties are accessible through another object property of the **UserControl**, the **Extender** object. The **Extender** object has five standard properties, as shown in Table 9.2. Other **Extender** properties are container-specific. Visual Basic adds about two dozen members to any control's **Extender** object that include not just properties, but also methods and events, as shown in Table 9.3. For the RolloverMenu control, we don't need to read or modify any of the properties provided by the **Extender** object—we can just let the **UserControl** take care of them for us.

Table 9.2 The standard properties of the Extender object.

Name	Type	Description
Name	Read-only **String**	The name of the current control instance.
Visible	Read/write **Boolean**	Specifies whether the control is visible at runtime.
Parent	Read-only **Object**	References the control's container objects, such as a Visual Basic form.
Cancel	Read-only **Boolean**	Indicates whether the control is the default Cancel button of the container.
Default	Read-only **Boolean**	Specifies whether the control is the default button for the container.

Table 9.3 Additional members that Visual Basic contributes to the Extender object.

Name	Type	Description
Container property	Read-only **Object**	The visual container of the control.
DragIcon property	Read/write **Picture**	The icon to use when control is dragged.
DragMode property	Read/write **Integer**	Specifies whether the control will automatically drag.
Enabled property	Read-only **Boolean**	Specifies whether the control is enabled. Requires additional preparation.
Height property	Read/write **Integer**	Height of the control in the container's scale units.
HelpContextID property	Read-only **Integer**	Specifies the context ID for help.
Index property	Read-only **Integer**	Specifies position in a control array.
Left property	Read/write **Integer**	Specifies horizontal position of the control in the container.
TabIndex property	Read/write **Integer**	Specifies control's Tab order position among container's controls.

continued

Table 9.3 Additional members that Visual Basic contributes to the Extender object (continued).

Name	Type	Description
TabStop property	Read/write **Boolean**	Determines whether Tab will stop on the control.
Tag property	Read/write **String**	Any user-defined string expression.
ToolTipText property	Read/write **String**	The pop-up text displayed when the cursor lies over the control.
Top property	Read/write **Integer**	Specifies the vertical position of the control within the container.
WhatsThisHelpID property	Read/write **Integer**	Specifies the help context ID for use with the What's This pop-up.
Width property	Read/write **Integer**	Specifies the control's width within the container.
Drag method	Method	Controls drag operation.
Move method	Method	Moves the control to a new position within the container.
SetFocus method	Method	Sets focus to the control.
ShowWhatsThis method	Method	Displays a help topic for What's This pop-up.
ZOrder method	Method	Changes control's position within the graphical z-order.
DragDrop event	Event	Occurs when another control is dropped on this control.
DragOver event	Event	Occurs when another control is dragged over this control.
GotFocus event	Event	Occurs when the control receives the focus.
LostFocus event	Event	Occurs when the control loses the focus.

Using Property Pages For Complex Properties

Now that you've seen how we use property procedures to implement control properties, you may be wondering why **MenuOptions** is declared as a **Public** variable. Each of the control's menu options actually comprises three distinct elements: a menu option **Caption**, an extended **Description**, and a **TargetURL** that will be passed in the **Click** event. But you can't set compound properties, or properties that consist of multiple elements in the Properties Window. For such situations, the Windows operating systems support a special type of object called a **PropertyPage**. If you've worked with Visual Basic for any length of time, you're already familiar with the property pages that let you select font settings or colors. You can also build custom property pages for your controls that enable your users to view and modify complex properties, such as object properties or properties whose values are interdependent. Before I explain why I've included the **MenuOptions** variable, let's build the Menu Options property page, which is shown in Figure 9.5.

The Menu Options property page is the only place—from within Visual Basic's development environment, anyway—where the user can add or remove menu options and set their **Captions**, **Descriptions**, and **TargetURLs**. Building a property page is similar to building a Visual Basic form. You draw your controls and define

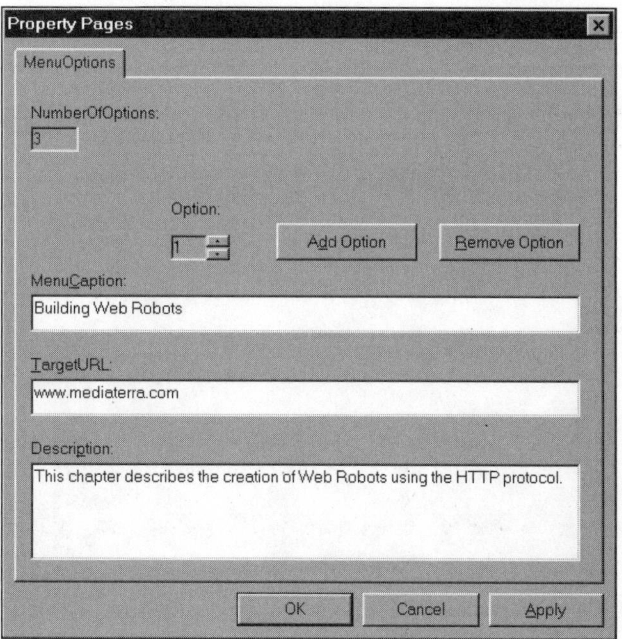

Figure 9.5
The Menu Options property page from the RolloverMenu ActiveX control.

their behavior with code. As a programming task, the key difference between property pages and forms lies in what happens when they open and close. While a Form raises a **Load**() event when it opens, a property page raises the **SelectionChanged**() event. **SelectionChanged**() receives no arguments, but the **PropertyPage** object owns an object called **SelectedControls**, which is a collection of all the controls currently selected in the host application—and I do mean all controls, not just controls of a specific type. If any of the selected controls do not support the property linked to the active property page, you will not see that property, nor will you be able to open the property page. If the property page is already open, it will become unavailable, as shown in Figure 9.6.

The primary purpose of the **SelectionChanged**() event procedure is to copy the current values of the control's properties to the property page. The Menu Options property page, **ppgMenuOptions**, maintains its own internal variables that shadow the properties of the RolloverMenu control, including the **Captions**, **Descriptions**, and **TargetURLs** arrays. The **PropertyPage_SelectionChanged**() event procedure shown in Listing 9.6 copies the control's current property values to the variables in the property page, which act as temporary storage for the duration of the edit session.

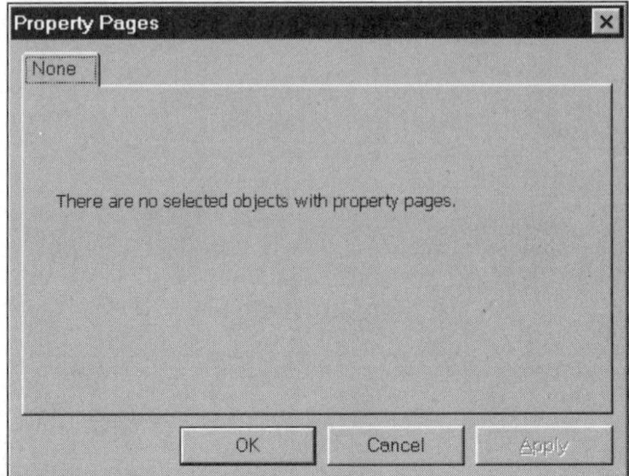

Figure 9.6
The Menu Options property page after selecting an incompatible control.

Listing 9.6 The **PropertyPage_SelectionChanged()** event procedure from RolloverMenu_MenuOptions.PAG.

```
Private Sub PropertyPage_SelectionChanged()
    Dim Counter As Integer

    With SelectedControls(0)
        lblNumberOfOptions.Caption = .NumberOfOptions
        m_NumberOfOptions = .NumberOfOptions
        If m_NumberOfOptions > 0 Then
            ReDim m_TargetURLs(.NumberOfOptions)
            ReDim m_Captions(.NumberOfOptions)
            ReDim m_Descriptions(.NumberOfOptions)
            For Counter = 1 To .NumberOfOptions
                m_TargetURLs(Counter) = .TargetURL(Counter)
                m_Captions(Counter) = .Caption(Counter)
                m_Descriptions(Counter) = .Description(Counter)
                Next Counter
            lblNumberOfOptions.Caption = CStr(m_NumberOfOptions)
            udCurrentOption.Min = 0
            udCurrentOption.Max = m_NumberOfOptions
            udCurrentOption.Value = 1
            lblCurrentOption.Caption = "1"
          End If
    End With
End Sub
```

If the user cancels the property page, the original properties of the control will remain unchanged. However, if the user decides to apply the values stored and displayed in the property page, they will be copied to the control's properties in the **PropertyPage_ApplyChanges**() event procedure, shown in Listing 9.7. Until the user (remember that the "user" in this context is the programmer) clicks the OK or Apply buttons on the Property Pages dialog box, the property values stored in the property page are supposed to be scratch values. That's why it's important not to update the control's properties from any other procedure in the property page than the **PropertyPage_ApplyChanges**() event procedure.

Listing 9.7 The **PropertyPage_ApplyChanges()** event procedure from RolloverMenu_MenuOptions.PAG.

```
Private Sub PropertyPage_ApplyChanges()
    Dim Counter As Integer
```

```
With SelectedControls(0)
    'Transfer the array values from the property
    ' page's arrays to the control's arrays.
    For Counter = 1 To m_NumberOfOptions
        .TargetURL(Counter) = m_TargetURLs(Counter)
        .Caption(Counter) = m_Captions(Counter)
        .Description(Counter) = m_Descriptions(Counter)
        Next Counter
    ' Re-assign NumberOfOptions property to run its
    ' Let procedure, so it will update the menu option
    ' labels with the latest values.
    .NumberOfOptions = m_NumberOfOptions
    End With
End Sub
```

The **PropertyPage_SelectionChanged**() and **PropertyPage_ApplyChanges**() event procedures mark the birth and death of a property page instance. But what happens in between? Anything you wish. The Menu Options property page incorporates 13 controls—quite a few when you consider that the **RolloverMenu** control itself begins life with just 2. And those 13 controls are all used to update just 4 of the control's properties.

Okay, I'll admit that the real work is done by just six of the controls—the rest are labels. The **udCurrentOption** UpDown control lets the user select one of the existing menu options, displaying its number in the Label **lblCurrentOption**. The user is never given the opportunity to change the **NumberOfOptions** property directly. To add or remove options, the user must use the two CommandButton controls, **cmdAddOption** and **cmdRemoveOption**. Although the current value of **m_NumberOfOptions** appears on the property page in **lblNumberOfOptions**, its value is changed indirectly by adding or removing options one at a time with the command buttons. Once an option has been added, the user may leave and return to it freely to update its **Caption**, **Description**, or **TargetURL**, which appear in the three TextBox controls: **txtMenuCaption**, **txtDescription**, and **txtTargetURL**, respectively.

The **cmdAddOption_Click**() event, shown in Listing 9.8, inserts a new menu option after the currently displayed option and changes the current position to the new option. The process of inserting a new option consists primarily of expanding the three arrays and moving the existing options up one position to make room for the new one. The procedure then updates the **udCurrentOption** and **lblNumberOfOptions** controls. The final line sets the property page's own **Changed** property to **True**, indicating that it will be necessary to raise the **ApplyChanges** event if the user accepts the current property values by clicking OK or Apply.

Listing 9.8 The **cmdAddOption_Click()** event procedure from RolloverMenu_MenuOptions.PAG.

```
Private Sub cmdAddOption_Click()
    Dim CurrentOption As Integer
    Dim Counter As Integer

    CurrentOption = CInt(lblCurrentOption.Caption)
    m_NumberOfOptions = m_NumberOfOptions + 1
    ReDim Preserve m_Captions(m_NumberOfOptions)
    ReDim Preserve m_TargetURLs(m_NumberOfOptions)
    ReDim Preserve m_Descriptions(m_NumberOfOptions)
    For Counter = UBound(m_Captions) To (CurrentOption + 2) Step -1
        m_Captions(Counter) = m_Captions(Counter - 1)
        m_TargetURLs(Counter) = m_TargetURLs(Counter - 1)
        m_Descriptions(Counter) = m_Descriptions(Counter - 1)
        Next Counter
    udCurrentOption.Max = m_NumberOfOptions
    CurrentOption = CurrentOption + 1
    udCurrentOption.Value = CurrentOption
    m_Captions(CurrentOption) = ""
    m_TargetURLs(CurrentOption) = ""
    m_Descriptions(CurrentOption) = ""
    lblCurrentOption.Caption = CStr(CurrentOption)
    lblNumberOfOptions.Caption = CStr(m_NumberOfOptions)
    Changed = True
    End Sub
```

The **cmdRemoveOption_Click()** event procedure, shown in Listing 9.9, performs a similar series of steps, inverted to reduce the number of options, and hence the size of each array of temporary property values. This procedure, and each of the **Change** event procedures, also shown in Listing 9.9, set the property page's **Changed** property to **True**. If this step is omitted, the property page will not execute its **ApplyChanges()** event procedure, meaning that any edits performed to the properties from within the property page will be ignored.

Listing 9.9 The complete listing of RolloverMenu_MenuOptions.PAG.

```
Option Explicit

Private m_NumberOfOptions As Integer
Private m_TargetURLs() As String
Private m_Captions() As String
Private m_Descriptions() As String

Private Sub cmdAddOption_Click()
    Dim CurrentOption As Integer
    Dim Counter As Integer

    CurrentOption = CInt(lblCurrentOption.Caption)
    m_NumberOfOptions = m_NumberOfOptions + 1
    ReDim Preserve m_Captions(m_NumberOfOptions)
    ReDim Preserve m_TargetURLs(m_NumberOfOptions)
    ReDim Preserve m_Descriptions(m_NumberOfOptions)
    For Counter = UBound(m_Captions) To (CurrentOption + 2) Step -1
        m_Captions(Counter) = m_Captions(Counter - 1)
        m_TargetURLs(Counter) = m_TargetURLs(Counter - 1)
        m_Descriptions(Counter) = m_Descriptions(Counter - 1)
        Next Counter
    udCurrentOption.Max = m_NumberOfOptions
    CurrentOption = CurrentOption + 1
    udCurrentOption.Value = CurrentOption
    m_Captions(CurrentOption) = ""
    m_TargetURLs(CurrentOption) = ""
    m_Descriptions(CurrentOption) = ""
    lblCurrentOption.Caption = CStr(CurrentOption)
    lblNumberOfOptions.Caption = CStr(m_NumberOfOptions)
    Changed = True
    End Sub

Private Sub cmdRemoveOption_Click()
    Dim CurrentOption As Integer
    Dim Counter As Integer

    CurrentOption = CInt(lblCurrentOption.Caption)
    For Counter = CurrentOption To (UBound(m_Captions) - 1)
        m_Captions(Counter) = m_Captions(Counter + 1)
        m_TargetURLs(Counter) = m_TargetURLs(Counter + 1)
        m_Descriptions(Counter) = m_Descriptions(Counter + 1)
        Next Counter
    m_NumberOfOptions = m_NumberOfOptions - 1
```

```
    udCurrentOption.Max = m_NumberOfOptions
    ReDim Preserve m_Captions(m_NumberOfOptions)
    ReDim Preserve m_TargetURLs(m_NumberOfOptions)
    ReDim Preserve m_Descriptions(m_NumberOfOptions)
    lblNumberOfOptions.Caption = CStr(m_NumberOfOptions)
    Changed = True
    End Sub

Private Sub lblCurrentOption_Change()
    Dim CurrentOption As Integer

    CurrentOption = CInt(lblCurrentOption.Caption)
    If CurrentOption > 0 Then
        txtMenuCaption.Text = m_Captions(CurrentOption)
        txtTargetURL.Text = m_TargetURLs(CurrentOption)
        txtDescription.Text = m_Descriptions(CurrentOption)
        txtMenuCaption.Enabled = True
        txtTargetURL.Enabled = True
        txtDescription.Enabled = True
        cmdRemoveOption.Enabled = True
      Else
        txtMenuCaption.Text = ""
        txtTargetURL.Text = ""
        txtDescription.Text = ""
        txtMenuCaption.Enabled = False
        txtTargetURL.Enabled = False
        txtDescription.Enabled = False
        cmdRemoveOption.Enabled = False
      End If
    End Sub

Private Sub PropertyPage_ApplyChanges()
    Dim Counter As Integer

    With SelectedControls(0)
        ' Transfer the array values from the property
        ' page's arrays to the control's arrays.
        For Counter = 1 To m_NumberOfOptions
            .TargetURL(Counter) = m_TargetURLs(Counter)
            .Caption(Counter) = m_Captions(Counter)
            .Description(Counter) = m_Descriptions(Counter)
            Next Counter
        ' Re-assign NumberOfOptions property to run its
        ' Let procedure, so it will update the menu option
        ' labels with the latest values.
        .NumberOfOptions = m_NumberOfOptions
```

```
        End With
    End Sub

Private Sub PropertyPage_SelectionChanged()
    Dim Counter As Integer

    With SelectedControls(0)
        lblNumberOfOptions.Caption = .NumberOfOptions
        m_NumberOfOptions = .NumberOfOptions
        If m_NumberOfOptions > 0 Then
            ReDim m_TargetURLs(.NumberOfOptions)
            ReDim m_Captions(.NumberOfOptions)
            ReDim m_Descriptions(.NumberOfOptions)
            For Counter = 1 To .NumberOfOptions
                m_TargetURLs(Counter) = .TargetURL(Counter)
                m_Captions(Counter) = .Caption(Counter)
                m_Descriptions(Counter) = .Description(Counter)
                Next Counter
            lblNumberOfOptions.Caption = CStr(m_NumberOfOptions)
            udCurrentOption.Min = 0
            udCurrentOption.Max = m_NumberOfOptions
            udCurrentOption.Value = 1
            lblCurrentOption.Caption = "1"
          End If
        End With
    End Sub

Private Sub txtDescription_Change()
    If CInt(lblCurrentOption.Caption) > 0 Then
        m_Descriptions(CInt(lblCurrentOption.Caption)) = _
            txtDescription.Text
        Changed = True
      End If
    End Sub

Private Sub txtMenuCaption_Change()
    If CInt(lblCurrentOption.Caption) > 0 Then
        m_Captions(CInt(lblCurrentOption.Caption)) = _
            txtMenuCaption.Text
        Changed = True
      End If
    End Sub

Private Sub txtTargetURL_Change()
    If CInt(lblCurrentOption.Caption) > 0 Then
```

```
        m_TargetURLs(CInt(lblCurrentOption.Caption)) = _
            txtTargetURL.Text
        Changed = True
      End If
    End Sub

Private Sub udCurrentOption_Change()
    lblCurrentOption.Caption = CStr(udCurrentOption.Value)
    End Sub
```

Adding a property page to your project isn't enough to make it available to the user. First, you must *connect* the property page to a particular control (remember, each ActiveX component project can contain multiple controls). Then you must *associate* the property page with a particular property or properties. To connect **ppgMenuOptions** to the RolloverMenu control, first use the Project Explorer window to open the control designer—right-click it in the Project Explorer, then select View Object from the context menu. Locate the control's **PropertyPages** property and click its ellipsis button to open the Connect Property Pages dialog box, as shown in Figure 9.7.

The Available Property Pages list will display the three standard property pages (which are available to all control projects), along with any property pages you've added to the current project. Select the **ppgMenuOptions** property page, then click OK to dismiss the dialog box.

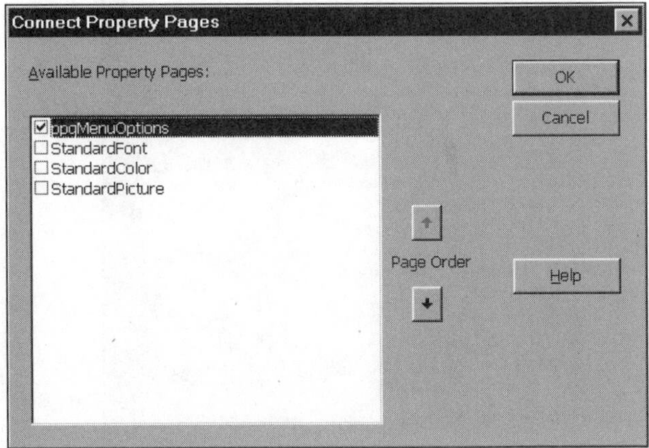

Figure 9.7
The Connect Property Pages dialog box.

To associate the property page with a particular property, open the control's code window. Open the Procedure Attributes dialog box by selecting Procedure Attributes from the Visual Basic Tools menu. Click Advanced to open the extended version of the dialog box, as shown in Figure 9.8.

Select the **MenuOptions** property from the Name drop-down list at the top of the dialog. Then, in the drop-down list labeled Use This Page in Property Browser, select **ppgMenuOptions** and click Apply or OK.

To see the effects of these changes, you must place an instance of the RolloverMenu control on a Form. If you haven't already done so, add a new Standard EXE project to the project group. When you close the control's designer window, the control's Toolbox button will become enabled. Click the button and draw the control on the new Form. The Properties Window will now display the current list of properties exposed by the RolloverMenu control. Notice that Visual Basic assigns it a **Name** of **RolloverMenu1**. As with other controls, Visual Basic constructs a default identifier for each instance of the control by appending an integer to the control's class name, which we defined above when we assigned the name RolloverMenu to the **UserControl** object.

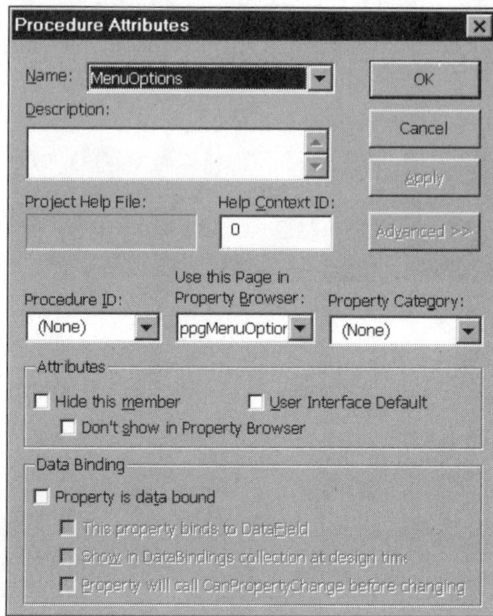

Figure 9.8
The advanced features version of the Procedure Attributes dialog box.

Locate the **MenuOptions** property. You'll see that it displays an ellipsis button. Now you can see what I meant when I said that **MenuOptions** wasn't a real property. **MenuOptions** itself has no particular meaning as a property; it's just a proxy, holding a place in the Properties Window for the Menu Options property page. It never receives or returns any value of its own.

I've made one other adjustment to accommodate the Menu Options property page. I've suppressed the appearance of **NumberOfOptions** in the Properties Window. This property must be set by **ppgMenuOptions**, which means that we need to declare it **Public**. We never want the user to set **NumberOfOptions** directly; but as a **Public** property, it will automatically appear in the Properties Window, so we need to hide it. We do this also in the Advanced Procedure Attributes dialog; choose the **NumberOfOptions** property and select Hide This Member in the Attributes section. That's it. The property will now appear only in the Menu Options property page.

Beware The Wizards

Visual Basic comes with a pair of Wizards that are meant to simplify the process of implementing ActiveX controls: the VB ActiveX Control Interface Wizard and the VB Property Page Wizard. I've chosen not to use them in this project for three reasons. First, they're well explained in other sources, including Visual Basic's extensive documentation. Second, by handling the details for us, Wizards limit our understanding of what they're actually doing. And third, what the Wizards do requires so much modification that they don't really help that much. Despite these reservations, you'll notice that the Control Interface Wizard has had some influence on my code. For example, I've adopted some of the naming conventions used by the Wizards for naming object members. I don't necessarily recommend against using the Wizards. I've just chosen to do things the hard way to gain a better grasp of the process.

Storing And Retrieving Properties

When you use controls in your programs or Web pages, you expect them to retain the settings you apply to their properties. The controls you create will need to do the same. ActiveX provides a special storage interface called the **PropertyBag** object, which provides methods we can use to store and retrieve properties and their assigned values. Each container may provide its own storage system for the properties.

For example, Visual Basic stores the properties for a Form and its controls in its FRM file. In an HTML document, the properties are stored as **<PARAM>** tags. The **PropertyBag** object provides a simple standard interface to the property store, independent of the container's data storage system. However, you do need to watch out for a few pitfalls. Let's look at the two **UserControl** events and two **PropertyBag** methods that implement this interface.

The **UserControl** object supports two event procedures that team up with the **PropertyBag** object to help us manage the storage and retrieval of property values. The **UserControl_WriteProperties()** event procedure, shown in Listing 9.10, receives a single argument, **PropBag**, which represents the data store of the current container.

Listing 9.10 The **UserControl_WriteProperties()** event procedure from RolloverMenu.CTL.

```
Private Sub UserControl_WriteProperties(PropBag As PropertyBag)
    Dim Counter As Integer

    On Error Resume Next
    With PropBag
        .WriteProperty "NumberOfOptions", m_NumberOfOptions, 0
        For Counter = 1 To m_NumberOfOptions
            .WriteProperty "TargetURLs" & Counter, _
                m_TargetURLs(Counter), ""
            .WriteProperty "Captions" & Counter, _
                m_Captions(Counter), ""
            .WriteProperty "Descriptions" & Counter, _
                m_Descriptions(Counter), ""
            Next Counter
        .WriteProperty "BackColor", m_BackColor, Ambient.BackColor
        .WriteProperty "BackStyle", m_BackStyle, m_def_BackStyle
        .WriteProperty "BorderStyle", m_BorderStyle, _
            m_def_BorderStyle
        .WriteProperty "OptionFontName", _
                       lblOptions(0).Font.Name, _
                       Ambient.Font.Name
        .WriteProperty "OptionFontSize", _
                       lblOptions(0).Font.Size, _
                       Ambient.Font.Size
        .WriteProperty "OptionFontBold", _
                       lblOptions(0).Font.Bold, _
                       Ambient.Font.Bold
```

```
        .WriteProperty "DescFontName", _
                       lblTargetDescription.Font.Name, _
                       Ambient.Font.Name
        .WriteProperty "DescFontSize", _
                       lblTargetDescription.Font.Size, _
                       Ambient.Font.Size
        .WriteProperty "DescFontBold", _
                       lblTargetDescription.Font.Bold, _
                       Ambient.Font.Bold
        .WriteProperty "DescriptionProportion", _
                       m_DescriptionProportion,
                       m_def_DescriptionProportion
    End With
End Sub
```

The **PropertyBag** object, **PropBag**, supports just two methods, **ReaderProperty()** and **WriteProperty()**. **WriteProperty()** accepts three arguments. The first is a string expression, the **DataName**, which will become the identifier for the property value in the **PropBag**. Although the **PropertyBag** doesn't enforce any naming requirements, it's a good idea to use the property names for the sake of clarity. You'll use the same names later, in the **UserControl_ReadProperties()** event procedure, to retrieve the property values. In the second argument, **Value**, we pass the value that needs to be stored, the current value of the property. In the optional third argument, we can specify the **DefaultValue** of the property. If the values passed in the second and third arguments match, the property is not written to the **PropBag**. This prevents the **PropertyBag** from becoming bloated with values that can be set just as easily by an initialization procedure.

In many of the calls to **WriteProperty()**, I've passed in properties of the **AmbientProperties** object, **Ambient**, as defaults. A well-behaved control often needs to match many of its own properties to the corresponding settings of its container. The **AmbientProperties** object contains many of the container's properties in read only form, as shown in Table 9.4, such as its current background color and font

Table 9.4 The members of the **Ambient** object.

Name	Type	Description
BackColor	Color	The background color.
DisplayAsDefault	Boolean	Specifies whether this is the default control.

continued

Table 9.4 The members of the **Ambient** object (continued).

Name	Type	Description
DisplayName	String	The name the control should display for itself.
Font	Font	The current text font of the container.
ForeColor	Color	The foreground color.
LocaleID	Long	Identifies the country and language of the user.
MessageReflect	Boolean	The container supports message reflection.
Palette	Picture	The current color palette of the container.
RightToLeft	Boolean	The direction in which text is added to the display.
ScaleUnits	String	The name of the container's current coordinate system.
ShowGrabHandles	Boolean	Indicates whether the container is capable of showing the grab handles for sizing controls.
ShowHatching	Boolean	Indicates whether the container is capable of showing hatching.
SupportsMnemonics	Boolean	Indicates whether the container handles access keys for its controls.
TextAlign	Integer	Indicates how the container will align text it displays.
UserMode	Boolean	True if the control is in a runtime; false at design time.
UIDead	Boolean	If True, indicates that the user interface does not respond.

settings. To keep the control's properties synchronized with the container, you can use the **UserControl**'s **AmbientChanged** event.

The **UserControl_WriteProperties()** event procedure occurs only when a design time instance of the control is terminated; property values of controls that have been set at runtime are not persistent.

As I said, property storage has a few pitfalls, even with the handy **PropertyBag** object—or perhaps because of it. You may have wondered why the RolloverMenu control exposes so many separate font-related properties. Why couldn't we have declared two object properties: **DescriptionFont** As **Font**, and **CaptionFont** As **Font**? If we had, the **Font** data type would indicate to the Visual Basic IDE that it should offer the standard system Font dialog to set the **Font** object's various properties. That would work fine in development environments that support object properties, such as Visual Basic and Delphi. Unfortunately, it would make it difficult for the **PropertyBag** object to store and retrieve the property in an HTML document. When you pass a binary object to the **WriteProperty**() method of an HTML-hosted **PropertyBag**, it may store it in a special **DATA** attribute as a MIME data object, as shown in Listing 9.11.

Listing 9.11 An HTML **<OBJECT>** tag with binary persistent properties.

```
<HTML>
<HEAD>
<TITLE>New Page</TITLE>
</HEAD>
<BODY>
    <OBJECT ID="ShapeLabel1" WIDTH=252 HEIGHT=173
 CLASSID="CLSID:32AAACE1-93C9-11D0-B8EF-00608CC9A71F"
 DATA="DATA:application/x-oleobject;BASE64,4ayqMsmTOBG4
7wBgjMmnH5OyAABIAAAAAwAIAAvyV0cgAAAAXwBlAHgAdABlAG4AdAB
4ANYUAAADAAgACvJXR+D///9fAGUAeABOAGUAbgBOAHkAYw4AAA==">
    </OBJECT>
</BODY>
</HTML>
```

The example in Listing 9.11—which I've edited slightly to exclude unprintable characters—was created by dropping a Visual Basic demonstration control, **ShapeLabel**, into a Web document with the Microsoft ActiveX Control Pad. In fact, I've found that whenever any of the properties are large or complex binary objects, the **PropertyBag** object in the ActiveX Control Pad stores all the properties in a single encoded **DATA** attribute, making it all but impossible to identify or modify them directly in the HTML **<OBJECT>** tag. By breaking down the **Font** object into its constituent member properties and by declaring separate control properties for each element, we expose properties with simple—or *primitive*—data types. Simple data elements can be represented within the HTML **<OBJECT>** tag by **<PARAM>** tags, as shown in Listing 9.12.

Listing 9.12 An HTML <OBJECT> tag with persistent properties stored in <PARAM> tags.

```
<HTML>
<HEAD>
<TITLE>New Page</TITLE>
</HEAD>
<BODY>

<OBJECT ID="RolloverMenu1" WIDTH=313 HEIGHT=217
 CLASSID="CLSID:6772DD8D-9E1F-11D0-B8EF-00608CC9A71F">
    <PARAM NAME="_ExtentX" VALUE="6625">
    <PARAM NAME="_ExtentY" VALUE="4593">
    <PARAM NAME="NumberOfOptions" VALUE="2">
    <PARAM NAME="Captions1" VALUE="Menu Option 1">
    <PARAM NAME="Descriptions1"
        VALUE="Description of first option.">
    <PARAM NAME="Captions2" VALUE="Menu Option 2">
    <PARAM NAME="Descriptions2"
        VALUE="The second option has this description.">
    <PARAM NAME="BackStyle" VALUE="1">
    <PARAM NAME="OptionFontSize" VALUE="9.6">
    <PARAM NAME="DescFontSize" VALUE="12">
</OBJECT>

</BODY>
</HTML>
```

The **UserControl_ReadProperties**() event procedure shown in Listing 9.13 also receives the single argument, **PropBag**.

Listing 9.13 The UserControl_ReadProperties() event procedure from RolloverMenu.CTL.

```
Private Sub UserControl_ReadProperties(PropBag As PropertyBag)
    Dim Counter As Integer

    On Error Resume Next
    With PropBag
        m_NumberOfOptions = .ReadProperty("NumberOfOptions", 0)
        ReDim m_TargetURLs(m_NumberOfOptions)
        ReDim m_Captions(m_NumberOfOptions)
```

```
        ReDim m_Descriptions(m_NumberOfOptions)
        For Counter = 1 To m_NumberOfOptions
            m_TargetURLs(Counter) = _
                .ReadProperty("TargetURLs" & Counter, "")
            m_Captions(Counter) = _
                .ReadProperty("Captions" & Counter, _
                    "Default Caption " & Counter)
            m_Descriptions(Counter) = _
                .ReadProperty("Descriptions" & Counter, "")
            Next Counter
        NumberOfOptions = m_NumberOfOptions
        BackColor = .ReadProperty("BackColor", Ambient.BackColor)
        BackStyle = .ReadProperty("BackStyle", m_def_BackStyle)
        BorderStyle = .ReadProperty("BorderStyle", m_def_BorderStyle)
        lblOptions(0).Font.Name = _
            .ReadProperty("OptionFontName", Ambient.Font.Name)
        lblOptions(0).Font.Size = _
            .ReadProperty("OptionFontSize", Ambient.Font.Size)
        lblOptions(0).Font.Bold = _
            .ReadProperty("OptionFontBold", Ambient.Font.Bold)
        lblTargetDescription.Font.Name = _
            .ReadProperty("DescFontName", Ambient.Font.Name)
        lblTargetDescription.Font.Size = _
            .ReadProperty("DescFontSize", Ambient.Font.Size)
        lblTargetDescription.Font.Bold = _
            .ReadProperty("DescFontBold", Ambient.Font.Bold)
        DescriptionProportion = _
            .ReadProperty("DescriptionProportion", _
                m_def_DescriptionProportion)
        End With
    End Sub
```

To retrieve the value of a stored property, we assign the return value of **ReadProperty()** to either the property procedure or directly to the **Private** property storage variable. If you need your property to perform some sort of process whenever it changes, you should let the property procedure handle things. The **ReadProperty()** method takes two arguments, a **DataName** and a **DefaultValue**. The **DataName** is a string and will accept any valid string expression. The second argument, **DefaultValue**, lets you assign a value to the target property in the event that the property value has never been saved to the **PropBag**. As I explained above, the **WriteProperty()** method doesn't need to write a property name value to the **PropBag** unless it differs from the specified default value.

The control raises the **ReadProperties** event at startup, immediately following the initialization event. The initialization event depends on two factors: whether the property is in its runtime or design time state, and whether the design time instance is new. When a new instance of the control enters design mode, it executes three event procedures, in the following order:

1. **UserControl_Initialize()**
2. **UserControl_InitProperties()**
3. **UserControl_Resize()**

When the control enters run mode, it also executes three event procedures:

1. **UserControl_Initialize()**
2. **UserControl_ReadProperties()**
3. **UserControl_Resize()**

The second time a control instance enters design mode—and all subsequent times—it executes the same three events as a runtime instance. **UserControl_InitProperties()** occurs only once—when the control is first created. From that time forward, the control retrieves its persistent property values from the **PropertyBag**. The **UserControl_InitProperties()** event procedure is the place where we set all our properties to their default values.

The **UserControl_WriteProperties()** event procedure occurs only when a design time instance of the control closes. The **UserControl_Terminate()** event procedure occurs when any instance of the control closes—whether design time or runtime.

Typically, you would use the **Initialize()** and **Terminate()** event procedures to build and tear down object instances or complex data structures. I realize that, at this point, the word "simple" seems inappropriate. Nevertheless, the *relatively* simple RolloverMenu control doesn't have any hidden data structures, and therefore doesn't need any general initialization or termination code.

The Resize Event

The other key event in the lifetime of a control is **Resize**. Whether at design time or runtime, the **UserControl_Resize()** event procedure executes immediately following the initialization and **ReadProperties** events, and then again every time the control changes size. The **UserControl_Resize()** event for the RolloverMenu control, shown in Listing 9.14, requires a little explanation.

Listing 9.14 The **UserControl_Resize()** event procedure from RolloverMenu.CTL.

```
Private Sub UserControl_Resize()
    Dim OptionHeight As Long
    Dim Counter As Integer

    lblTargetDescription.Top = 0
    lblTargetDescription.Left = 0.33 * UserControl.ScaleWidth
    lblTargetDescription.Width = _
        ScaleWidth - lblTargetDescription.Left
    lblTargetDescription.Height = _
        (m_DescriptionProportion / 100) * _
        UserControl.ScaleHeight
    OptionHeight = (UserControl.ScaleHeight - _
                    lblTargetDescription.Height - _
                    15 * NumberOfOptions) \ _
                   NumberOfOptions
    lblOptions(0).Left = 0
    lblOptions(0).Top = lblTargetDescription.Height + 15
    lblOptions(0).Width = UserControl.ScaleWidth
    lblOptions(0).Height = OptionHeight
    lblOptions(0).Caption = m_Captions(1)
    lblOptions(0).Visible = True
    For Counter = 1 To (NumberOfOptions - 1)
        lblOptions(Counter).Width = UserControl.ScaleWidth
        lblOptions(Counter).Top = lblOptions(Counter - 1).Top + _
                                  lblOptions(Counter - 1).Height
        lblOptions(Counter).Height = OptionHeight
        lblOptions(Counter).Left = 0
        lblOptions(Counter).Caption = m_Captions(Counter + 1)
        Next Counter
    End Sub
```

In terms of its appearance, the RolloverMenu control is an odd beast. Not only is it made from constituent controls, but the user can change the number of constituents by changing **NumberOfOptions**. And to make matters worse, the font settings can also affect the sizes of all the constituent controls, creating a few problems with the control's layout. RolloverMenu has two major display sections: the list of options and the extended description that appears when the cursor lies over each of the options. I've created a property called **DescriptionProportion** that enables the user to determine what percentage—expressed as a whole integer from 1 to 100—of the controls **ScaleHeight** should be occupied by **lblTargetDescription.** The **Resize()** event procedure then divides the remaining vertical space equally among the members of the **lblOptions** control array, separating them with 15 vertical twips. It's an awkward solution, but it works reasonably well. I've also determined arbitrarily that **lblTargetDescription** should indent itself one-third of the way from the left edge. You may want to add additional properties to control such fine points of the control's appearance.

Raising Events

No matter how many properties it has, a control doesn't do much without events. Events are the mechanism by which a developer can incorporate your control into useful programs. While a control's properties and methods provide the host program with functions that can be called to manipulate information, events enable the control to request a response from the host program. But the only events that your control will offer by default are the four events supported by the **Extender** object: **DragDrop**, **DragOver**, **GotFocus**, and **LostFocus.**

The **UserControl** object does supply about 30 intrinsic events to which you, the control developer, can respond. In addition, each constituent control supplies its own set of events. But none of these events will become available to users of your control until you use them to *raise* events of your own.

As I explained above, you can expose properties of the **UserControl** object, or any of the constituent controls, through a process called delegation. We'll use a similar technique to raise events. The RolloverMenu control really needs just two events to perform its essential functions. First, to display the extended option descriptions in **lblTargetDescription**, it will need to detect the presence of the cursor over the **lblOptions** label controls. Second, to enable users to select a menu option, it will also need to detect a mouse click on any of the options.

It takes just two lines of code to raise an event. In the declarations section, you must declare it, as shown in Listing 9.15. Next, you must use a **RaiseEvent** statement somewhere within your code to trigger the event. The two procedures shown in Listing 9.16 each raise one of the RolloverMenu's two events.

Listing 9.15 Event declarations from RolloverMenu.CTL.

```
Event Click(ByVal TargetURL As String)
Event MouseMove(MenuOption As Integer, Shift As Integer, _
                X As Single, Y As Single)
```

Listing 9.16 The **lblOptions_Click()** and **lblOptions_MouseMove()** event procedures from RolloverMenu.CTL.

```
Private Sub lblOptions_Click(Index As Integer)
    If Index < UBound(m_TargetURLs) Then
        RaiseEvent Click(m_TargetURLs(Index + 1))
      End If
    End Sub

Private Sub lblOptions_MouseMove(Index As Integer, _
                                 Button As Integer, _
                                 Shift As Integer, _
                                 X As Single, Y As Single)

    Static CurrentIndex As Integer

    If (Index < UBound(m_Descriptions)) And _
       (Index <> CurrentIndex) Then
        lblTargetDescription.Caption = m_Descriptions(Index + 1)
        CurrentIndex = Index
      End If
    RaiseEvent MouseMove(Index + 1, Button, X, Y)
    End Sub
```

The VB ActiveX Control Interface Wizard tosses in declarations for nine event procedures, including such popular events as **MouseMove()**, **MouseUp()**, and **KeyDown()**. These are just suggestions for the events that users expect most controls to support. You aren't required to implement any of them. And neither are you limited to the standard events—you may implement as many events as you wish, including any of your own design.

Complete Listing

In previous chapters, I've provided a table of controls and their salient properties, then listed just the code that would appear in Visual Basic's Code Window. For this project, I've chosen to omit the control table (after all, the project only has two base controls) and show you the complete contents of the file RolloverMenu.CTL. In previous versions of Visual Basic, the main difference between these two views of the code was the section at the top of the file that listed the controls, their property values, and their parent/child relationships. In a Visual Basic ActiveX control project, the file listing now includes additional information that is hidden from view in the Code Window. In particular, watch for the **Attribute** statements, found most commonly just before the declarations section and in the property procedures.

Listing 9.17 The complete contents of RolloverMenu.CTL.

```
VERSION 5.00
Begin VB.UserControl RolloverMenu
   BackColor       =   &H00C0C0C0&
   BackStyle       =   0  'Transparent
   ClientHeight    =   2592
   ClientLeft      =   0
   ClientTop       =   0
   ClientWidth     =   3756
   PropertyPages   =   "RolloverMenu.ctx":0000
   ScaleHeight     =   2592
   ScaleWidth      =   3756
   Begin VB.Label lblOptions
      BackStyle       =   0  'Transparent
      BorderStyle     =   1  'Fixed Single
      Height          =   252
      Index           =   0
      Left            =   120
      TabIndex        =   1
      Top             =   2160
      Width           =   3492
   End
   Begin VB.Label lblTargetDescription
      BackStyle       =   0  'Transparent
      Caption         =   "Option Target Description"
      BeginProperty Font
         Name            =   "MS Sans Serif"
         Size            =   12
```

```
            Charset         =   0
            Weight          =   400
            Underline       =   0   'False
            Italic          =   0   'False
            Strikethrough   =   0   'False
         EndProperty
         Height          =   1692
         Left            =   1200
         TabIndex        =   0
         Top             =   120
         Width           =   2412
      End
   End
Attribute VB_Name = "RolloverMenu"
Attribute VB_GlobalNameSpace = False
Attribute VB_Creatable = True
Attribute VB_PredeclaredId = False
Attribute VB_Exposed = True
Attribute VB_Ext_KEY = "PropPageWizardRun" ,"Yes"
Option Explicit

Public Enum RolloverMenuBackStyleConstants
    rmbsTransparent
    rmbsOpaque
    End Enum

Public Enum RolloverMenuBorderStyleConstants
    rmbdNone
    rmbdSingle
    End Enum

Public MenuOptions As Variant
Attribute MenuOptions.VB_VarProcData = "ppgMenuOptions"

'Default Property Values:
Const m_def_NumberOfOptions = 1
Const m_def_BackColor = 0 ' Not Used
Const m_def_ForeColor = 0 ' Not Used
Const m_def_Enabled = True
Const m_def_BackStyle = rmbsOpaque
Const m_def_BorderStyle = rmbdSingle
Const m_def_DescriptionProportion = 40

' Private Member Declarations
'      These values are exposed, when necessary,
'      with Get/Let/Set property procedures.
```

```
Private m_NumberOfOptions As Integer
Private m_TargetURLs() As String
Private m_Captions() As String
Private m_Descriptions() As String

Private m_BackColor As Long
Private m_ForeColor As Long
Private m_Enabled As Boolean
Private m_BackStyle As Integer
Private m_BorderStyle As Integer
Private m_DescriptionProportion As Integer

' Event Declarations
Event Click(ByVal TargetURL As String)
'Event DblClick()
'Event KeyDown(KeyCode As Integer, Shift As Integer)
'Event KeyPress(KeyAscii As Integer)
'Event KeyUp(KeyCode As Integer, Shift As Integer)
'Event MouseDown(Button As Integer, Shift As Integer, _
    X As Single, Y As Single)
Event MouseMove(MenuOption As Integer, Shift As Integer, _
    X As Single, Y As Single)
Attribute MouseMove.VB_UserMemId = -606
'Event MouseUp(Button As Integer, Shift As Integer, _
    X As Single, Y As Single)


Private Sub lblOptions_Click(Index As Integer)
    If Index < UBound(m_TargetURLs) Then
        RaiseEvent Click(m_TargetURLs(Index + 1))
      End If
    End Sub

Private Sub lblOptions_MouseMove(Index As Integer, _
                                Button As Integer, _
                                Shift As Integer, _
                                X As Single, Y As Single)

    Static CurrentIndex As Integer

    If (Index < UBound(m_Descriptions)) And _
       (Index <> CurrentIndex) Then
        lblTargetDescription.Caption = m_Descriptions(Index + 1)
        CurrentIndex = Index
```

```
    End If
   RaiseEvent MouseMove(Index + 1, Button, X, Y)
   End Sub

Private Sub UserControl_InitProperties()
    ReDim m_Captions(1)
    ReDim m_TargetURLs(1)
    ReDim m_Descriptions(1)
    Caption(1) = "Menu Option 1"
    NumberOfOptions = m_def_NumberOfOptions
    BackColor = Ambient.BackColor 'm_def_BackColor
    ForeColor = Ambient.ForeColor
    Enabled = m_def_Enabled
    OptionFontName = Ambient.Font.Name
    OptionFontSize = Ambient.Font.Size
    OptionFontBold = Ambient.Font.Bold
    DescFontName = Ambient.Font.Name
    DescFontSize = Ambient.Font.Size * 1.5
    DescFontBold = Ambient.Font.Bold
    BackStyle = m_def_BackStyle
    BorderStyle = m_def_BorderStyle
    DescriptionProportion = m_def_DescriptionProportion
    End Sub

Private Sub UserControl_ReadProperties(PropBag As PropertyBag)
    Dim Counter As Integer

    On Error Resume Next
    With PropBag
        m_NumberOfOptions = .ReadProperty("NumberOfOptions", 0)
        ReDim m_TargetURLs(m_NumberOfOptions)
        ReDim m_Captions(m_NumberOfOptions)
        ReDim m_Descriptions(m_NumberOfOptions)
        For Counter = 1 To m_NumberOfOptions
            m_TargetURLs(Counter) = _
                .ReadProperty("TargetURLs" & Counter, "")
            m_Captions(Counter) = _
                .ReadProperty("Captions" & Counter, _
                "Default Caption " & Counter)
            m_Descriptions(Counter) = _
                .ReadProperty("Descriptions" & Counter, "")
            Next Counter
        NumberOfOptions = m_NumberOfOptions
        BackColor = .ReadProperty("BackColor", Ambient.BackColor)
```

```
            BackStyle = .ReadProperty("BackStyle", m_def_BackStyle)
            BorderStyle = .ReadProperty("BorderStyle", _
                          m_def_BorderStyle)
            lblOptions(0).Font.Name = _
                .ReadProperty("OptionFontName", Ambient.Font.Name)
            lblOptions(0).Font.Size = _
                .ReadProperty("OptionFontSize", Ambient.Font.Size)
            lblOptions(0).Font.Bold = _
                .ReadProperty("OptionFontBold", Ambient.Font.Bold)
            lblTargetDescription.Font.Name = _
                .ReadProperty("DescFontName", Ambient.Font.Name)
            lblTargetDescription.Font.Size = _
                .ReadProperty("DescFontSize", Ambient.Font.Size)
            lblTargetDescription.Font.Bold = _
                .ReadProperty("DescFontBold", Ambient.Font.Bold)
            DescriptionProportion = _
                .ReadProperty("DescriptionProportion", _
                    m_def_DescriptionProportion)
            End With
        End Sub

    Private Sub UserControl_Resize()
        Dim OptionHeight As Long
        Dim Counter As Integer

        Debug.Print "Resizing"
        lblTargetDescription.Top = 0
        lblTargetDescription.Left = 0.33 * UserControl.ScaleWidth
        lblTargetDescription.Width = _
            ScaleWidth - lblTargetDescription.Left
        lblTargetDescription.Height = (m_DescriptionProportion / 100) _
                                      * UserControl.ScaleHeight
        OptionHeight = (UserControl.ScaleHeight - _
                        lblTargetDescription.Height - _
                        15 * NumberOfOptions) \ _
                       NumberOfOptions
        lblOptions(0).Left = 0
        lblOptions(0).Top = lblTargetDescription.Height + 15
        lblOptions(0).Width = UserControl.ScaleWidth
        lblOptions(0).Height = OptionHeight
        lblOptions(0).Caption = m_Captions(1)
        lblOptions(0).Visible = True
        For Counter = 1 To (NumberOfOptions - 1)
            lblOptions(Counter).Width = UserControl.ScaleWidth
            lblOptions(Counter).Top = lblOptions(Counter - 1).Top + _
                                      lblOptions(Counter - 1).Height
```

```
        lblOptions(Counter).Height = OptionHeight
        lblOptions(Counter).Left = 0
        lblOptions(Counter).Caption = m_Captions(Counter + 1)
        Next Counter
    End Sub

Private Sub UserControl_WriteProperties(PropBag As PropertyBag)
    Dim Counter As Integer

    On Error Resume Next
    With PropBag
        .WriteProperty "NumberOfOptions", m_NumberOfOptions, 0
        For Counter = 1 To m_NumberOfOptions
            .WriteProperty "TargetURLs" & Counter, _
                m_TargetURLs(Counter), ""
            .WriteProperty "Captions" & Counter, _
                m_Captions(Counter), ""
            .WriteProperty "Descriptions" & Counter, _
                m_Descriptions(Counter), ""
            Next Counter
        .WriteProperty "BackColor", m_BackColor, Ambient.BackColor
        .WriteProperty "BackStyle", m_BackStyle, m_def_BackStyle
        .WriteProperty "BorderStyle", m_BorderStyle, _
            m_def_BorderStyle
        .WriteProperty "OptionFontName", _
                       lblOptions(0).Font.Name, _
                       Ambient.Font.Name
        .WriteProperty "OptionFontSize", _
                       lblOptions(0).Font.Size, _
                       Ambient.Font.Size
        .WriteProperty "OptionFontBold", _
                       lblOptions(0).Font.Bold, _
                       Ambient.Font.Bold
        .WriteProperty "DescFontName", _
                       lblTargetDescription.Font.Name, _
                       Ambient.Font.Name
        .WriteProperty "DescFontSize", _
                       lblTargetDescription.Font.Size, _
                       Ambient.Font.Size
        .WriteProperty "DescFontBold", _
                       lblTargetDescription.Font.Bold, _
                       Ambient.Font.Bold
        .WriteProperty "DescriptionProportion", _
                       m_DescriptionProportion, _
                       m_def_DescriptionProportion
        End With
    End Sub
```

```
Public Property Get NumberOfOptions() As Integer
Attribute NumberOfOptions.VB_MemberFlags = "40"
    NumberOfOptions = m_NumberOfOptions
    End Property

Public Property Let NumberOfOptions _
    (ByVal New_NumberOfOptions As Integer)
    Dim Counter As Integer
    Debug.Print "Setting NumberOfOptions to " & New_NumberOfOptions

    ' Remove all but the first option label control.
    If lblOptions().UBound > 0 Then
        For Counter = 1 To m_NumberOfOptions - 1
            Unload lblOptions(Counter)
            Next Counter
      End If
    m_NumberOfOptions = New_NumberOfOptions
    lblOptions(0).Caption = m_Captions(1)
    Debug.Print "Set first label caption to " & lblOptions(0).Caption
    lblOptions(0).BackStyle = 0
    lblOptions(0).BorderStyle = 0
    lblOptions(0).Visible = True
    If m_NumberOfOptions > 1 Then
        ' Expand the label control array to the current
        ' number of options. The control array is zero-based,
        ' while the three property arrays are treated as
        ' if they are one-based; i.e., each array element
        ' corresponds to the position of a menu option.
        For Counter = 1 To New_NumberOfOptions - 1
            Load lblOptions(Counter)
            lblOptions(Counter).Top = _
                lblOptions(Counter - 1).Top + _
                lblOptions(Counter - 1).Height + 10
            lblOptions(Counter).BackStyle = 0
            lblOptions(Counter).BorderStyle = 0
            lblOptions(Counter).Visible = True
            Set lblOptions(Counter).Font = lblOptions(0).Font
            lblOptions(Counter).Caption = _
                m_Captions(Counter + 1)
            Next Counter
        UserControl_Resize
      End If
    PropertyChanged "NumberOfOptions"
    End Property
```

```
Public Property Get TargetURL(ByVal Index As Integer) As String
    TargetURL = m_TargetURLs(Index)
    End Property

Public Property Let TargetURL(ByVal Index As Integer, _
                             ByVal New_TargetURL As String)
    If (UBound(m_TargetURLs) < Index) And _
       (m_NumberOfOptions <= Index) Then
        ReDim Preserve m_TargetURLs(Index)
      End If
    m_TargetURLs(Index) = New_TargetURL
    PropertyChanged "TargetURL"
    End Property

Public Property Get Caption(ByVal Index As Integer) As String
    Caption = m_Captions(Index)
    End Property

Public Property Let Caption(ByVal Index As Integer, _
                           ByVal New_Caption As String)
    If (UBound(m_Captions) < Index) And _
       (m_NumberOfOptions <= Index) Then
        ReDim Preserve m_Captions(Index)
      End If
    m_Captions(Index) = New_Caption
    If Index <= (lblOptions.UBound + 1) Then
        lblOptions(Index - 1).Caption = m_Captions(Index)
      End If
    PropertyChanged "Caption"
    End Property

Public Property Get Description(ByVal Index As Integer) As String
    Description = m_Descriptions(Index)
    End Property

Public Property Let Description(ByVal Index As Integer, _
                               ByVal New_Description As String)
    If (UBound(m_Descriptions) < Index) And _
       (m_NumberOfOptions <= Index) Then
        ReDim Preserve m_Descriptions(Index)
      End If
    m_Descriptions(Index) = New_Description
    PropertyChanged "MenuOptions"
    End Property
```

```
Public Property Get BackColor() As OLE_COLOR
Attribute BackColor.VB_ProcData.VB_Invoke_Property = ";Appearance"
Attribute BackColor.VB_UserMemId = -501
    BackColor = m_BackColor
    End Property

Public Property Let BackColor(ByVal New_BackColor As OLE_COLOR)
    Dim Counter As Integer

    m_BackColor = New_BackColor
    UserControl.BackColor = m_BackColor
    For Counter = 0 To (NumberOfOptions - 1)
        lblOptions(Counter).BackColor = m_BackColor
        Next Counter
    lblTargetDescription.BackColor = m_BackColor
    PropertyChanged "BackColor"
    End Property

Public Property Get BackStyle() As RolloverMenuBackStyleConstants
Attribute BackStyle.VB_ProcData.VB_Invoke_Property = ";Appearance"
Attribute BackStyle.VB_UserMemId = -502
    BackStyle = m_BackStyle
    End Property

Public Property Let BackStyle _
    (ByVal New_BackStyle As RolloverMenuBackStyleConstants)
    Dim Counter As Integer

    m_BackStyle = New_BackStyle
    UserControl.BackStyle = m_BackStyle
    PropertyChanged "BackStyle"
    End Property

Public Property Get ForeColor() As OLE_COLOR
Attribute ForeColor.VB_UserMemId = -513
    ForeColor = m_ForeColor
    End Property

Public Property Let ForeColor(ByVal New_ForeColor As OLE_COLOR)
    Dim Counter As Integer

    m_ForeColor = New_ForeColor
    UserControl.ForeColor = m_ForeColor
    For Counter = 0 To (NumberOfOptions - 1)
        lblOptions(Counter).ForeColor = m_ForeColor
        Next Counter
```

```
    lblTargetDescription.ForeColor = m_ForeColor
    PropertyChanged "ForeColor"
    End Property

Public Property Get BorderStyle() As _
                    RolloverMenuBorderStyleConstants
    BorderStyle = m_BorderStyle
    End Property

Public Property Let BorderStyle(ByVal New_BorderStyle As _
                                RolloverMenuBorderStyleConstants)
    m_BorderStyle = New_BorderStyle
    UserControl.BorderStyle = m_BorderStyle
    PropertyChanged "BorderStyle"
    End Property

Public Property Get Enabled() As Boolean
Attribute Enabled.VB_UserMemId = -514
    Enabled = m_Enabled
    End Property

Public Property Let Enabled(ByVal New_Enabled As Boolean)
    UserControl.Enabled = New_Enabled
    PropertyChanged "Enabled"
    End Property

Public Property Get OptionFontName() As String
    OptionFontName = lblOptions(0).Font.Name
    End Property

Public Property Let OptionFontName(ByVal New_FontName As String)
    Dim Counter As Integer

    lblOptions(0).Font.Name = New_FontName
    PropertyChanged "OptionFontName"
    End Property

Public Property Get OptionFontSize() As Integer
    OptionFontSize = lblOptions(0).Font.Size
    End Property

Public Property Let OptionFontSize(ByVal New_FontSize As Integer)
    lblOptions(0).Font.Size = New_FontSize
    PropertyChanged "OptionFontSize"
    End Property
```

```
Public Property Get OptionFontBold() As Boolean
    OptionFontBold = lblOptions(0).Font.Bold
    End Property

Public Property Let OptionFontBold(ByVal New_FontBold As Boolean)
    lblOptions(0).Font.Bold = New_FontBold
    PropertyChanged "OptionFontBold"
    End Property

Public Property Get DescFontName() As String
    DescFontName = lblTargetDescription.Font.Name
    End Property

Public Property Let DescFontName(ByVal New_FontName As String)
    lblTargetDescription.Font.Name = New_FontName
    PropertyChanged "DescFontName"
    End Property

Public Property Get DescFontSize() As Integer
    DescFontSize = lblTargetDescription.Font.Size
    End Property

Public Property Let DescFontSize(ByVal New_FontSize As Integer)
    lblTargetDescription.Font.Size = New_FontSize
    PropertyChanged "DescFontSize"
    End Property

Public Property Get DescFontBold() As Boolean
    DescFontBold = lblTargetDescription.Font.Bold
    End Property

Public Property Let DescFontBold(ByVal New_FontBold As Boolean)
    lblTargetDescription.Font.Bold = New_FontBold
    PropertyChanged "DescFontBold"
    End Property

Public Property Get DescriptionProportion() As Integer
    DescriptionProportion = m_DescriptionProportion
    End Property

Public Property Let DescriptionProportion _
    (ByVal New_DescriptionProportion As Integer)
    If (New_DescriptionProportion > 0) And _
       (New_DescriptionProportion <= 100) Then
        m_DescriptionProportion = New_DescriptionProportion
```

```
    Else
      Err.Raise 380
    End If
  PropertyChanged "DescriptionProportion"
  UserControl_Resize
  End Property
```

Compiling An ActiveX Control

As you work on your new ActiveX control, you'll want to test it. For most purposes, you can set up to test with just a few steps:

1. Add a Standard EXE project to the current Project Group.
2. Drop in an instance of your control.
3. Close the control's designer window.
4. Run the project.

When you're about ready to release your control into the world, you'll want to compile it as an OCX file and test it in a standalone project. But before you begin running or compiling the control and its test project, you should take a few simple precautions.

Open the Visual Basic Project menu and select the Properties option to open the Project Properties dialog for the control project, as shown in Figure 9.9.

Select the Component tab to display the Version Compatibility options. Each time we compile a version of our control, it must be registered with the operating system before it can be activated. The ActiveX specification tries to manage compatibility from one version to the next.

Each time you compile a new control, Visual Basic uses a standard algorithm to assign it a unique identifier—its *Globally Unique Identifier*, or GUID. The GUID of an ActiveX component is also known as its *Class ID*. Once a component is registered under a particular Class ID, all applications that use that component will assume that they can continue to use that component as if it never changed. In other words, the *interface* of the component must remain backward-compatible. This means that we can add all the new properties, methods, and events we wish—as long as we don't remove any, and we don't change any of the existing argument lists. If we choose to implement a non-compatible version of the control, we must assign it a

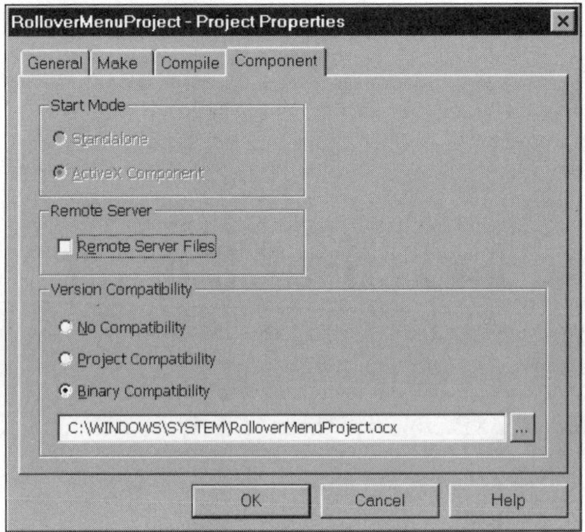

Figure 9.9
The Project Properties dialog for RolloverMenuProject.

new Class ID and leave the older version in place. If we choose to replace an existing control with a new, backward-compatible version, we need to ensure that it maintains the same Class ID. The Version Compatibility options in the Project Properties dialog offers three choices that determine how Visual Basic will manage the registration of newly compiled components: no compatibility, project compatibility, and binary compatibility.

No Compatibility

When this option is selected, Visual Basic will generate and register a new Class ID each time the project is compiled. This can get out of hand quickly. Don't forget, each time you close the control's designer window, Visual Basic registers the control. Your registry can become cluttered with incompatible versions of the same control.

Project Compatibility

Project Compatibility is the default option for new ActiveX component projects. Each time Visual Basic recompiles your control, it removes the previous instance from the registry, generates a new GUID, and registers the newly compiled control, as if it had never existed before. In this mode, you may modify your new control as extensively and as often as you wish, without regard to interface compatibility. That is, until you have compiled a version into OCX form.

Binary Compatibility

Once you compile a new control as an OCX file, you must select Binary Compatibility. A compiled OCX is treated as a veteran control, which may be used by existing applications anywhere in the system. To prevent you from breaking any applications that depend on the control, Visual Basic's compiler will check your modifications against the existing OCX and warn you when you make changes that alter the existing interface. If the code passes the compatibility test, it will be compiled and re-registered under the existing Class ID. The only way to recompile a control with an incompatible interface is to delete the old OCX and remove the previous version from the Registry. You may modify the Windows Registry with the RegEdit program (select Run from the Windows 95 Start menu and type RegEdit.EXE).

Compiling The Control Into An OCX

To compile your control, select the Make option from Visual Basic's File menu. OCX files are usually installed to the WINDOWS\SYSTEM directory, so you may want to compile the OCX to that location. Your Visual Basic project file will keep track of the location of the compiled control. After you compile the control for the first time, open the Project Properties dialog, select Binary Compatibility, and verify that the text box in the Version Compatibility section contains the correct path and file name of the OCX. If it does not, click the ellipsis button to locate and select it.

Creating An Internet Setup File

Before you can place your new control into a Web document, you must create a setup file for it. The Application Setup Wizard—found in the Visual Basic 5.0 program group, not in the Add-Ins menu—offers an option to build a special *cabinet file*, or *CAB* file, for Internet download. CAB files compress the OCX and all its support files into a single downloadable package. An ActiveX-compatible client, such as Internet Explorer, can automatically download and unpack the CAB file and install the control.

On the first screen in the Application Setup Wizard, you will need to specify the location of the control's project file, as shown in Figure 9.10.

In the Options section, choose Create Internet Download Setup. Click Next to proceed to the next step. The Wizard will display its Internet Distribution Location dialog, as shown in Figure 9.11.

By default, the Wizard will specify the target directory for the setup file as \WINDOWS\TEMP\SWSETUP. You may change it if you wish. When you click Next, the Wizard will display its Internet Package dialog, as shown in Figure 9.12.

Some of the runtime components required by your control can be downloaded separately—in particular, the Visual Basic runtime library. Separating these modules into their own CAB files minimizes the number of bytes required by any particular client. Once a user has downloaded a Visual Basic ActiveX control, he won't need to download the standard runtime library for any subsequent controls. If all the support files were stored in the same CAB, the client browser would need to download them every time it encountered a Visual Basic control.

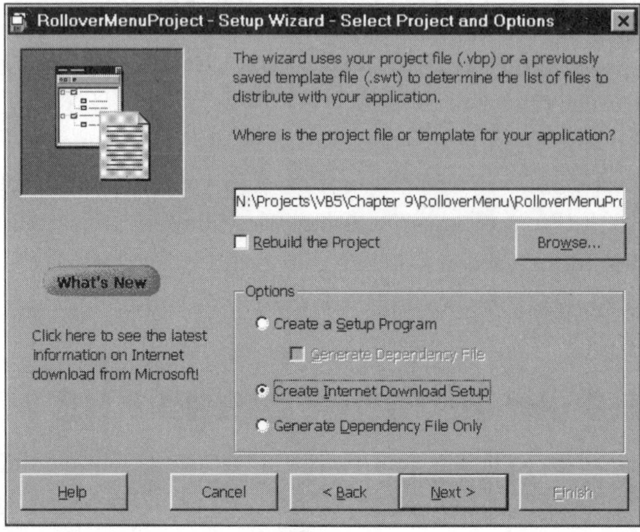

Figure 9.10
The first dialog of the Application Setup Wizard.

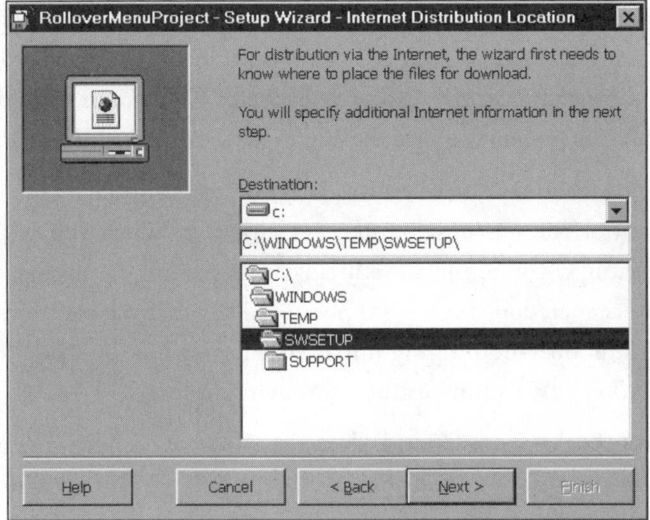

Figure 9.11
The Internet Distribution Location dialog.

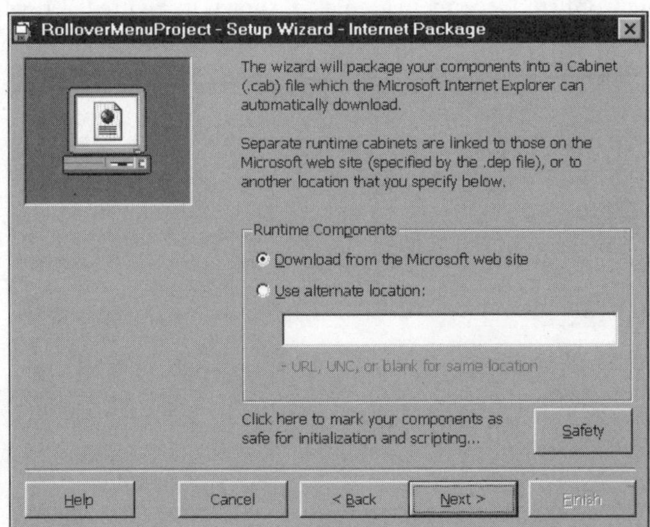

Figure 9.12
The Internet Package dialog.

You may choose either to download the support components from the Microsoft Web site, or from some other site. The advantage of downloading from Microsoft—other than placing the data transfer burden on Microsoft's Web servers instead of yours—is that your users will always receive the latest releases of the runtime libraries.

From this dialog, you may also select the Safety button to specify whether you consider your control safe for initialization and scripting. When you select either of these safety settings, you are not modifying your control or placing any kind of constraint on its operation. You are simply promising that the control will not perform any harmful operation during initialization or cannot be made to perform a harmful operation by activating features through scripting.

The next dialog in the Setup Wizard, shown in Figure 9.13, identifies any ActiveX server components that your control uses. If the Wizard fails to detect any such dependencies, you must add them to the list manually. You may even add remote servers—servers that will run at remote locations on the network.

After you verify or update the list of ActiveX servers used by the control, you may proceed to the Confirm Dependencies dialog, shown in Figure 9.14, which will list

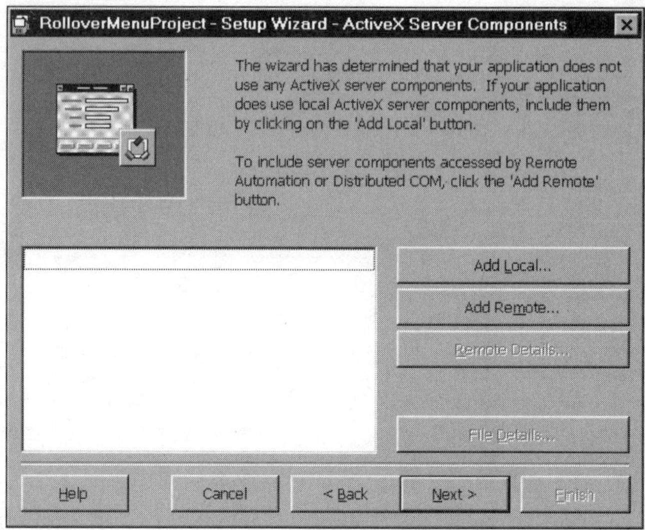

Figure 9.13
The ActiveX Server Components dialog.

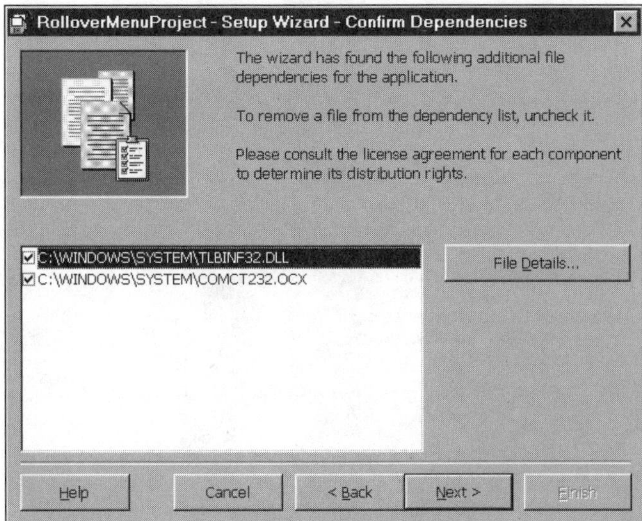

Figure 9.14
The Confirm Dependencies dialog.

any other files that the control requires for its operation. This information is taken primarily from your project file and from built-in knowledge of the Visual Basic runtime systems.

When you click Next, the Wizard will look for additional dependencies based on the files listed. If the control requires property pages, it will also ask whether you wish to include the property page support DLL. It will then display the File Summary dialog, shown in Figure 9.15.

The Finished dialog, shown in Figure 9.16, offers the opportunity to save a template of the current setup, so you may regenerate the setup file without reconstructing the dependency lists. If you found the Wizard's automatic detection accurate, then you probably don't need to save the settings. When you are ready to generate the setup file, click Finish.

The CAB file will be placed in the directory specified as the target, usually WINDOWS\TEMP\SWSETUP, along with an HTM file with the same root name. The HTM file contains an example that demonstrates how to incorporate the control into a Web document using the **<OBJECT>** tag, along with instructions on how to incorporate a license package file if needed, as shown in Listing 9.18.

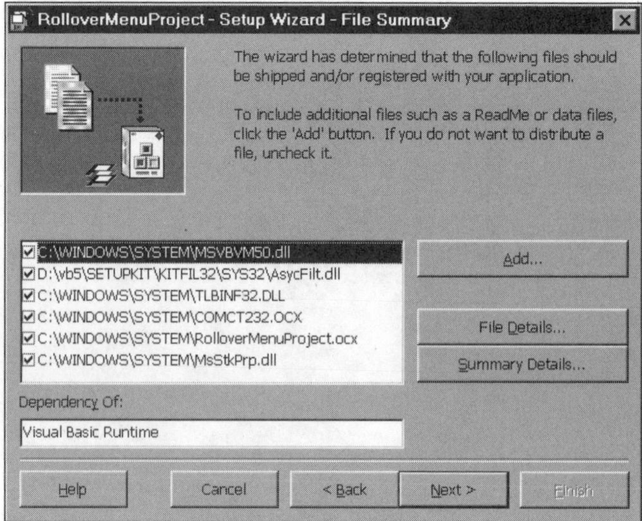

Figure 9.15
The File Summary dialog from the Setup Wizard.

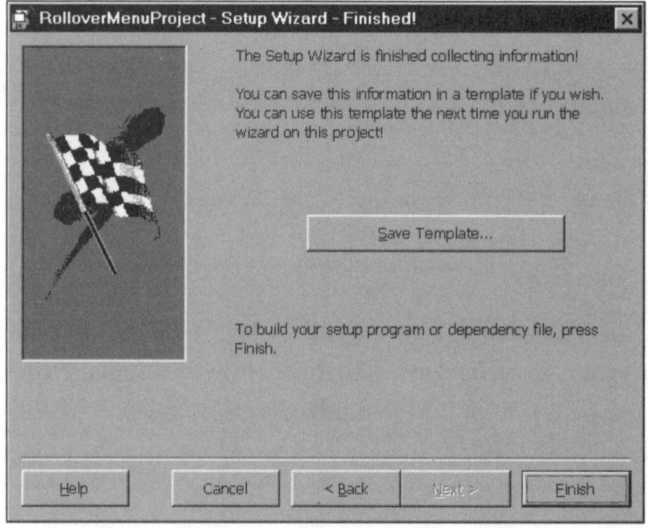

Figure 9.16
The Finished dialog from the Application Setup Wizard.

Listing 9.18 The RolloverMenuProject.HTM file produced by the Setup Wizard.

```
<HTML>
<!--If any of the controls on this page require licensing, you must
create a license package file. Run LPK_TOOL.EXE to create the
required LPK file. LPK_TOOL.EXE can be found on the ActiveX SDK,
http://www.microsoft.com/intdev/sdk/sdk.htm. If you have the Visual
Basic 5.0 CD, it can also be found in the \Tools\LPK_TOOL directory.

The following is an example of the Object tag:

<OBJECT CLASSID="clsid:5220cb21-c88d-11cf-b347-00aa00a28331">
<PARAM NAME="LPKPath" VALUE="LPKfilename.LPK">
</OBJECT>
-->

<OBJECT ID="RolloverMenu" WIDTH=313 HEIGHT=216
CLASSID="CLSID:6772DD8D-9E1F-11D0-B8EF-00608CC9A71F"
CODEBASE="RolloverMenuProject.CAB#version=1,0,0,0">
</OBJECT>
</HTML>
```

ActiveX Code Signing

The ActiveX technology found in Microsoft's Internet Explorer is designed to make rich content available to users without the hassle of trying to figure out which software components are installed, where to get them, what version is the most current, and so on. By enabling software components to "automagically" install themselves to the user's computer as necessary, ActiveX and MSIE have done a great deal for both the user and developer communities.

With software components and digital content being transparently installed to users' computers all over the world, the hazard that someone in the developer community will develop and distribute a software component that either maliciously or unknowingly does some sort of damage to a user's computer has greatly increased. ActiveX technology addresses the potential of unsafe code through code-verification systems or code signing. For you to effectively use ActiveX technology, you must register yourself or your company as a developer and get a verification certificate. The process is simple and relatively inexpensive, and you'll find all the information you need at ***http://www.microsoft.com/intdev/controls/signmark-f.htm****.*

Basically, code signing and verification identifies developers of software components so that a developer cannot anonymously create an ActiveX component that, for example, deletes your hard drive. MSIE, by default, has maximum security enabled. That means that no ActiveX content can be downloaded unless it is digitally signed. The medium level of security (recommended for developers) warns before any unsigned content is to be downloaded and allows the user to decide whether to allow it. There is an option for no security, but it is not recommended. Only under limited conditions, such as closely monitored intranets not wired to the Internet, would turning security off be an option.

Adding Controls To Web Documents

To incorporate the **RolloverMenu** control, we can just add an **<OBJECT>** tag to any Web document. The **CLASSID** attribute uniquely identifies the control, while the **CODEBASE** attribute tells the client where to find its setup file. The **CODEBASE** tag shown earlier in Listing 9.18 includes no path, which means that the client—and therefore the Web server—will expect to find the RolloverMenuProject.CAB file in the same directory as the Web document in which the control is referenced. You may add relative or absolute path information, or even a complete URL to specify an alternative location.

To set the properties of the control, you must add **<PARAM>** tags to the **<OBJECT>** tag, as shown earlier in Listing 9.12. To set each property, we set the **NAME** attribute in each **<PARAM>** tag to the same names expected by the **ReadProperty()** functions in the control. This control supports three array properties, whose values are set by appending an index value to the property names. Object browsers will not reveal this little secret, so users will need some documentation to make use of this control.

Use A Web Editor To Insert <OBJECT> Tags

*To simplify the incorporation of ActiveX controls into your Web documents, many Web authoring tools now support object editing. For the most rudimentary form of Web object manipulation, download a copy of the Microsoft ActiveX Control Pad. It's free. You'll find it at **http://www.microsoft.com/sitebuilder/**.*

Once you've placed an instance of the RolloverMenu control on the document, you can add some VBScript to activate it. Let's just add a simple Click() event procedure, as shown in Listing 9.19.

Listing 9.19 The RolloverMenu control activated with VBScript.

```
<HTML>
<HEAD>
<TITLE>New Page</TITLE>

<SCRIPT LANGUAGE="VBS">
sub RolloverMenu1_Click(TargetURL)
    MsgBox "URL: " & TargetURL
end sub
</SCRIPT>

</HEAD>
<BODY>

<OBJECT ID="RolloverMenu1" WIDTH=313 HEIGHT=217
 CLASSID="CLSID:6772DD8D-9E1F-11D0-B8EF-00608CC9A71F">
   <PARAM NAME="_ExtentX" VALUE="6625">
   <PARAM NAME="_ExtentY" VALUE="4593">
   <PARAM NAME="NumberOfOptions" VALUE="2">
   <PARAM NAME="Captions1" VALUE="Menu Option 1">
   <PARAM NAME="Descriptions1" VALUE="Description of first option.">
   <PARAM NAME="TargetURLs1" VALUE="http://www.yourfirstchoice.com">
   <PARAM NAME="Captions2" VALUE="Menu Option 2">
   <PARAM NAME="Descriptions2" _
       VALUE="The second option has this description.">
   <PARAM NAME="TargetURLs2" VALUE="http://www.yoursecondchoice.com">
   <PARAM NAME="BackStyle" VALUE="1">
   <PARAM NAME="OptionFontSize" VALUE="9.6">
   <PARAM NAME="DescFontSize" VALUE="12">
</OBJECT>

</BODY>
</HTML>
```

A Word About ActiveX Documents

The next level in the ActiveX universe is ActiveX documents. Instead of discrete controls linked together in HTML documents with VBScript or JavaScript, ActiveX documents are entire application interfaces that display themselves in a host application, known as an ActiveX container application. Writing an ActiveX document is similar to writing ordinary Visual Basic standard EXEs. Unlike standard applications, however, ActiveX documents can be packaged for automatic download and installation, just like ActiveX controls. ActiveX documents are Web documents that contain no HTML—just objects and program code—which means they can achieve the full interactivity of conventional applications.

ActiveX documents are contributing to the fading distinction between browsers and operating system desktops. In forthcoming versions of the Windows operating systems, for example, the desktop will become the browser, displaying not only Web documents, but all information available on the system.

ActiveX documents are leading the way toward smarter management of network-based applications. Soon it may be possible to set up LANs and larger networks with applications that install and update themselves automatically. This is good news for Visual Basic programmers. Visual Basic 5.0 will generate ActiveX document applications just as easily as previous versions created form-based applications.

ActiveX technology will likely become a driving force in the next generation of networked computing.

Talk Talk Talk

CHAPTER 10

Have your people get in touch with their people with live, realtime communications. With the Winsock control, we can create our own Internet applications that enable servers and clients to exchange information in any format we wish.

Talk Talk Talk

In Chapter 1, we built a simple application that enabled two Internet nodes to communicate with the TCP/IP protocol. We used the Winsock control to build a server application that waited for a client to request a connection, and a client that could link itself to the server and exchange messages. In this chapter, we'll expand on the concepts we briefly demonstrated in that project and build an Internet chat application that again comprises two separate applications—a client and a server. Once the basic program is working, we'll convert the client into an ActiveX control that we can embed in any Web page.

Revisiting Winsock

The Windows Sockets (Winsock) interface is a feature of the Windows operating system that enables Windows applications to exchange information with other nodes on the Internet, while hiding the details of how that information is packaged and transmitted. The Microsoft Winsock ActiveX control encapsulates the functions of Windows Sockets in a component that we can incorporate into any Visual Basic application. In Chapters 5 and 6, we used the Winsock control to implement the key elements of the Network News Transfer Protocol (NNTP). As I explained then, the Winsock control itself offers no intrinsic support for any of the common Internet service protocols such as FTP, HTTP, Gopher, NNTP, and SMTP. It merely provides an interface to the Internet's data transfer system that we can use to implement those higher-level protocols, or any protocol of our own design.

The Winsock control supports 15 properties, 8 methods, and 7 events, as shown in Table 10.1. To create a complete application, with both a client and a server, we'll use most of the Winsock control's members.

As we saw in Chapter 1, a Winsock dialog consists of a few essential operations:

1. Set the server to listen for a connection request on a specific IP port.
2. Tell the client to connect to a server at the appropriate IP address and port.

Table 10.1 The members of the Winsock ActiveX control.

Member	Type	Description
BytesReceived	Property	Returns number of bytes received.
Index	Property	Identifies the control's position in a control array, if an array has been declared.
LocalHostName	Property	Returns the name of the local machine.
LocalIP	Property	Returns the IP address of the local machine.
LocalPort	Property	Returns or specifies the port number.
Name	Property	Identifies the control instance.
Object	Property	Returns a reference to an object for use in automation tasks.
Parent	Property	Returns a reference to the control's container.
Protocol	Property	Specifies whether to use the TCP or UDP protocol.
RemoteHost	Property	Sets or returns the machine name of the remote computer.
RemoteHostIP	Property	Sets or returns the IP address of the remote computer.
RemotePort	Property	Sets the port number to connect to on the remote computer.
SocketHandle	Property	Returns a handle to the attached socket instance.
State	Property	Indicates the current connection status of the socket.
Tag	Property	User-definable string.
Accept()	Method	Accepts a connection request.
Bind()	Method	Binds the socket to a specific port and adapter for a UDP protocol connection.
Close()	Method	Used to close a connection.
Connect()	Method	Used to request a connection to a remote node.
GetData()	Method	Used to retrieve incoming data from the buffer.
Listen()	Method	Causes the socket to await connection requests.
PeekData()	Method	Retrieves data from the input buffer without removing it.
SendData()	Method	Used to send data to the remote node.

continued

Table 10.1 The members of the Winsock ActiveX control (continued).

Member	Type	Description
Close()	Event	Raised when the remote node closes the connection.
Connect()	Event	Raised when a connection is established.
ConnectionRequest()	Event	Raised when a node requests a connection to a server application.
DataArrival()	Event	Raised when data arrives over the active connection.
Error()	Event	Raised when an error occurs.
SendComplete()	Event	Raised at the completion of a send operation.
SendProgress()	Event	Raised to indicate the number of bytes sent versus the number of bytes remaining to send.

3. On the server, respond to the connection request by accepting the connection.
4. Send data from client to server or from server to client.
5. On either the server or client, retrieve incoming data from the buffer.
6. Repeat steps 4 and 5 as necessary.
7. Close the connection.

The Winsock control makes it easy to exchange data over the Internet between clients and servers located anywhere in the world.

A Winsock Chat Application

In the project WinsockExperiment1.VBP, we wrote a simple application with two forms, **frmClient** and **frmServer**, which would run simultaneously in the Visual Basic development environment. These two forms demonstrated a simple one-to-one TCP connection. In the next project, we'll split the client and server into two independent programs and expand them to enable multiple clients to connect to a single server.

Running The Winsock Chat Programs

Copy all the files in the \WINSOCK CHAT subdirectory to your hard drive. Then open the project group WinsockChat.VBG. This group contains two projects: WinsockChatClient and WinsockChatServer. Since you can run only one application at a time within the Visual Basic development environment, you'll need to compile at least one of these two programs into an EXE before you can try them out. I would recommend compiling the server. To do so, select WinsockChatServer in the Project Explorer window, then from the Visual Basic menu select File|Make ChatServer.EXE. You can save the executable version in any directory. Start the server by double clicking it in Windows 95 Explorer, or use the Run option on the Windows 95 Start Menu.

Open the code window for **frmClient**. In the declarations section, locate the **String** constant **ChatHost**, then set it to the IP address displayed by the server, as shown in Figure 10.1. To run the client, shown in Figure 10.2, from within the Visual Basic IDE, first right click the project in the Project Explorer, and select "Set as Start Up" from the context menu. Then run the project.

You may run the server and client either on separate machines or together on the same machine. You may also run the client on multiple machines by compiling it and invoking from each machine on your network.

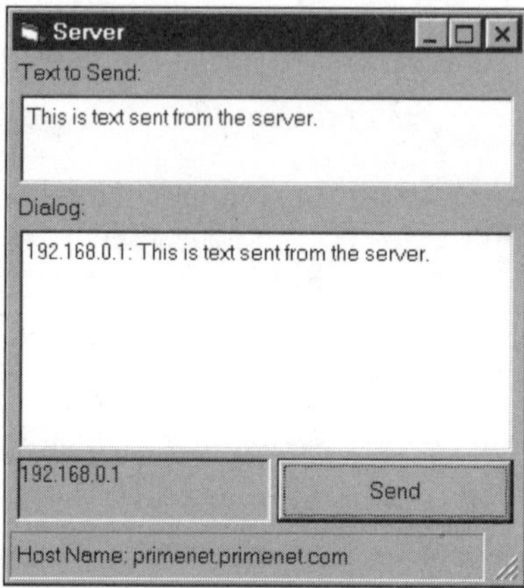

Figure 10.1
The WinsockChatServer at runtime.

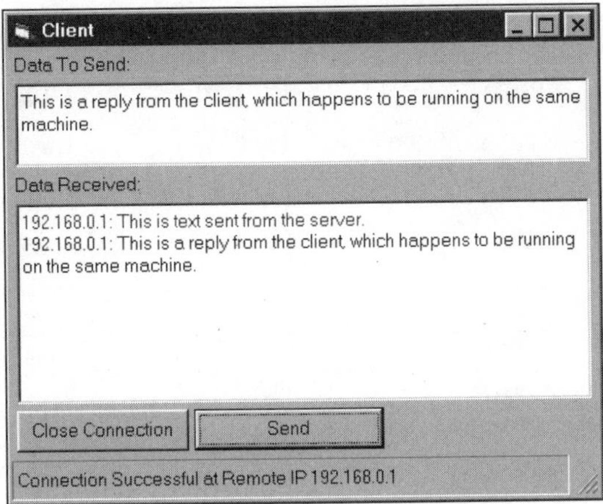

Figure 10.2
The WinsockChatClient at runtime.

Running Multiple Instances Of The Client

If you do not have Visual Basic 5 installed on every machine, you'll need to create a setup program for the client program. The Application Setup Wizard will create a setup script that will enable you to copy and install the client program and all the required Visual Basic runtime support files to any machine on your network.

On the client, click the Connect button to establish a TCP connection to the server. You may then type messages in the upper text box of either program and transmit it by clicking the Send button. If you have multiple clients connected to the server, the text transmitted by any client node—or by the server—will appear in the Data Received text box of all active nodes.

Designing The Server Form

The server form contains two rich text boxes, a command button, a status bar, three labels, and one Winsock control, as shown in Table 10.2. To communicate with multiple clients, a TCP server application must open one Windows socket for each connection, so we'll set the **Index** property of the Winsock control to 0, effectively declaring it as the first member of a control array. To establish a control array, we need at least one member. We can then expand or contract the control array at runtime.

Table 10.2 The controls in frmServer1.FRM.

Name	Type	Property	Value
cmdSendData	CommandButton	Caption	"Send"
lblDataReceived	Label	Caption	"Data Received:"
lblDataToSend	Label	Caption	"Data to Send:"
lblIPAddress	Label	Caption	""
sbWinsockStatus	StatusBar	(Custom)	
sktTCPChatServer	Winsock	Index	0
		Protocol	0 - sckTCPProtocol
txtDataReceived	RichTextBox	MultiLine	True
		RightMargin	1
		ScrollBars	3 - rtfBoth
txtDataToSend	RichTextBox	MultiLine	True
		RightMargin	1
		ScrollBars	3 - rtfBoth

As in previous projects in this book, the layout of the controls isn't critical. If you're building the project from scratch, just drop them on the form in roughly the configuration shown in Figure 10.1. We'll tidy them up with code in the **Resize**() event procedure, shown later in Listing 10.6.

Accepting Connections To The Server

A server needs to monitor the Internet for connection requests. To place our server in this mode, we need to invoke the Winsock control's **Listen**() method. In this project, we'll let the server activate itself immediately upon loading by calling **Listen**() from the **Form_Load**() event procedure, shown in Listing 10.1.

Listing 10.1 The **Form_Load()** event procedure from frmServer1.FRM.

```
Private Sub Form_Load()
    ReDim gActiveSockets(0)
```

```
sktTCPChatServer(0).LocalPort = 1600
sktTCPChatServer(0).Listen
lblIPAddress.Caption = sktTCPChatServer(0).LocalIP
sbWinsockStatus.Panels(1) = "Host Name: " & _
    sktTCPChatServer(0).LocalHostName
End Sub
```

To listen for connection requests, all the server needs is a home on a TCP/IP node and a port number. I've selected the arbitrary port number 1600. You may use any port number you wish, although it's a good idea to avoid the well-known port numbers used by major Internet services, which are shown in Table 10.3.

Assigned Port Numbers

For an extensive—though not necessarily comprehensive—list of assigned port numbers, see RFC 1700 at ***http://ds.internic.net/std/std2.txt****. The well-known port numbers are assigned by an organization known appropriately as the Internet Assigned Numbers Authority (IANA). Although the common Internet services use just a handful of port numbers, the IANA has actually assigned hundreds of numbers to various services developed by both commercial and academic users. As long as you don't intend to distribute your application to other users, you may use any port number you wish; your server program will not cause a conflict unless a computer at a particular IP address tries to run your server concurrently with another server application that listens on the same port. If you do plan to distribute your server, you must apply to the IANA for a reserved port number. RFC 1700 explains how to contact the IANA.*

Table 10.3 Some of the well-known Internet port numbers.

Protocol	Port Number
File Transfer Protocol	21
Telnet Protocol	23
Simple Mail Transfer Protocol	25
Whois Protocol	43
Gopher Protocol	70
Finger Protocol	79
Hypertext Transfer Protocol	80
Network News Transfer Protocol	119

When the Winsock control receives a connection request from a client, it raises its **ConnectionRequest** event. The **sktTCPChatServer_ConnectionRequest()** event procedure, shown in Listing 10.2, spawns a new Windows socket and hands off the pending connection.

Listing 10.2 The **sktTCPChatServer_ConnectionRequest()** event procedure from frmServer1.FRM.

```
Private Sub sktTCPChatServer_ConnectionRequest(Index As Integer, _
                                        ByVal requestID As Long)
    Dim ArrayIndex As Integer
    Dim OpenSocketPos As Integer
    Dim Dummy As String

    ArrayIndex = 0
    OpenSocketPos = 0
    Do While (OpenSocketPos = 0) And _
            (ArrayIndex < UBound(gActiveSockets))
        ArrayIndex = ArrayIndex + 1
        If Not gActiveSockets(ArrayIndex).Connected Then
            OpenSocketPos = ArrayIndex
          End If
        Loop

    If OpenSocketPos = 0 Then
        OpenSocketPos = UBound(gActiveSockets) + 1
        ReDim Preserve gActiveSockets(OpenSocketPos)
      End If

    Load sktTCPChatServer(OpenSocketPos)
    gActiveSockets(OpenSocketPos).Connected = True
    sktTCPChatServer(OpenSocketPos).Accept requestID
    gActiveSockets(OpenSocketPos).ClientIPAddress = _
        sktTCPChatServer(OpenSocketPos).RemoteHostIP
    sbWinsockStatus.Panels(1) = "Connecting Socket " & _
        OpenSocketPos & " to " & _
        gActiveSockets(OpenSocketPos).ClientIPAddress

    End Sub
```

To manage the server's connections, we use two parallel arrays. The Winsock control array is shadowed by **gActiveSockets()**, a dynamic global array comprising elements of the user-defined type **tActiveSocket**:

```
Private Type tActiveSocket
    Connected As Boolean
    ClientIPAddress As String
    ClientName As String
    End Type

Private gActiveSockets() As tActiveSocket
```

As the server creates and destroys instances of **sktTCPChatServer**, it may leave gaps in the numbering sequence of the control array's **Index** property. The array **gActiveSockets** keeps track of which socket instances are in use and which can be reassigned to new control instances. When we get a new connection request, we first step through **gActiveSockets** to determine whether any existing positions are available. If not, we **ReDim** the array, increasing its size by one element. We then use the **Load** statement to create a new instance of **sktTCPChatServer** at the new or available **OpenSocketPos**. We call the Winsock **Accept()** method to establish the connection between the new Winsock control and the remote client, passing it the **requestID** received as an argument to the **ConnectionRequest()** event procedure. We also set the **Connected** and **ClientIPAddress** fields in the corresponding element of **gActiveSockets**.

The type **tActiveSocket** defines one other field, **ClientName**, which I have left unused here. Although the Winsock control is capable of returning the remote computer's host name, it cannot do so without the aid of a domain name server, or DNS. If you use this program over the Internet, chances are that you already use a DNS. But many local area networks have no DNS, and the Winsock control cannot easily determine the remote machine name. If the program will have access to a DNS, you may wish to set the **ClientName** field.

Sending Text From The Server

The server program needs to send its messages to all connected clients. The array **gActiveSockets** makes this easy. In the **cmdSendData_Click()** event procedure, shown in Listing 10.3, we step through the array seeking **Connected** sockets. For each connection, we use the Winsock **SendData()** method to transmit the server's IP address, followed by the contents of the **txtDataToSend.Text**.

Listing 10.3 The **cmdSendData_Click()** event procedure from frmServer1.FRM.

```
Private Sub cmdSendData_Click()
    Dim ArrayIndex As Integer

    For ArrayIndex = 1 To UBound(gActiveSockets)
        If gActiveSockets(ArrayIndex).Connected Then
            sktTCPChatServer(ArrayIndex).SendData _
                sktTCPChatServer(0).LocalIP & ": " & _
                txtDataToSend.Text
            'Must allow Windows to service its event queue:
            DoEvents
          End If
        Next ArrayIndex
    txtDataReceived.SelColor = vbButtonText
    txtDataReceived.SelText = sktTCPChatServer(0).LocalIP & ": " & _
        txtDataToSend.Text & vbCrLf
    txtDataReceived.UpTo vbEOF
    End Sub
```

Notice the **DoEvents** statement inside the **For Next** loop. Without this statement, Windows does not have a chance to service its event queue until all the transmissions have been initiated. You wouldn't expect this to make much difference; the Winsock controls should queue up their data, then fire when Windows gives them the signal. However, when you run this program without **DoEvents**—for some reason that I cannot explain—only the last Winsock control in the array actually transmits its data. The data waiting in each of the other transmission buffers remains there until you disconnect the client attached to the next higher array member. Then, when you transmit again, all the backed-up data appears in a single surge. This may be a bug in the Winsock control, or it may be a normal characteristic of the Windows Sockets interface. Whatever the cause, a simple call to **DoEvents** will keep things flowing smoothly.

After sending the string to each client, the procedure updates its local chat dialog display, **txtDataReceived**, which provides a scrolling display of all chat activity. I've used the **SelText** property of the RichTextBox control to add the new text at the current insertion point, which will normally be the end of the document. To force the display to scroll to the end of the document, call the RichTextBox's **UpTo()** method, passing it the Visual Basic constant **vbEOF**, the end-of-file marker. To make the RichTextBox controls wrap their text properly, set their **RightMargin** properties to 1. The help file for the late pre-release beta version of Visual Basic 5 states that the default **RightMargin** value of 0 should cause text to wrap at the control's rightmost edge, but that was not the case: a value of 0 resulted in no automatic wrapping at all.

Receiving Text From The Clients

In the project WinsockExperiment1.VBP, we established simple two-way communications between a single client and a server. The server in this project, however, acts more as a moderator than a participant. The purpose of a real chat server is to relay messages among all participants. The **cmdSendData_Click**() procedure (discussed earlier) enables one participant to send messages from the server to all the clients, but the server must also forward all messages received from each client to all the other clients. That way every user in the chat session will see the complete text of the discussion.

The **sktTCPChatServer_DataArrival**() event procedure, shown in Listing 10.4, begins by using the Winsock control's **GetData**() method to remove incoming data from the receive buffer. It then takes one of two paths.

If a **sktTCPChatServer** control receives the string "QUIT", it then calls the **sktTCPChatServer_Close**() event procedure, passing it the **Index** of that control. (I'll explain shortly why we're using this roundabout method to close the connection.) If the server receives any other text string, it appends the message to the client's IP address, re-transmits the message to each of the clients, and updates **txtDataReceived**—just as it did in the **cmdSendData_Click**() event procedure described earlier.

Listing 10.4 The **sktTCPChatServer_DataArrival()** event procedure from frmServer1.FRM.

```
Private Sub sktTCPChatServer_DataArrival(Index As Integer, _
                                         ByVal bytesTotal As Long)
    Dim DataReceived As String
    Dim ArrayIndex As Integer

    sktTCPChatServer(Index).GetData DataReceived, vbString
    If CStr(DataReceived) = "QUIT" Then
        sktTCPChatServer_Close Index
```

```
    Else
      For ArrayIndex = 1 To UBound(gActiveSockets)
          If (ArrayIndex <> Index) And _
             (gActiveSockets(ArrayIndex).Connected) Then
              sktTCPChatServer(ArrayIndex).SendData _
                  gActiveSockets(Index).ClientIPAddress & _
                  ": " & DataReceived
              'Must allow Windows to service its event queue:
              DoEvents
            End If
          Next ArrayIndex

      txtDataReceived.SelColor = vbHighlight
      txtDataReceived.SelText = _
          sktTCPChatServer(Index).RemoteHostIP & _
          ": " & DataReceived & vbCrLf
      txtDataReceived.UpTo vbEOF
    End If

  End Sub
```

Closing A Server Connection

Similar to the "QUIT" command we used in Chapters 5 and 6 to disconnect from an NNTP server, the "QUIT" command sent by the client instructs our server to disconnect itself from the client. While it's true that the Winsock control supports a **Close**() method, and that the client could disconnect itself from the server just as easily as the server can disconnect itself from the client, that more direct method causes problems at the client side of the connection.

In the **sktTCPChatServer_Close**() event procedure, shown in Listing 10.5, we call the Winsock control's **Close**() method before we **Unload** the control instance.

Listing 10.5 The sktTCPChatServer_Close() event procedure from frmServer1.FRM.

```
Private Sub sktTCPChatServer_Close(Index As Integer)
    sbWinsockStatus.Panels(1) = _
        "Disconnecting from " & sktTCPChatServer(Index).RemoteHostIP

    sktTCPChatServer(Index).Close
    Unload sktTCPChatServer(Index)
```

```
    gActiveSockets(Index).Connected = False
    gActiveSockets(Index).ClientIPAddress = ""
    End Sub
```

Remember, for each connection to the server, we create a new instance of the Winsock control. So when we close a connection, we must remove the idle socket. This preserves system resources and ensures that the connection will be completely terminated. Of the two Winsock controls that constitute a single connection between a client and the server, the one that first calls its **Close**() method does not receive the **Close** event. This doesn't make much difference on the server because we tear down the control instance anyway, which cleans up any unfinished business as it goes. On the client, however, we may want to reuse the Winsock control to establish a new connection. Unfortunately, when we close the connection from the client, it does not entirely reset the socket, preventing us from making such a request. However, if the server closes the connection, the client will raise the **Close** event, enabling us to call the **Close**() method on the client's Winsock control *post mortem*. This will properly reinitialize the control in preparation for a new TCP session. As terribly convoluted as all of this may seem, it is still the most reliable way to terminate a connection.

Listing 10.6 contains all the code required for frmServer1.FRM.

Listing 10.6 The complete listing of frmServer1.FRM.

```
Option Explicit

Private Type tActiveSocket
    Connected As Boolean
    ClientIPAddress As String
    ClientName As String
    End Type

Private gActiveSockets() As tActiveSocket
Private Const FormSpace = 50

Private Sub cmdSendData_Click()
    Dim ArrayIndex As Integer

    For ArrayIndex = 1 To UBound(gActiveSockets)
        If gActiveSockets(ArrayIndex).Connected Then
            sktTCPChatServer(ArrayIndex).SendData _
```

```
                sktTCPChatServer(0).LocalIP & ": " & _
                txtDataToSend.Text
            'Must allow Windows to service its event queue:
            DoEvents
          End If
        Next ArrayIndex
    txtDataReceived.SelColor = vbButtonText
    txtDataReceived.SelText = sktTCPChatServer(0).LocalIP & ": " & _
        txtDataToSend.Text & vbCrLf
    txtDataReceived.UpTo vbEOF
    End Sub

Private Sub Form_Load()
    ReDim gActiveSockets(0)

    sktTCPChatServer(0).LocalPort = 1600
    sktTCPChatServer(0).Listen
    lblIPAddress.Caption = sktTCPChatServer(0).LocalIP
    sbWinsockStatus.Panels(1) = "Host Name: " & _
        sktTCPChatServer(0).LocalHostName
    End Sub

Private Sub Form_QueryUnload(Cancel As Integer, _
                             UnloadMode As Integer)
    Dim ArrayIndex As Integer

    For ArrayIndex = 1 To UBound(gActiveSockets)
        If gActiveSockets(ArrayIndex).Connected Then
            sktTCPChatServer(ArrayIndex).Close
            Unload sktTCPChatServer(ArrayIndex)
          End If
        Next ArrayIndex
    End Sub

Private Sub Form_Resize()
    Dim MinFormHeight As Long
    Dim MinFormWidth As Long
    Dim FreeSpace As Long

    If frmServer.WindowState = vbMinimized Then
        Exit Sub
      End If

    MinFormHeight = (Height - ScaleHeight) + _
                    sbWinsockStatus.Height + _
                    cmdSendData.Height + _
```

```
                  lblDataToSend.Height + 100 + _
                  lblDataReceived.Height + 100 + _
                  8 * FormSpace
    MinFormWidth = (Width - ScaleWidth) + _
                  cmdSendData.Width + _
                  3 * FormSpace + 100
    frmServer.Height = MaxLong(frmServer.Height, MinFormHeight)
    frmServer.Width = MaxLong(frmServer.Width, MinFormWidth)

    cmdSendData.Left = ScaleWidth - _
        (cmdSendData.Width + FormSpace)
    cmdSendData.Top = ScaleHeight - _
        (sbWinsockStatus.Height + cmdSendData.Height + FormSpace)
    FreeSpace = (cmdSendData.Top - 3 * FormSpace)

    lblIPAddress.Left = FormSpace
    lblIPAddress.Top = cmdSendData.Top
    lblIPAddress.Height = cmdSendData.Height
    lblIPAddress.Width = cmdSendData.Left - 2 * FormSpace

    lblDataToSend.Left = FormSpace
    lblDataToSend.Top = FormSpace
    txtDataToSend.Left = FormSpace
    txtDataToSend.Top = lblDataToSend.Top + lblDataToSend.Height
    txtDataToSend.Width = ScaleWidth - (2 * FormSpace)
    txtDataToSend.Height = (FreeSpace * 0.33) - _
                          lblDataToSend.Height
    lblDataReceived.Left = FormSpace
    lblDataReceived.Top = txtDataToSend.Top + _
                          txtDataToSend.Height + FormSpace
    txtDataReceived.Left = FormSpace
    txtDataReceived.Top = lblDataReceived.Top + _
                          lblDataReceived.Height
    txtDataReceived.Width = txtDataToSend.Width
    txtDataReceived.Height = (FreeSpace * 0.67) - _
                            lblDataReceived.Height

    End Sub

Private Sub sktTCPChatServer_Close(Index As Integer)
    'MsgBox Index & " Closing Connection"
    sbWinsockStatus.Panels(1) = _
        "Disconnecting from " & sktTCPChatServer(Index).RemoteHostIP

    sktTCPChatServer(Index).Close
    Unload sktTCPChatServer(Index)
```

```
    gActiveSockets(Index).Connected = False
    gActiveSockets(Index).ClientIPAddress = ""
    End Sub

Private Sub sktTCPChatServer_Connect(Index As Integer)
    ' This event never executes on a server.
    MsgBox "Connect Event"
    gActiveSockets(Index).Connected = True
    gActiveSockets(Index).ClientIPAddress = _
        sktTCPChatServer(Index).RemoteHostIP
    sbWinsockStatus.Panels(1) = "Connected to " & _
        sktTCPChatServer(Index).RemoteHostIP
    End Sub

Private Sub sktTCPChatServer_ConnectionRequest(Index As Integer, _
                                        ByVal requestID As Long)
    Dim ArrayIndex As Integer
    Dim OpenSocketPos As Integer
    Dim Dummy As String

    ArrayIndex = 0
    OpenSocketPos = 0
    Do While (OpenSocketPos = 0) And _
             (ArrayIndex < UBound(gActiveSockets))
        ArrayIndex = ArrayIndex + 1
        If Not gActiveSockets(ArrayIndex).Connected Then
            OpenSocketPos = ArrayIndex
          End If
        Loop

    If OpenSocketPos = 0 Then
        OpenSocketPos = UBound(gActiveSockets) + 1
        ReDim Preserve gActiveSockets(OpenSocketPos)
      End If

    Load sktTCPChatServer(OpenSocketPos)
    gActiveSockets(OpenSocketPos).Connected = True
    sktTCPChatServer(OpenSocketPos).Accept requestID
    gActiveSockets(OpenSocketPos).ClientIPAddress = _
        sktTCPChatServer(OpenSocketPos).RemoteHostIP
    sbWinsockStatus.Panels(1) = "Connecting Socket " & _
        OpenSocketPos & " to " & _
        gActiveSockets(OpenSocketPos).ClientIPAddress
    'Dummy = sktTCPChatServer(OpenSocketPos).LocalHostName

    End Sub
```

```
Private Sub sktTCPChatServer_DataArrival(Index As Integer, _
                                    ByVal bytesTotal As Long)
    Dim DataReceived As String
    Dim ArrayIndex As Integer

    sktTCPChatServer(Index).GetData DataReceived, vbString
    If CStr(DataReceived) = "QUIT" Then
        sktTCPChatServer_Close Index
      Else
        For ArrayIndex = 1 To UBound(gActiveSockets)
            If (ArrayIndex <> Index) And _
               (gActiveSockets(ArrayIndex).Connected) Then
                sktTCPChatServer(ArrayIndex).SendData _
                    gActiveSockets(Index).ClientIPAddress & _
                    ": " & DataReceived
                'Must allow Windows to service its event queue:
                DoEvents
              End If
            Next ArrayIndex

        txtDataReceived.SelColor = vbHighlight
        txtDataReceived.SelText = _
            sktTCPChatServer(Index).RemoteHostIP & _
            ": " & DataReceived & vbCrLf
        txtDataReceived.UpTo vbEOF
      End If

    End Sub

Public Function WinsockStateString(WinsockState As Integer) As String
    Select Case WinsockState
      Case sckClosed
        WinsockStateString = "Closed"
      Case sckClosing
        WinsockStateString = "Closing"
      Case sckConnected
        WinsockStateString = "Connected"
      Case sckConnecting
        WinsockStateString = "Connecting"
      Case sckConnectionPending
        WinsockStateString = "Connection Pending"
      Case sckHostResolved
        WinsockStateString = "Host Resolved"
      Case sckError
        WinsockStateString = "Error"
```

```
    Case sckListening
      WinsockStateString = "Listening"
    Case sckResolvingHost
      WinsockStateString = "Resolving Host"
    Case sckOpen
      WinsockStateString = "Open"
    Case Else
      WinsockStateString = "Unknown State"
    End Select
  End Function
```

Next, we'll create a client that will connect to and communicate with our custom chat server.

Designing The Client Form

The client form closely resembles the server form, with just a few small but significant differences. Many of the controls on the client form even share the same names with their counterparts on the server form, as shown in Table 10.4. But the client form has an additional CommandButton (**cmdConnect**), and its Winsock control (**sktTCPChatClient**) does not belong to a control array, as determined by its null **Index** property.

Table 10.4 The controls in frmClient1.FRM.

Name	Type	Property	Value
cmdConnect	CommandButton	Caption	"Connect"
cmdSendData	CommandButton	Caption	"Send"
lblDataReceived	Label	Caption	"Data Received:"
lblDataToSend	Label	Caption	"Data to Send:"
sbWinsockState	StatusBar	(Custom)	
sktTCPChatClient	Winsock	Protocol	0 - sckTCPProtocol
txtDataReceived	RichTextBox	MultiLine	True
		RightMargin	1
		ScrollBars	3 - rtfBoth
txtDataToSend	RichTextBox	MultiLine	True
		RightMargin	1
		ScrollBars	3 - rtfBoth

Controlling The Connection To The Server

The client's **cmdConnect_Click()** event procedure, shown in Listing 10.7, actually performs both the connect and disconnect operations. The binary variable **bConnected** keeps track of the current program state, determining which operation will be performed by the procedure.

Listing 10.7 The **cmdConnect_Click()** event procedure from frmClient1.FRM.

```
Private Sub cmdConnect_Click()
    If bConnected Then
        sbWinsockState.Panels(1) = "Closing Connection"
        cmdSendData.Enabled = False
        cmdConnect.Enabled = False
        sktTCPChatClient.SendData "QUIT"
      Else
        'Close connection as a (unreliable) precaution:
        sktTCPChatClient.Close
        With sktTCPChatClient
            .RemoteHost = ChatHost
            .RemotePort = 1600
            End With
        sktTCPChatClient.Connect
        sbWinsockState.Panels(1) = "You are at IP Address " & _
            sktTCPChatClient.LocalIP
        cmdConnect.Enabled = False
        Do
            DoEvents
            Loop Until sktTCPChatClient.State = sckConnected Or _
                       sktTCPChatClient.State = sckError
        If sktTCPChatClient.State = sckError Then
            cmdConnect.Enabled = True
            sbWinsockState.Panels(1) = "Unable to connect to host."
            sndPlaySound "Exclamation", SND_ASYNC
          Else
            cmdConnect.Caption = "Close Connection"
            bConnected = True
            cmdConnect.Enabled = True
            cmdSendData.Enabled = True
          End If
      End If
    End Sub
```

The first major section of the procedure, the main **Then** clause, initiates the close operation. After sending the "QUIT" command to the server, it disables the two command buttons, effectively disabling the entire program until it receives a response from the server. When the server responds to the "QUIT" command by ordering its Winsock control to close the connection, **sktTCPChatClient** will execute its **Close()** event procedure, shown in Listing 10.8.

Listing 10.8 The **sktTCPChatClient_Close()** event procedure from frmClient1.FRM.

```
Private Sub sktTCPChatClient_Close()
    cmdConnect.Enabled = False
    cmdSendData.Enabled = False
    sktTCPChatClient.Close
    Do
        sbWinsockState.Panels(1) = "Status: " & _
            WinsockStateString(sktTCPChatClient.State)
        DoEvents
        Loop Until sktTCPChatClient.State = sckClosed
    bConnected = False
    cmdConnect.Caption = "Connect"
    cmdConnect.Enabled = True
    End Sub
```

The **sktTCPChatClient_Close()** event procedure calls the **Close()** method on **sktTCPChatClient**. That's right—the **Close()** event procedure calls the **Close()** method to complete the close operation. The **Close()** event procedure then enters a loop, where it waits for the Winsock control's **State** property to change to **sckClosed**.

The **cmdConnect_Click()** procedure's lengthier **Else** clause handles the process of connecting to the server. After calling the Winsock control's **Connect()** method, it enters a loop where it waits for the **State** to change either to **sckConnected** or **sckError**. An error at this point would usually indicate a timeout, most likely caused by either an inactive server or an invalid **RemoteHost** or **RemotePort**. If the connection fails—which may take some time—the procedure reports the error and re-enables **cmdConnect**. I've thrown in a call to the Windows API here: I'm using the function **sndPlaySound()** to play the system sound called "Exclamation." You'll find the declaration for this library function in the declarations section of frmClient1.FRM in Listing 10.9.

If the connection succeeds, the **cmdConnect_Click()** procedure changes the **Caption** of the **cmdConnect** button to "Close Connection", sets **bConnected** to **True**, and enables both command buttons.

The other operations performed by the client work much like their counterparts in the server. For example, the **cmdSendData_Click()** event procedure, shown in Listing 10.9, calls the Winsock control's **SendData()** method to transmit the contents of **txtDataToSend.Text**, then updates the display by appending the same text to the contents of **txtDataReceived**. Other standard event procedures, all shown in Listing 10.9, handle the basic housekeeping tasks, such as resizing the form and enabling the appropriate command buttons.

Listing 10.9 The complete listing of frmClient1.FRM.

```
Option Explicit

Private bConnected As Boolean

Private Const SND_ASYNC = &H1
Private Const FormSpace = 50
Private Const ChatHost = "192.168.0.1"

Private Declare Function sndPlaySound Lib "winmm.dll" _
    Alias "sndPlaySoundA" _
    (ByVal lpszSoundName As String, _
     ByVal uFlags As Long) As Long

Private Sub cmdConnect_Click()
    If bConnected Then
        sbWinsockState.Panels(1) = "Closing Connection"
        cmdSendData.Enabled = False
        cmdConnect.Enabled = False
        sktTCPChatClient.SendData "QUIT"
      Else
        'Close connection as a (unreliable) precaution:
        sktTCPChatClient.Close
        With sktTCPChatClient
            .RemoteHost = ChatHost
            .RemotePort = 1600
            End With
        sktTCPChatClient.Connect
        sbWinsockState.Panels(1) = "You are at IP Address " & _
            sktTCPChatClient.LocalIP
```

```
        cmdConnect.Enabled = False
        Do
            DoEvents
            Loop Until sktTCPChatClient.State = sckConnected Or _
                       sktTCPChatClient.State = sckError
        If sktTCPChatClient.State = sckError Then
            cmdConnect.Enabled = True
            sbWinsockState.Panels(1) = "Unable to connect to host."
            sndPlaySound "Exclamation", SND_ASYNC
          Else
            cmdConnect.Caption = "Close Connection"
            bConnected = True
            cmdConnect.Enabled = True
            cmdSendData.Enabled = True
          End If
      End If
    End Sub

Private Sub cmdSendData_Click()
    sktTCPChatClient.SendData txtDataToSend.Text
    txtDataReceived.SelColor = vbButtonText
    txtDataReceived.SelText = sktTCPChatClient.LocalIP & ": " & _
        txtDataToSend.Text & vbCrLf
    txtDataReceived.UpTo vbEOF
    End Sub

Private Sub Form_Load()
    bConnected = False
    cmdSendData.Enabled = False
    sbWinsockState.Panels(1) = "You are at IP Address " & _
        sktTCPChatClient.LocalIP
    End Sub

Private Sub Form_QueryUnload(Cancel As Integer, _
                             UnloadMode As Integer)
    sktTCPChatClient.Close
    End Sub

Private Sub Form_Resize()
    Dim MinFormHeight As Long
    Dim MinFormWidth As Long
    Dim FreeSpace As Long

    If frmClient.WindowState = vbMinimized Then
        Exit Sub
      End If
```

```
    MinFormHeight = (Height - ScaleHeight) + _
                    sbWinsockState.Height + _
                    cmdConnect.Height + _
                    lblDataToSend.Height + 100 + _
                    lblDataReceived.Height + 100 + _
                    8 * FormSpace
    MinFormWidth = (Width - ScaleWidth) + _
                   cmdSendData.Width + _
                   3 * FormSpace + 100
    frmClient.Height = MaxLong(frmClient.Height, MinFormHeight)
    frmClient.Width = MaxLong(frmClient.Width, MinFormWidth)

    cmdConnect.Left = FormSpace
    cmdConnect.Top = sbWinsockState.Top - _
                     (cmdConnect.Height + FormSpace)
    cmdSendData.Top = cmdConnect.Top
    cmdSendData.Left = cmdConnect.Left + _
                       cmdConnect.Width + FormSpace
    cmdSendData.Height = cmdConnect.Height
    FreeSpace = (cmdConnect.Top - 3 * FormSpace)

    lblDataToSend.Left = FormSpace
    lblDataToSend.Top = FormSpace
    txtDataToSend.Left = FormSpace
    txtDataToSend.Top = lblDataToSend.Top + lblDataToSend.Height
    txtDataToSend.Width = ScaleWidth - (2 * FormSpace)
    txtDataToSend.Height = (FreeSpace * 0.33) - _
                           lblDataToSend.Height
    Debug.Print txtDataToSend.Height
    lblDataReceived.Left = FormSpace
    lblDataReceived.Top = txtDataToSend.Top + _
                          txtDataToSend.Height + FormSpace
    txtDataReceived.Left = FormSpace
    txtDataReceived.Top = lblDataReceived.Top + _
                          lblDataReceived.Height
    txtDataReceived.Width = txtDataToSend.Width
    txtDataReceived.Height = (FreeSpace * 0.67) - _
                             lblDataReceived.Height

    End Sub

Private Sub sktTCPChatClient_Close()
    cmdConnect.Enabled = False
    cmdSendData.Enabled = False
    sktTCPChatClient.Close
    Do
```

```
        sbWinsockState.Panels(1) = "Status: " & _
            WinsockStateString(sktTCPChatClient.State)
        DoEvents
        Loop Until sktTCPChatClient.State = sckClosed
    bConnected = False
    cmdConnect.Caption = "Connect"
    cmdConnect.Enabled = True
    End Sub

Private Sub sktTCPChatClient_Connect()
    If sktTCPChatClient.State = sckConnected Then
        sbWinsockState.Panels(1) = _
            "Connection Successful at Remote IP " & _
            sktTCPChatClient.RemoteHostIP
        End If

    End Sub

Private Sub sktTCPChatClient_DataArrival(ByVal bytesTotal As Long)
    Dim DataReceived As String

    sktTCPChatClient.GetData DataReceived, vbString
    txtDataReceived.SelColor = vbHighlight
    txtDataReceived.SelText = DataReceived & vbCrLf
    txtDataReceived.UpTo vbEOF
    End Sub

Public Function WinsockStateString(WinsockState As Integer) As String
    Select Case WinsockState
      Case sckClosed
        WinsockStateString = "Closed"
      Case sckClosing
        WinsockStateString = "Closing"
      Case sckConnected
        WinsockStateString = "Connected"
      Case sckConnecting
        WinsockStateString = "Connecting"
      Case sckConnectionPending
        WinsockStateString = "Connection Pending"
      Case sckHostResolved
        WinsockStateString = "Host Resolved"
      Case sckError
        WinsockStateString = "Error"
      Case sckListening
        WinsockStateString = "Listening"
```

```
    Case sckResolvingHost
      WinsockStateString = "Resolving Host"
    Case sckOpen
      WinsockStateString = "Open"
    Case Else
      WinsockStateString = "Unknown State"
    End Select
  End Function
```

The projects ChatServer.VBP and ChatClient.VBP constitute a basic Internet chat system. But to use that system, participants must acquire and install the ChatClient.EXE. In the next project we'll take advantage of ActiveX technology to turn the chat client into a self-installing ActiveX control.

ActiveX Chat On The Web

An embedded chat system offers Web developers the advantage of being able to build virtual communities around their Web sites. Like talk radio, a Web site that encourages a lively exchange between its audience members has the best chance of attracting and keeping that audience—and therefore the greatest opportunity to communicate its message.

With just a few simple modifications, we can convert the **WinsockChatClient** into an ActiveX control that transparently connects Web site visitors to an ongoing, online discussion.

From EXE To OCX

As we discussed in Chapter 9, an ActiveX control has many features in common with an ordinary application—known in Visual Basic as a Standard EXE. It differs primarily in its initialization and termination events, and in its ability to expose properties, methods, and events to a host application (or "container"). In this project, we'll modify the user interface of the chat client by eliminating the **cmdConnect** button, replacing it with an automatic connection feature. We'll also define two properties and four event procedures that can be used to operate and respond to the control from within a Web document.

Connecting With Web Chat

The ChatterBox control (shown in operation in Figure 10.3) automatically connects to the server when it loads. We accomplish this by adding a Timer control, **tmrConnect**, and by moving the code from the old **cmdConnect_Click**() event procedure into a new **Private Sub** procedure called **Connect**(), shown in Listing 10.10.

Listing 10.10 The general procedure **Connect()** from ChatterBox.CTL.

```
Private Sub Connect()
    ' Connect only at runtime:
    If Not Ambient.UserMode Then
        Exit Sub
      End If

    tmrConnect.Enabled = False

    'Close connection as a (unreliable) precaution:
    sktTCPClient.Close
    With sktTCPClient
        .RemoteHost = HostIPAddress
        .RemotePort = 1600
        End With
    sktTCPClient.Connect
    sbWinsockState.Panels(1) = "You are at IP Address " & _
        sktTCPClient.LocalIP
    Do
        DoEvents
        Loop Until sktTCPClient.State = sckConnected Or _
                   sktTCPClient.State = sckError
    If sktTCPClient.State = sckError Then
        sbWinsockState.Panels(1) = "Unable to connect to host."
        tmrConnect.Enabled = True
      Else
        cmdSendData.Enabled = True
      End If

    End Sub
```

The **Connect**() procedure begins by checking the **Ambient.UserMode** property. As with any ActiveX control, we frequently need to adjust the control's behavior according to whether it is in runtime mode or design mode. We don't want the control

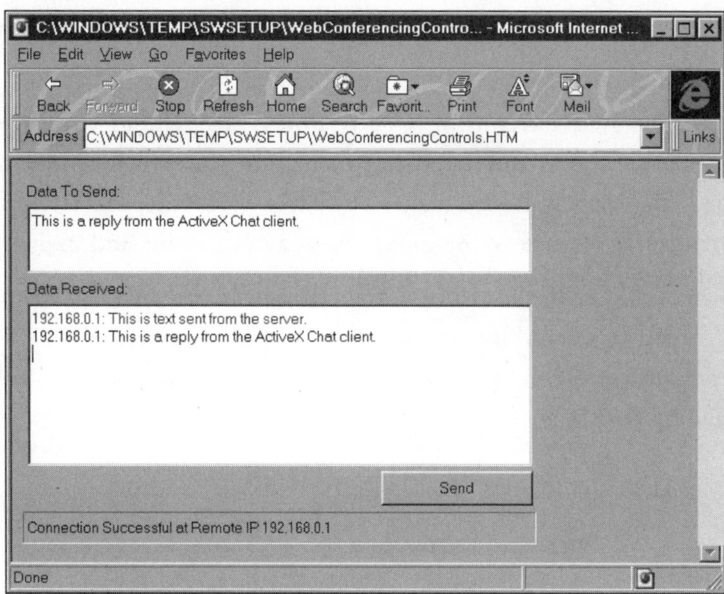

Figure 10.3
The ChatterBox ActiveX chat control in Internet Explorer.

to connect to the server at design time—only at runtime, as indicated by an **Ambient.UserMode** value of **True.**

If the control is in run mode, the procedure continues by disabling **tmrConnect** and attempting to connect to the server. Notice that it sets the Winsock control's **RemoteHost** property to **HostIPAddress**, which is a property of the ChatterBox control itself. You'll find the simple **Property Get** and **Let** procedures that define **HostIPAddress** in Listing 10.11.

After calling the Winsock control's **Connect**() method, the procedure enters a **Do** loop, where it awaits either a successful connection or an error condition. If the connection fails, the procedure re-enables **tmrConnect**, causing the control to attempt another connection after the delay specified in the ChatterBox control's **ReconnectInterval** property.

The timer control has only one purpose: to call **Connect**(), which it does from the **tmrConnect_Timer**() event procedure, as shown in Listing 10.11. When a user navigates to a Web page that contains the ChatterBox ActiveX control, the control will automatically try to connect to the chat server. If the server does not respond, the control will repeat the attempt until it succeeds or until the user navigates to another document.

Like almost any ActiveX control, ChatterBox.CTL includes **InitProperties()**, **ReadProperties()**, and **WriteProperties()** event procedures—all shown in Listing 10.11. Since the control exposes only two simple properties, **HostIPAddress** and **ReconnectInterval**, all three of these event procedures are brief and straightforward.

This version of the ChatterBox control supports just six members, as shown in Table 10.5. To fill out this control, you may wish to add a more complete selection of standard properties, such as **Enabled**, and the various properties that control appearance, including **BackStyle**, **BackColor**, and **BorderStyle**.

Table 10.5 The members of the ChatterBox ActiveX control.

Member	Type	Description
Connect()	Event	Raised when the control connects to the server.
Disconnect()	Event	Raised when the control loses its connection to the server.
HostIPAddress	Property	IP address of the chat host program, ChatServer.EXE.
ReceivedData()	Event	Raised when data arrives from the server.
ReconnectInterval	Property	Delay in milliseconds between connection retries.
SentData()	Event	Raised when data is transmitted to the server.

Listing 10.11 The complete listing of ChatterBox.CTL from WebConferencingControls.VBP.

```
VERSION 5.00
Object = "{248DD890-BB45-11CF-9ABC-0080C7E7B78D}#1.0#0"; _
    "MSWINSCK.OCX"
Object = "{3B7C8863-D78F-101B-B9B5-04021C009402}#1.1#0"; _
    "RICHTX32.OCX"
Object = "{6B7E6392-850A-101B-AFC0-4210102A8DA7}#1.1#0"; _
    "COMCTL32.OCX"
Begin VB.UserControl ChatterBox
   ClientHeight    =   3972
   ClientLeft      =   0
   ClientTop       =   0
   ClientWidth     =   5736
   ScaleHeight     =   3972
```

```
ScaleWidth      =   5736
Begin VB.Timer tmrConnect
   Enabled         =   0   'False
   Interval        =   3000
   Left            =   240
   Top             =   3120
End
Begin ComctlLib.StatusBar sbWinsockState
   Align           =   2  'Align Bottom
   Height          =   372
   Left            =   0
   TabIndex        =   5
   Top             =   3600
   Width           =   5736
   _ExtentX        =   10118
   _ExtentY        =   656
   SimpleText      =   ""
   _Version        =   327680
   BeginProperty Panels {0713E89E-850A-101B-AFC0-4210102A8DA7}
      NumPanels       =   1
      BeginProperty Panel1 {0713E89F-850A-101B-AFC0-4210102A8DA7}
         AutoSize        =   1
         Object.Width           =   10075
         TextSave        =   ""
         Key             =   ""
         Object.Tag             =   ""
      EndProperty
   EndProperty
   MouseIcon       =   "ChatterBox.ctx":0000
End
Begin VB.CommandButton cmdSendData
   Caption         =   "Send"
   Height          =   372
   Left            =   3960
   TabIndex        =   4
   Top             =   3120
   Width           =   1692
End
Begin RichTextLib.RichTextBox txtDataReceived
   Height          =   852
   Left            =   120
   TabIndex        =   3
   Top             =   2040
   Width           =   5532
   _ExtentX        =   9758
```

```
         _ExtentY         =   1503
         _Version         =   327680
         Enabled          =   -1  'True
         TextRTF          =   $"ChatterBox.ctx":001C
      End
      Begin RichTextLib.RichTextBox txtDataToSend
         Height           =   1092
         Left             =   120
         TabIndex         =   1
         Top              =   480
         Width            =   5532
         _ExtentX         =   9758
         _ExtentY         =   1926
         _Version         =   327680
         Enabled          =   -1  'True
         TextRTF          =   $"ChatterBox.ctx":00E5
      End
      Begin MSWinsockLib.Winsock sktTCPClient
         Left             =   840
         Top              =   3120
         _ExtentX         =   593
         _ExtentY         =   593
      End
      Begin VB.Label lblDataReceived
         Caption          =   "Data Received:"
         Height           =   252
         Left             =   120
         TabIndex         =   2
         Top              =   1800
         Width            =   1452
      End
      Begin VB.Label lblDataToSend
         Caption          =   "Data To Send:"
         Height           =   252
         Left             =   120
         TabIndex         =   0
         Top              =   240
         Width            =   1692
      End
   End
   Attribute VB_Name = "ChatterBox"
   Attribute VB_GlobalNameSpace = False
   Attribute VB_Creatable = True
   Attribute VB_PredeclaredId = False
   Attribute VB_Exposed = True
   Option Explicit
```

```
Private Const SND_ASYNC = &H1
Private Const FormSpace = 50

Private m_HostIPAddress As String

Private Declare Function sndPlaySound Lib "winmm.dll" _
    Alias "sndPlaySoundA" _
    (ByVal lpszSoundName As String, _
     ByVal uFlags As Long) As Long

Event ReceivedData(ByVal DataReceived As String)
Event SentData(ByVal DataSent As String)
Event Connect(ByVal HostIP As String)
Event Disconnect()

Private Sub cmdSendData_Click()
    sktTCPClient.SendData txtDataToSend.Text
    txtDataReceived.SelColor = vbButtonText
    txtDataReceived.SelText = sktTCPClient.LocalIP & ": " & _
        txtDataToSend.Text & vbCrLf
    txtDataReceived.UpTo vbEOF
    RaiseEvent SentData(txtDataToSend.Text)
    End Sub

Private Sub sktTCPClient_Close()
    sndPlaySound "Exclamation", SND_ASYNC
    cmdSendData.Enabled = False
    sktTCPClient.Close
    Do
        sbWinsockState.Panels(1) = "Status: " & _
            WinsockStateString(sktTCPClient.State)
        DoEvents
        Loop Until sktTCPClient.State = sckClosed
    tmrConnect.Enabled = True
    RaiseEvent Disconnect
    End Sub

Private Sub sktTCPClient_Connect()
    If sktTCPClient.State = sckConnected Then
        sbWinsockState.Panels(1) = _
            "Connection Successful at Remote IP " & _
            sktTCPClient.RemoteHostIP
        End If
    RaiseEvent Connect(sktTCPClient.RemoteHostIP)
    End Sub
```

```
Private Sub sktTCPClient_DataArrival(ByVal bytesTotal As Long)
    Dim DataReceived As String

    sktTCPClient.GetData DataReceived, vbString
    txtDataReceived.SelColor = vbHighlight
    txtDataReceived.SelText = DataReceived & vbCrLf
    txtDataReceived.UpTo vbEOF
    RaiseEvent ReceivedData(DataReceived)
    End Sub

Private Sub tmrConnect_Timer()
    Connect
    End Sub

Private Sub UserControl_InitProperties()
    HostIPAddress = sktTCPClient.LocalIP
    ReconnectInterval = 0
    End Sub

Private Sub UserControl_ReadProperties(PropBag As PropertyBag)
    With PropBag
        HostIPAddress = _
            .ReadProperty("HostIPAddress", sktTCPClient.LocalIP)
        ReconnectInterval = _
            .ReadProperty("ReconnectInterval", 0)
        End With
    cmdSendData.Enabled = False
    sbWinsockState.Panels(1) = "You are at IP Address " & _
        sktTCPClient.LocalIP
    Connect
    End Sub

Private Sub Connect()
    ' Connect only at runtime:
    If Not Ambient.UserMode Then
        Exit Sub
      End If

    tmrConnect.Enabled = False

    'Close connection as a (unreliable) precaution:
    sktTCPClient.Close
    With sktTCPClient
        .RemoteHost = HostIPAddress
        .RemotePort = 1600
        End With
```

```
    sktTCPClient.Connect
    sbWinsockState.Panels(1) = "You are at IP Address " & _
        sktTCPClient.LocalIP
    Do
        DoEvents
        Loop Until sktTCPClient.State = sckConnected Or _
                   sktTCPClient.State = sckError
    If sktTCPClient.State = sckError Then
        sbWinsockState.Panels(1) = "Unable to connect to host."
        tmrConnect.Enabled = True
      Else
        cmdSendData.Enabled = True
      End If

    End Sub

Public Property Get HostIPAddress() As String
    HostIPAddress = m_HostIPAddress
    End Property

Public Property Let HostIPAddress(ByVal New_HostIPAddress As String)
    m_HostIPAddress = New_HostIPAddress
    PropertyChanged "HostIPAddress"
    End Property

Private Sub UserControl_Resize()
    Dim MinFormHeight As Long
    Dim MinFormWidth As Long
    Dim FreeSpace As Long

    MinFormHeight = (Height - ScaleHeight) + _
                    sbWinsockState.Height + _
                    cmdSendData.Height + _
                    lblDataToSend.Height + 100 + _
                    lblDataReceived.Height + 100 + _
                    4 * FormSpace
    MinFormWidth = (Width - ScaleWidth) + _
                   cmdSendData.Width + _
                   3 * FormSpace + 100
    UserControl.Height = MaxLong(UserControl.Height, MinFormHeight)
    UserControl.Width = MaxLong(UserControl.Width, MinFormWidth)

    cmdSendData.Top = sbWinsockState.Top - _
                      (cmdSendData.Height + FormSpace)
    cmdSendData.Left = ScaleWidth - _
                       (cmdSendData.Width + FormSpace)
    FreeSpace = (cmdSendData.Top - 3 * FormSpace)
```

```
    lblDataToSend.Left = FormSpace
    lblDataToSend.Top = FormSpace
    txtDataToSend.Left = FormSpace
    txtDataToSend.Top = lblDataToSend.Top + lblDataToSend.Height
    txtDataToSend.Width = ScaleWidth - (2 * FormSpace)
    txtDataToSend.Height = (FreeSpace * 0.33) - _
                           lblDataToSend.Height
    lblDataReceived.Left = FormSpace
    lblDataReceived.Top = txtDataToSend.Top + _
                          txtDataToSend.Height + FormSpace
    txtDataReceived.Left = FormSpace
    txtDataReceived.Top = lblDataReceived.Top + _
                          lblDataReceived.Height
    txtDataReceived.Width = txtDataToSend.Width
    txtDataReceived.Height = (FreeSpace * 0.67) - _
                             lblDataReceived.Height

    End Sub

Public Function WinsockStateString(WinsockState As Integer) As String
    Select Case WinsockState
      Case sckClosed
        WinsockStateString = "Closed"
      Case sckClosing
        WinsockStateString = "Closing"
      Case sckConnected
        WinsockStateString = "Connected"
      Case sckConnecting
        WinsockStateString = "Connecting"
      Case sckConnectionPending
        WinsockStateString = "Connection Pending"
      Case sckHostResolved
        WinsockStateString = "Host Resolved"
      Case sckError
        WinsockStateString = "Error"
      Case sckListening
        WinsockStateString = "Listening"
      Case sckResolvingHost
        WinsockStateString = "Resolving Host"
      Case sckOpen
        WinsockStateString = "Open"
      Case Else
        WinsockStateString = "Unknown State"
      End Select
    End Function
```

```
Private Sub UserControl_WriteProperties(PropBag As PropertyBag)
    With PropBag
        .WriteProperty "HostIPAddress", _
                       m_HostIPAddress, _
                       sktTCPClient.LocalIP
        .WriteProperty "ReconnectInterval", _
                       tmrConnect.Interval, _
                       0
        End With
    sktTCPClient.Close
    End Sub

Public Property Get ReconnectInterval() As Long
    ReconnectInterval = tmrConnect.Interval
    End Property

Public Property Let ReconnectInterval _
                  (ByVal New_ReconnectInterval As Long)
    tmrConnect.Interval = New_ReconnectInterval
    PropertyChanged "ReconnectInterval"
    End Property
```

Compiling And Using The ChatterBox Control

Before you can use the ChatterBox control in a Web page, you must compile it and generate its Internet setup file. The Application Setup Wizard will make a sample HTM file similar to the one shown in Listing 10.12.

Listing 10.12 The file WebConferencingControls.HTM generated by the Application Setup Wizard.

```
<HTML>
<!--If any of the controls on this page require licensing, you must
    create a license package file. Run LPK_TOOL.EXE to create the
    required LPK file. LPK_TOOL.EXE can be found on the ActiveX SDK,
    http://www.microsoft.com/intdev/sdk/sdk.htm. If you have the
    Visual Basic 5.0 CD, it can also be found in the
    \Tools\LPK_TOOL directory.

    The following is an example of the Object tag:

<OBJECT CLASSID="clsid:5220cb21-c88d-11cf-b347-00aa00a28331">
    <PARAM NAME="LPKPath" VALUE="LPKfilename.LPK">
</OBJECT>
-->
```

```
<OBJECT ID="ChatterBox" WIDTH=478 HEIGHT=331
CLASSID="CLSID:225DDCA3-ADAC-11D0-B8EF-00608CC9A71F"
CODEBASE="WebConferencingControls.CAB#version=1,0,0,0">
    <PARAM NAME="ReconnectInterval" VALUE="3000">
    <PARAM NAME="HostIPAddress" VALUE="192.168.0.3">
</OBJECT>
</HTML>
```

I've already modified this file slightly by adding the two **<PARAM>** tags to set the **ReconnectInterval** and **HostIPAddress**. Before this document will work on your own system, you must set the **HostIPAddress** to the IP address of the machine on which you are running the ChatServer.EXE.

Name Your Controls Uniquely

Visual Basic has made it easy to create ActiveX controls, and the many books available that explain how to design and implement controls simplify the process even further. However, they do create another problem: name and class ID conflicts. If you decide to create a distributable control based on the ChatterBox project, you should do two things to minimize the chance of a conflict with another control based on the same project. First, name your OCX file to something other than WebConferencingControls.OCX, the name I have used for the ChatterBox project. Also, before you compile your component for the first time, disable Binary Compatibility in the Version Compatibility section of the Project Options dialog box so that Visual Basic will generate a new Class ID for you. Immediately after your first compilation, re-enable Binary Compatibility and set the file reference to your newly generated OCX.

Knock My Socks Off

As ActiveX controls go, the ChatterBox is a little plain. To fit into a sharp-looking Web site, it will probably need some visual and functional enhancements. Here are a few suggestions:

- Implement a chat protocol that supports more meaningful user identification such as names or "handles."

- Add support for multiple chat sessions.
- Convert the ChatterBox to an invisible control by removing all its visual elements. You could then use VBScript to implement more flexible document layouts, using other visual ActiveX controls to construct the user interface.

Design Your Own Internet Protocol

By building our own servers and compatible client applications, we can invent any kind of Internet service we wish. And thanks to Visual Basic and ActiveX technology, we can easily incorporate our new services into Web pages that automatically distribute and install the latest versions of our client applications.

In Chapters 5 and 6, we used the Winsock control to implement part of NNTP, which enabled us to communicate with Internet News servers. NNTP defines numerous commands and responses, each of which consists of a simple text string. The conventions used to structure the commands and responses in an NNTP transaction appear in other Internet protocols as well. You can use the same techniques to define your own Internet services. And if you come up with an idea for a new service that might benefit the entire Internet community, you can write your own Request for Comments (RFC).

Index

—D—

—E—

—F—

—N—

—O—

—P—